ALTERNATIVE NARRATIVES IN CERAMIC HISTORY

ALTERNATIVE NARRATIVES IN CERAMIC HISTORY

Intermediaries and the Anglo-American Ceramic Trade

Neil Ewins

BLOOMSBURY VISUAL ARTS
LONDON • NEW YORK • OXFORD • NEW DELHI • SYDNEY

BLOOMSBURY VISUAL ARTS
Bloomsbury Publishing Plc, 50 Bedford Square, London, WC1B 3DP, UK
Bloomsbury Publishing Inc, 1359 Broadway, New York, NY 10018, USA
Bloomsbury Publishing Ireland, 29 Earlsfort Terrace, Dublin 2, D02 AY28, Ireland

BLOOMSBURY, BLOOMSBURY VISUAL ARTS and the Diana logo are
trademarks of Bloomsbury Publishing Plc

First published in Great Britain 2026

Cover design: Louise Dugdale
Cover image: Interior view of C. I. Filley's crockery store from "Direct Importation of Queensware to St. Louis, Mo: Chauncey I. Filley's Extensive Queensware Importing House—The Queensware Trade in the Mississippi Valley," *Frank Leslie's Illustrated Newspaper*, November 24, 1860.

A catalogue record for this book is available from the British Library.

Library of Congress Cataloging-in-Publication Data
Names: Ewins, Neil author
Title: Alternative narratives in ceramic history : intermediaries and the
Anglo-American ceramic trade / Neil Ewins.
Description: London : Bloomsbury Visual Arts, 2026. |
Includes bibliographical references and index.
Identifiers: LCCN 2025026545 | ISBN 9781350538337 hardback |
ISBN 9781350543935 paperback | ISBN 9781350538344 pdf | ISBN 9781350538351 epub
Subjects: LCSH: Pottery industry –Great Britain –History –19th century | Pottery industry – United States –History –19th century | Great Britain –Commerce –United States –History – 19th century | United States –Commerce –Great Britain –History –19th century
Classification: LCC HD9612.5 .E95 2026 | DDC 338.4/76663 –dc23/eng/20250813
LC record available at https://lccn.loc.gov/2025026545

ISBN: HB: 978-1-3505-3833-7
ePDF: 978-1-3505-3834-4
eBook: 978-1-3505-3835-1

Typeset by Integra Software Services Pvt. Ltd.
Printed and bound in Great Britain

For product safety related questions contact productsafety@bloomsbury.com.

To find out more about our authors and books visit www.bloomsbury.com
and sign up for our newsletters.

To my Mum.
Thank you for everything.

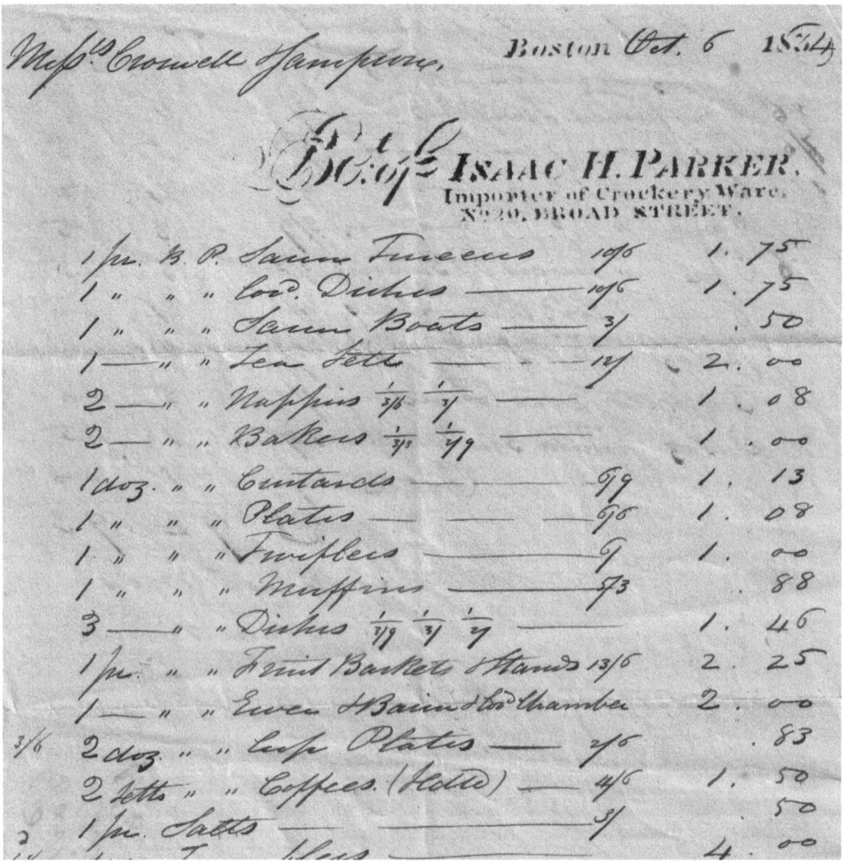
Messrs. Croswell & Sampson, Boston Oct. 6 1834

Bo't of Isaac H. Parker,
Importer of Crockery Ware,
No. 20, Broad Street.

1 pr.	B. P. Sauce Tureens	10/6	1.75
1 "	" " Cov'd. Dishes	10/6	1.75
1 "	" " Sauce Boats	3/	.50
1	" " Tea Setts	12/	2.00
2	" " Nappies 3/6 3/		1.08
2	" " Bakers 3/3 2/9		1.00
1 doz.	" " Custards	6/9	1.13
1 "	" " Plates	6/6	1.08
1 "	" " Twifflers	6/	1.00
1 "	" " Muffins	5/3	.88
3	" " Dishes 3/9 3/ 2/		1.46
1 pr.	" " Fruit Baskets & Stands	13/6	2.25
1	" " Ewer & Basin for Chamber		2.00
3/6 2 doz.	" " Cup Plates	2/6	.83
2 setts	" " Coffees (Hdld)	4/6	1.50
1 pr.	Salts	3/	.50
			4.00

Frontispiece Invoice (extract), Isaac H. Parker, importer of crockery ware, Boston, addressed to Croswell & Sampson. Dated October 6, 1834. It is recorded that a Thomas Croswell and his nephew, Benjamin Sampson, ran a store at Farmington Falls, Maine (Butler 1885: 268).

CONTENTS

List of Figures viii
List of Pedigrees xv
Acknowledgements xvi

INTRODUCTION 1

Chapter 1
COLLECTING AND PERCEPTIONS OF PRODUCTION 17

Chapter 2
CONSUMPTION AND PERCEPTIONS OF DEMAND 47

Chapter 3
BACKGROUNDS AND KINSHIP 89

Chapter 4
POLITICS AND MARKETING 123

Chapter 5
DYNASTIES AND INTERCONNECTIONS 143

Chapter 6
RELIGION AND ABOLITIONISM 169

Chapter 7
MORALITY AND RACE 197

CONCLUSION 233

References 240
Pedigrees 255
Glossary 269
Index 271

FIGURES

Author's collection and photography, unless otherwise stated.

Introduction

Frontispiece Invoice (extract), Isaac H. Parker, importer of crockery ware, Boston. Dated October 6, 1834 vi

Chapter 1

1.1 Jug, creamware, black printed, commemorating President George Washington (1732–1799). Probably Herculaneum Pottery, Liverpool, c.1800–05 18
1.2 A range of American-themed blue printed wares, Staffordshire, c.1820s 18
1.3 Trade card, for Maddock & Co., New York, sole agents for John Maddock & Sons' "Royal Vitreous Dinner Ware", c.1890 21
1.4 Figurine, earthenware, enamel and gilt decoration, of Dr. Benjamin Franklin, signed as "General Washington", c.1860–70 27
1.5 Plate, earthenware, blue printed, depicting Pittsfield, Massachusetts. Impressed, "Clews Warranted, Staffordshire", Cobridge, c.1825–28 30
1.6 Printed backstamp on Figure 1.5. American Seal, "Winter View of Pittsfield, Mass" 31
1.7 A range of Staffordshire wares with impressed backstamp for Peter Morton, importer, Hartford, Connecticut, c.1823–30 33
1.8 Jug, earthenware, black printed with luster decoration, signed "Henshaw & Jarves, Importers of Earthen and China ware, Boston, from Wood & Caldwells, Manufactory, Burslem, Staffordshire," c.1814–18 34
1.9 Side view of jug, Figure 1.8 34
1.10 Side view of jug, Figure 1.8 35
1.11 Plate, creamware, enamel decoration providing a sample of different rim patterns. Signed "Joseph Allen Crocker/China Glass/ Earthen ware, Dealer/ Boston." Impressed mark for Davenport, Longport. Staffordshire, c.1809–1817. Bequest of Henry Francis du Pont. Courtesy Winterthur Museum, Garden & Library 36

1.12 Cup plate, earthenware, blue transfer printed in a willow pattern. Probably Staffordshire, c.1819–44. Museum purchase. Courtesy Winterthur Museum, Garden & Library 37
1.13 Backstamp on cup plate, Figure 1.12. Museum purchase. Courtesy Winterthur Museum, Garden & Library 37
1.14 Cup plate, earthenware, light-brown printed with faint enamel decoration, "Peking Japan" pattern. Manufactured by C.J. Mason, Fenton, Staffordshire, c.1825–35 38
1.15 Backstamp on Figure 1.14, printed in blue as, "Imported By/ T. T. Kissam 99 Water Street/ New York," c.1825–1835 38
1.16 Auction catalogue (extract), "The William Randolph Hearst Collection, Part II …", Parke-Bernet Galleries, November 1938, pp. 98–99 42
1.17 Cup plate, pearlware, brown printed, with brown enamel decoration, depicting La Fayette and Washington, below an eagle. Enoch Wood & Sons, Burslem, c. 1825–30 43

Chapter 2

2.1 *Columbian Register*, New Haven, Connecticut May 11, 1833 54
2.2 *Norfolk Democrat*, Dedham, Massachusetts December 19, 1845 54
2.3 Plate, earthenware, blue printed, depicting a warehouse (detail), backstamped, "Mitchell & Freeman, China & Glass warehouse, Chatham St., Boston". Impressed mark, "Staffordshire Warranted, Adams [Stoke]," surrounding an American Seal, c.1829–32 55
2.4 View of C. I. Filley's crockery store from, "Direct Importation of Queensware to St.Louis, Mo: Chauncey I. Filley's Extensive Queensware Importing House—The Queensware Trade in the Mississippi Valley," *Frank Leslie's Illustrated Newspaper*, November 24, 1860, p.13 57
2.5 Interior view of C. I. Filley's crockery store from "Direct Importation of Queensware to St. Louis, Mo: Chauncey I. Filley's Extensive Queensware Importing House—The Queensware Trade in the Mississippi Valley," *Frank Leslie's Illustrated Newspaper*, November 24, 1860, p. 13 58
2.6 Range of ceramics and glass cup plate with marks relating to E.A. & S.R. Filley and C.I Filley 59
2.7 Printed backstamp on white granite soup plate shown in Figure 2.6 59
2.8 Engraving entitled, "Chauncey I. Filley, Esq—Photographed by G. Elliot, Staffordshire Potteries, England', from "Direct Importation of Queensware to St. Louis, Mo: Chauncey I. Filley's Extensive Queensware Importing House—The Queensware Trade

in the Mississippi Valley," *Frank Leslie's Illustrated Newspaper*, November 24, 1860, p. 13 60
2.9 Invoice (extract), Abram French & Co., Boston, showing an image of the emporium. Dated May 22, 1873 60
2.10 Jugs, depicting American naval heroes from the 1812–14, Anglo-American war, Staffordshire, c.1815–20 62
2.11 Ceramics depicting Boston State House, Staffordshire, c.1818–20 63
2.12 *Columbian Centinel*, Boston April 20, 1822 64
2.13 Plate, earthenware, blue printed transfer. Backstamp, "Opaque China, Christ Church, Oxford, J.& W. Ridgway," Shelton, Staffordshire, c.1822 64
2.14 *Alexandria Herald*, Virginia September 28, 1830 65
2.15 *Augusta Chronicle*, March 13, 1846 66
2.16 *Alexandria Herald*, Virginia, June 3, 1822 67
2.17 Davenport backstamp from a green edged plate, c.1810–20 67
2.18 Printed circular of Simpson & Caldwell, Boston, to Brown & Co., Norway, Maine, August 8, 1848 68
2.19 Letter on reverse of printed circular (Figure 2.12), Simpson & Caldwell, Boston, August 8, 1848 69
2.20 Invoice (extract), J. & W. P. Fogg, Cleveland, Ohio, referring to "Jenny Lind" tea-ware. Dated, July 27, 1852 70
2.21 Plate, earthenware, grey transfer printed with enamel decoration, depicting a stylized landscape with figures, backstamped "Jenny Lind/ CM & S [Charles Meigh & Sons, Hanley]," impressed "Improved Stone China," c.1850 71
2.22 *Columbian*, New York June 5, 1819 72
2.23 Auction catalogue of David Dunham & Co., New York, May 6, 1818. Courtesy of the New York Historical Society 73
2.24 Plate, earthenware, purple printed, depicting the burning of the Merchants' Exchange, New York, December 1835. Backstamped, "D/ Stone Ware/Exchange/New York." Probably Staffordshire, c.1836 75
2.25 Plate, earthenware, blue printed design known as "Castle," manufactured by R. & J. Clews, Cobridge, Staffordshire, c.1825–1835 76
2.26 Backstamps on plate (Figure 2.25) 76
2.27 *Evening Post*, New York September 30, 1845 78
2.28 Invoice of Tyndale & Mitchell, Philadelphia, addressed to Thomas I. Wharton, Philadelphia. Dated December 31, 1849 79
2.29 Diagram from Catharine Beecher's *Domestic Receipt Book: Designed as a Supplement to her Treatise on Domestic Economy*, New York, 1846, p. 244 81

Chapter 3

3.1 *Massachusetts Centinel*, Boston March 13, 1790 91
3.2 *Independent Chronicle*, Boston January 5, 1804 94
3.3 *Philadelphia Gazette* January 5, 1808 98
3.4 Printed circular, March 19, 1834. Kress Collection, Baker Library, Courtesy of, Harvard Business School 100
3.5 *Poulson's American Daily Advertiser*, Philadelphia September 8, 1820 102
3.6 *Evening Post*, New York, May 28, 1823 105
3.7 *Auburn Journal and Advertiser*, New York June 12, 1844 108
3.8 Invoice (extract), Norcross, Mellen & Co., importers of crockery, Boston Dated February 11, 1860 111
3.9 *Evening Post*, New York June 19, 1821 111
3.10 *Spectator*, New York, September 17, 1830 113
3.11 *Western Monitor*, Lexington, Kentucky, July 18, 1815 114
3.12 Invoice (extract), John F. Seymour & Co., New York, to Messrs. Rohrbought [sic] & Moore, Kinmudy, Illinois. Dated March 29, 1871 117
3.13 *The Sun*, New York, July 5, 1879 118
3.14 Invoice (extract), Enoch Wood & Sons, Burslem, to J. A. Brown & Co., Philadelphia. Dated May 6, 1833 119
3.15 Declaration (extract), made at the United States Consular Agency, Tunstall by Edward Asbury of Longton, agent of Asbury & Young, Philadelphia. Dated April 21, 1869 121

Chapter 4

4.1 Jug, creamware, black printed, commemorating President George Washington, "Washington in Glory, Born Feb.11th 1752, Died December 14, 1799, America in Tears." Staffordshire, or Liverpool, c.1800–1810 124
4.2 Blue edged wares, adapted to the American market, English, c.1810–1830 124
4.3 *Poulson's American Daily Advertiser*, Philadelphia December 4, 1823 126
4.4 Tea-wares, bone china, transfer printed in variety of colors, with enamel and luster decoration, depicting Mount Vernon. Probably Staffordshire, c.1820s 126
4.5 *The Independent Chronicle*, Boston February 5, 1807 129
4.6 *Poulson's American Daily Advertiser*, Philadelphia November 6, 1805 132

4.7 Jug, creamware, printed and gilt decoration, entitled "Jefferson." Possibly Herculaneum Pottery, Liverpool, c.1801–9, Gift of S. Robert Teitelman. Courtesy Winterthur Museum, Garden & Library 133
4.8 Jugs, earthenware, luster, printed and enamel decoration, depicting front and back in each case, a portrait of General "La Fayette," and the surrender of Cornwallis at York Town. Staffordshire, c.1825 136
4.9 *Alexandria Gazette*, Virginia July 4, 1825 137
4.10 *Alexandria Gazette*, Virginia December 20, 1828 138
4.11 Cup plate, earthenware, black printed and black enamel rim, depicting Andrew Jackson. Enoch Wood & Sons, Burslem, c.1824–28 139
4.12 Miniature cup and saucer, earthenware, blue printed image of a log cabin. Backstamped as "Columbian Star, 444, Oct [October] 28th 1840, Jno [John] Ridgway." John Ridgway, Shelton, Staffordshire, c.1840 140

Chapter 5

5.1 *The Daily Union*, Washington DC January 2, 1846 145
5.2 *New York Gazette* June 20, 1821 147
5.3 *Evening Post*, New York April 9, 1824 147
5.4 *Evening Post*, New York, June 14, 1830 148
5.5 *American and Commercial Advertiser*, Baltimore, September 21, 1844 149
5.6 Invoice, Shirley & Son, Baltimore. Dated July 26, 1873 150
5.7 Side dish, earthenware, blue printed, "Sydenham" pattern, Joseph Clementson, Hanley, c.1856–70 152
5.8 Backstamp (of Figure 5.7), "Manufactured For/ Davenport Bro/ 203 Greenwich St / N.Y" 152
5.9 Invoice (extract), ceramics and glass sold by Davenport Brothers, importers and manufacturers, City Pottery, Trenton, NJ. Dated February[?] 13, 1879 153
5.10 Cup plate, earthenware, blue edged, Staffordshire, c.1820–30 154
5.11 Backstamp on Figure 5.10, "S. Tams & Co. Warranted, Staffordshire, Semi China," c.1820–30 155
5.12 Cup and saucer, earthenware, blue printed, floral pattern 156
5.13 Backstamp on Figure 5.12, impressed and printed "Tams, Anderson & Tams, Warranted Staffordshire", c.1822–27 156
5.14 Sugar, earthenware, flow blue printed, Staffordshire, c.1840s 157
5.15 Backstamp on Figure 5.14, "James Tams & Co./ Importers Philadelphia/ Rock Stone" 157
5.16 Invoice (extract), Mellor, Venables & Co., Burslem, addressed to S. & J. Tams & Co., Philadelphia. Dated January 28, 1836 158

5.17 *The Press*, Philadelphia October 19, 1859 159
5.18 Invoice, China Hall, J. & J. K. Kerr. Dated May 28, 1862 160
5.19 Jersey City Pottery, New Jersey 162
5.20 *Public Ledger*, Philadelphia June 29, 1836 165
5.21 Invoice of E. & J. Tams, Philadelphia, addressed to E. H. Pickett, Tippecanoe, Ohio. Dated May 13, 1849 166

Chapter 6

6.1 Plate and mug, earthenware, transfer printed, with additional enamel decoration on the plate, based on the maxims of Dr. Benjamin Franklin. English, c.1830–40 170
6.2 Sugar, earthenware, blue printed, depicting two fishermen beside a ruin. Impressed "Field & Clark, Importers of Earthenware, Utica." Enoch Wood & Sons, Burslem, Staffordshire, c.1820s 175
6.3 Plate, earthenware, blue printed, "The Grand Erie Canal, A Splendid monument …", Staffordshire, c.1824 176
6.4 Plate, earthenware, blue printed, "Utica, A village in the State of New York …", Staffordshire, c.1824 177
6.5 Plates, earthenware, pink and brown printed, inscribed, "Peace on Earth". Printed backstamp, "Millenium" [sic], Staffordshire, c.1833 178
6.6 *Christian Watchman*, Boston September 6, 1833 181
6.7 *Columbian Register*, New Haven August 3,1833 181
6.8 Plate, earthenware, blue printed, "Lovejoy … Congress shall make no law …". Staffordshire, c.1838 184
6.9 *The Emancipator*, New York October 11, 1838 185
6.10 Detail of Figure 6.8, showing the inscription "LOVEJOY, The First Martyr to American LIBERTY, at ALTON NOV.7. 1837." Staffordshire, c.1838 186
6.11 *Spectator*, New York March 18, 1839 187
6.12 Plate, earthenware, black printed, entitled "The Rule of Three." English, c.1840–50 189
6.13 Plate, earthenware, blue printed. Backstamped, "Beauties of America/ City Hall/ New York/J.& W. Ridgway." Manufactured by J. & W. Ridgway, Cauldon Place works, Shelton, Staffordshire, c.1823–25 192

Chapter 7

7.1 Plate, earthenware, blue printed, depicting business premises and members of the firm, Jones, McDuffee & Stratton, Boston,

celebrating one hundred years of business. Manufactured by Wedgwood, Etruria, Staffordshire, c.1910 199
7.2 Invoice (extract), Jones, McDuffee & Stratton. Dated November 25, 1879 200
7.3 Parian, bust of Charles Sumner, impressed, "Published by J McD & S, Equally of Rights is the first of Rights, Charles Sumner, Copyright." Probably manufactured by Robinson & Leadbeater, Stoke-upon-Trent, c.1875 202
7.4 *New-York Gazette & General Advertiser,* December 8, 1818 205
7.5 Reverend William H. Bakewell, frontispiece, from W.H. Bakewell's *Vision of Faith in the Dream of Time …* 1888 206
7.6 Engraving, "Peggy", in Reverend C. Carey Willett, ed., *Memories of Britain By Rev. W. H. Bakewell,* Darius D. Thorp, Lansing, Michigan, 1892, pp. 8–9 208
7.7 Engraving, entitled "Spring Vale, near Stone, Staffordshire, seat of T. Bakewell, Esq," c.1830.
7.8 *New-York Baptist Register,* Utica, December 19, 1828 209
7.9 *The New-York Recorder,* March 27, 1850 211
7.10 Toothbrush holder, earthenware, blue printed. Josiah Wedgwood & Sons, Etruria, Staffordshire, c.1870–80 212
7.11 Backstamp and printed mark on Figure 7.9. Impressed "Wedgwood" and blue printed mark, "Brooklyn/ Ovingtons/ Chicago" 213
7.12 Plate and figurine based on Harriet Beecher Stowe's *Uncle Tom's Cabin,* c.1852–60 214
7.13 Engraving, "Plymouth Church (Henry Ward Beecher's), Brooklyn, New York," *Harper's Weekly,* August 11, 1866, p.500 215
7.14 Plate (detail), earthenware, blue printed, entitled, "Uncle Tom's Cabin. Emmeline about to be sold to the highest bidder." English, c.1860s 216
7.15 Plate, earthenware, blue printed, depicting the arrival of General La Fayette at New York on "August 16, 1824." Impressed, "R. & J. Clews," Cobridge, Staffordshire, c.1825 220
7.16 *The Brooklyn Daily Eagle,* April 21, 1881 222
7.17 Engraving, "Crockery ware and vases," Horace Greeley et al., *The Great Industries of the United States,* 1872, Plate 345, p. 833 224
7.18 The Brooklyn district with key addresses 227
7.19 Engraving, "The Tilton-Beecher Trial – Portraits and Incidents," *Frank Leslie's Illustrated Newspaper* March 20, 1875, p. 24 229
7.20 Parian, statuette of Henry Ward Beecher, manufactured by W. T. Copeland and Sons, Staffordshire, c.1875. Courtesy of, The Green-Wood Historic Fund Collections, Brooklyn, New York 230

PEDIGREES

1	Wainwright	256
2	Cauldwell	257
3	Hewitt	258
4	Wetmore and Tredwell	259
5	Tredwell and Kissam	260
6	Hastings, Blanchard, and Sampson	261
7	Norcross	262
8	Homer	263
9	Mellen	264
10	Eddowes	265
11	Collamore	266
12	Shirley	267
13	Ovington	268

ACKNOWLEDGEMENTS

Any research project is reliant on the help, goodwill, and encouragement of a whole range of individuals and institutions. I am grateful to the *Conference on Historical Analysis and Research in Marketing* for their enthusiastic response to a research paper, given at their Ottawa Conference. Their feedback encouraged me to continue with this area of research. I am deeply grateful to *The Transferware Collectors Club* for providing me with a Richards Foundation grant to study the Peter Wainwright papers at the New York Public Library. I thank Philip Dempsey, a member of Plymouth Church, and author of *From Enslavement to Freedom in Brooklyn: The Story of Rose Ward Hunt, A Nine Year Old Freed at Plymouth Church*, who gave me a fascinating tour of the Brooklyn district.

The following museums, university libraries, and archives have been invaluable in helping me produce this book. I thank the staff from the Baker Library, Harvard Business School; Brooklyn Public Library, Center for Brooklyn History; the David M. Rubenstein Rare Book & Manuscript Library, Duke University, Durham, North Carolina; Green-Wood Collections, Brooklyn, New York; the New York Historical Society; the New York Public Library; the Massachusetts Historical Society, Boston; the Potteries Museum and Art Gallery, Hanley, Stoke-on-Trent; and the Walter P. Reuther Library, Wayne State University, Detroit, Michigan. I am particularly grateful to Jeanne Solensky, Librarian, Nicole Schnee, Imagine Manager Coordinator, and Leslie Grigsby, Senior Curator of Ceramics & Glass, all of Winterthur Museum, Garden & Library, Delaware. Also, to Hilary Anderson Stelling, Director of Collections and Exhibitions, Scottish Rite Masonic Museum & Library, Lexington, MA.

For helpful guidance and comments over the years I thank, Lucie Ewins, Pat Halfpenny, Ron Fuchs II, and Amanda Lange, and Dan Sousa of Historic Deerfield, Massachusetts. Thanks to Andrea, Emilia, and Estella for putting up with me. Finally, I am grateful to Suzie Nash and Joe Skingsley of Bloomsbury for bringing this book into fruition.

INTRODUCTION

On October 6, 1834, Isaac H. Parker of Boston sold a range of ceramics and glass to a firm called Croswell & Sampson, who appear to have been located at Farmington Falls, Maine. The surviving invoice, headed as, "Isaac H. Parker, Importer of Crockery Ware, No. 20 Broad Street," with its handwritten list of merchandise, is just one example of the thousands of transactions that occurred between those involved in the ceramic and glass trade. This invoice amounted to $92.93 and consisted of a mixture of "B.P" [blue printed] table, toilet, and teaware, "1 sett china," "CC" [cream colored] chambers and mugs, and 100 tumblers. (For readers less familiar with ceramic terminology, a glossary is provided at the end of the book). The ceramics are priced in shillings and pence, followed by the selling price given in dollars, suggesting that these goods had been imported from Britain. Indeed, on occasion, Parker's own advertisements in Boston newspapers mention how his ceramics were imported from Liverpool. In all likelihood, his ceramic stock was acquired from the Staffordshire Potteries. Surviving invoices, such as the one mentioned above, provide fragmentary insight into the demand for goods in the New England area by the 1830s (Frontispiece).

When Isaac H. Parker died in 1867, his obituary establishes that he was a church member for fifty years, attending the Park Street Church under Dr. Dwight and then the Congregational Church on Bowdoin Street, where both Dr. Lyman Beecher and Dr. Hubbard Winslow had, at different times, been pastors (*Boston Recorder* November 14, 1867). It transpires that Isaac Parker was the son of Dr. Henry Parker and Mary Grosvenor, a daughter of Reverend Ebenezer Grosvenor of Harvard, Massachusetts. He was well connected and evidently a devout Christian.

Isaac Parker was a multidimensional individual, whose background and life, in the manner of the other importers and dealers explored in this book, was often more complex and layered than simply being involved in mercantile trade. Could a greater exploration of the backgrounds, culture, and identity of intermediaries serve as additional ways of enhancing our interpretations of ceramics made for, distributed, and consumed by the American market? In an attempt to shed more light on the relationship between supply and demand, this book examines the role and contribution of intermediaries.

Immediately, there may be limitations with this approach. French philosopher, Roland Barthes, in his insightful essay titled "Death of the Author," questioned the value of focusing too much on the personal lives of individuals when attempting to interpret what was produced. As he suggested:

> … the failure of Baudelaire the man, Van Gogh his madness, Tchaikovsky's his vice. The *explanation* for a work is always sought in the man or woman who produced it, as if it were always in the end … the voice of a single person, the *author* "confiding" in us.
>
> (Barthes [1968] 1977: 143)

Prioritizing the individual abilities of the producer was a tendency of the earliest ceramic-history publications. Simeon Shaw's *History of the Staffordshire Potteries: and the Rise and Progress of the Manufacture of Pottery and Porcelain … and the Notices of Eminent Potters* was concerned with the development of the industry and "the Persons whose genius and perseverance have raised it to its present celebrity" (1829: v). Even more extreme was Eliza Meteyard's two volumed analyses of *The Life of Josiah Wedgwood* published in 1865–6, where she informed the readers that:

> Nature had made Wedgwood a great artist. His was a poet's conception and interpretation of his art. What his hand touched, what his eye vitalised through form and colour, thereon was at once seen the impress of nature herself in delicacy and perfection of truth.
>
> (1865–66 Vol II: 26)

Today, such flamboyant, hyperbolic language would be avoided in literature concerning design or ceramic history. Even though a range of other talented artists (such as John Flaxman) were employed, as far as Meteyard was concerned, "Wedgwood exercised a controlling judgment" (1865–66 Vol I: xx). Clearly, the manufacturer becomes the central in the approaches of Simeon Shaw, or Eliza Meteyard, allowing limited scope for examining the degree to which producers responded to the desires of the market, or were entirely responsible for authorship.

Supply versus demand debate

Latterly, the pendulum has swung away from simply emphasizing the abilities of the producer, giving far greater consideration to the role of demand. There has been a surge of interest in the so-called consumer revolution and its impact on supply. In fact, some writers have increasingly related the actual roots of the industrial revolution to the influence of growing demand (Gilboy [1932] 1967: 121–38). Paralleling this shift in focus, research papers by Neil McKendrick in the *Economic History Review* of 1960, or in the *Royal Historical Transactions* of 1964, began to systematically address the business strategy of Josiah Wedgwood. While McKendrick focused on Wedgwood, it is pointed out how other Staffordshire manufacturers, such as Thomas Minton and Josiah Spode, also formed partnerships with merchants (1964: 32). Culminating in McKendrick, Brewer and Plumb's *The Birth of a Consumer Society: The Commercialization of Eighteenth-century England* of 1982, McKendrick's chapter on "Josiah Wedgwood and the Commercialization of the Potteries" examined how he made use of distribution warehouses, showrooms, exhibited and displayed new products, employed travelling salesmen, as well as utilizing "straight-forward" advertising (1982: 118). Wedgwood advertised widely, promoting outlets in Dublin and Bath, and advertisements placed in a Bath newspaper referred to his showroom on Soho Street, London (*Bath Chronicle and Weekly Gazette* October 10, 1776). McKendrick's analysis usefully began to bridge the gap between production and consumption.

McKendrick, Brewer and Plumb's *The Birth of a Consumer Society* ... outlines a "consumer revolution," where a range of sophisticated marketing techniques were developed and employed (1982: 9–13). Within this revolution considerable emphasis has been placed on the role of fashion and emulative behavior in accounting for how new markets were reached and demand stimulated. In fact, McKendrick argues that for British manufacturers, including Staffordshire potters, "Fashion was essential, if not sufficient, key to open up the necessary access to the market" (1982: 98). Therefore, McKendrick believed that fashion should be given far more attention by economic historians.

A view expressed in John Brewer and Roy Porter's *Consumption and the World of Goods* of 1993, was that *The Birth of a Consumer Society* ... of 1982, was a seminal text, which in turn created a surge of research into marketing and consumption (Brewer, J. 1993: 2). Brewer and Porter's *Consumption and the World of Goods* brought together some of the varied results, including a chapter titled, "Manufacturing, consumption and design in eighteenth-century England" by John Styles, a design historian.

It is noticeable how the interpretation of consumption has become increasingly weighted toward manufacturers, as well as merchants, responding to fashion and demand, rather than producers manufacturing novelty goods that they hoped to sell (Styles 1993: 528).

If producers were more inclined to respond to changing consumer demand, it has then become worthwhile to consider the mechanisms involved in conducting the ceramic trade. For instance, Hilary Young's *English Porcelain 1745-95: its Makers, Design, Marketing and Consumption* of 1999, refers to how porcelain manufacturers began to use outlets and warehouses in London. Young suggests how contact with these London outlets—considered to be the hub of the English ceramic trade—provided opportunities for customers to request adaptations to be made to the products (Young 1999:163).

Increasingly, the modern interpretation of ceramic design has accepted the significance of demand, and this has occurred in both British and American publications. Regina Blaszczyk's *Imagining Consumers: Design and Innovation from Wedgwood to Corning* even argues that "Make no mistake: supply did not create demand in home furnishings, but demand determined supply" (2000: 13). In her opinion, the role of Thomas Bentley should not be overlooked in the Wedgwood and Bentley relationship, since in his mercantile capacity, he had traveled abroad, acquiring greater knowledge of different markets.

Thus, more modern interpretations of ceramic design have begun to address the ways in which intermediaries steered production. In Blaszczyk's view, merchants usefully "harvested meaningful data about tastes and purchasing habits" (2000: 32–3). In fact, she argues that Bentley was "Wedgwood's secret weapon in the war to conquer the pottery trade" (2000: 7). If manufacturers did not have a merchant partner, as was the case with Wedgwood and Thomas Bentley, it has been proposed that shopkeepers, retail buyers, etc., acted as "*fashion intermediaries*" [Blaszczyk's italics] (Blaszczyk 2000: 12). The point being that any dialogue between the producers and actual consumers would have been logistically problematic, but it was far more feasible for manufacturers to interact with merchant buyers, importers, and dealers. The intermediary has assumed a more significant position in modern interpretations of ceramic history. Blaszczyk provides an example of Richard Briggs, a nineteenth-century crockery and glass importer of Boston who commissioned designs from Wedgwood, based on his own specifications (2000: 36–37). Even a high-end manufacturer was willing to produce goods initiated by market demands. When faced with the sizable geographical separation between the Staffordshire Potteries and the expansive market of the United States, this interpretation provides an explanation as to how manufacturers produced goods appropriate for the market.

The example of Richard Briggs also draws attention to how archival sources have shaped research and interpretations. American historians, such as Regina Blaszczyk, have been able to consider the records of importers and dealers, whereas British writers have often focused on factory-histories and production, based on the evidence available (Lockett 1997: 91–2). When American historians have examined the records of merchants, their perspective has often resulted in a consideration of whether particular designs were adapted for the market. This was the case with Arlene Schwind's research paper on "The Ceramic Imports of Frederick Rhinelander, New York Loyalist Merchant" (1984: 21–36). In fact, Schwind establishes that Rhinelander of New York did order ceramics that responded to his own specifications (1984: 32).

The perspective—not simply the scope of archival sources—has also made a difference in whether the demands of the market have been considered as a factor in influencing production and design. Researchers who examine ceramics imported into a particular country may be more inclined to consider whether these goods were adapted to suit the demands of the market. For instance, Godden's *Oriental Export Market Porcelain and its influence on European wares* of 1979 mentions how imported Chinese porcelains for the British and American markets were decorated with family coats of arms and patriotic emblems (1979: 195–220, 281–300).

The relationship between supply and demand is complex. Some writers have favored the role of the producer, while others higlight the significance of market demand. While the concept of "consumer sovereignty" is associated with Hutt's *Economists and the Public: A study of Competition and Opinion* (1936: 257–72), in the eighteenth century, Adam Smith's *Wealth of Nations* proposed that "Consumption is the sole end and purpose of all production; and the interest of the producer ought to be attended to, only so far as it may be necessary for promoting that of the consumer" ([1776] 1871: 523). Despite this observation, it was conceded by Smith that the mercantile system seemed "to consider production not consumption, as the ultimate end and object of all industry and commerce" ([1776] 1871: 523). Other economists have, therefore, preferred to continually emphasize the role of the producer. Referring to Parisian, haute couture fashion, Ernest Mandel, the Marxist economist, proposed that "Fashion is a typically social phenomenon, with the impetus coming from the side of the producer (the designers), not from that of the consumers" ([1968] 1971: 662). In a broader context, he argued:

> As for new products, their mass production and their "launching" on the market, that is, their large-scale distribution among consumers, is already determined by the firms that produce them and not by the whims of the consumers. It is thus well and truly "planned" – but planned by a handful of capitalist firms, in accordance with criteria of private profit alone, and not in accordance with the objective and rational needs of the community and of the individuals composing it.
>
> (Mandel [1968] 1971: 663)

Mandel even asked the rhetorical question, how could consumers have "urgent needs" if these have not been presented to the consumer yet? ([1968] 1971: 663). To ask another rhetorical question in reply: where did the inspiration come from for these new products? In the case of the ceramic trade, the solution is perhaps a complex interplay between the producer, intermediaries, and the consumer.

Anglo-American trade

From the evidence available, the ceramic trade did not entirely follow Mandel's model of new designs simply emanating and planned by the producers. Although Staffordshire exported huge quantities of ceramics to the United States, wares from other European and Chinese sources were also imported, creating possibilities for competition and stylistic emulation. Imported ceramics from different sources could potentially influence the "whims of the consumer" and then, in a more cyclical way, impact on the production of manufacturers anxious to compete. It is interesting that while Briggs of Boston commissioned Wedgwood to manufacture his "Elder Brewster" teapot, it transpires that the form of the design was based on a piece of imported Chinese porcelain, in the collection of a wealthy Bostonian (Blaszczyk 2000: 36). The impact of competition perhaps reduced the ability of individual producers to be in complete control of the market, as outlined by Mandel.

In terms of the Anglo-American ceramic trade, there was, in fact, evidence of manufacturers producing goods to appeal to the market and importers requesting styles that would suit their own markets. When John Ridgway of the Cauldon

Place works, Shelton, visited the United States in 1822, he commissioned an artist to produce imagery, which was apparently used (along with published engravings), for some of the images in a printed series titled "Beauties of America" (Ewins 1997: 84) (see Figures 1.12 or 6.13 for examples of this series). Alternatively, a Boston importer wrote to Staffordshire manufacturers in the 1810s, requesting darker-blue and brown printed wares, apparently responding to the whims of the consumer (Ewins 1997: 43, 135). Richard Briggs of Boston evidently ordered his *own* designs to be manufactured by Wedgwood (Blaszczyk 2000: 36–7).

Nevertheless, the perplexing question of what was more dominant in the Anglo-American trade has continued to preoccupy different writers and importantly, ceramic historians, giving rise to various interpretations. George Miller and Amy Earls' research article, "War on Pots: The Impact of Economics and Politics on Ceramic Consumption Patterns," points out that:

> Was there a consumer revolution as described by McKendrick, Brewer and Plumb? It should be clear that supply, not demand, was the driver in the nineteenth century. Changes in consumer preferences obviously would be affected by falling prices and availability. Those trying to describe changing consumption patterns in terms of the "fashion system," "social emulation," or changing roles of women as consumers without taking into consideration the role of falling prices and the changing nature of the ceramics will come up short in their understanding of the process.
>
> (2008: 102)

Indeed, Miller calculated that the price of English ceramics dropped significantly from 1809 to 1848 (2013: 341). Emulation and fashion do not account for all aspects of consumption, but neither does Miller and Earls' notion that the Anglo-American ceramic trade was predominantly controlled by manufacturers, and that significant changes in demand were manipulated by reductions in price. It perhaps depends on the function and purpose of consumption. It may be anticipated that the cheapest option would impact on the selection of kitchenware for everyday use, but this rule may not apply to ceramics with a symbolic meaning or purchases intended as a gift. As ceramics can have a variety of functions, it creates many challenges when considering what determined consumption.

Organization

The way in which the Anglo-American trade was organized gradually changed over time. Norman Buck's *The Development of the Organisation of Anglo-American Trade 1800-1850,* first published in 1925, initially identified the important role of merchants, and then British manufacturers, in supplying the American trade. The purpose of Neil Ewins' *"Supplying the Present Wants of Our Yankee Cousins ...": Staffordshire Ceramics and the American Market 1775–1880* of 1997 was to examine what was exported and the mechanisms by which English ceramic manufacturers developed an understanding of what was required by the American market. Merchants who traded in ceramics, as well as the more specialized ceramic importers and dealers in America, played an important part in sales and distribution, and it is these individuals who are the particular focus of this book.

It was not within the scope of Norman Buck's analysis of the Anglo-American trade or "*Supplying the Present Wants of Our Yankee Cousins ...*" to explore the individual backgrounds of those involved in mercantile activities. Although the importance of kinship when conducting a transatlantic trade (in terms of securing credit) has been regularly identified (McCusker and Morgan 2000), considering the actual cultural identities of intermediaries has become a growing area of research. In *The Creation of the British Atlantic World* of 2005, a variety of authors have examined the transatlantic economy in terms of "the role of trade, religion, ethnicity, and class" (Mancke and Shammas 2005: 7). Karin Wulf's chapter titled, "'Of the Old Stock': Quakerism and Transatlantic Genealogies in Colonial British America," discusses the influence of kinship on Philadelphian Quaker families, and how religious views impacted on attitudes to slavery and business (2005: 304–20). Alternatively, a chapter by James Horn and Philip D. Morgan titled, "Settlers and Slaves: European and African Migrations to Early Modern British America" discussed migration and raises the fundamental question, "What role did ethnicity play in constructing their lives in the New World?" (Horn, J. and P.D. Morgan (2005): 38).

This book proposes that the same questions need to be applied to the ceramic importers and dealers located in North America. It may be convenient to describe ceramic importers and dealers as "American," but in the following chapters, it becomes abundantly clear that some of them had moved to the United States. Some importers and dealers even returned to England. They lived and worked within a changing sociopolitical landscape of the eighteenth and nineteenth century. Unquestionably, the behavior of importers and dealers was shaped by the social, political, and economic context, and in the case of ceramics, a strong connection to a specialist trade. Yet it seems that the merchants, importers, and dealers who purchased, advertised, and distributed goods have not always been considered as actual personalities. They are often just perceived as anonymous people, simply located between the manufacturer and the consumer, with their chief roles defined as buying and selling appropriate merchandise, aware of changing fashions, and skillfully balancing the books (Price 1989: 278–9). But, merchants, importers, and dealers were, it appears, far from being secular.

Culture and identity

Sheryllynne Haggerty's *'Merely for Money'?: Business Culture in the British Atlantic, 1750–1815*, usefully develops the debate about merchants having "underlying personas" and how these individuals "coped with and reacted to, events that affected them commercially" (2012: 27). The point becomes whether crockery merchants, importers, and dealers invested anything of themselves in terms of their backgrounds, ethnicity, religious or political views into how they conducted their trade. Roland Marchand's *Advertising the American Dream ...*, referring to the 1920s to 1940s (not an era corresponding to this book), raised a similar point regarding the role of advertisers when he wrote:

> Did the content of advertisements mirror the consumers' actual conditions and behavior—or their fantasies and aspirations? Or did the ads reflect, even more faithfully, the particular values and preoccupations of the advertisers, advertising agents and copywriters?
>
> (1985: xvi)

Marchand continues, "... even a plausible explanation of the content of a group of advertisements, as intended by their creators, would prove nothing about the impact of the messages in those ads on consumers" (1985: xvi). In other words, Marchand did not pursue this line of research, but if ceramic importers and dealers dealt in goods that adhered to their backgrounds and values, this surely has implications on interpreting production and demand. So, while it is not necessarily a new idea to suggest that the "preoccupations" of sellers could be of significance, this still needs to be thoroughly documented as to whether it occurred in the eighteenth and nineteenth centuries. The case study used concerns those involved in the ceramic and glass trade.

Just as we are accustomed to consider how far the consumption of ceramics might be a reflection of people's access to markets and their own ethnicity, status, and religious affiliations (Majewski and O'Brien 1987: 187), why not attempt to apply a similar set of prerogatives to the intermediaries? This book attempts to examine the relevance of kinship, culture, and identity of those involved in the ceramic trade, developing the idea that they were not simply neutral dealers in ceramics. Thus, it moves the debate away from the central role of the supplier or the influence of consumer demand on production to a proposed conceptual model that acknowledges the role of the ceramic merchant, importer, or dealer.

All this analysis takes place in the context of the consumption in North America. T. H. Breen's chapter on "The meanings of things: interpreting the consumer economy in the eighteenth century" in John Brewer and Roy Porter's *Consumption and the World of Goods* points out how American views concerning consumption were not always framed around fashion, with some still advocating constraint (1993: 251). Breen mentions the case of Reverend Jonathan Mayhew of Boston, who published *Christian Sobriety* ... in 1763. He believed that it was to, "the great unhappiness and sin of many young people, that their hearts are set on gay and costly apparel, as if it were a matter of mighty consequence" (1763: 151). He added, "And all who know any thing of the holy Scriptures, know that extravagant expence [sic], and pride in the articles of dress, are often forbidden ..." (1763: 152). As it turns out, his son-in-law was Peter Wainwright, a Liverpool merchant who established a wholesale and retail store in Boston in the late 1780s. Judging by Wainwright's advertisements, crockery and glass was part of his trade, though he developed connections to tobacco manufacturing in Boston. He also had a direct connection to the Staffordshire Potteries, which became apparent because of an attempt on his life by a manufacturer (see Chapter 3). Interestingly, Peter Wainwright's own son, Jonathan Mayhew Wainwright, became the Bishop of New York. In a variety of ways, those who promoted a religious asceticism were not entirely divorced from those connected to mercantile activities.

Moving into the nineteenth century, David E. Shi's *The Simple Life: Plain Living and High Thinking in American Culture* points out how a desire for "simple living" was advocated for both secular and religious reasons (1985: 6). The Reverend Dr. Lyman Beecher, the minister of the Congregational Church of Boston (which was attended by Boston crockery dealer, Isaac H. Parker), remained uneasy about the effect materialism had on the basis of Christian piety (Shi 1985: 104). Should the assumption be that those adverse attitudes to fashion and materialism, as influenced by religion, were simply treated with a degree of skepticism by the mercantile class, and that these views gradually became irrelevant and outmoded? After all, Mayhew was particularly troubled by young people adopting fashionable clothing, potentially transgressing social boundaries, rather than a wider discussion of the acquisition of other commodities, such as ceramics and glass. Or, did religious values have a recognizable impact on the behavior of intermediaries, and even on their approaches to marketing?

As it turns out, more measured attitudes toward consumption were still expressed by American household management publications in the nineteenth century (Witkowski 2016: 47). For instance, Catharine Beecher, a daughter of Dr. Lyman Beecher, wrote household guides in the 1840s, which gave her an opportunity to discuss the wider domestic economy. In Beecher's opinion, American housekeepers, perceived as being predominantly of English descent ([1841] 1843: 39), were presented with different conditions, since there were "no distinct classes, as in aristocratic lands" ([1841] 1843: 40). With an opportunity to freely intermingle, there was "a constant temptation presented to imitate the customs, and strive for the enjoyments, of those who possess larger means" ([1841] 1843: 40). The result was, in Catharine Beecher's view, that, "the people of this Country are under the influence of high commercial, political and religious stimulus, altogether greater than what was known by any other nation" ([1841] 1843: 43). American society was a fusion of commercialization, combined with a duty to religion, and Beecher usefully provides advice about the consumption of ceramics, as discussed in Chapter 2.

In spite of McKendrick, Brewer, and Plumb's notion that fashion became the abiding force in a consumer revolution, views in America that were shaped by religion evidently survived. In the manner of the views of Mayhew or Beecher, did merchants, importers, and dealers also comprise of different socio-religious views? This brings us back to what will be center stage of this book—the backgrounds and cultural identities of merchants, importers, and dealers.

Ceramic merchants, importers, and dealers

As this book refers to intermediaries as either merchants, importers, or dealers, a brief explanation is required of how these roles are defined, and why these different terms have been used. Early Anglo-American merchants tended to deal in a range of goods. Norman Buck points out how merchants could also be wholesale dealers and not retailers ([1925] 1969: 5). Increasingly, city directories and newspaper advertising link individuals to particular commodities—in this case, china, glass, and earthenware were typically found together. Often, the importers and dealers of ceramics declared themselves to be wholesalers and retailers. As far as Norman Buck was concerned, from the 1830s:

> The American importer quite noticeably became a figure of greater importance in the Anglo-American trade. He was a purchaser of goods himself and not merely a consignee of goods from the British merchant or manufacturer.
> ([1925] 1969: 153)

The focus of this book is on merchants, "American" importers, and dealers who traded in ceramics and glass. The ceramic and glass trade did not always follow the broader organizational tendencies outlined by Buck, and it is argued that the reasons for this may be related to the specialized nature of production. Buck's treatment of the importer as "American" and the manufacturer or merchant as "British" somewhat avoids the continuous role of migration. Whether described as a merchant, importer, or a dealer, individuals began to focus on dealing in a more limited range of merchandise. This was no doubt facilitated in the case of some importers and dealers by having family ties to the Potteries. Those involved in the crockery trade tended to cluster on the same streets in major American cities and East Coast ports. Many of these crockery importers and dealers advertised in newspapers and were also active members of their communities. Culture and identity impacted on their connections to the trade, and individual behavior was shaped by political and religious affairs.

Previously, when there have been more attempts to research the backgrounds of importers and dealers, it has generally been motivated by the existence of backstamps applied to Staffordshire wares. For example, early research into the life of Peter Morton was initially stimulated by a curiosity of Staffordshire wares marked as "Peter Morton … Connecticut", or "Peter Morton, Hartford" (McKnight, 1906). Currently, John A. Walthall's *Queensware Direct from the Potteries: US Importers of Staffordshire Ceramics in Antebellum America 1820-1860* is the most comprehensive record of importers' marks (2013). However, not all importers had backstamps, and these individuals have remained somewhat under the radar of other research. There is still a gap in the knowledge of understanding how a wider range of intermediaries contributed to the development of the Anglo-American trade, as considered in this book.

Does it make any difference to know from where the importers and dealers originated, or what their particular political or religious views might be? The central argument of this book is that it can be significant, and this becomes more apparent when examining advertising in conjunction with what may be established about these merchants, importers, or dealers. In the past, Ernest S. Turner's assessment of American advertising was that "In content, the American advertisements were not vastly different from those in English newspapers," except "the British upper classes had ceased to advertise their black boys for sale, American advertisers still trafficked in human flesh" ([1952] 1968: 116). A view expressed in Hilary Young's *English Porcelain 1745-95: its Makers, Design, Marketing and Consumption* points out how newspaper advertising was used by both English porcelain manufacturers and ceramic merchants as a "conduit for basic sales information" (1999: 171). Although advertising of the late eighteenth-century in England and North America drew attention to the ceramic stock available, any new arrivals, and the sellers' competitive prices, moving into the nineteenth century, the backgrounds of importers and dealers, and then their own marketing strategies, becomes surprisingly intertwined. In the United States, the number of published newspapers rapidly increased from the eighteenth century, already reaching over 300 by 1810, with the American Congress actually contributing to their distribution by fixing low postal rates (Cunningham 1994: 6–7).

Methodology

As indicated above, Roland Barthes observed in his influential essay, "The Death of the Author" that, "The *explanation* for a work is always sought in the man or woman who produced it" ([1968] 1977: 143), and this was often paralleled by the approaches of the earliest ceramic historians. An emphasis on "his person, his life, his tastes, his passions …" (Barthes [1968] 1977: 143) does not readily appreciate the degree to which design was influenced by demand in the context of a consumer revolution. For this reason, it can be problematic to treat the manufacturer in the similar manner to that of the autonomous artist, as was the case with Meteyard's analysis of Wedgwood (1865–66).

As an alternative methodology, it may be possible to focus only on surviving ceramics, as evidence of production. But this approach also has its limitations. Objects in ceramic collections are inevitably evidence of production, but at the same time they have been conserved and subjected to a process of selection. What has been considered as worthy of preservation has changed over time. Early collectors have often focused on the renowned manufacturers, or only on certain types of wares, distorting our notions of production. Collections may also create the wrong impression of what was widely consumed, as has been the case with publications concerned with printed Staffordshire wares decorated with American themes (see Chapter 1). Significant private ceramic collections have then passed to major museums, leading to further questions as to what was typically produced and what was actually regularly consumed.

An archaeological approach may provide a less impartial view of the range of production, if examining a factory site. Likewise, an investigation of a domestic site may be more indicative of actual ceramic consumption in a certain place and time. However, archaeology does not necessarily produce an understanding of the motivation for why production occurred in the first place, unless it is generally assumed that the commodity was a response to fashion and demand. It has also been argued that production has received more attention in archaeology (Hollenback and Schiffer 2010: 323), although this depends on the country. In the United States, archaeology has also been undertaken on urban sites where there has been a stronger tendency to initially rely on the imported manufactured goods, as its society developed (Cressey et al. 1982).

In the United States, those involved in mercantile activities assumed a highly significant role. Thus, more recent American authors, such as Regina Blaszczyk, have argued that ceramic merchants, importers, and dealers were far more capable of influencing what manufacturers produced than has previously been acknowledged. Intermediaries, being closer to consumers, could potentially have an awareness of changes in demand. However, Blaszczyk's view assumes (not unreasonably, perhaps), that intermediaries were responding to changes in fashion in the pursuit of maximizing profits in a straightforward, capitalist way.

So, herein lies the paradox of the theoretical framework used in this book. In the following chapters, the *explanation* for the work is explored through the role of intermediaries. It is not disputed that manufacturers produced the ceramics, but the degree to which importers and dealers orchestrated what was produced needs to be thoroughly examined. In a sense, there are some grey areas between manufacturer and the importer—who could also act as the author. In this respect, there becomes a justification for examining the lives of these individuals, despite the reservations of Barthes. If the religious affiliations of importers made a difference to the distribution of these commissioned goods, through their networks, this is also of significance. Therefore, this book proposes that an *explanation* of why certain ceramics was produced may be enhanced by a greater knowledge of the backgrounds of the intermediaries. To totally disregard their lives, their tastes and passions may, in fact, be missing important insights into why certain ceramics were manufactured and marketed in the first place.

This investigation uses records and sources regularly utilized and identified by marketing history (Witkowski and Jones 2006: 70–9). City directories and advertising usefully shows who was connected to the ceramic and glass trade. The main approach is to juxtapose the examination of backgrounds with approaches to marketing, as located in newspapers. On occasion, newspapers report reactions to ceramics being offered to the market. The central idea is relatively a simple one, but it is only in more recent years that the digitalization of archival records and newspapers has made it more feasible to search, survey, and analyze a much broader range of resources. New technology allows for rapid searches of newspapers and other records when previously manual searches required months, if not years, to physically examine each newspaper, or review scans, through a microfilm reader. The sources used in this book are not necessarily new, but it is the digital methods that have enabled a more efficient examination of what is available, and what emerges is a fuller picture of the relationship between supply and demand.

The methodology involves two related stages. The first is to establish the names of importers and dealers involved in the ceramic and glass trade located along the eastern seaboard of the United States. Some of these individuals are known because of previous research, but the digitalization of records such as newspapers and city directories has further contributed to establishing who was involved in the ceramic and glass trade. Second, once ceramic importers and dealers have been identified, the research has involved searching for advertisements, articles, or obituaries that related to the identified importer or dealer. Tools such as Genealogybank.com or the Britishnewspaperarchive.co.uk (since early importers moved between England and the United States) have proved to be vital for this aspect of the research. Some American newspapers, such as *The Friend of Man*, are available through Cornell University, and may also be digitally searched. In addition, immigration and census records are available through Ancestry.com. The social lives of importers and dealers have also been supplemented by archival material relating to the Wainwright family (Liverpool and Boston merchants) and the Ovington family, who were involved in the crockery trade in Brooklyn. An exploration of the backgrounds and behavior of intermediaries provides additional ways of understanding the complexities of production and consumption of ceramics in America from the end of the eighteenth and during the nineteenth century.

Structure

The structure of this book highlights the different tendencies and debates that have developed in ceramic-history literature. Rather than arrange the text around specific individuals, the chapters are thematic. This has allowed for a range of crockery merchants, importers, and dealers to be discussed, demonstrating the influence of kinship, politics, and religion. The most expeditious way to gauge the range of Anglo-American crockery merchants, importers, and dealers included is to consult Pedigrees 1 to 13. By and large, the discussion of particular individuals is clustered within a single chapter, unless certain comparisons are being made.

Chapter 1 examines the work and impact of early collectors on early ceramic history literature and explores how the earliest publications focused on the central role of the producers as the drivers behind goods tailored toward the American market. Demand and consumption are examined in Chapter 2. As interpretations of ceramics have shifted toward the role of demand, rather than of supply, the influence of fashion has been greatly considered. But this chapter also introduces the idea of how there could be varying approaches to consumption. If attitudes to consumption varied, this leads to questions of whether the backgrounds of importers and dealers also varied due to their own cultures and identity, as discussed in Chapter 3. Chapter 4 explores how far political aspects influenced mercantile behavior, and in this context, how this was reflected in what some importers marketed. Chapter 5 considers the dynastic tendencies of families involved in the crockery trade, often further bound together by links to the same religion. Developing this idea, Chapter 6 examines the case of one crockery importer who was attached to the Baptist community in the United States. The impact of religion has often been in the context of the manufacturer, or the consumer, rather than the importer. Chapter 7 examines the issue of morality and race and discusses how one firm of Brooklyn ceramic importers and dealers was also linked to equality movements.

Hitherto, the discussion of African-American culture has either been confined to the analysis of objects that depicted enslavement (Margolin 2002) or the work of nineteenth-century enslaved American potters, such as Dave, owned by the Drake family (Goldberg and Witkowski 2006). There is still more that may be explored concerning the interracial experience in the context of the crockery trade. Intriguingly, we find that a crockery firm employed an African American china packer, who was also an established church minster.

In a sense, the final chapters turn back on themselves. The deficiencies of earlier forms of ceramic history literature, so often identified by more recent writers (Richards 1999: 7), are then used to an advantage. Although Chapter 1 outlines how early ceramic history publications focused on what was increasingly collected (ignoring broader patterns of ceramic production and consumption), this literature is still of value to the modern historian. Early writers often identified how some patterns were rarer than others. How is it possible to reconcile recent interpretations of ceramics, which believe that production was motivated by fashion and demand, with earlier observations that recognized how some designs produced for the American market, were unusual, or rare? It is believed that the notion of varying levels of rarity made by these early connoisseurs is a genuine observation, and this is not simply the result of the imbalance caused by evolving habits of collecting. In the final chapters and the conclusion, it is proposed whether, moving forward, new literature should include the role of the intermediary as a way of explaining what appears to be a contradiction.

Summary

"For too long, ceramic scholarship has focused primarily on the potters who produced the wares and on ceramic technology, chronology, and connoisseurship" (Miller and Earl 2008: 67). While this observation is true, the intention of *Alternative Narratives in Ceramic History* is to develop an approach that can unite various interpretations of ceramics. Interpretations of ceramics that have simply been weighted toward the role of producers or the manipulative role of marketing do not fully convey the complete picture of why ceramics were produced for the American market. Neither does the view that intermediaries helped steer manufacturers' production on the basis of having a deeper understanding of the demands of the market. The central theory becomes that the backgrounds, culture, and identities of those involved in importing, dealing, and marketing ceramics should be interrogated. Therefore, *Alternative Narratives …* sets out to explore the contextualization of ceramics through the activities of merchants, importers, and dealers, as positioned between the producers and the consumers.

This book does not seek to detract or entirely discredit the previous perspectives utilized by ceramic history. The main contention is to demonstrate the value in *additionally* considering the contributions of intermediaries. Even the employment of an African American ceramic packer potentially becomes useful evidence of the attitudes of the importer and, in turn, relates to what was commissioned. Rather than the view that design and consumption were either production-led, or alternatively, more market-led, it is proposed that the motivation to create ceramic designs could also be more expressive, or conscience-led. Conscience-led design did not reside in the hands of the producers but in the hopes and desires of the intermediaries. If importers and dealers marketed, or even commissioned goods that reflected their own religious or political views, this introduces other dimensions as to why certain ceramics were produced. While this was marginal behavior, it is nevertheless evidence of how intermediaries were not necessarily marketing goods that responded to demand or acting in emulative ways. The point is that intermediaries commissioned and marketed ceramics for different reasons, and the theory becomes that their failures, madness, and vices have to be given far greater recognition to further understand design and consumption.

Chapter 1

COLLECTING AND PERCEPTIONS OF PRODUCTION

Taken as a whole, the range of Staffordshire ceramics printed with American themes was clearly only a small proportion of what was exported to the United States (Figures 1.1 and 1.2). As an example, excavations of a rubbish pit belonging to a merchant-shopkeeper of Middletown, Connecticut, found only a small quantity of American-themed sherds. These included cups depicting a seated figure (long considered by the earliest collectors and writers to be the Marquis de Lafayette), beside Benjamin Franklin's tomb, and plates depicting the White House, Washington DC, and the State House of Hartford, Connecticut (Dyson 1982: 376). Even when American-themed sherds have been found in larger quantities, this could be a reflection of the significance of the locations where these designs were sold. Previous archaeological investigations in Alexandria DC (near to George Washington's home at Mount Vernon) have located a range of sherds incorporating patriotic emblems. Rather than being indicative of widespread distribution, these sherds parallel what was marketed by a crockery merchant of Alexandria DC (Magid 2006: 3–39).

There was growing interest in ceramic collecting in the United States, but this was not always confined to American-themed wares. In the period in which Governor Caleb Lyon's ceramic collection was auctioned off in New York in 1876, he was described as "one of the first victims of the choice ceramic-ware mania" (*Sunday Dispatch*, Philadelphia April 30, 1876). Based on contemporary descriptions in the press, Lyon's collection was a mixture of Far Eastern and European wares and, apparently, did not include Liverpool or Staffordshire wares made for the export trade. The closest Caleb Lyon came to acquiring ceramics associated with the American market was his possession of wares associated with different presidents. Apparently, Lyon had acquired a plate manufactured in France, owned by Martha Washington, which subsequently sold for a high price at the New York auction of 1876.

At this stage, collecting habits were not dissimilar to those of Britain. When the English writer, Joseph Marryat, published *Collections Towards a History of Pottery and Porcelain* ... in 1850, he provided an insightful list of what different private collectors owned. Typically, collections of Sèvres, Dresden, European faïence, Far Eastern and Cheslea porcelain were owned by the nobility, or wealthy bankers, such as members of the Rothschild family. Joseph Marryat appeared on this list, and he described himself as a collector of "Miscellaneous" ceramics, living at Whitehall, London (Marryat 1850: 365–8). Some years later, when his collection

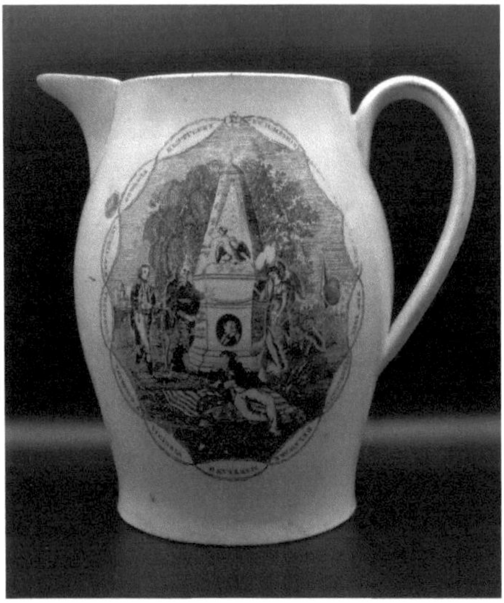

Figure 1.1 Jug, creamware, black printed, commemorating President George Washington (1732–1799), with an image of an unnamed ship on the reverse. Probably Herculaneum Pottery, Liverpool, c.1800–05.

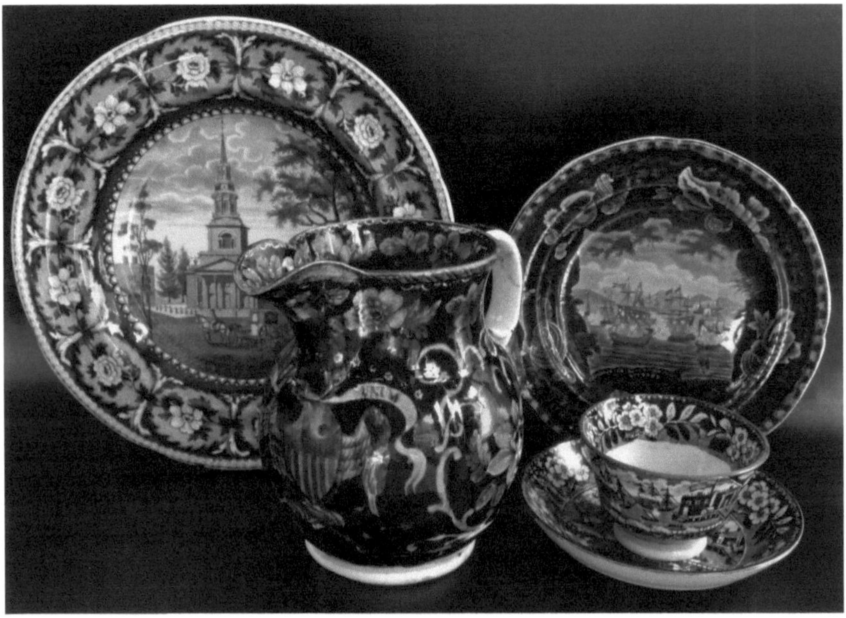

Figure 1.2 A range of American-themed wares. From left to right: Plate, earthenware, blue printed, backstamped, "Beauties of America/ Octagon Church, Boston/ J. & W. Ridgway", Shelton, c.1823–25. Jug, earthenware, blue printed, American Seal and inscription "E Pluribus Unum", impressed "Adams, Staffordshire Warranted", Stoke, c.1825–30. Plate, blue printed, depicting Commodore Macdonough's victory over the British at Lake Champlain in 1814, Enoch Wood, Burslem. c.1825–30. Cup and saucer, earthenware, blue printed commemorating General Lafayette's arrival in New York, August 16, 1824, impressed "[R. & J.] Clews, Staffordshire Warranted", Cobridge, c.1825.

was auctioned at Christie's, it was described as chiefly consisting of Far Eastern china, European wares, with some specimens of English porcelains, Staffordshire and Wedgwood ware (*The Daily News*, London February 8, 1867). Marryat was a member of parliament and the son of a wealthy merchant-banker and West Indian plantation owner who opposed abolitionism (Marryat 1816). When Joseph Marryat's father died in 1824, he was allegedly worth in the region of half a million pounds. As Joseph Marryat received £31,000 per annum from this estate, there then becomes the undeniable fact that his ability to travel, research, and collect ceramics was, in part, funded by an unsavory income inherited from his father (*Cambridge Chronicle and Journal* January 30, 1824).

American ceramic collecting began to deviate from British trends. William C. Prime's enormously ambitious, *Pottery and Porcelain of all Times and Nations*, was first published in New York in 1877. While contemporary reviews were quick to point out how a great deal of the book "could be found elsewhere" (*New York Herald* November 25, 1877), a significant aspect of this publication was Prime's examination of English pottery derived from his own extensive collection. Prime describes creamware pitchers printed with American themes (which he associated with the Herculaneum factory of Liverpool), and other wares depicting American scenery, characteristically printed in varying shades of under-glaze blue, manufactured in Staffordshire. Three Liverpool creamware pitchers and a plate depicting a Hudson River steamer, manufactured by Enoch Wood of Burslem, were illustrated in this book, all of which were described as, "T-P Coll". In other words, these items were part of the Trumbull-Prime collection, created by W. C. Prime and his wife, Mary Trumbull.

William Cowper Prime and Mary Trumbull formed a huge collection of ceramics from all around the world, estimated to be in the region of twenty to thirty thousand pieces, and embraced wares expressly made for the American market. Mary Trumbull died in 1872, and in her memory, this collection was gifted to Princeton University in 1890 (*New York Observer* April 11, 1872; *The New York Tribune* December 25, 1890). Prime was born in 1825 and initially trained as a lawyer at Princeton. Later, he became editor and part-owner of the *New York Journal of Commerce* and a Professor of Art History at Princeton University (*New York Daily Tribune* February 15, 1905). Prime was not the only American author of that era to write about ceramics, but he does appear to represent an early example of discussing English wares designed for export. Jennie J. Young's *The Ceramic Art: A Compendium of the History and Manufacture of Pottery and Porcelain* of 1878, first published in New York, broadly discussed British ceramics and the development of the American industry. However, she does not mention what was to become more widely known by collectors and writers as "historical Staffordshire" wares.

What inspired William C. Prime to write about ceramics that were, in effect, manufactured within his lifetime, is important. In part, the motivation seems to have stemmed from a growing recognition of the rarity of certain Liverpool and Staffordshire pieces. Prime already observed how, "American decorations" in dark blue, "common enough … forty years ago", were now "becoming scarce", and as a consequence, "collectors will do well to secure good specimens" ([1877] 1879: 346). However, he adds that these Staffordshire wares were "not prized, except by a few judicious collectors, who recognize in it a color that is rarely surpassed on pottery …" ([1877] 1879: 346). Apparently, there was only moderate interest in ceramics printed with American subjects in the 1870s, although some writers have suggested that the collecting of these types of wares had already commenced by 1865 (Laidacker 1939a: 125). Nevertheless, as late as 1907, Alexander M. Hudnut (a ceramic collector, museum director, and author) pointed out in *American Homes and Gardens* that, "There are only a few collections of Old Blue historical china in this country which are well known" (1907: 21).

In the United States, the urge to gradually collect Liverpool and Staffordshire wares was related to a realization that these ceramics provided a visual record of a rapidly changing world. Evidence for this may be derived from the introductory text provided by William C. Prime for a book, *The China Hunters Club*, published 1878. Originally published as by "The Youngest Member", *The China Hunters Club*, was actually written by Prime's sister-in-law, Annie Trumbull Slosson, who was another ceramic enthusiast. Despite the fact that women have often been so central to ceramic collecting, writing, and at times, engaged in the actual crockery business, it is unclear whether the book's anonymity was a reflection of the rise of a patriarchal society. With prophetic insight, Prime's introduction predicted that English ceramics printed with American themes would one day rank with the "vases of Greece" since they provided important visual evidence of the early development of the United States (Slosson 1878: 8). Annie Trumbull Slosson discusses Chinese and European porcelains, and then devotes a whole chapter to the theme of "American History Illustrated in Pottery". Once these types of ceramic wares had achieved a collectable status, it influenced perceptions of what was exported, as well as the nature of American ceramic demand.

Leon Rosenstein's *Antiques: The History of an Idea* outlines the evolution of collecting in the United States, and how it spread from the aristocracy to a wider bourgeoisie during the nineteenth century. American collecting habits developed a nostalgia for early colonialism, and items with historical associations, or objects that could be linked to places of national pride. Rosenstein recognizes how collecting antiques had a distinctive American flavor, and also how far systematic forms of research had emerged by the 1880s (2009: 132–8). However, the motivation to collect ceramics was still varied and complex. As early as 1883, it was recorded how:

> Mrs. Thomas Maddock, in Lafayette-place [New York City], has one of the best collections of British and American ware in this country, from royal china to the pioneer's stone mug, probably some thousands of pieces. Her husband was a native of the Staffordshire pottery district, and began making collections long ago. In blue and pink ware her specimens go back beyond the Hanoverian kings.
>
> (*The Indianapolis Journal* March 28, 1883)

Mrs. Thomas Maddock's name was Alice Capes, nee Patten, and she came from Marlborough, New York. Her second husband, Thomas Maddock, was a New York crockery importer and dealer, born in Burslem in c.1833. In 1868, a partnership between Thomas, William B. Maddock and William Steel (the husband of Betsy Maddock) was formed, although a John Maddock junior was already active as a New York crockery importer from at least the mid-1850s (Wilson 1855; *New York Commercial Advertiser* February 28, 1868; *New York Herald* April 23, 1891). By the 1870s, Thomas, William B. and a Henry Maddock, shared the same New York address, and the firm acted as an agency for John Maddock & Sons, earthenware manufacturers of Burslem (Trow 1876; *Pottery Gazette* June 1, 1881: 506). A trade card connecting John Maddock & Sons to Maddock & Co., of New York is shown in Figure 1.3. After Thomas Maddock died in 1889, Alice continued to be involved in the crockery importing business (*Pottery Gazette* June 1, 1889; *Savannah Morning News*, Georgia December 9, 1902). Widows running a business after the death of a husband occurred in eighteenth century (diZerega Wall 1994: 261), and this evidently still remained a characteristic for those connected to the crockery trade in the nineteenth century.

After Alice Maddock died, it was those involved in the crockery trade who became entrusted with preserving her collection. Her final will and testament gave her ceramic collection to Sidney Maddock, the son of Henry Maddock, who had also become involved in the New York firm. Although he was bequeathed the collection, it was Alice's desire that her ceramics be given to the city of Trenton and the Trenton School of Industrial Arts, New Jersey, shortly before she died in 1902 (*Trenton Evening Times* May 21, 1902; February 27, 1903). A bronze tablet, to be placed in the art school, was inscribed, "The Mrs. Alice Maddock Collection, presented to the city of Trenton, N. J., by Sidney Maddock of Brooklyn, N.Y., in cordial appreciation of her wishes, 1903" (*Trenton Times* July 23, 1904).

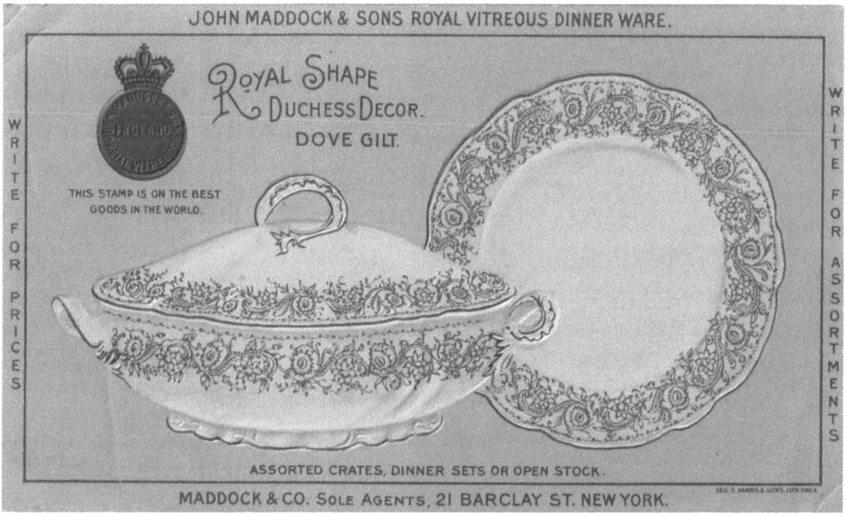

Figure 1.3 Trade card, for Maddock & Co., New York, sole agents for John Maddock & Sons' "Royal Vitreous Dinner Ware", c.1890.

The gift was made to Trenton, New Jersey, because of its strong links to the ceramic industry. Indeed, other members of the large and extended Maddock family were heavily involved in the development of pottery and sanitary ware production in Trenton. For instance, another Thomas Maddock (born Burslem, in c.1817) formed a partnership with Millington and Astbury, later to become Thomas Maddock & Sons (*Trenton Evening Times* June 17, 1899). It was believed that Thomas Maddock established the first sanitary ware manufactory in the United States (*Trenton Evening Times* June 20, 1899).

Around the time of Alice Maddock's gift to Trenton, an article indicated that she "began her collection when young and had every means of adding to it" (*New-York Tribune* February 22, 1903). Before marrying Thomas Maddock in 1882, Mrs. Alice Capes ran a Turkish bathhouse business, later bequeathed to a nephew. Alice and Thomas Maddock had no children of their own. Her collection was considered as "particularly valuable from an American point of view as there is only one other of a similar nature in the country," and this was identified as the Trumbull-Prime collection housed at Princeton University (*New-York Tribune* February 22, 1903). A large proportion of the Alice Maddock's collection was related to the American market, and this again, is evidence of the small number of collections that existed in museums, or institutions, in that period. The newspaper article described the Maddock collection as including Belleek ware, and "… six hundred blue print plates, representing the finest specimens of work done at the potteries of Staffordshire, the Ridgeway [sic], Adams, Davenport, Stubbs, Wood and other shops." It is worth quoting at length since it reveals what had been collected, and early assumptions made about demand:

> In the early part of the century it was the fashion to make souvenir plates to commemorate the historical events. Mrs. Maddock secured a great number of these, some of which are exceedingly rare. The landing Lafayette plate, dated 1824, is one especially sought by collectors. A fine one is in the collection.
>
> The English Anti-Slavery Society in 1837 sent a consignment of plates to New York Abolitionists to be sold at auction for the benefits of the cause. Though many were sold, and at complimentary prices, for some reason they have been poorly preserved, and there are few in existence. The one in the collection has scalloped edges and a scroll border dotted with stars, American eagles, shields and medallions. In the centre are appropriate quotations from the constitution of the United States.
>
> The only New Jersey plate in the collection shows the Stevens mansion, in Hoboken. A Baltimore and Ohio Railway plate, dark blue, shows the first train of cars on that road, drawn by the locomotive invented by Peter Cooper. A New York plate reproduces the old Park Theatre, built in 1797, and shows the old city in the vicinity of the present City Hall Park …
>
> (*New-York Tribune* February 22, 1903)

This highly significant and early description of Mrs. Maddock's collection draws attention to how it was "the fashion to make souvenir plate" but then paradoxically observes how some patterns were already considered as "poorly preserved." The article already begins to acknowledge that there were variations in what had survived and also expresses an uncertainty as to why some designs were scarce. In one account (which discussed the anti-slavery plate), it was observed how, "While the plate is not an antique, it is very rare" (*Trenton Sunday Advertiser* February 15, 1903). The important issue of rarity will be returned to in Chapter 6, when discussing the anti-slavery plate of 1837. In contacting Trenton City Museum, where Alice Maddock's collection resides, the current whereabouts of the anti-slavery plate is unknown.

An article titled "China Collecting" (which first appeared in the *New York Times* and was reprinted in the *Pottery Gazette*, published in England) suggested how there was "something peculiarly womany, if not womanly, about china collecting" (August 1, 1894).

Wealthy American women were certainly interested in forming collections, but men were involved, too. As it was stated, "Some of our New York collectors are Mrs. Livingstone [sic], Mrs. Maddock, Mrs. Benjamin Perrine Young, the late William Henry Harrison, and Mr. Henry Clews who comes naturally by his china culture, his father, Mr. James Clews, being a famous potter and designer and manufacturer of many now much-prized patterns" (August 1, 1894). Ceramic collecting was not just a manifestation of an "American appreciation of the antique" (Rosenstein 2009: 136). Some, although by no means all, collected because they had a vested interest in preserving their own heritage. It was felt that Henry Clews' Staffordshire connections had played a part in stimulating his collecting interests. Mrs. Livingston (nee Emily A. Green) was a daughter of Henry Woodhull Green, Chief Justice and Chancellor of New Jersey and was evidently from a wealthy background (*New York Daily Tribune* March 23, 1900). Her ceramic collection was given to Princeton University (Hasley [1899] 1974: xx–xxi).

Ralph and James Clews produced a range of blue printed wares, which included a scene of General Lafayette arriving in New York in 1824—an example of which was owned by Mrs. Alice Maddock (Figures 1.2 and 7.15). James Clews briefly moved to America and set up a pottery at Troy, Indiana, but this was unsuccessful, and he returned to Staffordshire (Stefano, [1974] 1980: 207–9). However, his son, Henry Clews, remained in New York, and became a successful, Wall Street banker. To some degree, collections formed in the United States were shaped by backgrounds, culture and identity, whereas Marryat's English-list, only mentions one Staffordshire manufacturer, Herbert Minton, as a collector of miscellaneous wares (1850: 367).

James Clews' attempt at establishing an American pottery was also briefly discussed in Edwin Barber's *The Pottery and Porcelain of the United States* published in 1893. At this point, the language used to describe Staffordshire wares is of significance. Barber provides some background about James Clews, and then observes that, "Many of his now highly prized pieces were decorated with dark-blue transfer prints of American views ..." (Barber, E. A. (1893): 158). It is notable how there was a shift from William C. Prime's comment in the late 1870s, that American-themed ceramics were "not prized, except by a few judicious collectors," to Barber's description of "highly prized" by the 1890s. The change in tone is indicative of the growth of collecting these types of wares. Early collectors would visit the "bric-a-brac shops of New York, Boston, and Philadelphia" or tour around remote villages offering to buy wares directly from the owners (Slosson 1878: 214). While the practice of visiting country homes continued, Alice Morse Earle's *China Collecting in America* of 1892, mentions how, "many of the finest specimens of American historical china that have been offered for sale in New York and Boston 'Antique shops' during the past year have been purchased and sent to California" (1892: 414–17). American-themed wares were evolving from being categorized as bric-a-brac to that of the antique.

Early writers tended to consider a broader range of ceramics found in the United States. So, Earle's *China Collecting in America* included chapters on "Oriental China," as well as on "Liverpool and other Printed Wares" and "Staffordshire Wares." She attempted to list the range of designs found in this category of wares and also documented Staffordshire backstamps that incorporated an American eagle (Earle 1892: 141, 324–31). Alice Earle was born in Worcester, New Hampshire, in 1853, and became fascinated with wider aspects of society and culture of New England. She also wrote, *The Sabbath in Puritan New England*, published in New York in 1891. When she died, prematurely, in 1911, her obituary pointed out how she, "had taught most of us that the accumulations of old New England and Dutch closets and attics were not rubbish" (*Columbus Dispatch* February 20, 1911). Another newspaper claimed that she had influenced "the cult of the antique." Due to the influence of her books, "the old, blue Staffordshire and brown Bennington pottery" had made its way "from kitchen shelves to the mantelpiece" (*Fairmont West Virginian* February 23, 1911). While Prime considered the ceramics printed with American scenes as important historical records of the past, Earle's motivation was more about preserving objects that would provide evidence of wider material culture.

By the late 1890s, there was scope for the publications to focus only on the printed wares, as manufactured in either Liverpool or Staffordshire. This applied to Richard Townley Haines Halsey's *Early New York Dark Blue Staffordshire Pottery* and Edwin Barber's *Anglo-American Pottery*, both published in 1899. Barber, as curator of the Pennsylvania Museum and School of Industrial Art, had already written about different aspects of American ceramics and glassware. At the forefront of Barber's analysis was the actual Staffordshire producers—to the extent that he included portraits of Enoch Wood, James Clews, and John Ridgway. Barber identified Enoch Wood of Burslem as one of the earliest to produce dark-blue printed ceramics for the American market (1899: 23). The work of both Haines Halsey and Barber was supplemented by the magazine, *Old China*, published in Syracuse, New York from 1901, that set out to bring collectors of "old china in closer contact with each other" (Robineau 1901: 1).

Both Haines Halsey and Barber attempted to catalogue the sheer variety of patterns produced in Liverpool and Staffordshire, and this required access to extensive collections. Indeed, Haines Halsey's *Early New York Dark Blue Staffordshire Pottery* acknowledges how, "Owing … to the foresight and generosity of Mr. William C. Prime, a large number of pieces of this ware can be seen in the Trumbull-Prime collection of Pottery and Porcelain which fills the beautiful Art Building on the historic campus of Princeton University" (1899: 273). Haines Halsey's research was enhanced by having access to the Trumbull-Prime collection. He was a member of the New York Stock Exchange, and later became involved in organizing the American wing of the Metropolitan Museum (*Boston Herald* February 8, 1942). But these individuals were often collectors in their own right, as well as influential writers. In an article titled "Some notable Collections of Old Blue Staffordshire China," published in *American Homes and Gardens* of 1907, it was indicated that Haines Halsey's collection of American views on dark blue Staffordshire was "well-known" (Hudnut 1907: 25). It was almost as though the earliest collectors and writers sought solace in their collections of historical Staffordshire wares, as the old and new world collided; this happened quite literally in the case of Haines Halsey, who died after being struck by an automobile in 1942 (*Boston Herald* February 8, 1942).

Dark-blue printed

The earliest ceramic historians recognized that the American views manufactured in Staffordshire were often printed in dark-blue (Figure 1.2). Edwin Barber expressed a view that a demand for dark-blue had originally evolved as a way of covering up blemishes on inferior ceramics (1899: 21–22). R. T. Haines Halsey's *Pictures of Early New York on Dark Blue Staffordshire Pottery* of 1899 reiterated a similar view. However, he also quotes William C. Prime who "twenty years ago," when researching this subject at the Trenton potteries in New Jersey, had established additional information from an Englishman involved in the ceramic industry. The story relayed to Prime was how, on one occasion, simply by chance, the printed blue decoration "overflowed." However, it was decided to ship the batch of ware to the United States, where it still sold remarkably well, and a preference for the darker printed blue was thus established (Haines Halsey 1899: 16).

Certainly, in the order book of Horace Collamore, a crockery importer of Boston, there is a reference to "blue printed dining ware new dark pattern State House …", as early as August 1818 (Ewins 1997: 136). This would appear to be the Boston State House pattern (see Chapter 2, Figure 2.11). Interestingly, Collamore also wrote to the Staffordshire suppliers complaining that the wares printed in blue were "not dark enough," which would imply how a taste for darker-blue printed ware was more of a gradual evolution (Ewins 1997: 43). In 1826, a letter from Matthew Smith of Baltimore states, "In Blue print'd the demand is still for dark & well cov'd patterns" (Pomfret 2010: 97). As importers stipulated what they wanted, this appears to suggest that there was an element of fashion involved, though as indicated above, early writers believed that the demand for dark-blue printed was something that initially occurred by chance.

What stimulated a demand for a darker blue in the first place is a difficult question. Instead of problems with firing, an alternative theory was suggested in

Ada Walker Camehl's *The Blue China Book* of 1916. She noted that while "the rich blue color" on Staffordshire wares could cover up imperfections, it was also "an echo" of imported Far Eastern and Delftwares (Camehl [1916] 1946: xiii). If this were the case, a demand for Staffordshire dark blue (which in reality embraced flora and fauna designs, Far Eastern themes, English views, as well as the collectable American subjects), may be related to a form of emulation. It is notable that when Samuel Sumner of Boston advertised in 1799, it was stipulated that he had just received from Canton, "Dark Blue Nankin-Colour Dinning sets China, with gilt edged Custard Cups to them …" (*Massachusetts Mercury* July 12, 1799). Likewise, James and John H. Cresson, crockery importers of Philadelphia, used the phrase "Dark blue" to describe a "complete assortment of China" advertised in 1804. Other advertisements placed by Cresson suggest that their supplies of china ware came from Canton (*Poulson' American Daily Advertiser* April 20, 1804; May 12, 1807). However, the view that imperfections were the reason for dark-blue production persisted well into twentieth century (Smith 1924: iv). Only in the 1970s did Marian Klamkin reintroduce a view, as expressed by Ada Walker Camehl, that the explanation for dark-blue printed could have related to imitating Chinese porcelain and Dutch Delft earthenware, also widely imported into the United States (1973: 22). As the scholarship of the subject evolved, it became apparent that demand shifted to a range of other printed colors in the 1830s (Smith 1924: iv; Larsen 1939: 25).

The research for the earliest books was also aided by the authors themselves, forming sizable collections. Ellouise Baker Larsen's *American Historical Views on Staffordshire China* of 1939, used many of her own wares as examples, which were later given to the Smithsonian Museum. The reputation of a collection was enhanced if it had been mentioned in a publication. Some of the illustrations in Haines Hasley's book were from the collection of one Miss Florence I. Chauncey, a daughter of a Brooklyn banker. Later, when her ceramic collection was advertised for sale by the American Art Association of New York, it was on the basis that her "Rare Blue and White Historical China" included "many Specimens of which are reproduced in Mr. R. T. Haines Hasley's Book, 'Early New York Dark Blue Staffordshire Pottery'" (*Sun and New York Press* April 1, 1917).

It seems that collections obtained an additional cachet if they were mentioned by key texts. Florence I. Chauncey's collection (along with ceramics belonging to the late Alfred D. Barnard of Baltimore) was exhibited by the American Art Association prior to the auction sale. The following description is evidence, yet again, of what had attracted the attention of the early collectors:

> There is, of course, much Lafayette, who is shown not only when he landed at Castle Garden applauded by 200,000 New Yorkers, but also at all his stopping places.
>
> The collection includes a great many specimens that have been reproduced to illustrate R. T. H. Halsey's work "Early New York", in spite of their great age have guarded their deep blue glazes intact. Of these are the famous "Baltimore and Ohio" plates, the "Ruins of the Merchants' Exchange, New York," "Gilpin's

Mills on the Brandywine Creek," the "City Hotel," and the "City Hall," of New York, the Franklin library of Philadelphia, The Charleston Exchange, the ship "Cadmus" that brought Lafayette to America and the "Deaf and Dumb Asylum of Hartford."

There are also statuettes in Staffordshire ware of Uncle Tom, Little Eva and Benjamin Franklin, a "millennium" plate, a copper lustre cream ewer, and Erie Canal "Eulogy" plate, a set of dishes bearing the arms of the various states, a set of plates with the famous "Syntax" decorations and several designed by Sir David Wilkie.

(*Sun and New York Press* April 27, 1917)

While Florence I. Chauncey had collected historical events and places in "deep blue glazes," this description provides early evidence of collecting Staffordshire figurines linked to American culture, such as Dr. Benjamin Franklin, or those inspired by Harriet Beecher Stowe's *Uncle Tom's Cabin* (Figures 1.4 and 7.12). Based on this auction notice, "historical china" wares were continuing to reach high prices. A platter described as depicting Castle Garden of New York sold for $310, and $225 was paid for a plate illustrating New York from Brooklyn Heights (*Sun and New York Press* May 2, 1917).

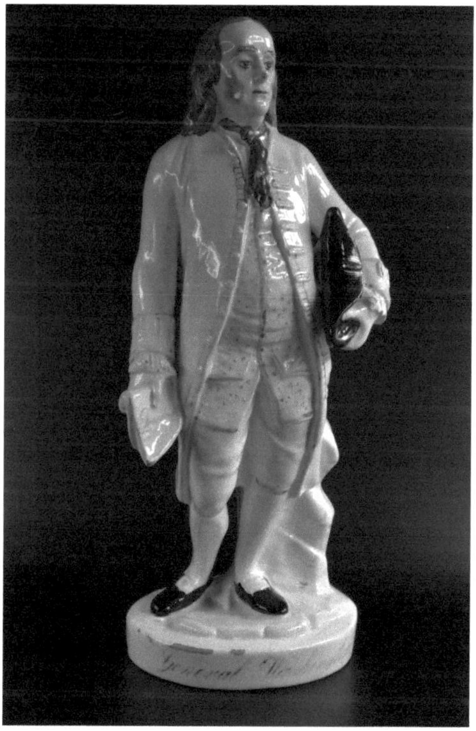

Figure 1.4 Figurine, earthenware, enamel and gilt decoration, of Dr. Benjamin Franklin, signed as "General Washington". The Figure holds a document signed "Freedom". Staffordshire, c.1860–70.

The ascendency of the producer

Most of the early authors addressed the fundamental questions—how and why were these designs manufactured for the American market? William C. Prime's *Pottery and Porcelain of all Times and Nations …* observed how as a "great variety" of Liverpool creamwares often included the names of ships and their captains, it was feasible that, "American ship-masters trading to Liverpool, and other Americans, had pitchers made to order with prints of local American interest" ([1877] 1879: 258, 361).

However, speculation as to the actual motivation continued. There was consideration of what had led to the production of printed creamwares (associated with Liverpool), and the Staffordshire earthenwares, produced after the Anglo-American War of 1812–14, in Annie Slosson's *The China Hunters Club* of 1878 (138–9, 155). Quoting from one of its club members, a Mr. Whitney, Slosson reported the belief that, "Sometimes pieces were made in obedience to American orders, and in other cases enterprising potters designed them for American sale" (1878: 155). The idea was, at least, proposed that American dealers may have sent prints to English manufacturers to be used for the surface pattern designs (1878: 159). In *The China Hunters Club,* Annie Slosson does not stipulate when this collecting society was founded, but importantly, she indicates that its formation was inspired by one of the members acquiring a copy of Meteyard's *Life of Wedgwood* published in 1865–66 (1878: 13–19). Mr. Whitney joined the organization because he discovered that the "ceramic art had some connection with American history" (1878: 137), and it was his opinions that were used extensively to inform her chapter titled, "American History Illustrated in Pottery" (1878: 137–64).

It is useful to know that Meteyard's publication influenced these early American collectors and writers, since this may help to explain why there was a tendency to be preoccupied with the role of the producer. Although America was a major destination for a variety of imported ceramics, this did not automatically translate into encouraging the earliest collectors, or writers, to consider whether importers and dealers had ever hugely influenced design. It appears that the model for approaching the subject of ceramic history was derived from writers such as Meteyard, who had focused on the entrepreneurial role of the manufacturer—namely, Josiah Wedgwood. Only when American authors discussed the Liverpool wares (as opposed to the Staffordshire wares) was it believed that these could represent instances of responding to American orders because existing examples occasionally incorporated the names of captains, or the names of actual ships. For instance, Barber's *Anglo-American Pottery* of 1899 pointed out that:

> Many pieces were ornamented with ships and maritime emblems and were brought to this country in large numbers by returning seaman. Frequently ship-owners ordered from Liverpool potters pieces bearing views of their own vessels. A pitcher of this character shows an engraving of the ship Astrea of Wiscasset, and it has been discovered that this vessel was built in 1793 by Gen. Abiel Wood, one of the largest ship-owners at that time in New England.
>
> (1899: 12)

However, other writers (even those interested in the Liverpool creamwares), gradually veered toward the idea of the entrepreneurial manufacturer. This was the case in Robert McCauley's *Liverpool Transfer Designs on Anglo-American Pottery* of 1942. For instance, when discussing a creamware pitcher, which depicted an American soldier standing on the foot of a British lion, McCauley's interpretation was, "we wonder at the business zeal which inspired them and the temerity of the English potter who marketed them" (1942: 24). By producing ceramics that were anti-British, this, in theory, was how manufacturers developed the Anglo-American market.

Increasingly, there was less recognition of the role of commissions but a focus on what each of the manufacturers had produced in terms of different patterns. What became the cornerstone of explaining why these wares were produced for the American market was how they represented a concerted effort on behalf of the manufacturer to appeal to consumers after the Revolutionary wars, and later still, the Anglo-American war. The irony of how British manufacturers were willing to produce goods that celebrated English defeats did not go unnoticed. Alice Morse Earle's *China Collecting in America* notes that:

> It seems odd that English potters should have made so many pitchers bearing testimony to the victories of their late enemies, unless they were ordered by American dealers specially for the American market; but I have never seen anything to prove that such orders were given.
>
> (1892: 142)

So while in this extract there was some speculation that American crockery dealers could have impacted on Staffordshire production, Earle had failed to find evidence to support this theory. Alternatively, R. T. Haines Halsey's *Pictures of Early New York on Dark Blue Staffordshire Pottery* simply argued that ceramics depicting American themes were "calculated to appeal to the national pride of their purchasers" (1899: 276). A few years later, N. Hudson Moore's *The Old China Book* ... mentioned how Enoch Wood produced wares that depicted "incidents and scenes which appealed in a peculiar way to the growing nation" (1903: 13). Later still, Ada Walker Camehl's *The Blue China Book* argued that in order to establish a profitable trade, English manufacturers "decorated the pottery destined for the new market with faithful views taken from America itself, many of which, by the way, have been perpetuated in no other manner" ([1916] 1946: ix).

As research developed during the early part of the twentieth century, the phrase "historical Staffordshire," or "historical china," became an established part of the nomenclature used to describe American-themed wares. The introduction to the first edition of Ellouise Baker Larsen's *American Historical Views on Staffordshire China* of 1939 was written by Homer Eaton Keyes, the editor of *The Magazine Antiques*. He points out how between 1922 and 1937, thirty-five articles on historical Staffordshire were published in *The Magazine Antiques*, and that this research often focused on the sources used by Staffordshire manufacturers (1939: x). Larsen's publication remains the most extensive catalogue of the underglaze American-themed printed wares.

In *American Historical Views*, there is evidence of Ellouise Baker Larsen already placing an emphasis on the role of manufacturers. In one instance, her thorough research referred to an example of a blue printed design titled "Winter View of Pittsfield, Mass [Massachusetts]," which was manufactured by Clews of Cobridge (Figures 1.5 and 1.6). While unable to reveal the source of the view, she added that, "Local historians discredit the story printed in *The China Hunters Club* (1878) that Mr Allen, a Pittsfield merchant, sent a view of the elm and the park to England in 1825, where it was transferred to Staffordshire" (1939: 72). Annie Slosson's book, *The China Hunters Club*, was published in 1878, and Larsen seems to have been content to follow the view of these local historians.

Turning to *The China Hunters Club*, Slosson mentions that her interpretation of the Pittsfield pattern had derived from "a newspaper paragraph which I had cut from a journal in 1864" (1878: 162). Using digital search tools to survey newspapers, it has been possible to locate Annie Slosson's somewhat vague reference. The *Boston Evening Transcript* contains a short report titled "The Old Elm at Pittsfield," which explains how a merchant called Allen had sent a view of Pittsfield to England to be "reproduced on blue crockery" around 1825 (August 5, 1864). A number of

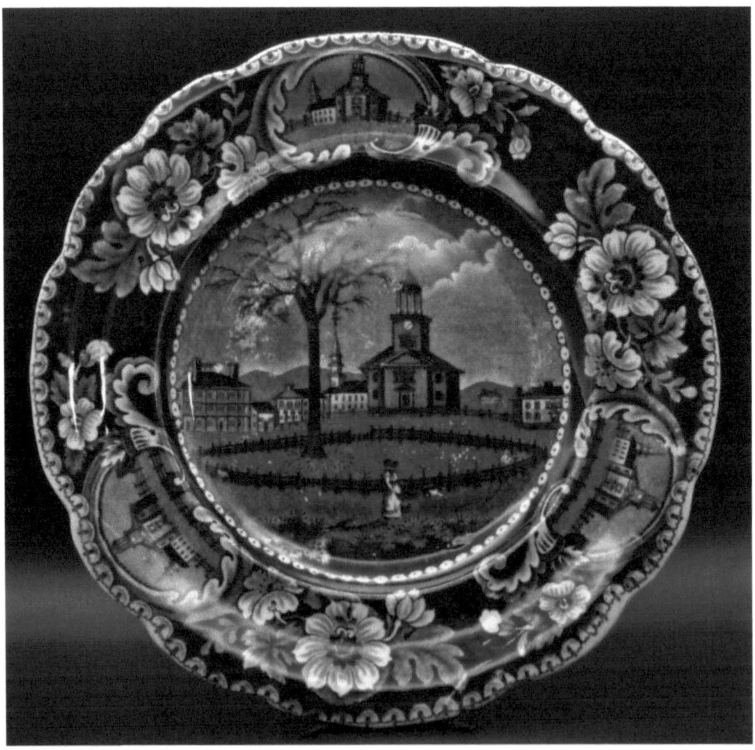

Figure 1.5 Plate, earthenware, blue printed, depicting Pittsfield, Massachusetts. Impressed, "Clews Warranted, Staffordshire," Cobridge, c.1825–28.

Figure 1.6 Printed backstamp on Figure 1.5, American Seal and text reading, "Winter View of Pittsfield, Mass".

store owners in Pittsfield stocked crockery ware (along with other merchandise), including a Charles J. F. Allen. Nevertheless, only Josiah Bissell of Pittsfield appears to have promoted "Of Crockery & Glass Ware we have a good supply, with or without the '*winter view of Pittsfield*'" (*The Pittsfield Sun* October 30, 1828). Whether Allen, or another merchant, exercised an influence on the manufacture of the Pittsfield's pattern still remains unclear, and Larsen seemed to increasingly gravitate toward the hegemony of the manufacturer. In fact, when her book was enlarged, she categorially expressed a view that in order to "win favor" with the American market, "The English potters realized their opportunity to furnish products of historical significance" (1950: 2).

Exactly how certain designs were produced for the American market was complex, but latterly, it became more straightforward for authors to emphasize the role of manufacturers in cultivating the American market. In the 1990s, Jeffrey Snyder's *Historical Staffordshire: American Patriots and Views* interpreted wares designed for the American market as manufacturers attempting to recapture trade after the Anglo-American War of 1812–14 by "plucking the patriotic heartstrings of the new nation" (1995: 6).

The role of importers and dealers

As a result of focusing on manufacturers, the earliest writers were slower in exploring the range of importers and dealers involved in the trade. Annie Slosson's *The China Hunters Club* of 1878 (based on the views of Mr. Whitney), noted:

> ... between 1815 and 1830 it is evident that English potters had established tolerably regular commercial relations with American merchants. In some cases, the wares were marked with the names of the American dealers. I find 'J. Greenfield, China, etc, New York,' and 'Peter Morton, importer, Connecticut,' on the backs of dinner-plates which date perhaps about 1825–30.
>
> (1878: 158)

This was early recognition of how some manufacturers had agents or established their own outlets. Trade was conducted through specialist importers and dealers, such as John Greenfield of New York and Peter Morton of Hartford. It is interesting that the importers and dealers were described as "American," whereas the potters were "English." The question of whether those involved in the trade were American, or more recent English migrants, was not considered relevant at that stage. As indicated by Alice Morse Earle's *China Collecting in America*, her assumption was also that manufacturers were English, whereas the dealers were simply "American" (1892: 142).

The existence of backstamps provided some of the earliest writers with a glimpse of the range of importers and dealers involved in the trade. However, examining their roles and their marketing strategy still remained on the periphery of mainstream research. In 1905, Dr. Everett McKnight presented a paper to the Connecticut Historical Society concerned with Peter Morton of Hartford, Connecticut, active from the 1820s, and briefly mentioned by Annie Slosson. An account of his lecture appeared in *The Hartford Courant* (December 6, 1905) and in more detail in *The Connecticut Magazine* of 1906. McKnight's opinion was that, "... Peter Morton seems to have been the only dealer or importer in this country who had his stamp impressed in the clay before the pieces were placed in the kiln" (1906: 353). The assertion was mistaken, but it does usefully convey the level of knowledge of crockery importers and dealers in that period (Figure 1.7).

In the late 1930s, Sam Laidacker, a dealer, as well as author and the editor of *The Antique Collector*, commented on how the study of importers' marks could result in some "interesting discoveries" (1939b: 150). This also suggests how this aspect of ceramics was still a relatively new area of research. The Maryland attorney and collector, Robert McCauley, who published *Liverpool Transfer Designs on Anglo-American Pottery*, lists a jug marked as "Henshaw & Jarves, importers of earthenware and china, Boston, and manufactured by Wood & Caldwell of Burslem," depicting a portrait of Massachusetts Congressman, Fisher Ames (1942: 69). This example was not recorded by Ellouise Baker Larsen's *American Historical Views ...* published just a few years before, in 1939.

As a collector and researcher, Robert McCauley was increasingly interested in the range of crockery importers and dealers. His short but pioneering article titled "American Importers of Staffordshire" appeared in *The Magazine Antiques* in 1944 and was based on a clear, central rational. Appreciating importers' business dates could provide additional ways of clarifying the dates of production of printed wares produced for the American market (McCauley 1944: 295–7). Based on city directories, McCauley provided the suggested business dates of Henshaw & Jarves of Boston. However, by surveying advertisements and notices in the press, it is now clear that the partnership of Joseph B. Henshaw and Deming Jarves was established in April 1814 and dissolved by May 1818 (Figures 1.8–1.10).

Robert McCauley's "American Importers of Staffordshire" focused on the sellers of American-themed Staffordshire wares and did not include importers' backstamps found on later flow-blue printed, or white ironstone, associated with period from the 1840s and 1850s. Even though McCauley describes,

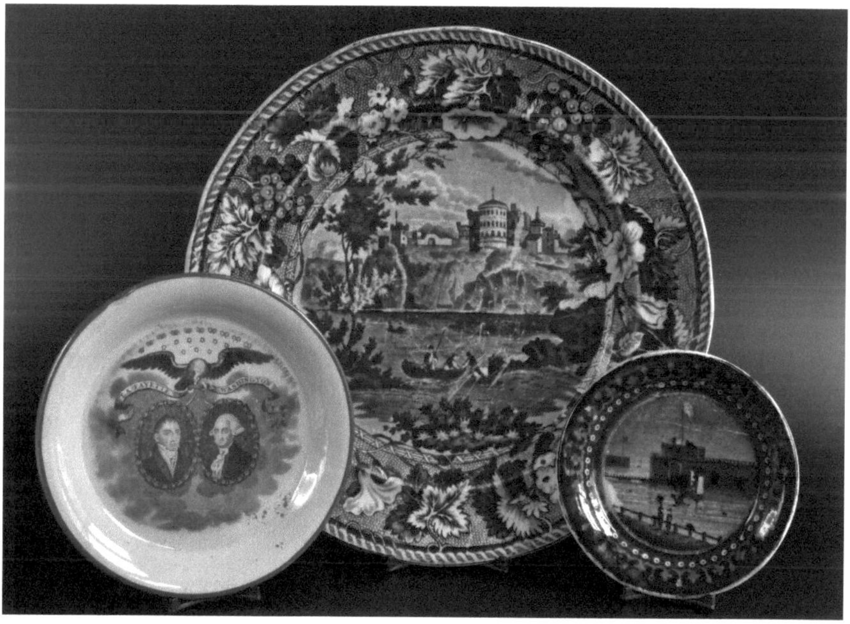

Figure 1.7 A range of Staffordshire wares with impressed backstamp for Peter Morton, Hartford, Connecticut. From left to right; Plate, earthenware, black printed, portraits of General Lafayette and George Washington, below an American Seal, impressed, "Peter Morton, Hartford," probably Enoch Wood & Sons, Burslem, Staffordshire, c.1825. Plate, blue printed, earthenware, titled "Culzean Castle, Ayrshire," impressed backstamp, "Peter Morton, importer of Earthenware, Connecticut," Enoch Wood & Sons, Burslem c.1823–25. Cup plate, earthenware, blue printed, depicting the Battery, New York, impressed, "Peter Morton, Hartford," Enoch Wood & Sons, Burslem, c.1825–30.

and illustrates a jug depicting General William H. Harrison, with the printed backstamp, "Manufactured/ for Robt. H. Miller. / Alexandria./ D.C.," the extent to which importers had influenced production was not fully explored (1944: 295). On closer analysis, the importer, Robert H. Miller, took an active part in political issues, as discussed in Chapter 4. Examining importers was perceived as a way of determining the dates of patterns rather than any notion that a greater knowledge of the intermediary could provide alternative perspectives as to the development of ceramic design. Recognizing the major contribution of importers and dealers, in developing the trade, was still in its infancy.

In reality, importers' backstamps or signed pieces can provide insight into the manufacturing dates of patterns, networks, and the distribution of English ceramics across the United States (Walthall 2013). The phenomena of having a business name on a vessel emerged as a marketing strategy in the 1810s, and its evolution is an interesting topic in its own right. At the Winterthur Museum, Delaware, there exists a large, creamware plate manufactured by Davenport of

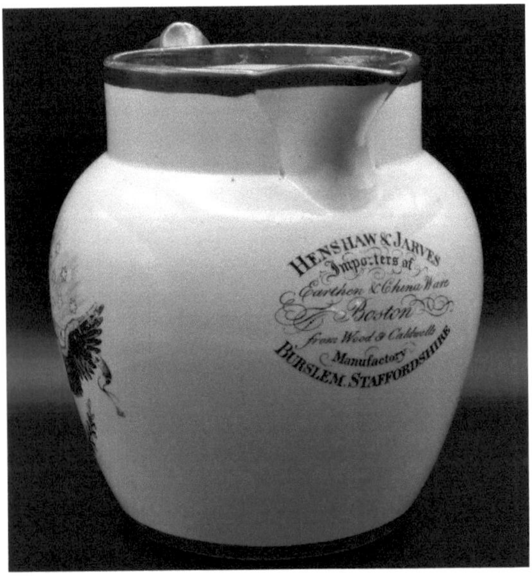

Figure 1.8 Jug, earthenware, black printed with luster decoration, signed "Henshaw & Jarves, Importers of Earthen and China ware, Boston, from Wood & Caldwells, Manufactory, Burslem, Staffordshire," c.1814–18.

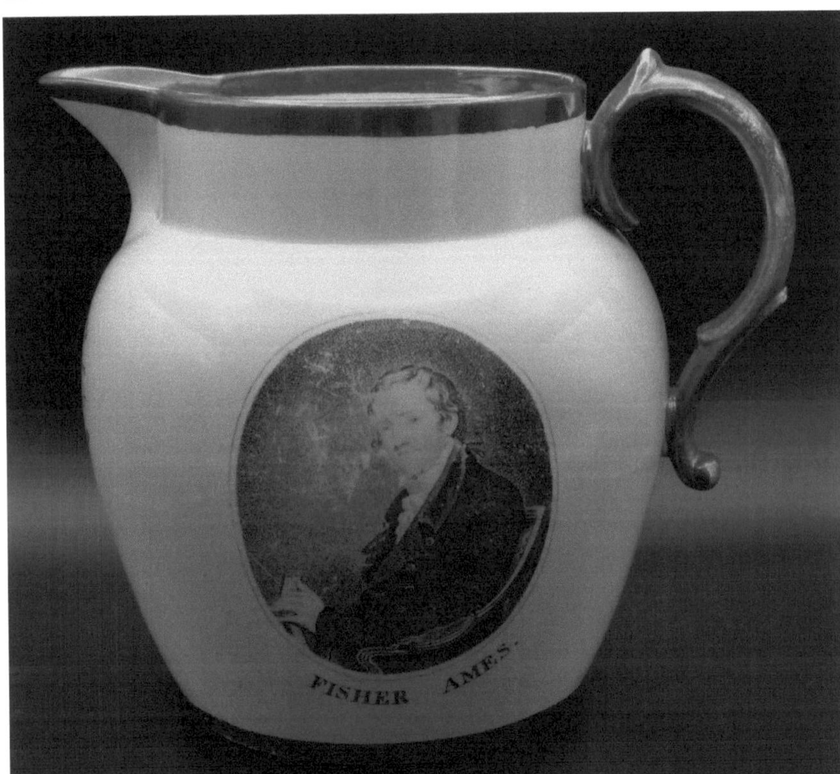

Figure 1.9 Side view of Figure 1.8, earthenware, black printed with luster decoration, depicting portrait of Congressman Fisher Ames (1758–1808). Manufactured by Wood & Caldwell, Burslem, c.1814–18.

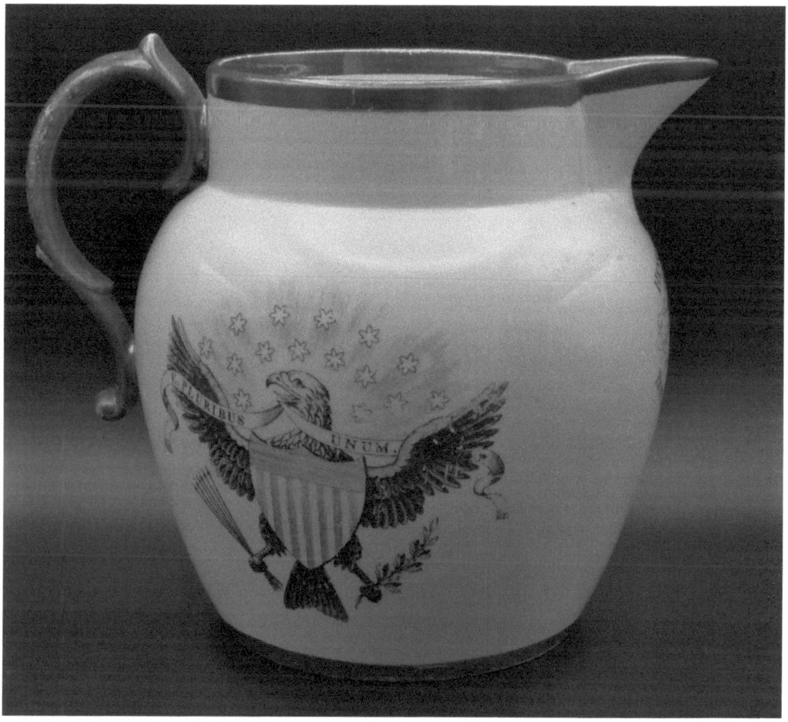

Figure 1.10 Side view of Figure 1.8, earthenware, black printed with luster decoration, depicting the American Seal. Manufactured by Wood & Caldwell, Burslem, c.1814–18.

Longport, decorated with samples of different hand-painted border designs, signed "Joseph Allen Crocker, China, Glass & Earthen Ware Dealer, Boston." This may date to c.1809, since Crocker advertised opening a new store, formerly occupied by William Andrews, in April 1809 (*Boston Gazette* April 1809). As Joseph Allen Crocker died in 1817, aged twenty-nine, the window of production was narrow (*Boston Daily Advertiser* May 2, 1817). This is certainly an early example of an American crockery importer referred to on the actual piece of pottery (Figure 1.11).

As the precise business dates of Joseph Crocker and Henshaw & Jarves (both of Boston) may be determined from newspaper notices, it suggests that signing the name of the importer on the front or the side of a ceramic vessel predates the use of the impressed, or printed, backstamp. Few importers had their names impressed onto the base of the ceramic vessel, but known examples include Peter Morton of Hartford, Connecticut (Figure 1.7); John Greenfield of New York; Thomas F. Field of Utica, New York (Figure 6.2); Kerr's China Hall of Philadelphia; and Henderson & Gaines of New Orleans.

Winterthur Museum, Delaware, has an unusual transfer printed cup plate bearing the impressed mark, "For Sale At The China, Glass & Earthenwarehouse[sic]/

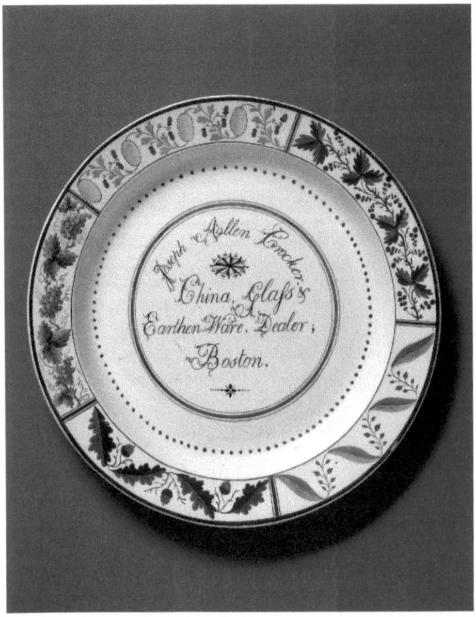

Figure 1.11 Plate, creamware, enamel decoration providing a sample of different rim patterns. Signed "Joseph Allen Crocker/China Glass/ Earthen ware, Dealer/ Boston." Impressed mark for Davenport, Longport. Staffordshire, c.1809–1817. Bequest of Henry Francis du Pont. Courtesy Winterthur Museum, Garden & Library.

Pearl St/ No.243/ New York" (Figures 1.12 and 1.13). This cup plate appears to be associated with John and George Tredwell. The Tredwells advertised bales of imported cotton from Georgia in 1809, but referred to china, glass and earthenware, available at 243, Pearl Street, New York, in 1819 (*Mercantile Advertiser*, New York, November 8, 1819). If this cup plate dates to c.1819, it is an early example of an importer with an impressed backstamp. Other examples (mentioned above) date from the 1820s onwards. Interestingly, only the New York address was considered relevant for marketing purposes, though the Tredwell family remained connected to 243, Pearl Street until c.1844 (Doggett 1843–44; Doggett 1844–45). Thus, providing a precise date for this cup plate is problematic.

Quite why the Tredwell family gravitated toward the crockery trade is unclear, although their nephew, Timothy Tredwell Kissam, also adopted the use of a backstamp as a promotional device (Pedigrees 4 and 5). Often (though not always), ceramics bearing an importer's mark avoided providing the name of manufacturer, such as a cup plate backstamped only as, T.T. Kissam of New York (Figures 1.14 and 1.15). In this instance, the printed pattern of "Peking Japan" is associated with C. J. Mason of Fenton, Staffordshire (Haggar and Adams 1977: Plates 101–2). Importers' backstamps provide evidence of the growing significance of the intermediary and help to show when business connections were formed. Kissam was located at 99 Water Street from c.1825, until December 1835, when the devastating New York fire destroyed his premises (Longworth 1825; Foster [1835] 2011: 31). Potentially, Kissam's link to C. J. Mason of Fenton dates from the mid-1820s.

A range of different examples of printed backstamps are shown in Figures 2.7, 2.26, 5.7, and 7.11. Backstamps were used by inland importers and dealers as the ceramic trade expanded westward. Printed backstamps were more typical

Figure 1.12 Cup plate, earthenware, blue transfer printed in a willow pattern. Probably Staffordshire, c.1819–44. Museum purchase. Courtesy Winterthur Museum, Garden & Library.

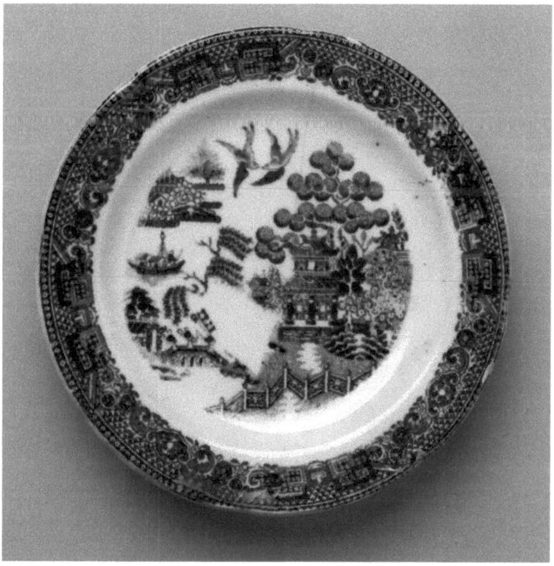

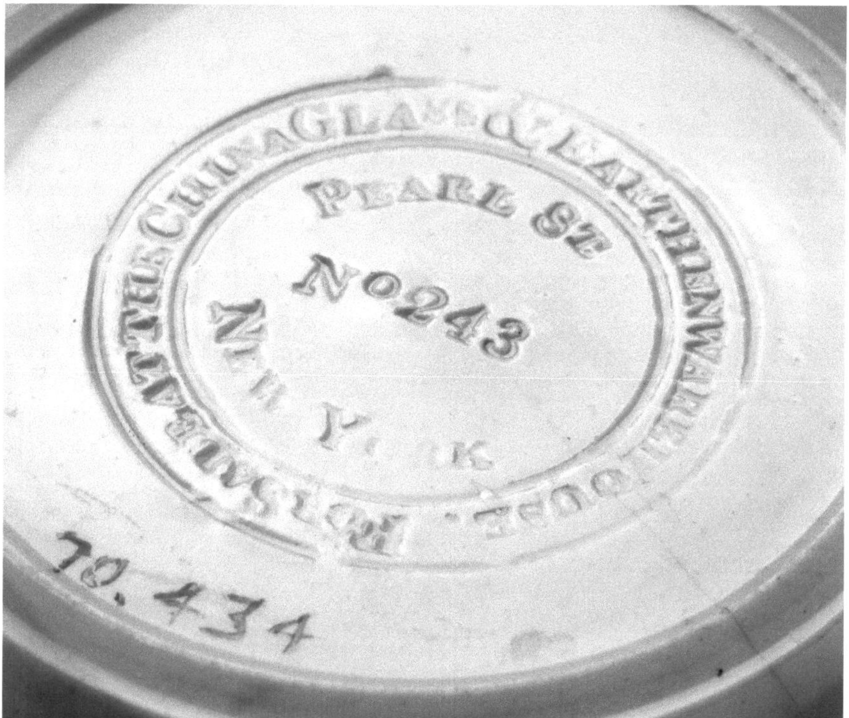

Figure 1.13 Backstamp on cup plate, Figure 1.12. Impressed, "For Sale At The China, Glass & Earthenwarehouse[sic]/ Pearl St/ No.243/ New York." Probably Staffordshire, c.1819–44. Museum purchase. Courtesy Winterthur Museum, Garden & Library.

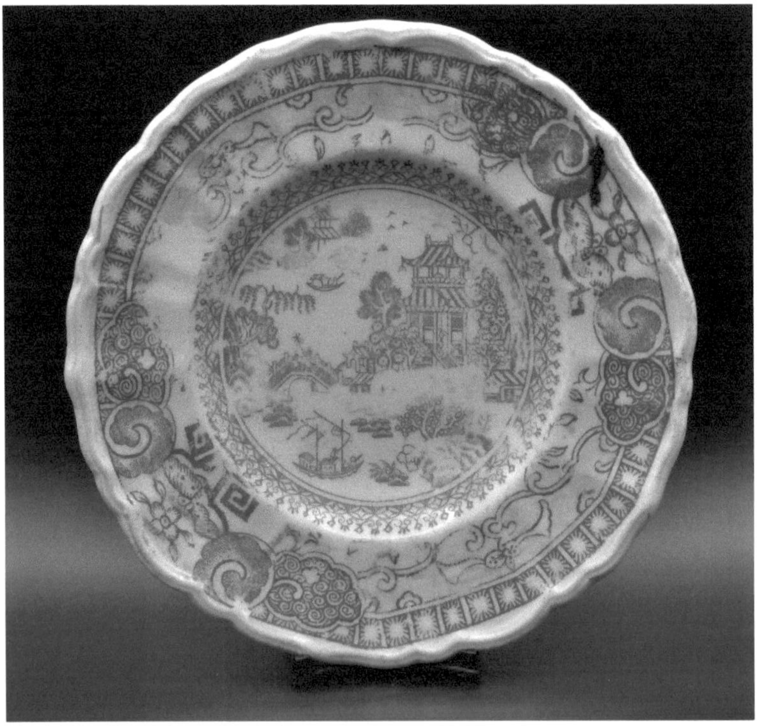

Figure 1.14 Cup plate, earthenware, light-brown printed with faint enamel decoration, "Peking Japan" pattern. Manufactured by C. J. Mason, Fenton, Staffordshire, c.1825–35. The date of the plate is determined by the backstamp (Figure 1.15).

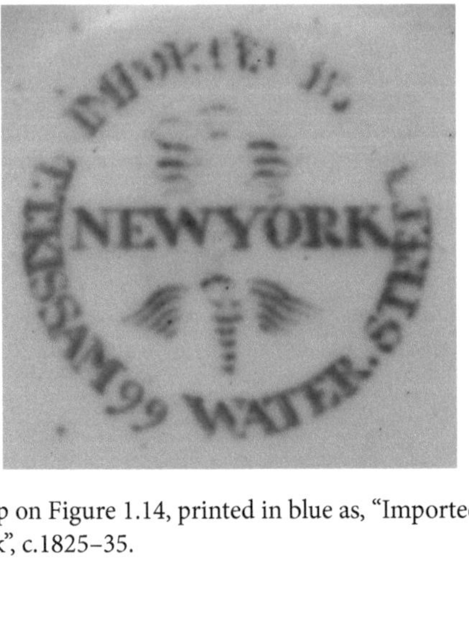

Figure 1.15 Backstamp on Figure 1.14, printed in blue as, "Imported By/ T. T. Kissam 99 Water Street/ New York", c.1825–35.

than impressed marks, although not all importers and dealers (known to us by numerous newspaper advertisements, city directories, and invoices) adopted this practice. There is still a need to consider the wider range of individuals involved in importing ceramics and glass.

Legacy

Although interest in other ceramic-types associated with the American market developed during the twentieth century—such as flow-blue, sponged and white ironstone wares—it seems that the early publications became a model of how to approach or structure ceramic-history literature. Typically, ceramic publications included some information about each manufacturer, and then catalogued the range of patterns and shapes associated with the producers (Greaser and Greaser 1973; Robacker and Robacker 1978; Williams 1971; Wetherbee 1996). This reflects how the writers were normally collectors of the actual wares, devoting many years to acquiring varieties and examples. However, by examining the activities of intermediaries in more depth, there is scope for ceramic-history literature to now consider wider, alternative narratives.

When John Spargo's *Early American Pottery and China* examined the development of the American industry and touched on the significance of British ceramics, it was explained how, "English manufacturers made desperate attempts to recover the important American market" after the Revolutionary wars (1926: 98). The early interpretation of what motivated the production of American-themed wares was adopted by other scholars. In another instance, Frank Thistlethwaite's "The Atlantic Migration of the Pottery Industry" of 1958, mentions how Staffordshire manufacturers produced wares for the American market, citing the authors Robert H. McCauley, N. Hudson Moore, and A. W. Camehl. As shown above, these were some of the earliest writers on American-themed ceramics. Thistlethwaite argued that apart from the Liverpool creamwares, which referred to ships and ship's captains, "Great pains were taken to cultivate American sentiment" by Staffordshire manufacturers, who accordingly decorated their ceramics with appropriate themes (1958: 267).

The onus was placed on the English manufacturer. In 1974, Ivor Nöel Hume, the chief archaeologist of Colonial Williamsburg, wrote of a willingness to "put pots before principle," which had resulted in Staffordshire potters producing transfer-printed wares by the 1820s that would have a "direct political or patriotic appeal" ([1974] 2009: 147). Only in more recent times has "for patrons to custom order their wares" been recognized as an alternative way designs were created (Teitelman et al. 2010: 97).

Cultural dimension

Collecting stimulated research, often resulting in notable publications. William C. Prime, who collected some examples of American-themed wares produced in Liverpool and Staffordshire, importantly appreciated how Staffordshire manufacturers supplied "regular patterns," along with "a great many special patterns of American subjects" ([1877] 1879: 420). Prime had a more measured opinion of production and built up a reputation as a lecturer, progressively recognizing how ceramics might provide insights into wider cultural issues. In 1877, Prime delivered a lecture titled "The Keramic Art" at the New York Academy of Design, where he proposed that:

> The prevalent idea that art is an aesthetic study … is untrue. Keramic art alone is the history of the human race and of nations.
>
> (*The New York Herald*, December 20, 1877)

Whereas other writers would increasingly focus on identifying the sheer variety of printed American-themed wares, consummate with what was becoming collectable, Prime was acutely aware of how the ownership of ceramics could also be linked to backgrounds and culture. In *Pottery and Porcelain of all Times and Nations* of 1877, Prime noted the case of an established American family, whose inheritance consisted of "services in Chinese, blue-and-white and polychrome, Japanese, Bow, Lowestoft, Worcester, and New Hall porcelains; and Jackfield, Liverpool, Cobridge, Shelton, and some other potteries." Alternatively, he observed how ceramics belonging to a French family (now living in America) were predominantly from Sèvres or Rouen. Likewise, a migrant family originally from Germany possessed ceramics from Dresden and Hochst (Prime [1877] 1879: 420). Naturally, it was recognized that Europeans had acquired what was simply available to them, whereas families who had settled earlier in North America had been supplied with ceramic imports from all across the globe, being presented with a considerable amount of choice. People's backgrounds, or origins, had made a difference to what they owned. Cultural identity played a part in ceramic ownership, and one wonders whether W. C. Prime's observation may also be applied to considering the backgrounds of importers and dealers who became involved in the ceramic trade. A cursory consideration of the surnames of individuals involved in the ceramic and glass trade reveals the influence of different cultural roots. So, for instance, in New York, we find Charles Ahrenfeldt selling "German glass ware," Coutan & Pillivuyt dealing in "French porcelain," and Peter Morton, described as an agent for Enoch Wood & Sons, of Burslem, Staffordshire (Ripley 1840). To a certain degree, the ethnic backgrounds of importers and dealers facilitated channels of supply, although a diverse range of imported ceramic and glass goods were typically sold.

Generally, however, research into the importing and retailing side of the ceramic trade remained limited. The earliest books stemmed from collecting, and then influenced how the subject was viewed. The next generation of enthusiasts had only these perspectives to go by as the basis of developing their own knowledge and interpretations. Outlining ways in which ceramics were described in the United States is thus revealing of how the relationship between supply and demand was originally perceived. In many respects, this has followed through into modern literature, still impacting on approaches and interpretations prevalent today.

Nevertheless, early publications made important, insightful observations. For instance, there was a growing realization that some designs manufactured for the American market were more readily available than others. Alice Morse Earle's *China Collecting in America* of 1892 points out how "Lafayette pieces of crockery" were typically found in better condition than other American-themed wares. Earle proposes that the possible explanation for this was that as Lafayette was venerated when he returned to the United States in 1824, these purchased commemorative pieces were carefully preserved (1892: 288). Earle even observed how "the most popular and universally widespread designs" were patterns such as Boston State House and the Landing of Lafayette (1892: 317–8; Figures 2.11 and 7.15). Meanwhile, N. Hudson Moore's *The Old China Book* pointed out how anti-slavery cup-plates had sold at a high price at a New York city auction (1903: 46). A whole article by Gregor Norman-Wilcox in *The Magazine Antiques* was devoted to "American-Historical Staffordshire Rarities" (1934: 178–82). This five-page illustrated survey draws attention to unusual patterns and designs on vessel-types all identified as rare. The article described how auction catalogues for "American-historical Staffordshire" might be found with descriptions such as "rare," "very rare," and even "unique". Despite Norman-Wilcox's theme, he does not address why some of these identified designs were rarer than others.

The earliest writers became locked into a notion that American-themed ceramics were designed to appeal to patriotism, without considering the implications of why some designs were apparently more common than others. Under the rubric of so-called industrialization, it is curious how there existed a degree of unevenness in the extent of production of so-called mass-produced commodities. If it is to be assumed that manufacturers produced ceramics that appealed to American patriotism, why were some of designs rarer than others? As an example, Mrs. Alice Maddock (the early collector), owned an anti-slavery plate commemorating an event of 1837 (Figure 6.8), which had already been identified as being "poorly preserved, and there are few in existence" (*New York Daily Tribune* February 22, 1903). It has not been the case that only latterly have some designs been identified as being rarer than others. Apart from the impact of certain designs being potentially more collectable than others, are there alternative explanations for this?

At first, it might be assumed that collectors were drawn to ceramics that depicted American themes because of the evidence they provided of the past, as well as being stylistically attractive (Anderson 2013). But, in another way, collecting contributed to forming a sense of American national identity. It is interesting how wealthy Americans, such as George Kellogg and William Randolph Hearst, had major collections of historical Staffordshire wares. When Kellogg's collection was auctioned off soon after he died, it was considered to be "by experts as probably the finest" (*Buffalo Evening News,* NY November 6, 1925). Hearst's "Historical Blue Staffordshire Ware" was auctioned-off due to the impact of the Great Depression (Parke-Bernet Galleries 1938). The New York sale catalogue described certain pieces as rare, including luster wares referring to Cornwallis and Lafayette, which had in turn been acquired from the Kellogg estate in 1925(Figure 1.16).

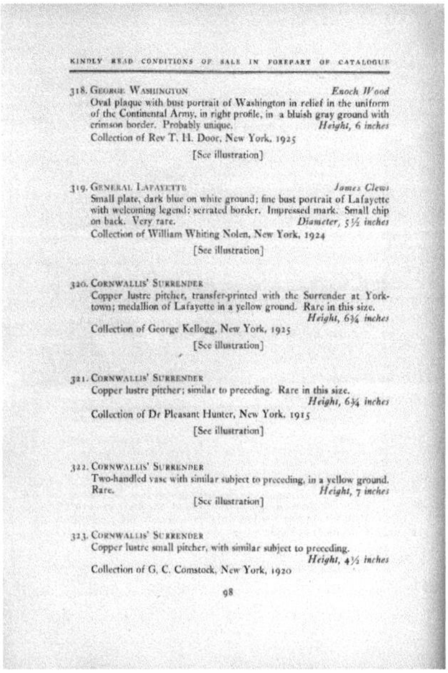

KINDLY READ CONDITIONS OF SALE IN FOREPART OF CATALOGUE

318. GEORGE WASHINGTON *Enoch Wood*
Oval plaque with bust portrait of Washington in relief in the uniform of the Continental Army, in right profile, in a bluish gray ground with crimson border. Probably unique. *Height, 6 inches*
Collection of Rev T. H. Door, New York, 1925
[See illustration]

319. GENERAL LAFAYETTE *James Clews*
Small plate, dark blue on white ground; fine bust portrait of Lafayette with welcoming legend; serrated border. Impressed mark. Small chip on back. Very rare. *Diameter, 5½ inches*
Collection of William Whiting Nolen, New York, 1924
[See illustration]

320. CORNWALLIS' SURRENDER
Copper lustre pitcher, transfer-printed with the Surrender at Yorktown; medallion of Lafayette in a yellow ground. Rare in this size. *Height, 6¾ inches*
Collection of George Kellogg, New York, 1925
[See illustration]

321. CORNWALLIS' SURRENDER
Copper lustre pitcher; similar to preceding. Rare in this size. *Height, 6¾ inches*
Collection of Dr Pleasant Hunter, New York, 1915
[See illustration]

322. CORNWALLIS' SURRENDER
Two-handled vase with similar subject to preceding, in a yellow ground. Rare. *Height, 7 inches*
[See illustration]

323. CORNWALLIS' SURRENDER
Copper lustre small pitcher, with similar subject to preceding. *Height, 4½ inches*
Collection of G. C. Comstock, New York, 1920

98

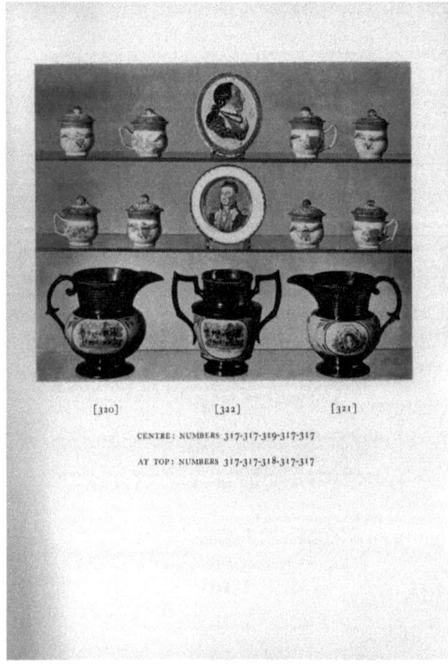

Figure 1.16 Auction catalogue (extract), Parke-Bernet Galleries, *The William Randolph Hearst Collection, Part II …*, November 1938, pp. 98–99.

Alternatively, collecting, as undertaken by individuals in America who had ties to the ceramic trade, or who were related to the actual Staffordshire manufacturers, conveys how culture and identity played a part in what was preserved; just as it is argued in the following chapters—how these factors influenced what was commissioned, or marketed by the intermediaries. Collecting also impacted what museums would later inherit, continuing to influence interpretations of the overall significance of American-themed printed wares.

Yet the modern era has witnessed the dismantling of ceramic collections by certain museums. As an example, a collection of over two hundred mainly "Historical Staffordshire China" wares was gifted to the Detroit Museum of Art in 1917. The collection was formed by Mrs. Arthur W. Soper (nee Hettie Mann Wardwell), the wife of a successful businessman, and presented to Detroit by their daughter, Mrs. Gustavus D. Pope (nee Mary Soper). At the time of the donation, Alexander M. Hudnut (an established authority on historical Staffordshire wares in that era), believed that the collection was worth in excess of $15,000 (Annual Report for the Year 1917: 8). In his estimation, the Soper collection was "one of the five or six best known collections of this kind of china in the world" (Hudnut 1917: 69). Despite its significance, reports in the press began to surface indicating how the Detroit Institute of Arts was deaccessioning some of its Staffordshire ceramics (*The Detroit News*, Michigan March 7, 1994). In due course, a cup plate, with an accession number matching the sequence used on ceramics retained by the Detroit collection (described as a "Gift of Mrs. Gustavus D. Pope") appeared on the open market (Figure 1.17).

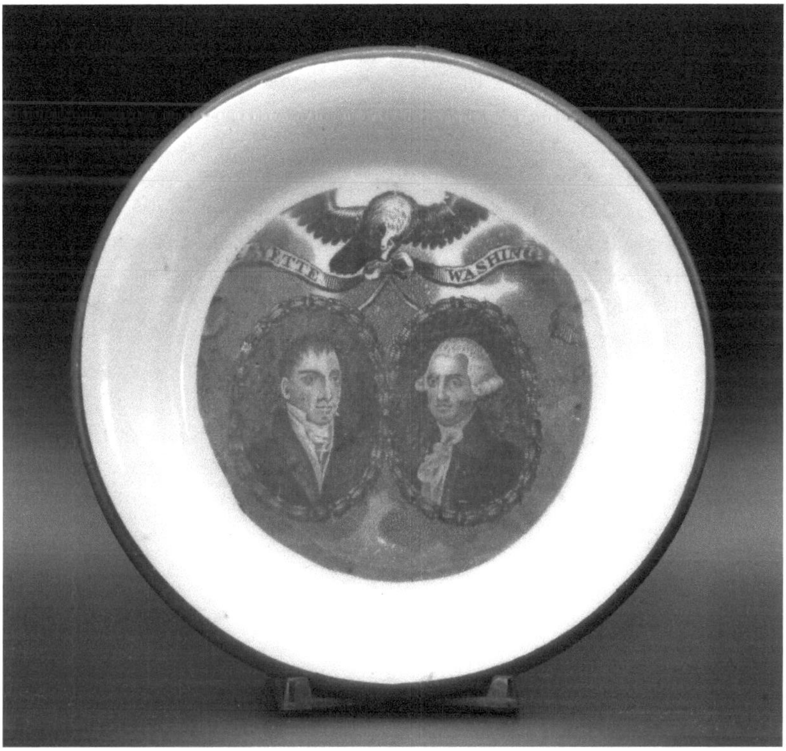

Figure 1.17 Cup plate, pearlware, brown printed, with brown enamel decoration, depicting La Fayette and Washington, below an eagle. Impressed "Wood." Manufactured by Enoch Wood & Sons, Burslem, c.1825–30. It still bears the accession number of "17.117.P165" and appears to have originally been in the Mrs. Arthur W. Soper collection, New York.

Similarly, a creamware jug depicting naval heroes of the Anglo-American War was originally part of a bequest made to the Philadelphia Museum of Art by millionaire attorney, R. Wistar Harvey, in 1940 (Figure 2.10). This huge bequest consisted of nearly six hundred wares produced for the American market. Between 2012 and 2014, it was decided to deaccession some of this collection on the basis of duplication, or condition issues, to benefit future acquisitions. The financial implications of conservation, storage, and display, have created a variety of problems for museums, as have curating ceramics in ways that will engage with changing audiences. Philadelphia confirmed the provenance of the jug shown in Figure 2.10, whereas Detroit never replied to a request for more information concerning the cup plate shown in Figure 1.17. What, potentially, has taken decades of painstaking collecting might be so easily lost. In the future, just how will the *history* of collecting be understood if precious pieces are misplaced, or deaccessioned, from some of the earliest, and arguably, the most important collections ever formed of ceramics produced for the American market?

Summary

Early literature concerned with American-themed wares normally focused on issues of attribution and compiling catalogues of the range of patterns produced. As pattern-driven research evolved, differences in economic value became apparent and an important issue. Variations in the price of American-themed wares, as determined by notions of rarity, still exist to this day. The more modern interpretation of American-themed wares has been that, due to extended periods of collecting, their original significance has been distorted and somewhat exaggerated (Ewins 1997: 39–40; Emmerson, 2010: 250). Demand for wares adapted for the American market was not necessarily extensive. In 1816, Jonathan Ogden, a New York crockery merchant, when writing to his Liverpool supplier, pointed out how, "... I never knew of General Heads or any National devices in any Article ever to meet a ready sale in any Country" (Miller et al. 1994: 232). Based on this observation, it is more straightforward to dismiss American-themed wares as having a minor importance—even at that time. Paradoxically, when discussing Liverpool creamware decorated with the apotheosis of Washington, it has been pointed that, "One would assume that the American market for these products was large enough to encourage such enterprises" (Cunningham 1994: 18). Could exploring the role of intermediaries provide additional insights into what motivated the production of these types of wares?

Increasingly, the phrase "historical Staffordshire" gained currency, as a convenient, short-hand way to describe wares printed with themes related to the American market. However, when ceramics were produced in Liverpool and Staffordshire, depicting a mixture of political figures, wars, buildings, canals, and landscapes, the subjects were, at the time, a reflection of culture, identity, progress, and modernity. Might the fact that ceramic imagery referred to contemporaneous sociopolitical issues or the industrial development of certain regions actually help to explain why these wares represented only a smaller part of American consumption? For example, the crockery importers Field & Clark of Utica, New York, advertised ceramics celebrating the opening of the Erie Canal in 1824. It was then noted by the press that they had received "several orders from New York and Albany for Canal Pattern Earthenware," implying that these designs tended to have a localized, not universal, American appeal (*City Gazette* Charleston, South Carolina August 2, 1824; Figure 6.3). R. T. Haines Halsey (one of the earliest writers on American-themed wares), described these wares as "Erie Canal Inscription," and while he suggested that, in this instance, the English manufacturers were probably provided with illustrations, how far the motivation for production was derived by American intermediaries was not fully explored ([1899] 1974: 142).

Using terminology such as "historical Staffordshire" simplifies what, on closer inspection, is more complex. This becomes apparent when exploring the backgrounds of those selling and marketing ceramics expressly produced for the American market, in the following chapters. Appreciating that there could be different reasons for producing certain ceramics is another reason why preserving particular collections intact is vital. Early collections still have the capacity to provide insight into what was readily available, or felt to be unusual, or rare. Regardless of condition, or duplication, early collections of so-called historical Staffordshire provide a narrative of the process of collecting. The deaccessioning of wares may, unwittingly, discard evidence of variations in the proportion of production, which is significant. As influential ceramic-history publications began to focus on "historical Staffordshire," there was a tendency to assume that manufacturers developed designs for the American market. Only in more recent times have merchants, importers, and dealers been acknowledged as influencing production, on the basis of having a clearer understanding of demand and being closer to the consumer (Blaszczyk 2000: 32–3). At this point, it is now necessary to consider the significance of consumption, fashion, and demand.

Chapter 2

CONSUMPTION AND PERCEPTIONS OF DEMAND

Early ceramic history literature did not greatly explore, or question, the degree to which ceramic importers and dealers influenced production. The earliest ceramic historians tended to believe that English manufacturers produced ceramics depicting American views, or patriotic themes, as a way of expanding their export trade. As research developed, publications began to distinguish between the monetary values of these increasingly collectable, American-themed wares (Laidacker 1938), as well as continue to compile comprehensive lists of identified patterns (Larsen 1939; enlarged 1950). Only in more recent times did alternative ideas and theories concerning consumption and demand begin to develop, moving the debate away from the role of supply. Historians began to consider marketing and sales techniques and the role of fashion in influencing the rise of consumption. If there were variations in ceramic consumption because of the impact of culture and identity (more complex than acquiring what was simply in vogue), this lays the foundation for considering whether the same forces should be applied to interpreting the behavior of intermediaries.

Fashion and demand

Export figures convey the volume of ceramics shipped to North America from England, and how these quantities were subject to wars and fluctuations in the economy (Ewins 1997: 5–6). The American historian, T. H. Breen pointed out in "An Empire of Goods: The Anglicization of Colonial America, 1690-1776" that "For all these Americans, drinking tea required cups that could hold extremely hot liquids and that, in turn, forced them to import the technically advanced ceramics that originated in Staffordshire" (1986: 488). Though the American colonies regularly used Chinese porcelains (Schwind 1984; Howard 1984), the suggestion is that in the case of certain commodities, as there were few alternatives, consumers relied on affordable English earthenware. In this way, Breen developed a view whereby any notion of colonial "self-sufficiency" (1986: 485) was a myth to the extent that:

> Without too much exaggeration, Staffordshire pottery might be seen as the Coca Cola of the eighteenth century. It was a product of the metropolitan economy that touched the lives of people living on the frontier of settlement, eroding

> seventeenth-century folkways and bringing scattered planters and farmers into dependence on a vast world market that they did not yet quite comprehend.
>
> (1986: 496–7)

Furthermore, Breen argues that as "American buyers became more dependent on British suppliers, the British business community became more dependent on the colonial market" (1986: 486). Due to this interdependence, commodities such as English ceramics continued to influence American society, and as a consequence, social and economic ties remained strong. Contemporary observations testify to the extent to which the United States relied on imported ceramics, although in reality the suppliers varied. A late eighteenth-century serialised report titled "On the Trade of France with the United States," published in a New York newspaper, *The Time Piece*, declared that as the French porcelain manufactories were so great, "we are justly entitled to an exporting trade in this article." The report continued:

> … tea, coffee, chocolate, &c. are used twice a day in every family; and various liquors, for refreshment, and drank out of the same ware. Hence arises a great consumption. The cups must be manufactured in a bowl-like form, which in America has usually the preference, I will say whether from habit, or because this form of vessel is more easily washed or wiped than others.

This also provides evidence of how French porcelain was already being adapted for the American market. By comparison, this report noted that "EARTHEN WARE … On scrutiny, it will be found, that notwithstanding their home manufactures of this kind, the greater part made use of in the United States is English" (*The Time Piece*, New York November 13, 1797). This report was attributed to one H. Caritat, who also ran a circulating library on Pearl Street, and is early evidence of the American market developing its own preferences (*Chronicle Express*, New York February 21, 1803).

Although some ceramic publications have remained preoccupied with the range of patterns produced for the American market (Snyder 1995; Arman 1998), new perspectives that considered the role of sales and marketing emerged from the 1960s. Neil McKendrick's "Josiah Wedgwood: An Eighteenth Century Entrepreneur in Salesmanship and Marketing Techniques" examined the factors which drove consumption. As an historian rather than a collector, McKendrick explored Wedgwood's marketing strategy in the context of emulative behavior. Consumption, it was believed, could be further stimulated by reducing prices, enabling "middling People" to further copy their peers (1960: 413–5, 428). Production was perceived as being far more tailored toward the desires of the market, so that in one instance, Wedgwood wrote to Thomas Bentley (his merchant-partner in Liverpool) in 1766:

> What do you think of sending Mr. Pitt upon Crockery ware to America. A Quantity might certainly be sold there now & some advantage made of the American prejudice in favour of the great Man.
>
> (1960: 422)

William Pitt openly opposed the American Stamp Act of 1765. McKendrick also points out how Wedgwood responded to other movements, such as the rise of Methodism and the contentious issue of the slave trade (1960: 422). These, and other themes, were viewed as potential "commercial" opportunities. Wedgwood and his merchant partner, Thomas Bentley, had their fingers on the pulse of market, and on other occasions, they attempted to catch up with sudden changes in the demands of market. McKendrick provides an example of Admiral Keppel, who was acquitted from a court martial during the American War of Independence. As a response, Wedgwood's travelling salesman noted that Keppel's portrait on ceramics could be sold at any price (1960: 422). This hints at how the addition of novelty might increase the actual sale-value of the commodity, if responding to political events.

McKendrick, Brewer and Plumb's *The Birth of a Consumer Society: The Commercialization of Eighteenth-century England* of 1982 developed the thesis whereby fashion played a significant role in stimulating the so-called birth, or growth of consumption. Indeed, in the chapter titled "Commercialization of Fashion", McKendrick argued:

> … in the late eighteenth century large numbers in society felt that they *must*[McKendrick's italics] be in fashion, whether they liked it or not, even to the point of ridicule. It was no longer forbidden fruit or an atypical social need.
>
> (1982: 40)

This represents a significant departure from previous attempts to explain the reasons for the success of Josiah Wedgwood. As *The Birth of a Consumer Society* pointed out, Eliza Meteyard's *The Life of Josiah Wedgwood* of the 1860s, had devoted limited attention to the themes of sales and distribution (1982: 109). To be fair, Meteyard does, on some occasions, mention how Wedgwood altered products, such as responding to female taste (Meteyard 1865–66 Vol II: 156). Furthermore, Meteyard mentions a letter to Sir William Meredith of 1765, in which Josiah Wedgwood expressed concerns over the loss of the American market due to the development of its own industry. Uncharacteristically for Meteyard, she expressed a criticism of Wedgwood by pointing out how "a better knowledge of economic science would have taught Mr.Wedgwood that productive duties, or appeals to Parliament, are utterly inoperative …" (1865–66 Vol I: 366). However, she continues in her more typical, celebratory tone, adding:

> Mr. Wedgwood would have smiled at his own fears, had some one told him, that, at the date of a century from the period of his writing this [the letter of 1765], our export trade in earthenware with America would be multiplied a thousandfold, that it is still amongst our best markets, and one to which the manufacturing firm he founded still contributes.
>
> (1865–66 Vol. 1: 367)

McKendrick's views are based on a meticulous analysis of the Wedgwood papers, and his research reveals clear evidence of how this manufacturer responded to taste, or cleverly marketed goods, in ways that might appeal to the market. However, potentially producing images of William Pitt on ceramics for the American market was, in part, motivated by a conversation with an aristocratic visitor to the factory. An additional part of the letter written to Thomas Bentley (after the extract quoted by McKendrick), reads as:

> Ld [Lord] Gower bro[t] [brought] his family to see my works the other day & asked me if I had not sent Mr. Pitt over in shoals to America. If you happen to do anything in that way we can divide a tolerable proffit [sic] & sell at the same price with Sadler.
>
> (Trustees of the Wedgwood Museum 1973: 96)

In other words, here is evidence of how Wedgwood responded to a suggestion from an aristocratic visitor rather than being the instigator of a design. Sadler and Green were printers of Liverpool, decorating wares supplied by Wedgwood.

McKendrick reveals the significance of appreciating the needs of different markets and the role of marketing, although he was also aware that Wedgwood's approach could have been an exception rather than the rule (1982: 147). The onus of initiating sophisticated marketing strategies was still placed on Josiah Wedgwood and Thomas Bentley. As Paul Glennie points out, McKendrick's sources relate to the producers and traders, making it hard to identify the role of "new consumers, and how and why their demand changed" (1995: 167). Another issue is that (as McKendrick himself points out), Wedgwood did not manufacture cheap goods (1982: 105). As far as Wedgwood and Bentley were concerned in the 1760s, the American market was a useful destination for off-loading unwanted stock (Trustees … 1973: 127) and was not ideally suited for their expensive products (McKendrick 1964:19). Although Wedgwood and Bentley were not necessarily convinced by the economic potential of the American market, there is evidence of a trade conducted with a variety of merchants, including Frederick Rhinelander of New York (Ewins 1997:19–23; Schwind 1984: 28–9). But, overall, this still leaves gaps in understanding how the advertising of ceramics evolved in the United States. A thorough examination of marketing is required in order to ascertain whether it was focused on promoting fashionable goods, and whether consumption was always emulative.

Advertising

If fashion was the main catalyst for growing consumption, it might be assumed that advertising in newspapers would have played a significant role in introducing consumers to the array of new imported commodities. Unlike England, there was no tax on American newspapers or advertisements (Presbery [1929] 1968: 75), and according to Edd Applegate's *The Rise of American Advertising*, it was from the mid-1780s that newspapers such as the *New York Daily Advertiser* became even more focused on advertising commodities instead of providing news (2012:18–9). Paradoxically, despite Dr. Benjamin Franklin's own apprehensive views toward extreme consumption (discussed in Chapter 6), as editor of the *Pennsylvania Gazette*, he has been credited as a pioneer of early newspaper advertising. Franklin considered the typographic layout, used basic illustrated imagery, and actually increased the number of advertisements in each edition (Applegate 2012: 8–12). Newspapers were very accessible to American consumers.

Typically, American crockery importers and dealers, in the manner of their English counterparts, drew attention to the wide range of ceramic stock available, the new arrivals, and the sellers' competitive prices. Sheenah Smith's examination of Norwich, England, from the mid- to late eighteenth century, shows the growing tendency of china dealers to widely advertise in newspapers. Advertisements might indicate that the crockery dealer had just returned from the place where goods were obtained, such as London or Staffordshire, and alternatively, notices might be used to indicate how ceramics could be purchased through local auction sales (1974: 193–211). The way crockery and glass were advertised in American newspapers was not dissimilar at this stage, but the details might vary depending on where the advertisements were placed. Those placed by importers in east-coast newspapers could be more elaborate in listing the merchandise available, probably because they were attempting to attract other dealers responsible for shipping goods further inland. Inland advertising in newspapers was often less detailed, and this may be related to it being simply aimed at more local, domestic buyers. Auctions were also an important way of speedily offloading ceramic merchandise, and notices for such sales often provided a fair amount of information regarding what was being sold—the types of wares, and even the names of the Staffordshire manufacturers responsible for producing the goods. This again could be a reflection of whom these notices were aimed at—the potential buyers being bulk dealers rather than domestic consumers (Cohen 2017: 94).

Maxine Berg's analysis of advertisements placed in the *Pennsylvania Gazette* found frequent references to the significance of price, but as this marketing technique evolved in the 1760s and 1770s, advertisements increasingly emphasized how the available merchandise was new and fashionable (2005: 321–2). This corresponds to McKendrick's overriding thesis that fashion became the central factor in contributing to rising consumption. In different aspects of design, such as British textiles, other historians have also noted how advertisements in American newspapers promoted goods on the basis of being new, and thus, more desirable patterns (Morgan 2000: 57–8). In 1761, corresponding to a wave of interest in what was fashionable, Keeling & Morris of New York advertised their imported stock from Liverpool as, "cups and saucers of the newest patterns" (*New York Gazette* October 13, 1761). James McCartney of New York advertised a "neat and new assortment" of stoneware and "table plates of different patterns" (*New-York Mercury* December 29, 1766). Here, perhaps there is evidence of promoting design on the basis of new fashions and novelty.

However, when Gilbert and Lewis Deblois used the phrase "Fashionable Goods, Just Arrived," on closer analysis the expression, "Fashionable Shawls—Callicoes[sic], Chints[sic]- Linens—Fans, &c," was applied to their range of clothing, whereas their stock of ceramics was simply described as "Crockery Ware, by the crate" (*American Herald*, Boston May 14, 1787). Likewise, Amos Atwell & Son's "New Crockery Store" of Providence, Rhode Island, advertised "An Assortment of Crockery and Glass Ware." It was their stock of clothing (which, interestingly, they also sold) that was described as "Winter Goods, Useful and Fashionable" (*United States Chronicle* Providence, Rhode Island December 8, 1791). Edward Brown & Co., of Albany, New York, simply advertised their "Black and Red Earthenware" as "very cheap" (*Albany Gazette* November 28, 1796). In this period, there was some unevenness as to what merchandise was particularly earmarked as being especially fashionable. Clothes might be treated differently from ceramics, and where the merchandise was sold could have influenced the significance of either price or fashion.

If the marketing of some ceramics was, at first, slower to reinforce that the imported merchandise was new or fashionable, it does, interestingly, appear to have become more of a prerogative of some American consumers. George Washington, when principally still a Virginian planter, ordered from his English agent, "ye most fashionable kind of Queen's Ware" in 1769 (Halfpenny 2010: 30). In 1787, when Mrs. Fuller of Philadelphia ordered Chinese porcelain through Captain Thomas Truxton, she stipulated that this should be "of the most fashionable kind" (Howard 1984: 111). This relates to other interpretations of the evolving American market. In John Brewer and Roy Porter's *Consumption and the World of Goods* of 1993, a chapter by John Styles, titled "Manufacturing, consumption and design in eighteenth-century England," describes how, in broad terms, North America was a growing market, which typically relied on imported goods. But he adds:

> A significant and possibly growing proportion of them (though by no means all) were fashion products, in the sense that their successful sale depended on repeated changes in their visual appearance in accordance with changing metropolitan notions of what was fashionable.
>
> (1993: 528)

Inferring that ceramics were new and fashionable became a typical marketing strategy, although just using the words "new" and "fashionable" does not necessarily prove that the actual stock was up to date. Giles Dayton of Hudson, New York, described his stock as, "... an assortment of fashionable Crockery and Glass Ware" in an advertisement of 1804 (*The Bee*, Hudson, New York September 25, 1804). Winne & Evertsen of Utica, New York, used the phrase "China, Glass & Earthenware, of the newest and best patterns" in 1807. Their stock included blue and green edged dining sets, jasper pitchers, and sixty crates of cream-colored ware available as enameled, blue printed, and fancy pressed or glazed (*Columbian Gazette*, Utica November 24, 1807). R. Shelton & Co., of

New Haven, Connecticut, advertised "New Crockery" imported from Liverpool in 1812 (*Connecticut Herald*, November 10, 1812). Henshaw & Jarves of Boston advertised in Massachusetts, as well as in the adjacent states of Connecticut, Maine, New Hampshire, and Vermont, declaring that their ceramics and glass had been selected "at the Manufactories by an agent, and are of the first quality and most fashionable patterns" (*American Advocate*, Maine, January 6, 1816). Their close relationship with Staffordshire is borne out by vessels marked as Henshaw & Jarves, importers of earthenware and china manufactured by Wood & Caldwell of Burslem (Figure 1.8). In 1822, Henry V. Garretson of New York, who was in partnership with John Scott of New Brunswick, New Jersey, advertised that they sold a "general assortment of Ware from the Factories of first repute in Staffordshire, and of the newest Patterns" (*The Fredonian*, New Brunswick, New Jersey July 4, 1822).

In this respect, there are reasonable grounds to interpret growing consumption in terms of fashion, as proposed by McKendrick, Berg and Styles, and others. However, understanding how manufacturers produced goods for different markets becomes even harder, especially if there was a geographical gap between the producer and the market. For this reason, it has been proposed that merchants, or manufacturers, responded to demand that was "especially clear in the case of the American market, because of its size and appetite, the distances involved and the relative weakness of manufacturing in eighteenth-century North America ..." (Styles 1993: 528).

Modern interpretations of consumption have considered how manufacturers and merchants were more responsive to the market. Regina Blaszczyk's *Imagining Consumers: Design and Innovation from Wedgwood to Corning* doubts how far manufacturers and retailers were straightforward manipulators of demand, suggesting that sales were more likely enlarged by "studying consumers and responding to their desires rather than trying to build markets by creating new needs" (2000: 2). She adds that "producers had to remain flexible, which meant knowing how to switch from one style to another as fashions changed" (2000:3). Although Blasczczk places far more emphasis on the role of intermediaries in helping to steer this production, this is framed around a dominant role of consumer taste and fashion.

As the nineteenth century progressed, it appears that the significance of fashion, or the marketing of goods as being of the latest fashions, cannot be denied. Huggins & Bradley of New Haven, Connecticut, used the phrase "Fashionable Crockery and Glass Ware" in an advertising campaign of 1833, and others even incorporated imagery. For example, E. B. Mason's China Hall in Boston sold "new goods" combining an image of a person made out of ceramic vessels in a humorously and innovative way in an endeavor to draw attention to this wholesale and retail establishment. Advertising was regularly used, but in later chapters, it is important to consider the reactions to certain publicized ceramic designs in order to question the role of fashion (Figures 2.1 and 2.2).

AT 135,
Fashionable Crockery and
Glass Ware

HUGGINS & BRADLEY, have just re-
ceived and are now opening, a large as-
Sortment of English and French CHINA TEA-
-SETTS – Fine Printed Dining Ware – Cut and
Plain GLASS – Common, Edged and White
Ware. Prices much reduced, at wholesale or re-
tail HUGGINS & BRADLEY.
North side Chapel, four doors from State-st

Figure 2.1 *Columbian Register*, New Haven, Connecticut May 11, 1833.

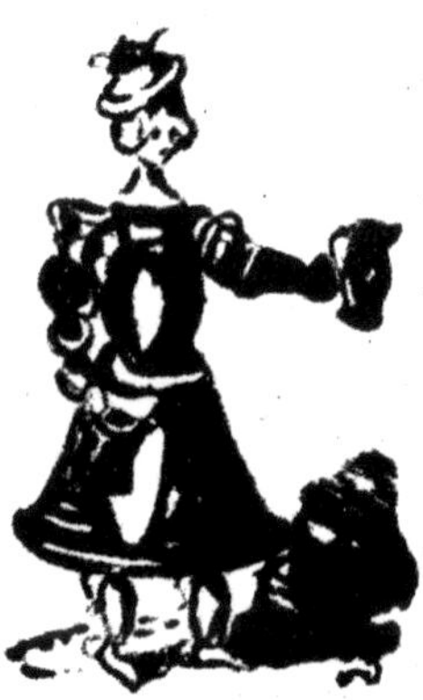

CROCKERY,
GLASS,
China,
AND
BRITTANIA
WARES.

E. B. MASON,
(Late E. B. McLaughlin,)
AT CHINA HALL. No.24 Hanover Street, near Court Street, Boston. has lately opened a large stock of new goods in the above line. His store is 82 feet by 33 feet,which enables him to exhibit a most extensive assortment. Prices low for ready cash at wholesale or retail.

Figure 2.2 *Norfolk Democrat*, Dedham, Massachusetts December 19, 1845.

Warehouses and stores

As major urban centers and ports developed, there were transitions in how the merchandise was presented and sold. When John Ridgway, a Staffordshire manufacturer, visited New York city in 1822, he was astonished by the amount of "imports & exports: the busy shops & bustling streets." His diary entry records how New York was "a sort of emporium to all Nations." Such scenes of mercantile activity impressed Ridgway to the extent that he noted that if he lived anywhere else than England, it would be New York (Diary, December 7, 1822).

Images of warehouses and stores provide important evidence of how these premises evolved in the United States. The company of Nathan Mitchell and Watson Freeman of Boston was established in around 1823. Dark-blue printed plates manufactured by William Adams of Stoke depict their warehouse-store at 12, Chatham Street, where they were located between c.1829 and 1832 (Figure 2.3). This appears to be the first example of depicting an image of the actual premises of an American crockery business on ceramic wares and was presumably used as a marketing device. Depicting business premises on ceramics would be repeated by another Boston crockery firm in a much later period (see Chapter 7, Figure 7.1).

Mitchell & Freeman's warehouse, with its Georgian-style windows, had only limited scope to display the merchandise to passersby, although it provides evidence of how premises in this period might be conveniently located near to

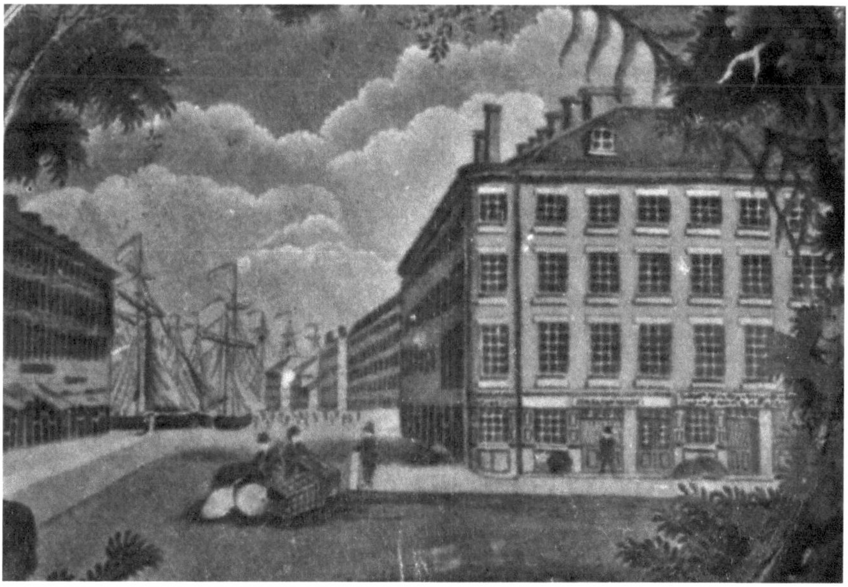

Figure 2.3 Plate, earthenware, blue printed, depicting a warehouse (detail), backstamped, "Mitchell & Freeman, China & Glass warehouse, Chatham St., Boston". Impressed mark, an American Seal surrounded by "Staffordshire Warranted, Adams [Stoke]," c.1829–32.

the docks, allowing for the convenient movement of crates and hogsheads loaded with ceramics. Crates and hogsheads are shown on the left-hand side of the image. Barrels (described as hogsheads) typically transported the more delicate and expensive china, whereas crates were used for earthenware. The amount of pottery in a crate varied depending on the proportion of packed flat or hollow ware, but it could amount to hundreds of pieces, based on an invoice of 1836 (Figure 5.16).

In this era, crockery stores or warehouses could be hazardous places to work. An apprentice of William F. Homer, crockery dealer of Boston, was almost killed when attempting to hoist a crate up to the third floor. Slipping over and falling through the scuttle, he momentarily hung onto the edge of the second story, only to end up on his back on the ground floor. He appeared to be lifeless, but it was reported that after being, "several times bled … we are happy to hear he is likely to recover" (*Daily Evening Transcript,* Boston September 5, 1831).

The prevailing view is that mercantile businesses were gradually transformed into safer, more sophisticated outlets. Joanna Cohen's *Luxurious Citizens: The Politics of Consumption in Nineteenth-Century America* outlines how elegant retail stores began to emerge in major cities. Served by eager assistants and clerks, these places were designed to entice more shoppers (2017: 155–7). In some respects, what Cohen proposes coincides with developments in selling crockery and glass. In 1833, a description of W. R. Kerr & Co.'s China Hall, located along the Arcade on Chestnut Street, Philadelphia, mentions how:

> Those gentlemen have filled eight compartments in the Arcade, – from No.41 to 48 inclusive, - and occupy in the same the whole cellar under the west avenue – through from Chestnut to Carpenter street … They have, - besides the usual supply of French, English and Canton ware, where most elegance or useful, and cut and plain glass and crockery, - numbers of other articles …
>
> (*Philadelphia Inquirer* December 24, 1833)

Furthermore, a description and images of Chauncey I. Filley's crockery business of St. Louis were featured in *Frank Leslie's Illustrated Newspaper*, in 1860 (Figures 2.4 and 2.5). Based on images of Filley's store, businesses now had the capacity to have large windows for displaying goods, in contrast to Mitchell & Freeman's warehouse of the late 1820s. The interior of Filley's store provides an impression of how ceramic merchandise was displayed, with attentive staff dealing with domestic buyers—not just other dealers. The customers wear hats, whereas the staff do not. Even though Filley's advertising emphasized how the business was wholesale, and their stock was for the trade, the image clearly shows how women, accompanied by men, shopped for ceramics. This coincides with an awareness of the growing significance of female consumers (Witkowski 2016: 46), although Figure 2.5 also shows evidence of how women were still accompanied by men when making purchases. The layout of Chauncey I. Filley's store relates to Joanna Cohen's view that far more attention was given to the display of goods during the nineteenth century.

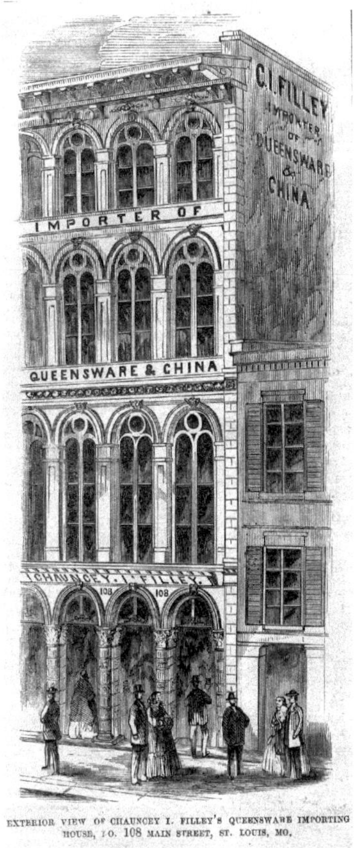

Figure 2.4 View of C. I. Filley's crockery store from, "Direct Importation of Queensware to St. Louis, Mo: Chauncey I. Filley's Extensive Queensware Importing House—The Queensware Trade in the Mississippi Valley," *Frank Leslie's Illustrated Newspaper* November 24, 1860, p. 13.

The article in *Frank Leslie's Illustrated Newspaper* also records how Filley's packing and shipping department alone employed fourteen men. Chauncey Filley even had a "department of design, in which new patterns of rare elegance and original styles are constantly being prepared by himself, to be forwarded to manufacturers in Europe, with whom he has immense contacts running through a series of years" (1860: 10). Chauncey was originally in partnership with his brothers, Edward Augustus and Samuel Roberts Filley, from the late 1840s. They were born in the state of New York, although their parents originated in Connecticut. It was a cousin, Giles F. Filley, who moved to St. Louis and established a crockery store in the early 1840s, which was subsequently sold to the Filley brothers (*St. Louis Republic*

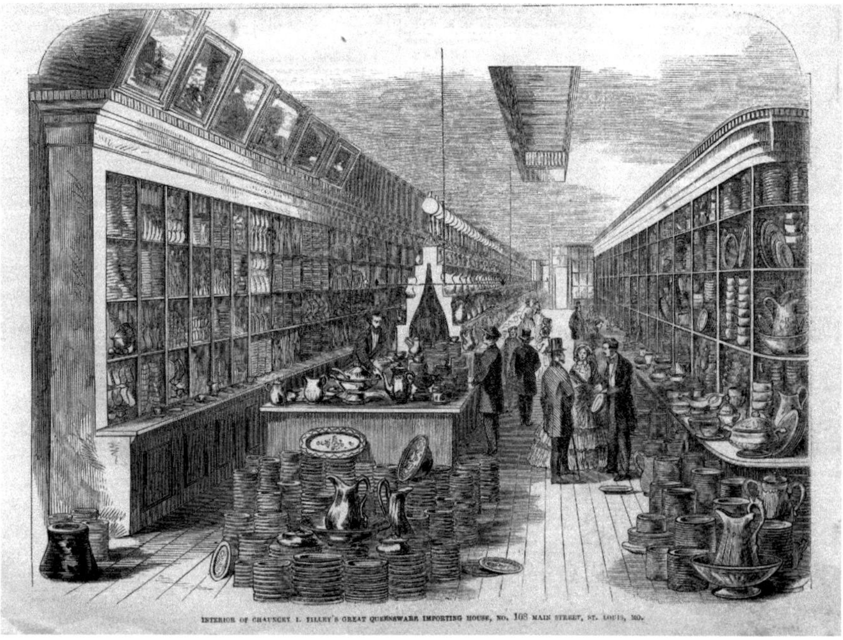

Figure 2.5 Interior view of C. I. Filley's crockery store from "Direct Importation of Queensware to St. Louis, Mo: Chauncey I. Filley's Extensive Queensware Importing House—The Queensware Trade in the Mississippi Valley," *Frank Leslie's Illustrated Newspaper,* November 24, 1860, p. 13.

February 4, 1895). Confirming their significant relationship with manufacturers are examples of ceramics backstamped "Manufactured For E. A. and S. R. Filley, St. Louis, Mo., By T. J. & J. Mayer, Longport" or "Manufactured For and Imported By Chauncey I. Filley, St Louis, M.O." Glass cup plates for advertising purposes were molded "E.A & S.R. Filley, Importer of China, Glass & Queensware, Saint Louis" (Figures 2.6 and 2.7). Chauncey Filley had such a close link to English manufacturers that his portrait (which appeared in the *Frank Leslie's Illustrated Newspaper* article) was derived from a photograph taken of him when visiting the Staffordshire Potteries (see Figure 2.8).

Equally revealing are the images that began to appear on invoices—described as billheads by American writers. From around the 1860s, invoices begin to incorporate images of the actual business establishments. These would tend to convey how there was growing interest in how these outlets appeared, and at the same time, suggest the level of success and prestige of some of these companies. For instance, an 1873 invoice of Abram French & Co., crockery importers, Boston, depicts a grand shop front, as shown in Figure 2.9. The invoice is also evidence of how businesses would invariably include a number of individuals. In the case of French & Co, the invoice mentions six members of the firm, and typically they would be connected by kinship.

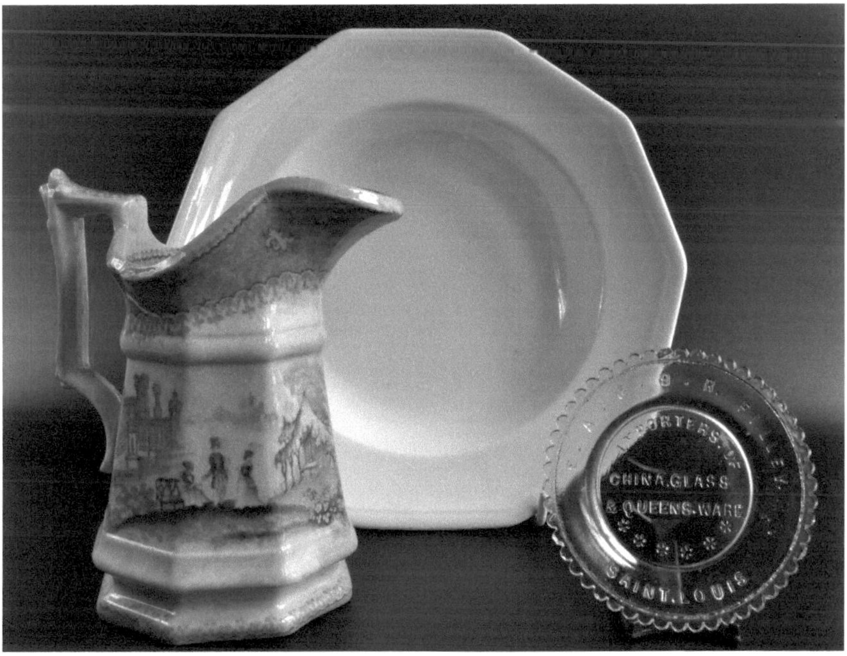

Figure 2.6 Range of ceramics and glass cup plate with marks for E.A. & S.R. Filley and C.I Filley. From left to right. Jug, earthenware, blue printed with a stylized landscape backstamped, "Manufactured For E. A. and S. R. Filley, St. Louis, Mo., By T. J. & J. Mayer, Longport," c.1849–55. Soup plate, white granite earthenware, with backstamp shown in Figure 2.7, impressed "Mayer & Elliott", Longport, Staffordshire, c.1858–60. Cup plate, pressed glass, with advertising inscription, "E.A & S.R. Filley, Importer of China, Glass & Queensware, Saint Louis." American, c.1850–60.

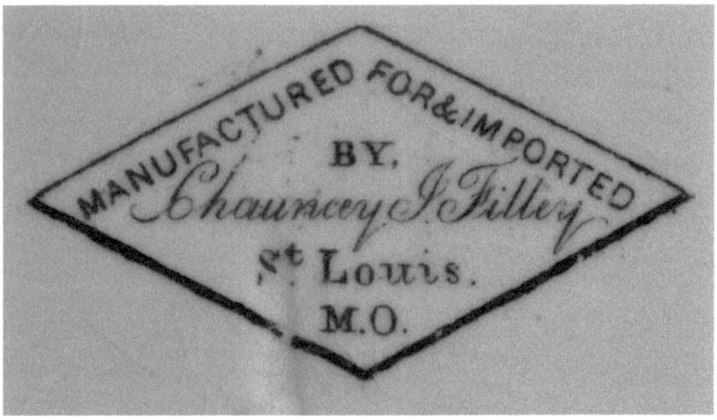

Figure 2.7 Printed backstamp on white granite soup plate shown in Figure 2.6.

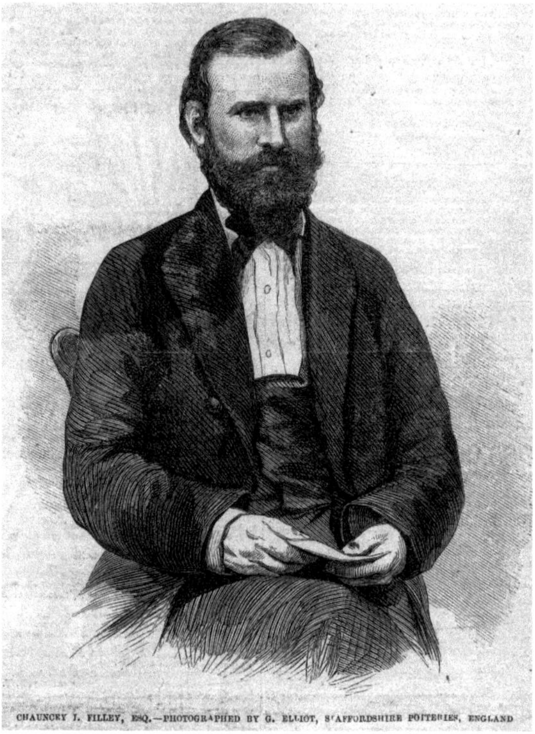

Figure 2.8 Engraving titled, "Chauncey I. Filley, Esq—Photographed by G. Elliot, Staffordshire Potteries, England" from "Direct Importation of Queensware to St. Louis, Mo: Chauncey I. Filley's Extensive Queensware Importing House—The Queensware Trade in the Mississippi Valley," *Frank Leslie's Illustrated Newspaper*, November 24, 1860, p.13.

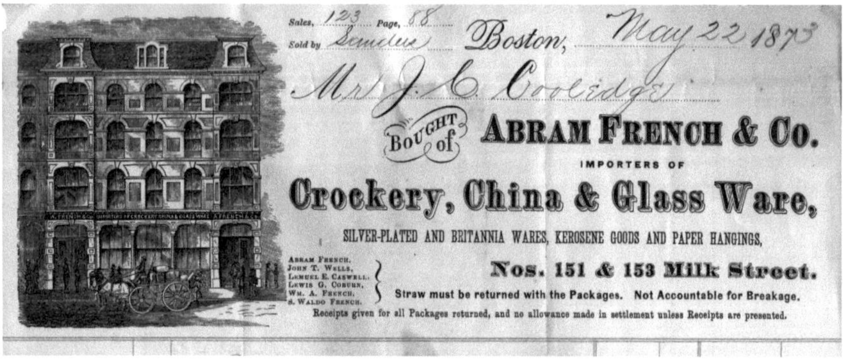

Figure 2.9 Invoice (extract), Abram French & Co., Boston, showing an image of the emporium. Dated May 22, 1873.

Based on these descriptions and images, it is hard to deny that there was not a huge demand for elegant and useful imported crockery in the wealthier, urban centers of the United States. But how widespread were these more sophisticated methods of display, and did the appreciation or demand for fashionable goods operate across the country, in a straightforward, all-at-once, way?

Motivation

The earliest writers, interested in the American-themed wares, assumed that these had evolved as a way to further entice consumers to purchase imported goods. Mabel Smith's *Anglo-American Historical China* is an early example of this, suggesting how these wares were designed to "appeal to our patriotism, a feeling which was then running very strong, and assured a ready sale" (1924: iv). Smith was not alone in expressing a view that ceramics based on American themes would be automatically popular, thus contributing to the development of a thriving Anglo-American trade (Larsen 1950: 2). However, it is curious to note how ceramics based on American themes were not widely advertised, when this technique seems to have been so widely exploited by merchants, importers and dealers, as outlined above.

The methodology used in this book reinforces this suggestion. As explained in the Introduction—physically surveying advertisements in American newspapers was in the past, an enormous undertaking, involving considerable time. However, it has become far more feasible to investigate ceramic marketing by using digital search tools. This approach reveals how the range of ceramic advertisements that referred to American-themed ceramics appears to vary, considerably. A digital research approach has, intriguingly, only uncovered one ceramic advertisement of 1805, which mentions pitchers, described as depicting a portrait of the American President—presumably, Thomas Jefferson, given the date. Such an unusual advertisement requires further discussion in Chapter 4.

While Otis Norcross of Boston advertised his stock as the "newest styles and patterns," consisting of 597 crates, there was only one reference to American-themed wares. These were luster jugs of "American navy and army heroes" in 1815 (*Boston Daily Advertiser* November 22, 1815). These perhaps relate to extant pieces shown in Figure 2.10, and if so, is evidence of when these items were manufactured. Along with ordinary cream colored [CC] and edged wares, a diverse range of other printed patterns were advertised, including Napoleonic themes, such as Wellington, Waterloo, Blucher [Gebhard Von Blücher], and the Prince of Orange, and blue printed dining sets, described as Zebra, Stag, Oriental, and Prince Regent. The subjects were eclectic and international and included enamel tea-ware described as Vandyke and Castlereagh and enameled and printed jugs described as Moscow, Leipsic, Cossacks, with one given the strange, macabre title of "Surgical Operations." Norcross' advertisement ends with the statement that the wares were selected by Mr. Collamore (another Boston Crockery importer) "while in Staffordshire." There is a sense of how crockery importers and dealers acted

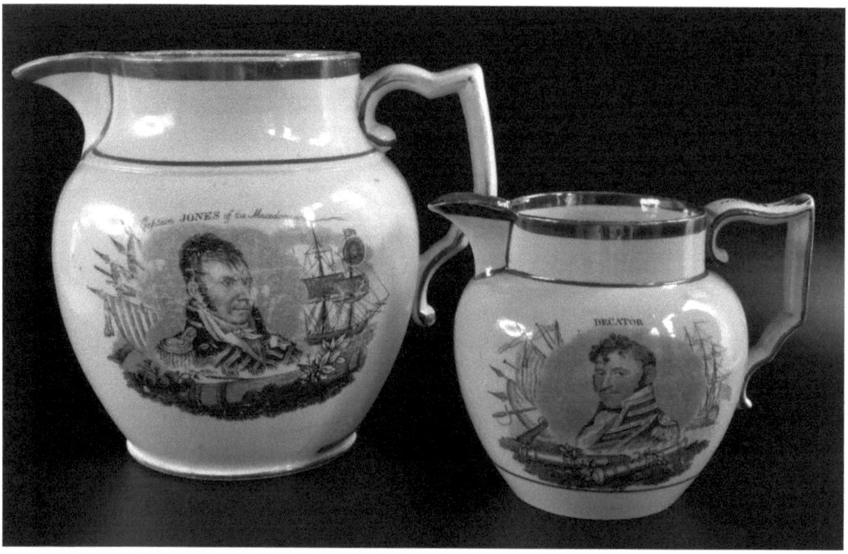

Figure 2.10 Jugs, depicting American naval heroes from the Anglo-American War, 1812–14. From left to right. Jug, cream colored, black printed and luster decoration, portrait of Captain Jones, titled "Captain JONES of the Macedonian." Accession number "40-16-95." Formerly in the collection of R.Wistar Harvey, Philadelphia Museum of Art. Manufactured, Staffordshire, c.1815–20. Jug, pearlware, black printed and luster decoration, portrait of Captain Decatur, titled "DECATOR"[sic]. Manufactured, Staffordshire, c.1815–20.

collectively rather than as competitors, and there is more evidence of this when considering the role of kinship in Chapter 3, Pedigrees 7 and 11.

Evidently, some American-themed blue-printed patterns were more widely advertised than others. For instance, the pattern called "State-House" was mentioned in the advertisements of Henshaw and Jarves (who imported wares manufactured by Wood & Caldwell, Burslem (Figure 1.8)) and Otis Norcross, both of Boston (*Columbian Centinel,* Boston April 29, 1818; *Boston Daily Advertiser* October 3, 1821). In the case of Norcross' advertisement, the stock was from the "first manufactories in Staffordshire, comprising blue printed, Zebra, Elephant and State-House patterns ..." in dining ware. The Boston State House is a well-known design, produced by manufacturers such as Enoch Wood and Joseph Stubbs, both of Burslem, and John Rogers & Son of Longport (Larsen 1950: 26–7, 117, 153). A whole article about the "State House" pattern appeared in *The Magazine Antiques* in 1931, inferring how this pattern was never particularly hard to find by early collectors (Norman-Wilcox: 363–66). As indicated in Chapter 1, the Boston importer, Horace Collamore specifically ordered "State House" in 1818 (Ewins 1997: 136). A combination of dates provided by merchant records and advertising would infer that Boston State House was one of the earliest underglaze blue printed-American-themed patterns, purposely developed for the export market (Figure 2.11), as opposed to overglazed, black printed wares, shown in Figures 1.1 and 4.1.

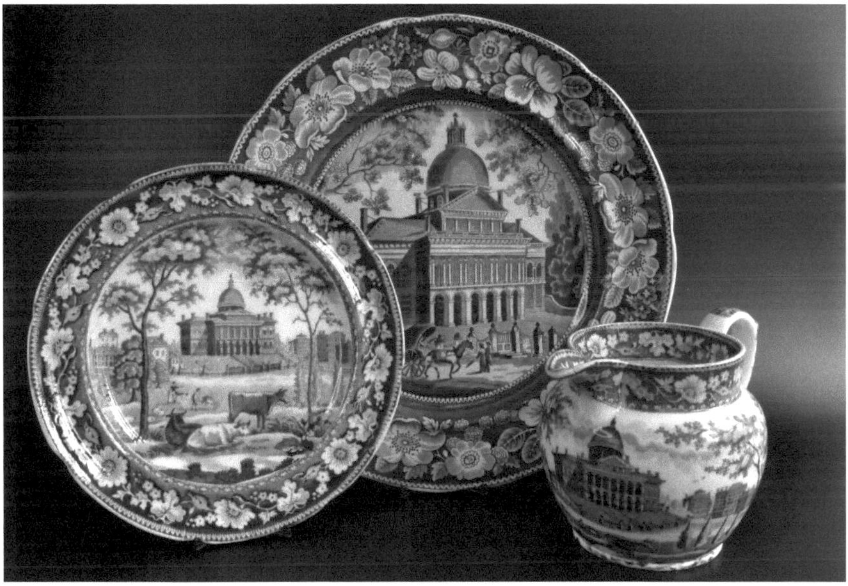

Figure 2.11 Ceramics depicting Boston State House, Staffordshire, c.1818–20. From left to right. Side plate, earthenware, blue transfer printed, impressed "Rogers," Longport, c.1820. Plate, earthenware, blue transfer printed, impressed "Enoch Wood & Sons," Burslem, c.1818–20. Jug, earthenware, blue transfer printed, unmarked, probably Rogers, Longport, c.1820.

Ironically, some of the most detailed advertisements (in terms of listing the actual patterns available) were not for American-themed wares at all. In the following advertisement, Charles Barrell of Boston regularly advertised John and William Ridgway's "College Views," depicting images of Oxford and Cambridge University during 1822 and 1823 (Figures 2.12 and 2.13).

Francis Wilby & Co., of Boston offered "blue printed Dinning ware of British Scenery, College, Oxford, India and Willow patterns" (*Independent Chronicle & Boston Patriot*, October 2, 1822), and Nathan Hastings (also of Boston) listed fourteen views of Oxford and Cambridge Universities (*Rhode Island American*, Providence May 24, 1822). The advertising of non-American printed themes was far more typical, and this coincides with the archaeological record, which shows widespread consumption of other patterns, such as those in a chinoiserie-style (Schwartz 2011: 84–5). Fifty-four crates of earthenware from "Spode & Copeland's manufactory, entirely new patterns, called 'French, Indian, Geranium, Grecian, Marbled,' &c." in dinner and tea sets were sold by Henry and George Barclay (*Evening Post*, New York November 13, 1822). Isaiah Atkins of Boston offered "blue printed dining ware, British views, Cascade, Waterloo, Quadrupeds, and other handsome patterns" (*Columbian Centinel*, Boston July 10, 1824). American consumers were offered a variety of patterns.

In the opinion of the earliest writers on American-themed Staffordshire wares, these were initially produced in dark-blue, followed by other colors during

COLLEGE VIEWS.

CHARLES BARRELL, *Agent*, has

received by the Mount Vernon, Triton and Hannah, part of his Spring supply of Ridgway's fine blue printed and Stone China, burnished gold DINING SETS – an elegant new pattern, called "College Views," embracing the following views of the public edifices in Oxford and Cambridge, viz : -

Downing College Cambridge;
Senate House, Cambridge;
Radcliffe Library Oxford;
Pembroke Hall, Cambridge;
Christ Church, Oxford;
Theatre, Printing-House, &c. Oxford;
Library of Trinity College, Cambridge;
Sidney Sussex College, do;
Caius College do;
St.Peter's College do;
Trinity Hall, do;
Trinity College, Oxford;
Wadham College, Oxford;
All Souls College and St.Mary's Church, &c from the finest point in High-street, Oxford.

Also – A superb assortment of Tea and Desert Services, and Ornaments.

Figure 2.12 *Columbian Centinel,* Boston April 20, 1822.

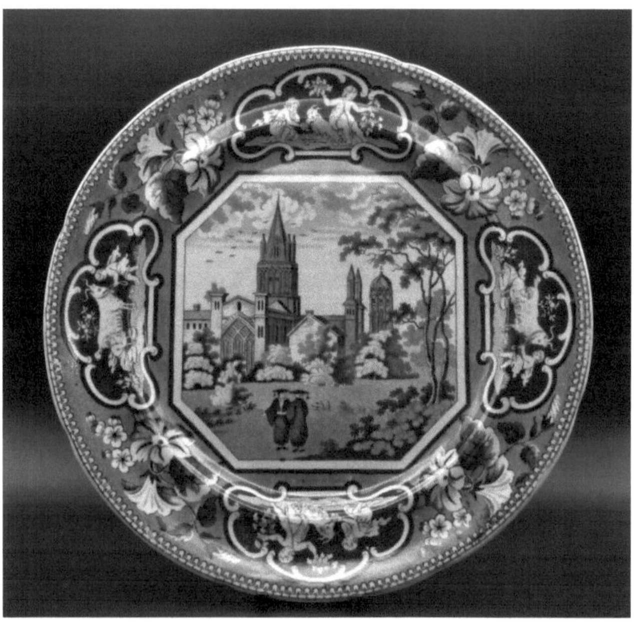

Figure 2.13 Plate, earthenware, blue printed transfer. Backstamp, "Opaque China, Christ Church, Oxford, J.& W. Ridgway," Shelton, Staffordshire, c.1822.

the 1830s (Larsen 1939: 26). To a degree, this corresponds to what is shown in advertisements. Alexander Walsh of Lansingburgh, Virginia, advertised "brown and pencilled earthen elegant new patterns" in 1830 (Figure 2.14).

These are views, associated with the manufacturers J. & R. Clews of Cobridge and Enoch Wood of Burslem, also printed in a variety of colors (Larsen 1950: 37, 62, 66, 69). Ellouise Baker Larsen's *American Historical Views on Staffordshire China* claimed that American-themed wares were produced into the 1840s, believing that "Few American historical scenes were launched on the market during the 1850s" (1939: 26). However, an advertisement placed by C. W. Churchill in the *Augusta Chronicle*, Georgia, of March 1846, advertised "an entire new pattern of Blue Printed EARTHENWARE, embracing views of American Scenery ..., " which is late to be still marketing these types of wares (Figure 2.15). By this era, it was more common to find references to flow blue and white granite in advertisements and invoices, suggesting regional differences in how demand evolved.

Despite Neil McKendrick's suggestion that Wedgwood was able to achieve "world-wide demand" (1982: 108), references to this company name did not appear that frequently in advertisements. Not all the links in the chain appear to be present. How did consumers hear of the fashionable goods they were supposed to be so desperate to acquire? Perhaps Thomas Bentley's view that the American

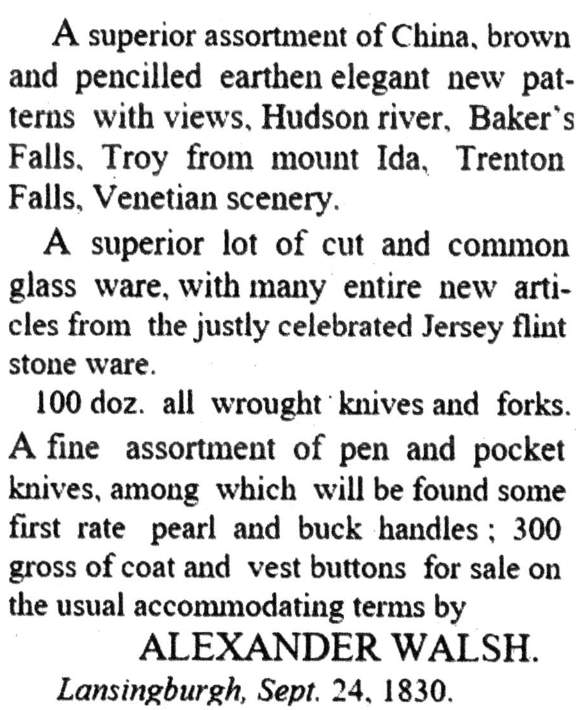
A superior assortment of China, brown and pencilled earthen elegant new patterns with views, Hudson river, Baker's Falls, Troy from mount Ida, Trenton Falls, Venetian scenery.

A superior lot of cut and common glass ware, with many entire new articles from the justly celebrated Jersey flint stone ware.

100 doz. all wrought knives and forks. A fine assortment of pen and pocket knives, among which will be found some first rate pearl and buck handles; 300 gross of coat and vest buttons for sale on the usual accommodating terms by

ALEXANDER WALSH.

Lansingburgh, Sept. 24, 1830.

Figure 2.14 *Alexandria Herald*, Virginia September 28, 1830.

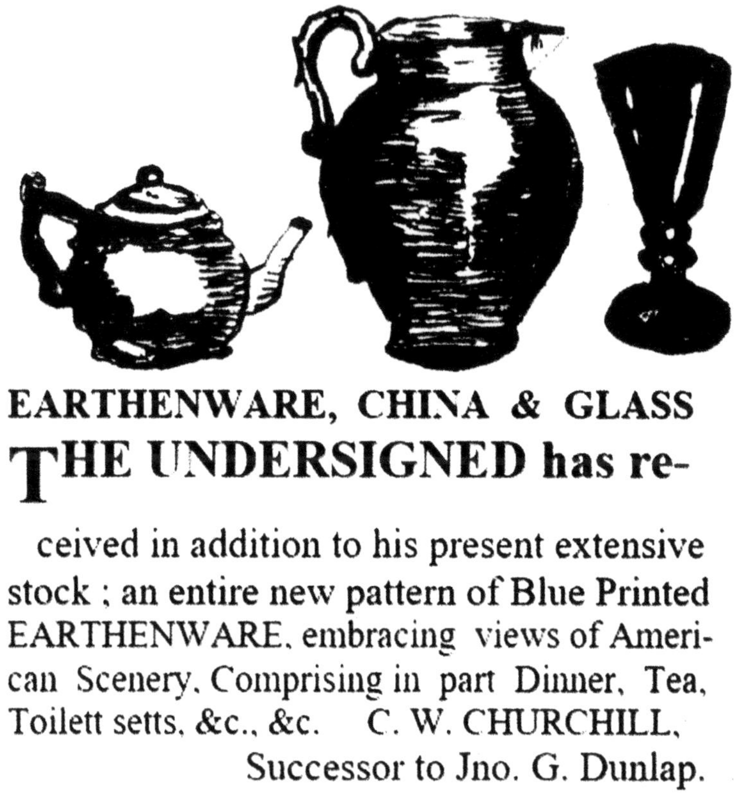

Figure 2.15 *Augusta Chronicle*, Georgia March 13, 1846.

market was “not ripe for expensive things at present” (McKendrick 1964: 19) remained the case in the immediate post-Josiah Wedgwood I period. A 1798 advertisement placed by Samuel Sumner of Boston mentions “N. B. A few Crates of Blue Printed and Enamelled Wedgwood” at the end, suggesting that it was not a major part of his trade (*Massachusetts Mercury* December 4, 1798). In later example of the 1830s, J. Kerr & Co., of Philadelphia headed their advertisement as “French China, at very reduced prices,” and briefly mention, “Also, just received, 6 crates of Wedgewood’s [sic] superior manufacture Table Services, Chamber sets, &c.” (*Philadelphia Inquirer* March 18, 1831). In this advertisement, the emphasis was placed on their French stock.

When surveying crockery advertisements placed in the American newspapers during the first half of the nineteenth century, it is more usual to find the names of many other Staffordshire manufacturers. An extract from an 1822 advertisement placed by George Grundy & Sons of Baltimore (in a Virginian newspaper) states that his stock consisted of 447 earthenware crates, using the generic phrase “Queen’s ware,” but stating that they had ware of the “anchor stamp, and put up to our order in the celebrated manufactory of Messrs. John & James Davenport, expressly for this market" (Figures 2.16 and 2.17). In a lower part of the advertisement, Grundy requested that this notice be reprinted by sixteen other newspapers, including the *Cincinnati Inquisitor*, the *Nashville Gazette*, and *Louisville Public Advertiser*. This is an early example of how the backstamp was viewed as having a brand value.

EARTHENWARE.

THE subscribers have received, by the recent arrivals at this port from Liverpool, their spring supply, consisting of

477 crates Earthenware,

comprising a very general and complete assortment of every article in the line. They will be sold to country merchants and others on better terms than they have been in the habit of buying. This ware is of anchor stamp, and put up to our order in the celebrated manufactory of Messrs. John & James Davenport, expressly for this market. 150 crates of the above number are variously and handsomely assorted, to suit every demand.

We have made arrangements to be regularly and constantly supplied with articles of Earthen and Queen's Ware, and invite examinations of prices and quality of ware, at our Warehouse, No.3, North Charles-street, Baltimore.

GEORGE GRUNDY & SONS.

N.B. We expect by the earliest fall arrivals, 580 crates,which will be sold on our usual terms.

Figure 2.16 *Alexandria Herald*, Virginia, June 3, 1822.

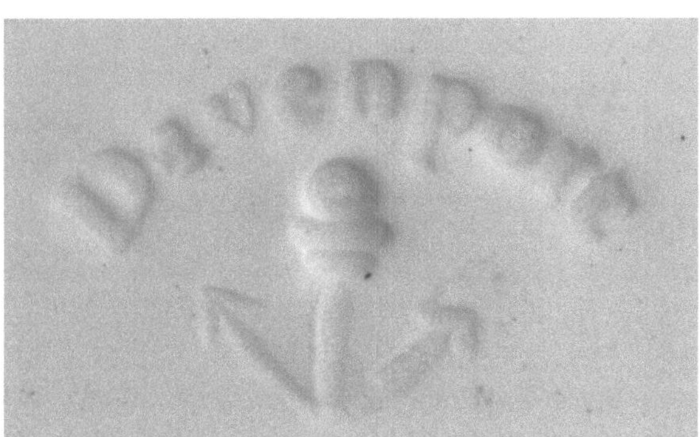

Figure 2.17 Davenport backstamp from a green edged plate, c.1810–20.

Davenport of Longport (near Burslem) was unusual in the sense that they produced china and earthenware, as well as flint and stained glass (Ward 1843: 156).

John Davenport was originally employed by Thomas Wolfe of Stoke to run his Liverpool warehouse, and when Davenport became a manufacturer in his own right, after purchasing a factory at Longport in the 1790s, he had already acquired knowledge of export markets (Emmerson 2010: 47). Wolfe's advertisements mention how the merchandise available was suitable for the West Indies and American markets, and John Davenport even established his own "Wholesale Staffordshire warehouse" in conjunction with his Longport factory (*Gore's Liverpool General Advertiser* April 30, 1795; March 13, 1800).

Not all researchers have been convinced by the critical role of fashion in stimulating demand, as outlined by McKendrick, Brewer and Plumb's rise of the "consumer revolution" (1982). George Miller and Amy Earls' "War on Pots: The

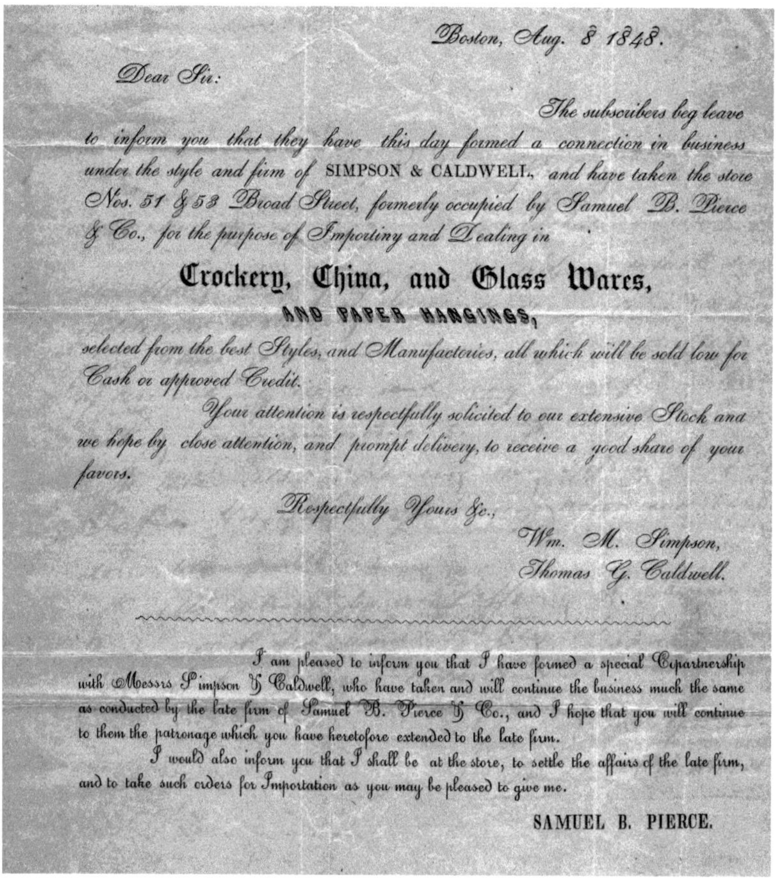

Boston, Aug. 8 1848.

Dear Sir:

The subscribers beg leave to inform you that they have this day formed a connection in business under the style and firm of SIMPSON & CALDWELL, and have taken the store Nos. 51 & 53 Broad Street, formerly occupied by Samuel B. Pierce & Co., for the purpose of Importing and Dealing in

Crockery, China, and Glass Wares,

AND PAPER HANGINGS,

selected from the best Styles, and Manufactories, all which will be sold low for Cash or approved Credit.

Your attention is respectfully solicited to our extensive Stock and we hope by close attention, and prompt delivery, to receive a good share of your favors.

Respectfully Yours &c.,

Wm. M. Simpson,
Thomas G. Caldwell.

I am pleased to inform you that I have formed a special Copartnership with Messrs Simpson & Caldwell, who have taken and will continue the business much the same as conducted by the late firm of Samuel B. Pierce & Co., and I hope that you will continue to them the patronage which you have heretofore extended to the late firm.

I would also inform you that I shall be at the store, to settle the affairs of the late firm, and to take such orders for Importation as you may be pleased to give me.

SAMUEL B. PIERCE.

Figure 2.18 Printed circular of Simpson & Caldwell, Boston, to Brown & Co., Norway, Maine, August 8, 1848.

Impact of Economics and Politics on Ceramic Consumption Patterns" (2008) expressed a skepticism. According to Miller and Earls, "Evidence from the nineteenth century suggests that oversupply and falling prices drove changing consumption patterns" (2008: 67). Their interpretation is based far more on the influential role of economics and price.

It is interesting to note how price was often mentioned in conjunction with novelty and fashion in marketing. Price was not irrelevant but nor, apparently, was design. Apart from newspaper advertisements, printed circulars were another way of directly reaching out to potential buyers, informing them of incoming merchandise. The firm of Simpson & Caldwell of Boston (successors to Samuel B. Pierce) sent a printed circular dated August 8, 1848 (Figure 2.18), to a dealer located at Norway, Maine, with a hand-written letter on the reverse, dated April 9, 1849.

The printed circular refers to the "best Styles." The hand-written note on the reverse reinforces how their spring supply of printed flowing blue, mulberry, and white goods was of "new patterns," but of the "lowest prices" (Figure 2.19). This

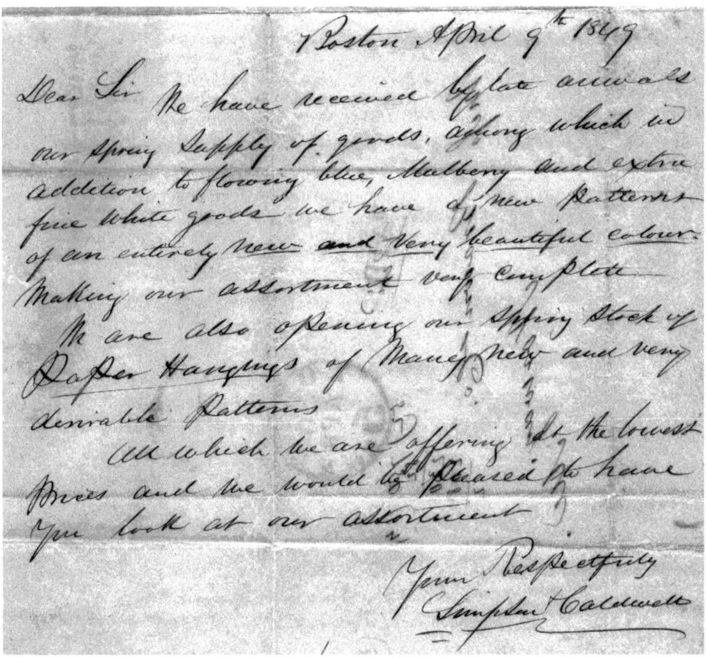
Boston April 9th 1849
Dear Sir We have received by late arrivals
our Spring Supply of goods, among which in
addition to flowing blue, Mulberry and extra
fine White goods we have a new Patterns
of an entirely new and Very beautiful colour
Making our assortment very Complete
We are also opening our Spring Stock of
Paper Hangings of Many new and very
desirable Patterns
All which we are offering at the lowest
Prices and we would be pleased to have
you look at our assortment
Yours Respectfully
Simpson & Caldwell

Figure 2.19 Letter on the reverse of printed circular (Figure 2.18), dated Boston April 9, 1849, reading "We have received by late arrivals our spring supply of goods, among which in addition to flowing blue, mulberry and extra fine white goods we have a new patterns [sic] of an entirely new and very beautiful colour making our assortment very complete … All of which we are offering at the lowest prices and we would be pleased to have you look at our assortment."

appears to suggest evidence of how contemporaries perceived price as inseparable from fashion and novelty. Offering affordable yet appropriate patterns was considered important when writing to this dealer in Norway, Maine.

A surviving invoice of J. and W. P. Fogg of Cleveland, Ohio, dated July 1852, illustrates the complexities of fashion and demand (Figures 2.20 and 2.21). In July 1852, Fogg sold tea-wares described as "Passiflora" and "Jenny Lind," both recorded as the printed patterns produced by the Staffordshire manufacturer, Charles Meigh of Hanley (Kowalsky and Kowalsky 1999: 494, 503). Conceivably, the motivation to produce a Jenny Lind design stemmed from the entrepreneurial manufacturer, since Lind, the Swedish opera singer, was renowned throughout Europe by the 1850s. However, what perhaps accounts for Foggs stocking the design was that Jenny Lind visited Cleveland, Ohio, between October to November 1851, and performed at Kelley's Hall. A temporary visit potentially created a sudden surge in interest in this opera singer, and crockery importers and dealers attempted to then capitalised on a local rather than national event.

If there is no definitive answer as to what always accounts for consumption, it does seem that the impact of fashion has remained a pervasive idea in attempting to interpret the relationship between production and demand.

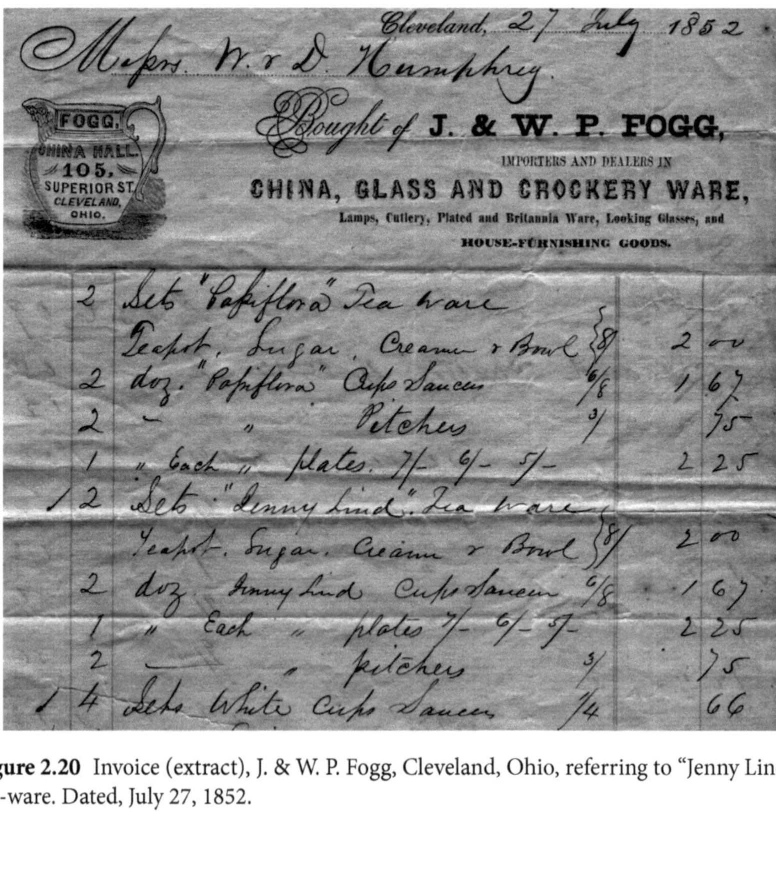
Cleveland, 27 July 1852
Messrs. W. & D. Humphrey
FOGG, CHINA HALL, 105, SUPERIOR ST, CLEVELAND, OHIO.
Bought of J. & W. P. FOGG,
IMPORTERS AND DEALERS IN
CHINA, GLASS AND CROCKERY WARE,
Lamps, Cutlery, Plated and Britannia Ware, Looking Glasses, and
HOUSE-FURNISHING GOODS.

2	Sets "Passiflora" Tea ware		
	Teapot, Sugar, Cream & Bowl	8/	2 00
2	doz. "Passiflora" Cups Saucers	6/8	1 67
2	" " Pitchers	3/	75
1	" Each " plates 7/- 6/- 5/-		2 25
2	Sets "Jenny Lind" Tea ware		
	Teapot, Sugar, Cream & Bowl	8/	2 00
2	doz. Jenny Lind Cups Saucers	6/8	1 67
1	" Each " plates 7/- 6/- 5/-		2 25
2	" pitchers	3/	75
4	Sets White Cups Saucers	1/4	66

Figure 2.20 Invoice (extract), J. & W. P. Fogg, Cleveland, Ohio, referring to "Jenny Lind" tea-ware. Dated, July 27, 1852.

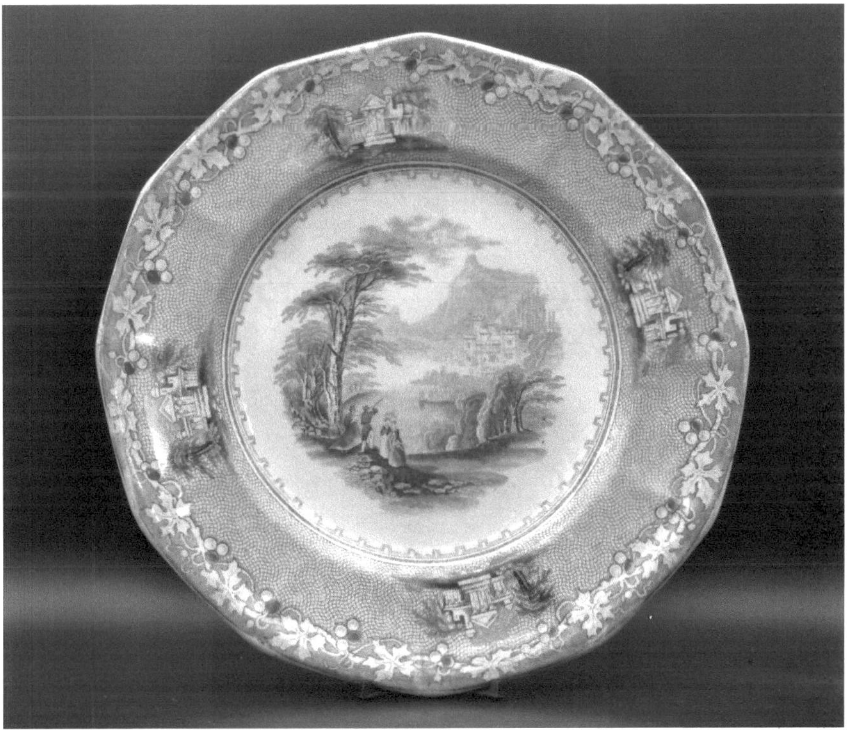

Figure 2.21 Plate, earthenware, grey transfer printed with enamel decoration, depicting a stylized landscape with Figures, backstamped "Jenny Lind/ CM & S [Charles Meigh & Sons, Hanley]," impressed "Improved Stone China," c.1850.

Auctioning stock

Advertisements for forthcoming auction sales were regularly placed in newspapers and provided a quick, albeit unpredictable, way of rapidly shifting stock. It has been proposed by historians that auctioning imported merchandise became a significant feature of the Anglo-American trade during and after the 1812–14 war, and generally how auctions were aimed at dealers, not individuals, buying larger quantities of merchandise (Buck [1925] 1969: 135–41; Cohen 2017: 94). David Dunham & Co., of 144 Pearl Street, New York, advertised ceramics manufactured by Harley & Sickerson [sic] in 1819 (Figure 2.22). The business of Harley & Sackerson of Longton existed from c.1809 until the mid-1820s, when their utensils were advertised for sale in a local newspaper (*Staffordshire Advertiser* September 10, 1825).

Later, "in front of their auction store," Dunham advertised sixty-one crates and hogheads of "very superior earthen and china ware, from the well known pottery of Messrs. Harley & Sickerson[sic]" (*New York Gazette* May 24, 1820). In 1823, "Two invoices, one of 108, one of 11 crates superior Earthen Ware, from the factory

By D. Dunham and Co.

To-morrow,

At half past 10 o'clock in front of their store, 144 Pearl-st. 83 crates & 6 hhds very superior crockery ware, from the manufactory of Harley & Sickerson, selected by a gentleman on the spot, particularly for this market (an entire invoice.) Catalogues will be ready on Wednesday previous to the sale – Terms liberal.

Figure 2.22 *Columbian*, New York June 5, 1819. (Extract of notice).

of Harley & Dickerson[sic], just arrived, and for sale by Dunham, Edgar & Co. 144 Pearl St." (*Commercial Advertiser*, New York, April 12, 1823). Again, in 1823, the phrase "the ware is in very fine order and from the well-known pottery of Harley & Sickerson[sic]" was used (*New York Daily Advertiser* May 23, 1823). What was described as produced by a "well-known" manufacturer is, from a contemporary ceramic-history perspective, totally obscure now.

Other American importers also mentioned Harley & Sackerson, suggesting how they had a regular export trade. For instance, N. & D. Talcott of New York offered sixty hogsheads and crates of "Herley & Seckerson's [sic] Staffordshire potteries, England; an unusually elegant assortment, of superior quality, put up with the greatest care expressly for this market …" (*Mercantile Advertiser*, New York January 19, 1819). But, despite these various notices to Harley & Sackerson, they have yet to have a recorded factory backstamp (Kowalsky and Kowalsky 1999; Henrywood 2002). Therefore, where exactly the ceramics produced by Harley & Sackerson reside in collections and museums remains unclear.

In 1820, it was announced that there would be a sale of:

> 61 crates and hhds [hogheads] of very superior earthenware and china ware from the well known pottery of Messrs. Harley & Sickerson. Catalogues will be ready on Tuesday, and a sample of the ware exhibited to save breakage.
>
> (*New-York Gazette & General Advertiser* May 24, 1820)

The reference to auction catalogues raises the question of whether these ever provided any detail of actual patterns, reinforcing the view that fashion was so important in facilitating the process of consumption. One such example of a catalogue, belonging to David Dunham & Co., survives in the archives of the New York Historical Society. While this catalogue promotes a sale to be held at the front of their store, at 144, Pearl-street, on May 6, 1818, it is somewhat vague. The list of merchandise does not refer to any actual manufacturers, and only infrequently to table-wares described as "Bath" pattern, or what was referred to as "fine enam. wreath border Blucher jugs." The catalogue does not appear to emphasize that the wares being sold were patterns of any particular, up-to-date, or fashionable merit (Figure 2.23).

From 1823, the business of Dunham & Co., became Edgar & Leffingwell. Life, it seems, was anything but predictable for intermediaries. David Dunham died in 1823, having been lost overboard from a sloop called the *Criterion* traveling along the North-river between Verplanck and Stony point, in the state of New York. Dunham assisted in taking in the sails, when faced by worsening windy weather. Alas, he was tragically thrown overboard, and all attempts to reach him failed. His family even put up a reward of $250 for the recovery of his body; it was noted at the time that Dunham was "an active and enterprizing[sic] citizen" (*American*, New York April 1, 1823). His body was not found until June 1823 (*Evening Post*, New York June 7, 1823).

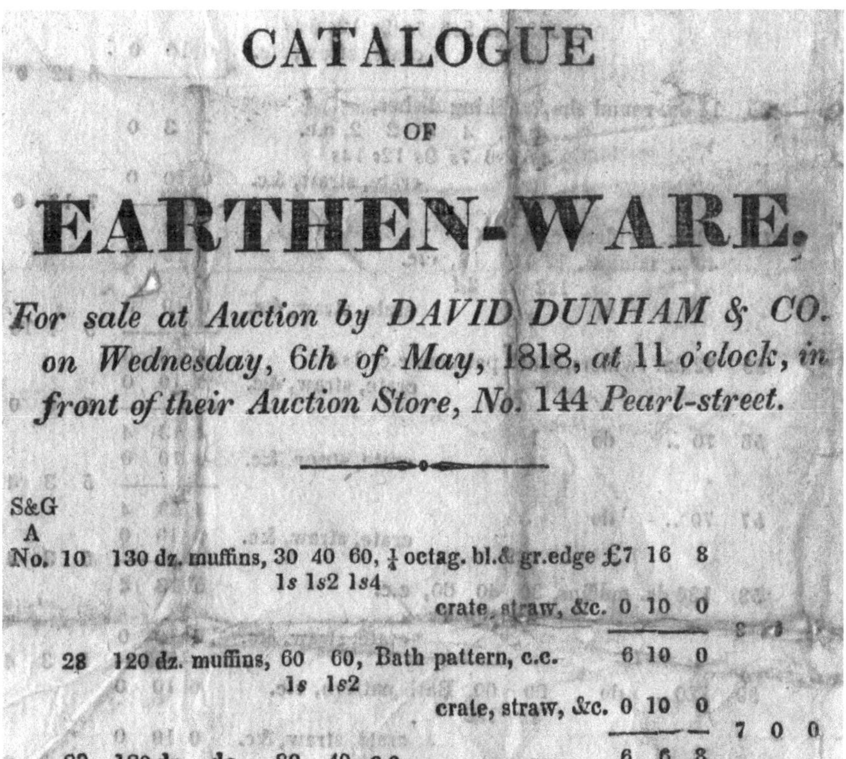
CATALOGUE
OF
EARTHEN-WARE.
For sale at Auction by DAVID DUNHAM & CO. on Wednesday, 6th of May, 1818, at 11 o'clock, in front of their Auction Store, No. 144 Pearl-street.

S&G
A
No. 10 130 dz. muffins, 30 40 60, ¼ octag. bl.& gr.edge £7 16 8
1*s* 1*s*2 1*s*4
crate, straw, &c. 0 10 0
28 120 dz. muffins, 60 60, Bath pattern, c.c. 6 10 0
1*s* 1*s*2
crate, straw, &c. 0 10 0
7 0 0
29 120 dz. do 80 40, c.c. 6 6 8

Figure 2.23 Auction catalogue (extract) David Dunham & Co., New York, May 6, 1818. Broadsides, SY1818 no. 31, New York Historical Society. ©New-York Historical Society.

Dunham's type of business was one of a quick turnover—so different from emerging elegant retail stores described by Cohen (2017: 155–7). But Edgar & Leffingwell continued to sell the wares of Harley & Sackerson. They advertised the auction sale of "200 crates Earthen-ware, comprising a general assortment of CC [cream colored], edged and blue printed, from the manufactory of Hardy [sic] & Sickerson [sic], lately imported and in excellent order." This auction was of smaller amount, but significantly included "23 hhds [hogsheads] and crates dark blue printed table and tea ware, American scenery …" (*New York Daily Advertiser* October 15, 1823). Ever since the rise of earliest collectors and writers (as outlined in the previous chapter), many have sought to document every pattern and maker of American-themed wares. But not once has the firm of Harley & Sackerson entered into their extensive lists. If this Longton firm, which apparently even lacked a backstamp, produced a dark-blue printed American view in c.1823, what design was it? In an instant, just by considering what the intermediaries actually advertised introduces alternative producers and intriguing results for the collector.

Fire and Theft

The downside of crockery businesses clustering on the same streets was how fires (which were not uncommon) easily wreaked havoc on an entire district devoted to selling the same kinds of merchandise. Dunham (later to be Edgar & Leffingwell) was on Pearl Street, as were many other crockery and glass warehouses. On the evening of December 16, 1835, a fire devastated sections of Water and Pearl Street and many other streets within the district of the First Ward. So cold and icy was that particular night that the hoses from fire engines froze and were then unable to effectively tackle the blaze (*New-York Commercial Advertiser* December 17, 1835). Some of the crockery businesses destroyed were huge concerns (Foster [1835] 2011: 31). Robert Charles Wetmore's crockery business was four stories high (see Pedigree 4), and H. W. Cauldwell's warehouse was five stories (see Pedigree 2). The disaster even became the subject of at least three images used on printed wares (Larsen 1950: 245–6). One version, depicting the destruction of the Merchant's Exchange on Wall Street, is shown in Figure 2.24.

As early as February 1, 1836, a "Circular" was printed in *Commercial Advertiser* of New York, signed by sixteen different "Importers and Dealers in China, Glass and Earthenware" whose businesses had been destroyed. It is interesting how even in the face of a catastrophe, this was turned into a marketing opportunity, since it was pointed out that:

> … From the large orders previously given to the manufacturers, it is expected that the assortment of the present season will, in quantity, be fully equal: and in its quality, superior to that of any former year—it being composed of the most recent and beautiful designs, without any mixture of old unsaleable patterns.
>
> (*Commercial Advertiser*, New York February 1, 1836)

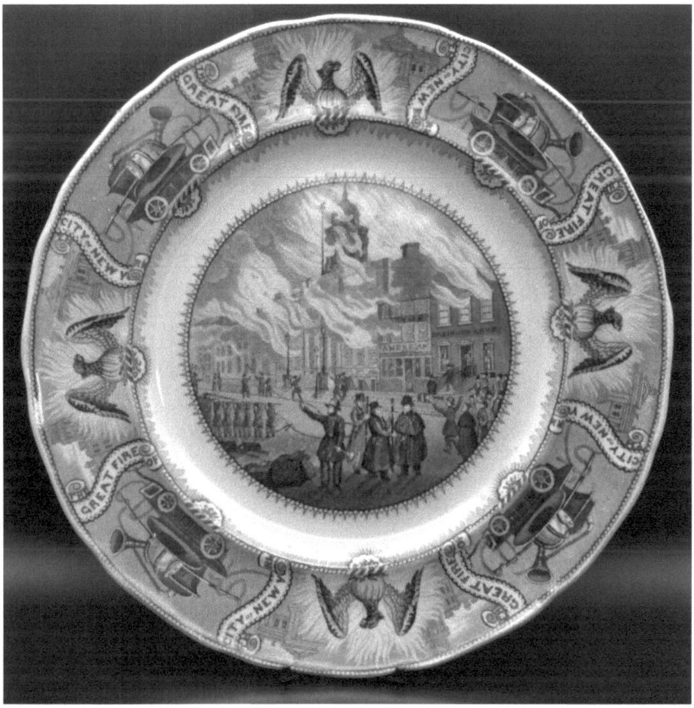

Figure 2.24 Plate, earthenware, purple printed, depicting the burning of the Merchants' Exchange, Wall Street, New York, December 1835. Backstamped, "D/ Stone Ware/ Exchange/New York." Probably Staffordshire, c.1836.

In an effort to entice customers, it is noticeable how the destruction of the fire was used to make a distinction between what was old, and then what would be, inevitably, new stock.

However, in the immediate aftermath of the fire, other possibilities of acquiring ceramics opened up. One New York visitor recorded in his diary how:

> I saw China stores where the masses of broken china was vitrified in clusters … I also brought away a whole Ewer, which had endured all the fire, at the China store of John Greenfield & Sons in Pearl St. close to where a China Store was blown up, & caused the arrest at the head of Coenties slips, on Pearl St.
>
> (Diary, John Fanny Watson, 1835: 7)

John Greenfield of New York is known to have sold the wares of R. & J. Clews of Cobridge, including a printed design known as "Castle" pattern. Examples marked as manufactured by Clews and signed "J. Greenfield's China Store, No.77 Pearl Street, New York" are recorded (see Figures 2.25 and 2.26). Greenfield was at this address from c.1825 until the fire of 1835.

Later, the same diarist recorded:

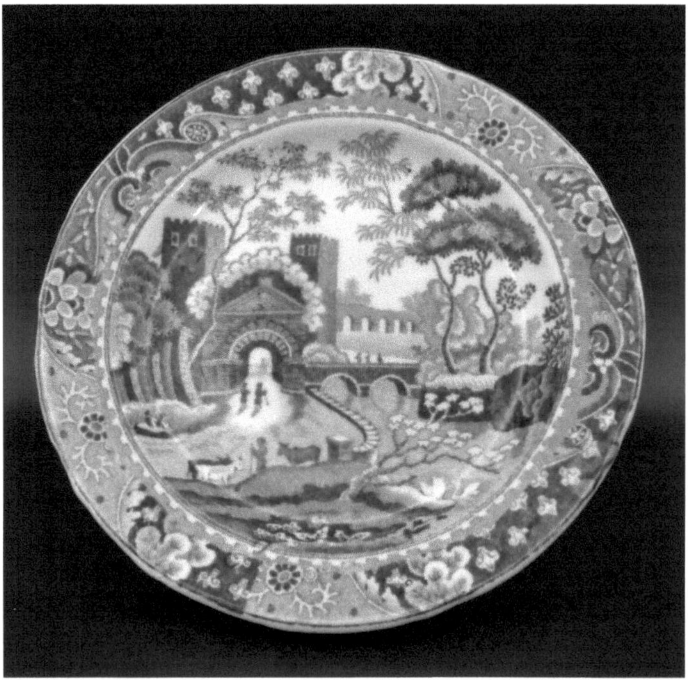

Figure 2.25 Plate, earthenware, blue printed design known as "Castle," manufactured by R. & J. Clews, Cobridge, Staffordshire, c.1825–35. The date derives from the importer's mark; see Figure 2.26.

Figure 2.26 Backstamps on plate (Figure 2.25), indicating manufacturer, Clews, Staffordshire, and J. Greenfield, importer, No. 77 Pearl Street, New York. Greenfield was at this address from c.1825–35.

> At the China Stores men, women and children were engaged raking among broken china & queens ware for small articles - In one such place I saw & purchased as a relic an ewer in good state.
>
> (Diary, John Fanny Watson, 1835: 22–3)

There were cases of goods being found and people scavenging for items that would be suitable for reselling. Another fire in 1840 along Pearl and Stone Street caused $30,000 worth of damage to the firm, John V. Greenfield & Co.'s crockery store (*New York Commercial Advertiser* January 29, 1840). John V. Greenfield was the son of John Greenfield.

Thus, the notion of middle-class buyers acquiring fashionable merchandise was not the complete picture of consumption. Indeed, Joanna Cohen's *Luxurious Citizens: The Politics of Consumption in Nineteenth-Century America* mentions how there existed second-hand stores in New York catering for those of lower incomes (2017: 171). Theft from stores was another means by which commodities could be acquired. In 1833, a spate of robberies from New York crockery stores occurred. Once article explained how:

> An extensive assortment of cut glass stolen in February last, has also been recovered, which he [Charles W. Webb] had packed up in boxes and stored in South Street, with a view to ship it to the South. The glass was stolen in February last from the Stores of Thomas Cook, No. 176 Broadway, James A. Dillinger No. 16 and William Odell No. 100 Bowery, which were entered by means of false keys, the most valuable property removed, and the doors left locked as they were found.
>
> (*Morning Courier and New-York Enquirer* August 23, 1833)

On the basis of the police investigation, it emerged that the perpetrator, Charles William Webb, was an Englishman who had arrived in the United States in 1830 and who was a glass cutter by trade (*Evening Post* August 23, 1833). In another instance, the crockery store of Sampson and James Tams on Market Street Philadelphia was burgled in 1839, and the thief stole $585 in Virginia bank notes, between $100,000 and $125,000 in bills, and "a quantity of valuable cut glass decanters" (*Philadelphia Inquirer* August 19, 1839). In 1842, two "colored men," Lewis Hewlett and George Dillen, were charged with breaking into the James M. Shaw's crockery store on 70, Chatham Street, New York, stealing two cut glass lamps, six dozen plain glass tumblers, and four decanters, worth $55 (*New York Journal of Commerce*, April 8, 1842). Money, or cut-glass items, rather than ceramics, was often the target for theft. In one case, an individual hid in the attic of John Y. Rushton's crockery store 245 Market Street, Philadelphia, opening the safe after closing time to steal money, cheques, and due bills (*Public Ledger* May 1, 1843). Ceramics were stolen when easily accessible. Ann Cunningham was arrested by a watchman for stealing eleven tea cups from a crate outside E. & J. Tams' store, on the corner of Fourth and Commerce Street, Philadelphia. Cunningham made no attempt to deny the charge (*North American*, Philadelphia August 18, 1849).

Not all shopping occurred in refined, convivial places, or in stores capable of employing "hundreds of clerks" (Cohen 2017: 155–7). For those involved in the crockery trade, the scale of businesses varied. Behind the facade of Henry Stevenson's advertisements for "newest shapes, patterns and styles," the reality could be rather different (Figure 2.27). An attempted robbery at Henry Stevenson's crockery store at 270, Pearl Street, on a Saturday in May 1845 reveals how his business was organized:

> A lad at present unknown, entered the crockery ware store of Mr. Henry Stevenson, and desired to purchase a dozen common pitchers. Mr. S. took the young gentleman up stairs, and showed him the pitchers, but these were two [sic] large, and those were two [sic] small, &c., and at last Mr. S. thought he couldn't suit the difficult young gentleman, and signified as much to him, whereupon they both came down stairs together. Just as they descended below the ceiling, Mr. S. discovered another young gentleman busily engaged at his desk with a chisel, endeavoring to pry it open …
>
> (*City Intelligence*, New York May 4, 1845)

The account of this robbery implies that Henry Stevenson was running his store unaided on that day, and in another press account, it was established that there was about $80 in the desk (*New York Herald* May 4, 1845). The young man who enquired to purchase the pitchers made a hasty retreat, while the other individual, armed with a chisel, was apprehended and taken to the police. His name was given as Joseph Williams, aged just ten years, and described as a copper plate printer.

The enquiry to purchase only a dozen pitchers did not avert any suspicion from Henry Stevenson, revealing how businesses were more than willing to cater for small orders. A surviving invoice belonging to Tyndale & Mitchell, crockery importers, Chestnut Street, Philadelphia, also confirms how this was often the case. In 1846, Tyndale & Mitchell sold one white granite ewer and basin, one

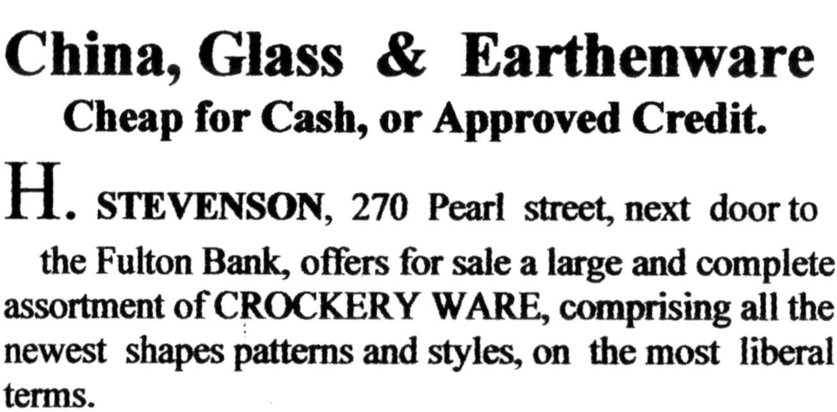
China, Glass & Earthenware

Cheap for Cash, or Approved Credit.

H. STEVENSON, 270 Pearl street, next door to the Fulton Bank, offers for sale a large and complete assortment of CROCKERY WARE, comprising all the newest shapes patterns and styles, on the most liberal terms.

Figure 2.27 *Evening Post* New York September 30, 1845.

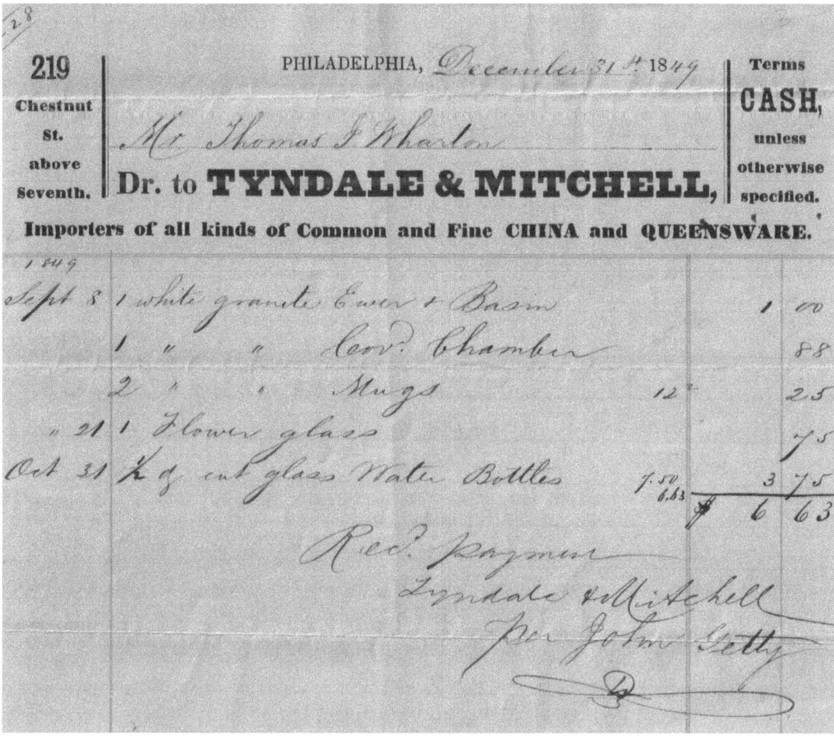

219 Chestnut St. above Seventh.

PHILADELPHIA, December 31st 1849

Terms CASH, unless otherwise specified.

Mr. Thomas I. Wharton

Dr. to TYNDALE & MITCHELL,

Importers of all kinds of Common and Fine CHINA and QUEENSWARE.

1849

Sept 8	1 white granite Ewer & Basin		1 00
	1 " " Cov'd Chamber		88
	2 " " Mugs	12½	25
" 21	1 Flower glass		75
Oct 31	½ d. cut glass Water Bottles	7.50	3 75
		6.63	$ 6 63

Rec'd Payment
Tyndale & Mitchell
per John Getty

Figure 2.28 Invoice of Tyndale & Mitchell, Philadelphia, addressed to Thomas I. Wharton, Philadelphia. Dated December 31, 1849.

chamber, and two mugs to a local attorney, Thomas I. Wharton, on nearby Walnut Street (Figure 2.28).

In another case of a theft from a crockery business, it becomes apparent just how ad hoc the arrangement was for storing imported stock. Kerr's China Hall was on Chestnut Street, Philadelphia, but their warehouse was located in the cellar of a nearby museum, enabling access to their merchandise by an employee. A "colored man named William Tillotson, who has recently been engaged to tend the furnace that heats the Philadelphia Museum," was arrested, and "A number of articles of crockery ware were found at his dwelling" (*The North American and Daily Advertiser* January 15, 1840).

Rituals: continuity or change?

T. H. Breen's argument that "... British imports provided white Americans with a common framework of experience" (1986: 496) is more complex when applied to ceramics of the nineteenth century. There has been speculation of how far North America followed the fashions of Europe, albeit at a different speed (Glennie

1995: 176), but there should be recognition of how America formed its own rituals, which in turn impacted on consumption. As an example, Miss Leslie's *The House Book, or a Manual of Domestic Economy*, first published in Philadelphia in 1840, notes how:

> Many of the saucers now made are but slightly concave, and turn outwards towards the edge which makes them useless to persons who do not like to take their tea out of the cup. As there are many who prefer drinking out of the saucer, it is well to buy them of a convenient shape, and also to have a set of little cup-plates or cup-mats.
>
> ([1840] 1844: 290)

Alternatively, Catharine Beecher's *Domestic Receipt Book: Designed as a Supplement to her Treatise on Domestic Economy*, published in New York in 1846, provided meticulous information concerning the "correct" way to set a dinner and tea table, reinforced by the inclusion of diagrams (Figure 2.29). These, and her accompanying discussion, suggest that "Small mats, or cup plates, should be placed at each plate, to receive the tea-cup, when it would otherwise be set upon the table-cloth and stain it" (1846: 243). She also indicates that "on the tea-table, by each plate is a knife, napkin, and small cup-plate" (1846: 246). The American habit of drinking tea from the saucer resulted in the need to rest the tea-cup on a mat or a cup plate.

A diagram provided by Beecher would imply that the ceramic or glass cup plate was a feature of refined American society. However, when an English writer, A. W. Coysh, published *Blue-Printed Earthenware, 1800-1850*, a whole section was devoted to "American Cup Plates," noting how:

> Cup plates are not listed in contemporary bills, accounts or inventories which list tea-wares. Indeed, they seem to be unknown in Britain and do not appear in the records of earthenware makers. Nor do contemporary prints show cup plates ... Can any *evidence* be provided to prove that these were items in tea services imported into America? Do they have counterparts in porcelain services? Or must one assume that earthenware cup plates are a myth?
>
> (1972: 110)

The cup plates illustrated in Coysh's publication—that is, small plates of between three or four inches in diameter—were interpreted as either being pattern-samples, or part of toy services. Coysh only located a reference to the cup plate in the American publication, N. Hudson Moore's *The Old China Book*, where there was an explanation of their function, as a place to rest a cup (1903: 45). While the phrase "cup plate" does not appear on Staffordshire invoices sent to American importers and dealers, these items were mentioned in household management books (as indicated above), and contrary to Coysh's view, the term was used on the invoices of American importers and dealers (Frontispiece). Some advertisements placed by crockery dealers in American newspapers also mention the availability

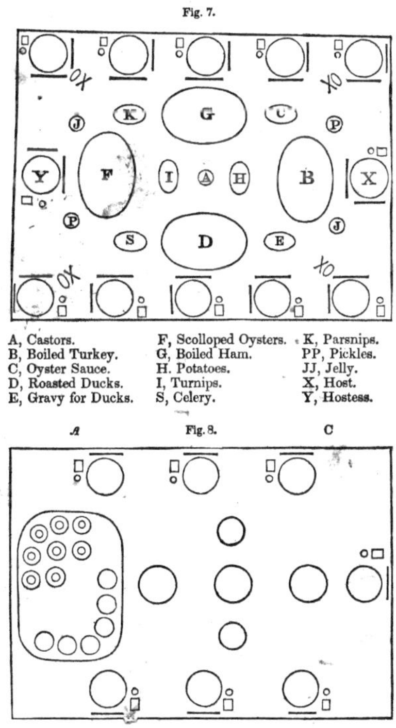

Figure 2.29 Diagram from Catharine Beecher's *Domestic Receipt Book: Designed as a Supplement to her Treatise on Domestic Economy*, "The proper mode of setting a dinner-table is shown at Fig. 7 and the proper way of setting a tea-table is shown at Fig. 8," New York, 1846, p.244.

of cup plates (*American and Commercial Daily Advertiser* Baltimore, May 9, 1832; *Springfield Republican*, Massachusetts, June 11, 1858). Plates that were produced from three to seven inches in size were simply called muffins by Staffordshire manufacturers on their invoices sent to the United States. Interestingly, a different vocabulary was used by English producers and American-based intermediaries. The cup plates serve to illustrate the ways in which English and American culture were moving apart. Cup plates were manufactured in both pottery and glass, and the case of a glass example, molded with the inscription "E.A & S.R. Filley, Importer of China, Glass & Queensware, Saint Louis," illustrates how they could be used as a marketing device (Figure 2.6).

It has been suggested in a chapter by Colin Campbell (an historical sociologist) in Brewer and Porter's *Consumption and the World of Goods* that the part of society that was the most heavily responsible for a "revolution in demand" was, in fact, the "middling classes." According to Campbell, the types of goods that showed a significant increase in consumption were pictures, china, mirrors, musical instruments and fashion, which he described as more "expressive goods" (1993: 54). Developing this idea further, Campbell's *The Romantic Ethic and the Spirit of Modern Consumerism* (taking its cue from Max Weber's *The Protestant Ethic and the Spirit of Capitalism* of 1904–05) debates whether:

> Perhaps there was a "Romantic ethic" working to promote the "spirit of consumerism" just as Weber had postulated that a "Puritan" ethic had promoted the spirit of capitalism? Certainly, it was a "romantic" cultural movement which was frequently identified as the "natural enemy" of Puritanism.
>
> (1987: 6)

This draws attention to another aspect of consumption relating to religious values. Max Weber's analysis of the rise of modern capitalism proposed that Protestants were against ostentatious consumption, veering instead toward simplicity ([1930] 2010: 115–6). Immediately, there arises the problem of attempting to reconcile McKendrick's view of a "consumer revolution" dominated by fashion with the values of Protestantism, apparently opposed to extravagant consumption. As Colin Campbell points out:

> … it was exactly the kind of conduct which, it could be assumed, would be the most likely to incur disapproval from those with a "Puritan" outlook which formed the very substance of this middle-class consumer revolution.
>
> (1987: 31)

The straightforward explanation proposed by historians is that attitudes shifted, making the consumption of fashionable goods more acceptable. A society eager to consume was emerging. Although Campbell's observations were focused on English behavior, from an American perspective, Joanna Cohen's *Luxurious Citizens: The Politics of Consumption in Nineteenth-Century America*, suggests how, fueled by distribution networks, urban expansion, and printing technology, a new kind of consumer emerged in the 1840s (2017: 149). The aversion to consume, as identified by T. H. Breen in the colonial period (1986: 478), and any notions of frugality advocated by Dr. Benjamin Franklin, were swept aside, or became outmoded (Cohen 2017: 18–9). A new political crusade emerged whereby American citizens were actively encouraged to participate in economic development through consumption (Cohen 2017: 151).

Based on the evidence available, Cohen's interpretation of shifting values is an appealing one. Yet it is still important to acknowledge how some people remained uneasy about extravagant forms of consumption. Terrence H. Witkowski draws attention to the phenomenon of "anti-consumption rhetoric" as being significant (2016: 47). Opposition to being fashionable or conforming to fashion still existed, and some American household guides espoused the values of the thrifty housewife. Catharine Beecher's *Domestic Receipt Book* of 1846 insisted that:

> where good taste exists, it leads a woman to wish to have her house, furniture, and style of living, in all its parts, exactly conformed to *her means,* and *her situation.* If she is not rich, she will not wish to have a house, or furniture, or dress like those who are rich, and will find pleasure in ... plain furniture, simple dress, and an economical table, so neat, and orderly, and comfortable, and tasteful, as to ensure comfort and satisfaction to all around her.
>
> (1846: 274)

Beecher added:

> She will not be so anxious to obtain admission into any circle as to seek it by a conformity to its fashions, which will involve her labor, or expenses that lessen her domestic comfort, or are inappropriate to her income.
>
> (1846: 275)

Beecher's views were a mixture of maintaining manners, respectability, and utility, somewhat coinciding with Max Weber's observation of how Protestantism opposed lavish consumption ([1930] 2010: 115–6). Catharine, a daughter of Reverend Dr. Lyman Beecher of the Presbyterian faith, came from a tradition of asceticism. In a sermon delivered by Lyman at Lichfield, Connecticut, in December 1819, he advocated, "setting our own houses in order, of checking, by our example, the innovation of expensive and gaudy fashions, of maintaining simplicity of living, and resisting that extensive luxury, which is creeping in under the cover of festivity, and the hospitalities of friendship, and of rearing up our families in habits of useful industry" (Carey et al. 1820: 285).

Prior to her *Domestic Receipt Book* of 1846, Catharine Beecher also published *A Treatise on Domestic Economy for the use of Young Ladies at Home and at School*, first published in 1841, and which was subsequently revised. Here, she also expressed her own apprehensions about the degree to which American society was "moving and changing" ([1841] 1843: 40). While this new society offered a range of possibilities for the American woman, she maintained that "Her responsibility, in reference to the institutions of benevolence and religion, is deeply realized" ([1841] 1843: 44). When it came to providing advice to "Young Ladies" about different commodities, she points out how "French China is deemed the nicest," but this was counterbalanced with the point of view that "it is liable to the objection of having plates, so made, that salt, butter and similar articles, will not lodge on the edge, but slip into the centre" ([1841] 1843: 307). Practical considerations were still at the heart of what influenced her assessment of the ceramics, rather than being judged by newest and fashion. The debate then becomes whether the views so powerfully expressed by members of the Beecher family were becoming increasingly marginalised in a wider context of this "moving and changing" society. Lyman Beecher's reference to the "fickle flood of fashion" was just becoming too much of an irreversible tide (Carey et al. 1820: 285).

Ethnicity and demand

Instead of those who were able and willing to clamber for the latest goods, was it possible that some "Americans" still continued to consume in different ways, responding to their own views, or expectations, or individual cultural, religious, and ethnic backgrounds? Cohen herself points out how American consumers have often only been portrayed as white middle-class, and if there were references to African Americans participating in a culture of consumption and fashion, they were simply lampooned in satirical prints for imitating white behavior (2017: 164–7). Bridget T. Heneghan's *Whitewashing America: Material culture and race in the antebellum Imagination* also explores the issue of ethnicity and consumption. As a result of slavery and a "flow of blackness" into the United States, she suggests that white material goods also became linked to race (2003: 4). Perceived in this way, the consumption of white commodities (which included ceramics), was used to express identity and reinforced boundaries between the different races (2003: 5). Heneghan argues that "Porcelain-quality ceramics appeared in specialized sets that required elaborated training for their proper use," whereas goods issued to slaves were "for contrast—dark color, coarse finish, chipped or broken or dilapidated condition, and unspecialised design" (2003: 5).

White, translucent porcelain bodies were expensive and, therefore, more likely to be found in the homes of the wealthier classes, but how far you can equate the use of commodities to different races is problematic. In reality, the ubiquity of Staffordshire ceramics is confirmed by an English traveler who, when visiting the "humble habitations" of the Seneca Indians near Buffalo in the 1830s, rather unexpectedly found among their furniture a "… display of Birmingham tea-trays, and blue and white Staffordshire crockery". As far as this traveler was concerned, this was "such an opposite picture of rural life" (Boardman 1833: 160–1). English earthenware was no longer the preserve of white settlers, and thus this account infers that ceramics were used by different ethnicities.

Importantly, Bridget Heneghan draws attention to a theory that cultural identities made a difference to ceramic usage. A demand for white ironstone ceramics (a form of undecorated earthenware, also known as white granite) emerged in the 1840s and became a major part of ceramic consumption in the United States. The popularity of undecorated ironstones could be because it was seen a cheaper alternative to French white china, and on a practical level, it was easier to match these ironstone wares regularly promoted as being suitable for use in hotels and on steamships (Ewins 1997: 47). Ascertaining why people purchased certain ceramics at given times is extremely hard. Unfortunately, contemporaries did not seem to record the actual motivation for selecting colors and styles, and so it has normally become the role of the historian to reconstruct the motivation, often, it seems, linked to aspiring to the latest fashion. One rare contemporary example that explored ceramic consumption in terms of culture and identity was written by an anonymous, presumably American writer, in an article titled, "About Breakfast Tables: The morning meal Here and Abroad: American and English Breakfast Tables—a British service Described—coffee-pots, egg-cups, and muffin-plates—breakfast parties," published in *The New York Times* in 1882. Even though the language used below was prone to hyperbole for editorial effect, the article usefully compares ceramics in England to those found in United States and provides an explanation for these differences:

> The average English mind has no independence. It is sufficient that a cup or plate, a jug or glass, has obtained the patronage of royalty or of some supposed authority upon the subject … when the upper classes happen to be cultured in

> art and capable of recognizing correct form and design, the taste spreads, not because the masses are educated up to the appreciation of the fact, but because it is a genuine article of faith with them that what is "the thing" in the rank above them is the thing to be imitated. This we know is true of more important things than china in the same way.
>
> (July 30, 1882)

Interestingly, emulative behavior within a hierarchical society was considered influential when describing English habits of consumption, which was not necessarily the case when describing America, so that:

> The average American is rarely swayed in his choice of cups and saucers by the fact that one enjoys the approval of the President and another does not, and as the average American is not highly cultivated in art principles, in spite of tremendous efforts upon the part of lectures and decorative agent, he is apt to buy the cup, saucer, or milk-jug which will stand the most wear and tear, or which commands itself to his individual taste. The result is a prevalence of white china for ordinary use unequaled except in France and Germany.
>
> (*The New York Times* July 30, 1882)

The proclivity for using white-wares in the United States, compared to Britain, was further reiterated by this writer when reporting:

> … we might pass reflection upon the extraordinary persistence with which white dishes appear upon the scenes at boarding-houses and smaller hotels. How ugly they are! The blue and white delf [sic] ware of England, be it only in the humble "Humphrey clock" or willow pattern is a thousand times better.
>
> (*The New York Times* July 30, 1882)

The reference to "Humphrey clock" patterns was alluding to how manufacturers produced printed wares inspired by a series of short stories written by Charles Dickens, which appeared in the periodical, *Master Humphrey's Clock*, published in the 1840s. A typical example of an undecorated white body produced for the American market, known to contemporaries as white granite [WG] ware, is shown is Figure 2.6.

Clear differences were perceived between American and British ceramic consumption, but importantly, the explanation for such distinctions was related to cultural factors—not entirely practical considerations or following the current fashion. The choice of ceramics was not a signifier of race distinctions, as outlined by Bridget Heneghan, but as this writer claimed, was due to the influence of migration:

> Who in the length and breadth of the British Isles would have a white dinner service? Occasionally, but very occasionally, white breakfast ware is seen, but more usually it has a gilded rim, or that solitary flower upon the centre which

> is inseparable from our recollection of the breakfast set in lodging-houses in London, Brighton, or any other popular resort. Its great merit, which commends the unblushing white ware to the American housekeeper lies in the fact that is so easily matched! We would say it is - in material, but perfectly unmatchable in hideous ugliness. There is some compensation in France and Germany for the ungainly thick white cups in the flavor and aroma of the coffee they contain ... but certainly if the prevalence of a thinner variety of the same is due to the tide of German immigration, that is a weighty reason for discountenancing it. The German propagator of the white ware of his native land is as injurious to the interests of trade as the Chinaman's delight in the wash-tub.
>
> (*The New York Times* July 30, 1882)

This highlights a contemporary awareness of how cultural factors shaped demand in a sense of German migration impacting on what ceramics were used in the United States, although the article was still based on the perspective of a spectator rather than a consumer recalling actual consumption behavior. Nevertheless, it is the case that the largest proportion of migrants to the United States came from Germany in the nineteenth century, and they were mostly Lutherans rather than Catholics (Dinnerstein and Riemers 1999: 6, 32). Interestingly, when the German writer Max Weber considered the impact of the values of Calvinism, Methodism, and the Baptists on consumption, he believed that this also resulted in a preference for "a sober simplicity," creating "the clean and solid comfort of the middle-class home as an ideal" ([1930] 2010: 114). If a variety of cultural influences existed, does this also begin to question how far American society was, on mass, simply clambering for one homogeneous fashion in ceramics? Was there an array of trends within the whole?

Summary

As outlined in Chapter 1, the extensive amount of literature focused on American-themed ceramics might imply that these wares represented a significant proportion of production. However, surveying advertisements and auction notices shows how their promotion was not widespread. Even some of the Staffordshire manufacturers who were mentioned in auction notices are obscure now. If American-themed ceramics were designed to appeal to patriotism, it might be anticipated that they would have been more widely advertised by those wishing to capitalize on their promotion and sale; however, this does rely on an assumption that the role of advertising was to draw attention to fashionable merchandise rather than stimulate the purchase of items proving harder to sell.

While more modern historians have begun to recognize how manufacturers responded to demand (rather than innovating different products which would appeal to the market), this interpretation has often been linked to the significance of fashion. For instance, when discussing the rising significance of the export markets, Maxine Berg's *Luxury and Pleasure in Eighteenth-Century Britain* points out how "products were defined and revised in response to the fastidious demands of American merchants and customers" (2005: 324). As mentioned above, Chauncey I. Filley, a crockery importer of St. Louis, designed his own ceramics, which were manufactured in Europe, and this would reinforce Berg's view of merchants taking control of their own demands. However, Berg also concedes that more research needs to undertaking, since there also existed "consumer protests in Britain and American against systems of slavery" (2005: 330). Commodities that incorporated anti-slavery imagery raises the issue of how production and consumption could be more symbolic, religious, moralistic, and political. Thus, the significance of American-themed wares (some of which addressed the issue of slavery) lies not in their proportion of manufacture but in how they reveal, in an inverse way, the existence of further complexities existing between the activities of the producer and the role of demand.

If consumption was entirely driven by fashion, how can there be such a thing as rarity? An assumption would be that consumer demand would be widespread for what was considered fashionable. Existing interpretations of supply and demand might suggest that if a design was initiated by a ceramic manufacturer and it failed to appeal to the market, this would have been quickly discontinued. The straightforward consequences of economics would prevail, and this might account for rarity. However, if production was driven by demands of the market (which have become the more modern way to consider supply), it would seem peculiar to produce a design, when there was already an inkling that demand was limited.

How might it be possible to reconcile the observations made by some of the earliest collectors and writers, which identified how certain designs were rare, with more modern theories that have given prominence on the role of demand in predetermining supply? It is not entirely clear how these observations, or interpretations, can co-exist. The impact of changing collecting habits might account for this paradox. Rarity is merely an illusion, or a construct. Ceramic objects that were readily discarded by contemporaries were subsequently rediscovered by the next generation of collectors and reassigned as culturally significant. But as an alternative conceptual model, is it possible that some ceramic designs were, from their initiation, a reflection of more marginal production? The explanation for why some designs were rarer than others is that they were not greatly produced, or widely consumed, in the first place. Instead of McKendrick's notion that "fashion was essential" (1982: 98), or that price factors accounted for changes in consumption (Miller and Earls 2008), the American market was far more multilayered. Rather than one abiding fashion, or how demand was influenced by variations in price, there were still aspects of American consumption shaped by different cultural sensibilities and divergent views.

Recognition of the sociopolitical, the second-hand, the scavenged, the bartered—begins to reveal how behavior was complex. Interestingly, there were still concerns about too much consumption within a society where there was allegedly more choice than ever before. Some American household management publications, such as those by Catharine Beecher, were influenced by what was perceived as following Christian piety. Printed ceramics referring to Dr. Benjamin

Franklin's maxims of hard work, self-help, and frugality, were available for children during the nineteenth century (Figure 6.1). The production and the buying of ceramics that promoted frugality was in itself paradoxical, although it could be argued that these vessels had a function of imbuing children with values far removed from fashion and excess.

Moving away from T. H. Breen's view that the colonial period was strongly Anglicized, during the nineteenth century, American society developed divergent rituals and different attitudes (1986: 496–9), such as a propensity to drink tea from a saucer well into the nineteenth century. The use of the cup plate to rest the tea cup was subsequently perceived as something quite alien by subsequent British ceramic historians. There was also an important contemporary observation that the demand for ceramic white-wares was related to the influence of German migration. Viewed in this way, ceramics ostensibly manufactured in Staffordshire were apparently being produced to respond to different needs and adapt to other changing cultural forces within American society.

An appreciation of the heterogeneity of the American market invites the question that if consumer consumption was subject to the impact of diverse identities and cultures, should the same principle be applied to the intermediaries? In the manner of consumers, they also had their own agendas, beliefs, and cultural backgrounds, which in turn influenced business behavior and what was commissioned and marketed. In fact, the wording of some advertisements implies that the importer and dealer had a significant impact on creating the particular design. These examples need to be analyzed in more detail, as do the individuals who placed these advertisements. To define crockery importers and dealers in the United States as only purveyors of fashionable goods in attempts to always maximize profits is a simplification of what actually occurred. At this point, the backgrounds, culture, and identities of importers and dealers must be explored in more depth.

Chapter 3

BACKGROUNDS AND KINSHIP

Writing in 1967, Elizabeth Collard's *Nineteenth-Century Pottery and Porcelain in Canada* suggested that "Crockery-selling in Canada was anybody's business" ([1967] 1984: 63). In much the same way in which Staffordshire manufacturers produced American-themed wares for the United States, transfer-printed ceramics depicting views of Canada were also produced (Collard 1983). The Canadian and American markets were not entirely dissimilar. Even though Collard mentions the example of Joseph Wedgwood, a cousin of Josiah Wedgwood of Etruria, who became a crockery dealer in Montreal, her overriding thesis insisted that, "The men who dealt in this china and earthenware for gain were as varied as their stock" (Collard [1967] 1984: 63). Contrary to Collard's view, this chapter sets out to show how involvement and the development of the crockery trade was influenced by backgrounds and kinship. As this chapter introduces a large number of names and families, it is well to use the Pedigrees (at the end of the book), in conjunction with the following text. Pedigrees are signposted when appliable and will assist in steering the reader through this material. In a further attempt to make the range of examples accessible, the structure is thematic and loosely chronological. The inclusion of such a large number of individuals is required to highlight the extent of interconnections and show how individuals were capable of moving back and forth between England and the United States.

Organization and business structure

Norman Buck's *The Development of the Organisation of Anglo-American Trade 1800-1850,* purposed that the Anglo-American trade initially relied on British merchants who "assumed the risk of commerce" ([1925] 1969: 99). This observation parallels certain creamware jugs decorated with American themes. For instance, the Winterthur collection houses a creamware jug attributed to the Herculaneum factory, printed with a memorial to George Washington and an image of a ship, accompanied by the name of shipper, Cropper, Benson & Co., of Liverpool. This seems to infer that production of this piece was based on an actual commission (Teitelman et al. 2010: 174–7). There has been recognition of the ways in which the Anglo-American trade was conducted, but with a tendency to describe those involved as either British or American. For instance, Norman Buck points out that before 1815, "the American importer, either himself purchasing in England or sending his orders to manufacturers or merchants was by no means an unimportant figure" (Buck [1925] 1969: 135). The purpose of this chapter is to examine the backgrounds of those involved in the Anglo-American ceramic trade and to highlight how the issue of culture and identity becomes relevant to a fuller understanding of ceramic design.

In the early eighteenth century, North American importers dealt in a variety of goods. Thus, Amos Wood advertised his Boston warehouse as stocking Cheshire cheese, ceramics, cutlery, and guns, in the 1730s (*New-England Weekly Journal* May 14, 1733). By the second half of the eighteenth century, merchants, importers, and dealers became more specialized. In 1763, James Gilliland marketed only ceramics and glass in New York (Schwind 1984: 21). James Christie ran a "china and glass shop" on New York's Maiden Lane, in the 1780s (Hodge et al. 1789). In the 1770s, Ebenezer Bridgham ran what was only termed a "Staffordshire & Liverpool Ware-house in King-Street" in Boston, in 1773. However, his stock was still supplemented by Cheshire cheese, Liverpool ale, and London porter (*Boston news-letter* April 29, 1773).

The ways in which merchants, importers, and dealers described themselves in east-coast city directories is also evidence of a growing tendency to focus on a limited range of merchandise. For instance, Norman's *The Boston Directory* of 1789 lists William Sumner and Benjamin Morgan Stillman as selling only "crockery-ware," while Ebenezer Frothingham ran a "china, glass and Staffordshire-ware" store. William Saxton was still described as a "grocer and Crockery-ware" dealer in 1789, but by 1796, a firm called Saxton & Wainwright was described as dealers in "crockery ware and dry goods" (West 1796: 90). Gradually, the number of specialist dealers increased. John West's *The Boston Directory* of 1796 lists dealers such as John Bennoch, "crockery ware;" Mary Butler, "crockery and toy shop;" Ebenezer Frothingham, "glass and earthen ware;" Harrison & Hall, "crockery ware," and Benjamin Sumner, junior, "crockery ware;" as well as Saxton & Wainwright, "crockery ware . . .". Saxton and Wainwright of Boston advertised the importation of a variety of goods, including earthenware, in 1789 (*Massachusetts Centinel* Boston July 1, 1789). Peter Wainwright was listed as a merchant in Boston in 1789 (Norman: 44), but an advertisement shows how he was intending to visit England (Figure 3.1).

Peter Wainwright remained in Liverpool during the 1790s (Barfoot and Wilkes 1791; Gore 1796). The Liverpool business was described as Wainwright, Howard & Co., or Wainwright, Cross and Howard. The firm frequently advertised freight and passage on ships bound for the United States (see Pedigree 1).

The term "China merchant" was used to describe several individuals listed in the census of Philadelphia of 1790, including John Morrell and Joseph Stansbury. This again infers a tendency to specialize along the eastern board. Stansbury first advertised "his shop" as dedicated to selling "a Variety of China, Glass, and Earthen wares" as early as 1769 (*Pennsylvania Gazette*, December 28, 1769), while John Morrell advertised as a wholesaler and retailer selling "blue printed,

Figure 3.1 *Massachusetts Centinel*, Boston March 13, 1790.

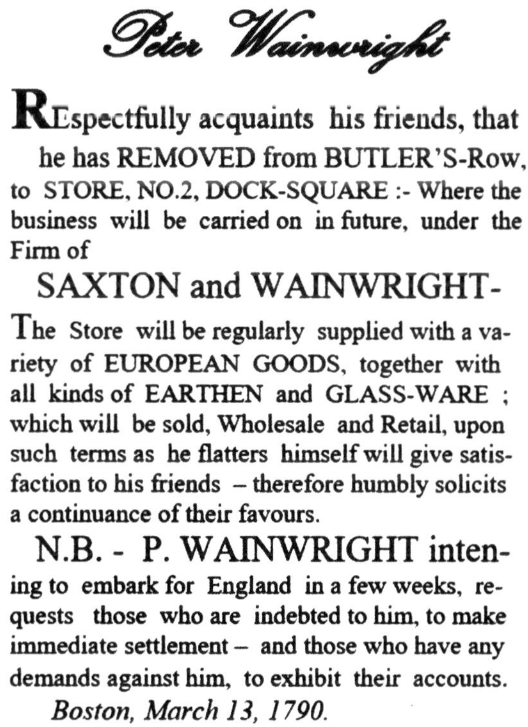

Peter Wainwright

REspectfully acquaints his friends, that he has REMOVED from BUTLER'S-Row, to STORE, NO.2, DOCK-SQUARE :- Where the business will be carried on in future, under the Firm of

SAXTON and WAINWRIGHT-

The Store will be regularly supplied with a variety of EUROPEAN GOODS, together with all kinds of EARTHEN and GLASS-WARE ; which will be sold, Wholesale and Retail, upon such terms as he flatters himself will give satisfaction to his friends – therefore humbly solicits a continuance of their favours.

N.B. - P. WAINWRIGHT intending to embark for England in a few weeks, requests those who are indebted to him, to make immediate settlement – and those who have any demands against him, to exhibit their accounts.

Boston, March 13, 1790.

enameled [sic] and plain QUEEN'S WARE" from the 1780s (*Independent Gazetteer,* Philadelphia April 17, 1784). When John Morrell, "late of this city" died in 1812, he left a substantial amount of mercantile property, including a three-storey brick warehouse on Front Street "lately occupied by John Morrell & Son" and a residential home in the village of Morrisville. The Morrells seem to be a well-established Philadelphian family, and many of them were active in the crockery trade for a lengthy period (McCarty and Davis 1821).

According to the Philadelphian census of 1810, involvement in dealing in ceramics was described in a variety of ways. Thus, Ben Cresson, John H., and Joseph Cresson were proprietors of "China stores," while William Baylis owned a "China & Glass Store." Joseph Cresson (evidently the same individual recorded twice) and a William Shufflebottom were both described as "China merchants." William Lindsay was listed as a dealer in "China, Glass & Queensware," and both R. jun. & J. Eddowes, and John Morrell jun. were described as "China, Glass &c." The Eddowes family are discussed in more detail in the following chapter because of the significance of their background and the ceramics they marketed.

Intrigue

With greater familiarity of those actually involved in the crockery trade becomes the possibility of considering the scope of business links and the issue of identity. In one instance, an attempted murder provides insight into Anglo-American connections. Simeon Shaw, the first, major historian of the Staffordshire Potteries, recalls how Theophilus Smith of the Smithfield Pottery, near Tunstall, attempted to murder his "kind friend, Mr. Wainwright, (who still survives, in the United States,) and subsequently in goal perished by his own hand" (1829: 20). Henry Wedgwood's *Romance of Staffordshire: A Collection of Historical, Biographic & Descriptive Sketches* ... published in 1877, re-examined the event in greater detail. In this account, it is alleged that the reason for Smith's assault on Peter Wainwright was that he had formed a romantic attachment with his wife, being a frequent visitor to Smithfield Hall, which "overlooked the valley of Chell," just outside Tunstall. Wedgwood finishes his account by explaining that:

> Mr. Wainwright stayed in Tunstall no longer than he was able to remove. Soon after he emigrated to America, where I believe he ended his days.
>
> (1877: 9)

At the time of the actual assault, the press reported how Theophilus Smith, earthenware manufacturer of Tunstall, traveled to Liverpool, June 1800, to meet Peter Wainwright, who was described as one of his principal creditors and "a respectable merchant of Liverpool" (*Staffordshire Advertiser* July 12, 1800). Wainwright agreed to travel back to Tunstall in order to attend a meeting with Smith's other creditors. At Golden Hill, near Tunstall, Theophilus Smith shot and then stabbed Peter Wainwright. After the attack, Wainwright was taken to the house of W. Adams of Tunstall. This would appear to be a reference to William Adams, a ceramic manufacturer (*Staffordshire Advertiser* July 12, 1800).

As Theophilus Smith absconded after the attempted murder, a notice was placed by Wainwright, Cross and Howard (who were all involved in the firm) in a Liverpool newspaper, offering a reward for his apprehension. The notice included a description of Smith, who was considered to be forty years old (*Gore's Liverpool General Advertiser* July 3, 1800). Smith was later captured and confined to Stafford goal. When his wife visited him, he attempted to murder her, only to shoot "himself thro' the head" (*Staffordshire Advertiser* January 3, 1801). Not surprisingly, national—even American—newspapers took a macabre interest in the story, and it was later reported how Mrs. Smith had survived (*Bath Chronicle and Weekly Gazette* February 26, 1801).

The central purpose of this book is to convey the value in exploring the backgrounds and the perspectives of merchants, importers, and dealers connected to the crockery trade. A range of Wainwright family papers survive, and these begin to cast doubt on Henry Wedgwood's 1870s account of Theophilus Smith. For instance, a letter sent to Mrs. Wainwright from Mary Adams of Tunstall, dated September 9, 1800 (over two months after Peter Wainwright's assault), enquired whether:

> you and Mr. Wainwright got home [to Liverpool]. We were extremely sorry when the Thunder came on, that you did not stay at Congleton …

Congleton, in Cheshire, is just a few miles north of Tunstall. The letter continues:

> My Father, and Mother, desire their best respect and if it is not too much trouble, will be happy to hear how you got home, and if Mr. Wainwright continues to gain strength … My brothers and sister send their remembrance. Smith's sale finished on Saturday, the things sold very well. Mrs. Smith is still at Chell.
>
> (Wainwright papers: Box 4, Folder 4.1, September 1, 1800)

In other words, Peter and Elizabeth Wainwright still had contact with the Adams family of Tunstall (presumably the ceramic manufacturers) in the period after the assault. The reference in the letter to a sale also coincides with the auction for Theophilus Smith's household goods being advertised in the summer of 1800 (*Staffordshire Advertiser*, August 16, 1800). In another letter, from Mary Adams of Tunstall to Mrs. Wainwright in Liverpool, it was requested:

> The present is to remind you of an old promise |viz| visiting Tunstall. Mr. Wainwright mentioned his intention of going soon to America and we are in hopes you will spend some time of his absence with us. The country is now very pleasant. Can you return with my Brothers?

She even adds that, "I cannot help indulging a secret wish that Mr. Wainwright may not go, in which case we shall expect to see him too" (Wainwright Papers: Box 4, Folder 4.7, July 18, no year).

The press described Theophilus Smith as a principal creditor of Peter Wainwright, and this parallels the primary evidence provided by members of the firm. John C. Howard, a half-brother of Elizabeth Mayhew Wainwright (the wife of Peter Wainwright) lived in either in Liverpool or Boston and was involved in the firm (see Pedigree 1). From Boston, John C. Howard wrote to Eliza Wainwright in Liverpool:

> I was made happy by your letter by the John Adams [the ship name] althou its contents was not of the most consolatory nature. It would not I confess be very pleasant to me at this moment that Mr. W. should relinquish the business in Liverpool. It has not certainly hitherto been productive of any thing but losses but I feel confident that for the future if we do not gain much we should not be exposed to the hazard of losing as by doing most of the business myself we shall not be under obligations to make advances where we do not ask commission. I think however it will be more agreeable to all parties concerned to dissolve at the expiration of our time of co-partners life. It is certain that I do not at present feel the confidence which I deem essentially requisite to the proper conduct of such a business as ours.
>
> (Wainwright, Box 4, Folder 4.2, April 8, 1801)

PETER WAINWRIGHT
At the New-Store, SCHOOL-STREET, *(next to Messrs.* TRAVERS, *Cornhill,)*

H as just opened an extensive and complete assortment of CROCKERY & GLASS,

with other articles, which he offers for Sales, upon such terms as he flatters himself will give satisfaction to those who may favour him with their custom – amongst which there are some neat and excellent low prices blue and brown line Table Services ; gilt and plan Tea Setts, Flower Pots, Jugs, Gravy Dishes, (the stands of which answer for milk pans,) selected by him at the manufactories previous to his leaving *England.* – in addition, he has on board the Hope, Capt. RIPLEY, (arrived on Saturday last.)

50 crates and casks, which, added to his former stock, makes upwards of three hundred Crates – *Also,* different kinds of chewing and smoaking Tobacco, Scotch & Rappee Snuff, supplied as above, or at his Manufactory (late SAXTON & WAINWRIGHTS, Mill-Bridge.

***N.B.* A liberal allowance made to those who buy largely.**

Figure 3.2 *Independent Chronicle*, Boston, January 5, 1804.

When writing to his sister, John C. Howard also complained how some people in America were slow to pay their debts (Wainwright, Box 4, Folder 4.2, April 27, 1801). Evidently, trading conditions were turbulent on both sides of the Atlantic, and in all likelihood, this contributed to Smith's deranged behavior.

Peter Wainwright remained in Liverpool and only left England toward the end of 1803. An advertisement placed in a Boston newspaper mentions that he had selected ceramics from English manufacturers and had established a new crockery and glass store after he arrived back in Boston (Figure 3.2).

Even if family relationships could become strained (as evidenced by the comments of John C. Howard), kinship helped to alleviate some of the financial problems associated with a transatlantic trade. Peter's brother, Henry Wainwright, was initially connected to Saxton & Wainwright of Boston. This partnership ended in 1804, but Henry remained connected to the crockery trade, forming a new partnership with Thomas Jackson (*Democrat*, Boston February 1, 1804). Although members of these partnerships changed, Wainwright & Jackson borrowed $500 from Peter Wainwright junior, who had become involved in the Union Bank of Boston (Wainwright Papers, Box 5, Folder 5.5, December 18, 1816).

While American city trade directories suggest a gradual tendency to focus on selling certain commodities, Peter Wainwright represents an exception to the rule. In 1801, Saxton & Wainwright advertised imported textiles, 114 crates of earthenware, and tobacco manufactured at Mill Bridge, Boston (*The Constitutional Telegraphe*, May 23, 1801). Peter Wainwright even advertised "100 crates earthen ware," including enameled tea ware and blue printed table ware, from his "Tobacco Manufactory" near Mill Bridge, Boston (*Boston Commercial Gazette* March 24, 1806).

A letter book belonging to Benjamin Eaton (who was employed by Wainwright) provides more information about this side of the business. Evidently, tobacco was purchased from the southern states, processed at the Mill Bridge works for smoking or chewing, and then sold or exported to Liverpool. Cigars were also manufactured and sent to Liverpool (Letter Book, Eaton, June 3, 1807). Apparently, ceramics continued to be shipped from Liverpool to Boston. A letter sent by Benjamin Eaton (addressed to Peter Wainwright in Liverpool) mentions:

> I also send you a box of papers† the amount of which you will see pr. the annexed bill. († See Crockery order book page 141).
>
> (Letter Book, Eaton, December 4, 1805)

When business was brisk, Benjamin Eaton mentioned how receiving payment from customers had enabled him to "pay your brother all the cash that I had borrowed of him" and then purchase more tobacco (Letter Book, Eaton, December 18, 1805). Kinship helped these different businesses to run and survive. A long winter had adversely affected business, causing Benjamin Eaton to write to Peter Wainwright in Liverpool:

> Sir, Herewith you will receive an account of the stock and statement of the same, as taken on 23rd of March which will give you some idea how the business stands at your tobacco manufactory. I am sorry to say that it has been dull with us for several months past which has obliged me to borrow so much money of your brother besides being so much indebt[sic] to the crockery department, however I suppose that is principally owing to a disagreeable broken up winter and very backward spring, which has discouraged the country people from coming to town.
>
> The roads are now drying up and I am in hopes that I shall have some money from the country people time enough to take up the two notes when they become due, and pay your brother, besides.
>
> (Letter Book, Eaton, April 18, 1807)

In the same era (of the quoted letter, above), Henry Wainwright advertised "crockery, glass and Japanned ware" available from his Dock Square store in Boston (*Boston Gazette* February 19, 1807). Jonathan Mayhew Wainwright, a nephew of Henry, and who in 1815 officiated at a church at Newton, near Boston, asked his brother who was on business in Louisville, Kentucky:

> What do you think of Debby Hammond's becoming married to Mr. Hastings. I do not know whether you are acquainted with him [sic] he is a crockery ware

> merchant & keeps in Dock square. It was thought a pretty strange thing as he is about forty & has grandchildren …
>
> (Wainwright papers, Box 1, Folder 1.5, April 24, 1815)

See Pedigree 6 for the Hastings family. Nevertheless, the Wainwright family had connections to different businesses, and this proved to be useful during difficult trading periods. As a consequence of European hostilities created by the Napoleonic war, an American trade embargo was temporarily introduced in 1807, restricting exports to, as well as imports from England (Ewins 1997: 86). When Jonathan Mayhew Wainwright wrote to his father, he adopted a consolatory tone, repeated a humorous, reassuring comment as:

> I heard a gentleman say the embargo would be a good thing for tobacconists, for those that use the leaf would expend double the quantity of what they did when they had nothing to trouble their minds.
>
> (Wainwright Papers, Box, folder 1.5, August 18, 1808)

Peter and Henry Wainwright were christened at Farnworth (near Liverpool), in 1759 and 1768, respectively, and both married into Bostonian families. Peter Wainwright married Elizabeth, daughter of the eminent Rev. Dr. Jonathan Mayhew of Boston in 1790, and Henry Wainwright married Lucretia Green in 1795 (*Massachusetts Mercury,* December 11, 1795). Henry died in Boston, in 1827 (*Universalist Magazine,* Boston, September 8, 1827), whereas family letters show how Peter and Elizabeth Wainwright moved between the United States and England. Their sons (the Rev. Jonathan Mayhew Wainwright, Bishop of New York, and Peter Wainwright jr. of Boston) were both born in Liverpool, but as young men in America, they inevitably became caught up in the political consequences of the Anglo-American War of 1812–14 (see Chapter 4).

Mrs. Elizabeth Wainwright died at Liverpool in 1829 aged 70 and was described as the "wife of Peter Wainwright esq. of Roxbury [Boston]" (*Christian Register* September 5, 1829). After the death of Elizabeth, Peter Wainwright spent a considerable amount of time in Liverpool, or Farnworth (where he still had a sister), or visiting the family of another sister who resided in Manchester. On one occasion, in a letter to his children in Boston, he refers to meeting his oldest acquaintance, a neighbor whom he had met while serving an apprenticeship in Liverpool, and who had become prosperous in business (Wainwright Papers, Box 3, Folder, 3.17, February 18, 1830). An apprenticeship in Liverpool perhaps accounts for Peter Wainwright's involvement in mercantile trade. While he was not from Staffordshire, he still used his mercantile contacts to benefit his wider family. The sister, who still lived in Farnworth, had a stepson. Writing to his son, Peter Wainwright jr., in Boston, he states:

> Last Wednesday I attended the Funeral of her step-son from his House. He was the son of her late Husband and the only Relative except very distant - twenty five years ago [c.1805] I procured for him a situation with one of the most respectable manufacturers in Staffordshire to learn the business, but

> unfortunately for himself and his Father he turned out an idle fellow and has hastened[?] his end[?] by folly and ardent spirits …
>
> (Wainwright Papers, Box 3, Folder 3.17, April 19, 1830)

Wainwright explains how his sister's stepson had been left with sufficient property by his father to live as a gentleman, and the family had "got him away from Staffordshire where he was wasting it," but he died in Manchester (Wainwright Papers, Box 3, Folder 3.17, April 19, 1830).

Surviving letters are revealing of Peter Wainwright's diverse range of connections. In a letter addressed to Peter Wainwright jr. of the Savings Bank, Boston, for the attention of his daughter, Eliza, wrote from Liverpool:

> The next mond [Monday?] I left for Manchester with an intention to have passd [passed] a few days in the Pottery but the day was very Rainy and disagreeable I Rode in the out sides[?] to the Pottery and had an opportunity of going inside I proceeded about[?] to Manchester where I arr'd about ten o clock. My sister B. had just gone un stairs came down again immediately on hearing me and gave me a cup of tea …
>
> (Wainwright Papers, Box 3, Folder 3.17, December 20, 1830)

The letter seems to imply that there was a connection to a pottery, located somewhere between Liverpool and Manchester.

In Henry Wedgwood's account of "Theophilus Smith, of Tuntstall," it was suggested that Peter Wainwright died in America (1877: 9). This provides the author with a fitting way to end the story, but it is wholly incorrect. A letter written by an English cousin to Peter Wainwright junior, in America, provides an account of what occurred, allowing our imagination to a reconstruction the scene. On Sunday, January 10, 1841, Peter Wainwright senior ventured into his garden at Farnworth, where a female servant was clearing the snow. Despite being aged around eighty-six, he insisted on doing the work himself. She returned ten minutes later to find him dead (Wainwright Papers, Box 2, Folder 2.5, January 13, 1841).

Peter Wainwright's death was reported in both the American and English newspapers, and based on the surviving family letters, there is definite evidence of merchants having "underlying personas," as proposed by Sheryllynne Haggerty's *Merely for Money'?: Business Culture in the British Atlantic, 1750-1815* (2012: 27). It is notable how Wainwright attempted to find work for members of his family, and how his children remained in the United States, whereas he and his American wife both died in England. Peter Wainwright was buried "in the Family Tomb at Prescott [sic]," and Prescot was near to his English home at Farnworth (Wainwright Papers, Box 2, Folder 2.5, January 13, 1841).

Staffordshire origins and a precursory stage

The backgrounds of the individuals involved in the crockery trade has a relevance. As an example, William Shufflebottom of Philadelphia was active as a china merchant, importer and dealer in the crockery and glass trade from c. 1800 until the early 1830s (Desilver 1831: 193). In 1800, Shufflebottom received a consignment of seventy-four crates and one cask of earthenware from Thomas Poulson, a Liverpool merchant (*Pennsylvania, U.S., Arriving Passenger and Crew Lists, 1800-1862*). In another instance, the manufacturers Ramsay, Gatchell and Barcroft, shipped five hogsheads of glassware from Waterford, Ireland, to William Shufflebottom, in 1805 (*Pennsylvania, U.S., Arriving Passenger and Crew Lists ...*). Shufflebottom's imports coincide with his advertisements for ceramics as well as glass in the 1800s (Figure 3.3).

In 1806, William Shufflebottom's application to become an American citizen declared that he had arrived in the United States in June 1798 and that he was "a native of England now of the city of Philadelphia, merchant" (*Pennsylvania, U.S., Federal Naturalization Records*, Roll 040, Petitions June 5, 1798–September 5, 1806). A notice in the *American Sentinel*, Philadelphia, announced that "Dr. Ralph Hammersley, son of William Shufflebottom" died in 1830, aged twenty-five. This indicates that one of William Shufflebottom's sons was called Ralph Hammersley Shufflebottom. William Shufflebottom died at Mauch Chunk (northwest of Philadelphia) in 1839, aged sixty-six, and so it may be established that he was born in c.1773 (*National Gazette*, Philadelphia August 22, 1839). In addition, the

Just Received,

AND for sale by the subscriber,

A HANDSOME ASSORTMENT OF

The best Burnished white and gold Tea Setts complete,

Ditto hair colored and burnished Gold do. do.

With a general assortment of the best Eng – lish Flint Glass, consisting of Decanters, Gob- lets, Jelly Glasses, best plain Wines, Cut Stem Wines, upright Tumblers plain and fluted, oval Salts of various shapes and patterns, &c. toge- ther with his usual assortment of

QUEEN's WARE.

All of which have been purchased for cash in the Manufactory, and will be sold at the lowest price. ***Wm. Shufflebottom.***

Figure 3.3 *Philadelphia Gazette* January 5, 1808.

Philadelphia Gazette reported that on, "Tuesday the 14th inst. [December 14, 1802] Mr. Ralph Shufflebottom, brother of Mr. William Shufflebottom, China merchant of this city," had died. Ralph Shufflebottom was also described as a merchant living in Philadelphia (*Philadelphia Gazette* December 24, 1802; *Boston Commercial Gazette* January 3, 1803). The records of the Second Presbyterian Church of Philadelphia indicate that Ralph was aged just twenty-three years, and so was born in c.1779 (Presbyterian Historical Society).

In all probability, William and Ralph Shufflebottom of Philadelphia were originally from the Potteries since the above information coincides with Staffordshire records. A William Shufflebotham[sic], e. p. [earth potter], married Sarah Hammersley in Stoke in 1772 (Adams, Part IV 1926–27: 40). Then, a William and Sarah Shufflebotham [sic], had a son called William, christened in the parish of Stoke-upon-Trent on September 19, 1773 (Adams, Part III 1925: 162). William and Sarah Shufflebotham[sic] also had a child called Ralph, christened at Stoke-upon-Trent on May 9, 1779 (Adams, Part III 1925: 192) During William Shufflebottom's long period of being in business, he regularly advertised, and in one instance, declared that his stock of "QUEEN's WARE … purchased for cash in the Manufactory" (Figure 3.3), suggesting how occasional return visits were made to England to acquire stock.

Although William Shufflebottom was listed in trade directories as still in business in 1831, his property on Second street, between Market and Arch, was advertised for sale in 1829. An impression of how early businesses and accommodation was arranged is provided by a description of the property. Conveniently located near to the Delaware River, it consisted of the store, out-buildings, brick stables, carriage house, a cistern in the yard, and a house, noted for having marble mantels. It was advertised as ideal for a large family and conducting an extensive trade in the "centre of business" (*The National Gazette and Literary Register*, Philadelphia August 5, 1829). Bearing in mind that Shufflebottom moved to No 42, Second street in 1809, it suggests how in the early period of trade, it was typical to live and work in the same location (*Philadelphia Gazette* December 30, 1809).

Merchandising agents

The end of the Anglo-American War of 1812–14 resulted in a temporary surge in exports (Ewins 1997: 6–9). In this context, it has been argued that British manufacturers, as opposed to merchants, became more dominant as "merchandising agents" (Buck [1925] 1969: 121). Coinciding with this view, some English ceramic manufacturers began to have agents helping to coordinate their American trade (Ewins 1997: 88–9; Frelinghuysen 2000: 330). For instance, Curtis Bolton of 129, Maiden Lane, New York, advertised that he was the agent for John and William Ridgway, offering their china and earthenware tea and table services (*American*, New York October 5, 1827). Or, a printed circular of 1834 concerning price-fixing mentions that Charles Cartlidge was acting as an agent for William Ridgway (Figure 3.4). A John Gray, who was in the chair, was described as the agent for Enoch Wood & Sons:

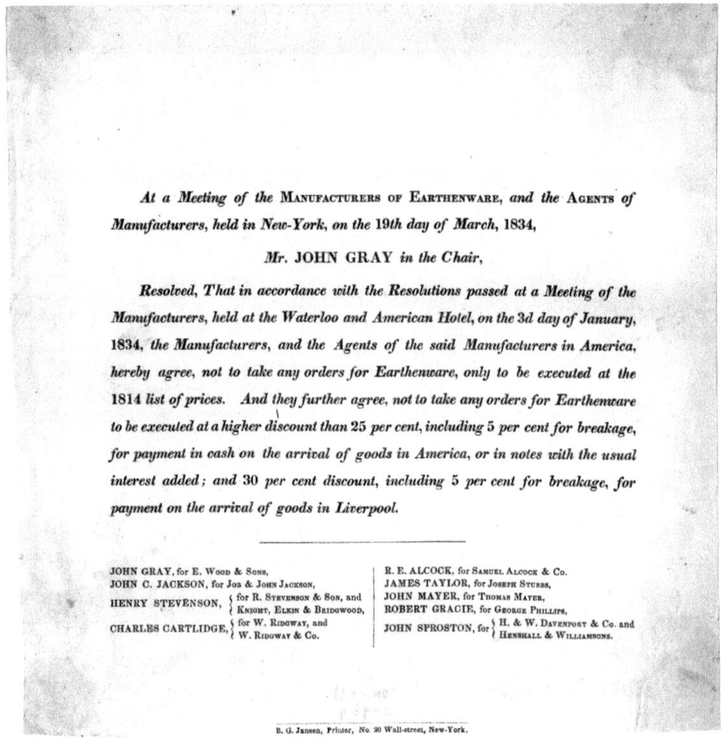

At a Meeting of the Manufacturers of Earthenware, *and the* Agents *of Manufacturers, held in New-York, on the 19th day of March,* 1834,

Mr. JOHN GRAY *in the Chair,*

Resolved, That in accordance with the Resolutions passed at a Meeting of the Manufacturers, held at the Waterloo and American Hotel, on the 3d day of January, 1834, *the Manufacturers, and the Agents of the said Manufacturers in America, hereby agree, not to take any orders for Earthenware, only to be executed at the* 1814 *list of prices. And they further agree, not to take any orders for Earthenware to be executed at a higher discount than* 25 *per cent, including* 5 *per cent for breakage, for payment in cash on the arrival of goods in America, or in notes with the usual interest added; and* 30 *per cent discount, including* 5 *per cent for breakage, for payment on the arrival of goods in Liverpool.*

JOHN GRAY, for E. Wood & Sons,
JOHN C. JACKSON, for Job & John Jackson,
HENRY STEVENSON, for R. Stevenson & Son, and Knight, Elkin & Bridgwood,
CHARLES CARTLIDGE, for W. Ridgway, and W. Ridgway & Co.
R. E. ALCOCK, for Samuel Alcock & Co.
JAMES TAYLOR, for Joseph Stubbs,
JOHN MAYER, for Thomas Mayer,
ROBERT GRACIE, for George Phillips,
JOHN SPROSTON, for H. & W. Davenport & Co. and Henshall & Williamsons.

B. G. Jansen, Printer, No. 30 Wall-street, New-York.

Figure 3.4 Printed circular, March 19, 1834. Kress Collection, Baker Library, Courtesy of, Harvard Business School.

The significance of John Gray (the representative of Enoch Wood & Sons) is considered in more detail below. Based on the printed circular, agents often shared the same surname as the Staffordshire manufacturer, and this suggest how having a family member in the United States further augmented the trade. John C. Jackson was a New York representative for Job Jackson of Cobridge; Henry Stevenson for Ralph Stevenson of Cobridge; R. E. Alcock was a representative for Samuel Alcock of Burslem; and John Mayer, the agent for Thomas Mayer of Stoke. John Clews Jackson was joined by his brother, Job, becoming crockery importers rather than manufacturers (Ewins 1997: 95–7). John Mayer, a brother of Thomas Mayer of Longport, Staffordshire was said to be worth $100,000 by the 1840s and was described as:

> … a high minded, honorable man, and blessed with no ordinary share of prudence. As a man of business, he is prompt and systematic, confining himself to exclusively to his own affairs.
>
> (*The Wealth and Biography* …, 1846: 20)

Apparently, all these individuals integrated into New York society, and all died in the United States: Richard Edward Alcock in 1854, Job Jackson in 1866, Henry Stevenson in 1877, John Mayer in 1881, and John C. Jackson in 1889.

On closer inspection, an examination of agents' backgrounds still yields some intriguing results. Henry Stevenson was listed as a New York importer on Water Street (Longworth 1826), but according to census records was born in Scotland, not Staffordshire (Census, New York City, 1860, 1870). His 1877 gravestone at the Green-Wood Cemetery, Brooklyn indicates that he was born in Dumbarton, near Glasgow, Scotland, on January 17, 1803 (findagrave.com #58036818). Prior to 1799, a partnership existed between James and Andrew Stevenson of Glasgow and Ralph Stevenson of Cobridge. James Stevenson continued to run a "Glass, China & Earthen Warehouse" in Edinburgh until 1806 (*Caledonia Mercury*, Edinburgh February 6, 1806). Ralph Stevenson's obituary mentions how, although he was born at Sneyd Green, near Burslem in 1775, at the age of only eleven, he was dispatched to Glasgow to live with his maternal uncle, Lieutenant John Adams (*Staffordshire Advertiser* February 5, 1853). Ralph Stevenson's father died, and his mother, Ann Adams, remarried. Presumably, Ralph and his brothers, James and Andrew Stevenson, were also sent to Scotland at this time. Henry Stevenson of New York (born in Scotland) was perhaps related to Ralph Stevenson of Cobridge. In this respect, there was an indirect connection to Staffordshire.

Nevertheless, the evolution of the crockery trade was more complex than the model proposed by Norman Buck (1969 [1925]). A characteristic of the ceramic trade was how individuals, apparently from Staffordshire, were established in the United States long before 1815—when Buck proposed that English manufacturers were more likely to have merchandising agents. In turn, these importers and dealers assisted manufacturers, as they developed their own links with the United States. When John Ridgway of the Cauldon Place Works, Shelton, visited Philadelphia in 1822, he turned to William Shufflebottom and the Tams family (also originally from the Potteries) for information about his business affairs. As Ridgway wrote in his diary:

> After breakfast I paid a visit to Mr. Shufflebottom, who gave me a candid statement of Haslam's ignorance of and inattention to business – and in short of his general bad conduct; I then saw Tams and Anderson who gave me a Second Edition of the thing … afterwards I called in at Haslam's late shop, a pretty place and fine situation, the rent moderate, the premises convenient.
>
> (Diary, John Ridgway, November 4, 1822)

Newspaper advertisements show that J. B. Haslam was a wholesale and retail crockery dealer in Philadelphia (Figure 3.5). Haslam had evidently been involved in selling J. & W. Ridgway's goods, but in the desired manner, and accounts of this emerged from conversations with Shufflebottom, and then Tams. William Shufflebottom had been in Philadelphia since the late 1790s, and Sampson Tams arrived in America in 1816. (The Tams family are discussed in Chapter 5). John Buckley Haslam was also English, and after failing in the crockery trade, served

J. B. HASLAM,
IMPORTER OF
And Wholesale and Retail Dealer
IN CHINA,
Glass and Earthenware, &c.
No.7 SOUTH THIRD STREET,

Has just opened, a very extensive assortment of RICH ENGLISH, NANKIN AND CANTON CHINA DINNER, DESERT AND TEA SERVICES, elegant scent and flower Vases, Mantle Ornaments, Figures, Flower Pots, and numerous other beautiful Fancy Articles of the richest China.

RICH CUT and PLAIN GLASS, &c.

He has likewise every description of LIVERPOOL and QUEENSWARE of the most superior quality, which he offers at the lowest cash prices.

Dealers are, as usual, supplied by the Package or Dozen, at the lowest Wholesale prices.

Figure 3.5 *Poulson's American Daily Advertiser*, Philadelphia September 8, 1820.

in the navy (until discharged), and finally moved into teaching. Mysteriously, Haslam died of injuries sustained from an assault in Baltimore in 1837. Although he briefly survived the assault and knew the attacker, Haslam refused to ever name the culprit (*The Sun*, Baltimore September 19, 1837).

Ridgway's diary mentions meeting other crockery merchants and dealers, such as the Cressons, when in Philadelphia. However, he socialized with "Mr. Shufflebottom & family—who were exceedingly kind" (Diary, John Ridgway, November 14, 1822). As ceramic manufacturers began forging their own links with the United States, they appear to have fallen back on the fraternalism of the crockery importers and dealers, who already had older ties to Staffordshire.

Backgrounds seem to have been an important element in developing the trade. When Matthew Smith, a crockery importer of Baltimore, visited Philadelphia in 1825, he records in a letter:

> In conversation with Wm Shufflebotham [sic] of Philadelphia, a very intimate friend of Ginder, he informed me he had suggested various improvements to them in regard to sizes, shapes, colours &c. which he expected they would adopt. I consider him a very shrewd man, and his suggestions well worth attending to.
> (Pomfret 2010: 93–4)

Shufflebottom, who by that period had acquired over twenty years of experience of American ceramic demand, was also familiar with various Staffordshire manufacturers, given his origins. Samuel Ginder & Co. were earthenware manufacturers of Lane End from the late 1810s until the early 1840s. Ginder had an American trade. An auction notice selling earthenware manufactured by Stubbs & Kent, Samuel Ginder & Co, Ralph Stevenson, and William Adams was placed by Bowen & Richards of Philadelphia in 1828 (*Poulson's American Daily Advertiser*, Philadelphia April 4, 1828).

The kinship nexus

There was a strong tendency of businesses to revolve around kinship. For those involved in the ceramic trade, links to the Staffordshire Potteries were often a characteristic in both Britain and the United States. James Stevenson, who ran a crockery warehouse in Edinburgh, was succeeded by "E. Cotton, from Staffordshire" in 1806 (*Caledonia Mercury* February 15, 1806). Elijah Cotton advertised, "Mason's Patent China, and Wedgewood's [sic] Queen's Ware" (*Caledonia Mercury*, August 15, 1807). It has been speculated that Miles Mason acquired a china patent belonging to Turner of Lane End, who was bankrupt by 1806 (Haggar and Adams 1977: 58). The reference in Elijah Cotton's 1807 advertisement, to Mason's Patent China (as a precursor of Ironstone China, patented by his son, Charles J. Mason, in 1813), confirms that this is a distinct possibility. Due to Elijah Cotton's Staffordshire connections, he was able to promote up-to-date goods.

Members of the Cauldwell family were crockery dealers in Birmingham, England, and had connections to Staffordshire before becoming importers in New York. They had prior knowledge of the crockery trade. A "Staffordshire warehouse" business called Lea and Cauldwell existed in Birmingham during the early 1790s (Pye 1791; Ward 1798). This consisted of Jacob Lea a potter of Longport, Staffordshire, and Joseph Cauldwell in Birmingham, although Jacob Lea was declared bankrupt in 1793 (*London Gazette* April 29, 1791; May 9, 1793). Perhaps not coincidentally, Joseph Cauldwell married a Maria Lea in Birmingham in 1787. His brother, John Cauldwell, moved to New York and advertised metal buttons, stockings, and forty crates of "assorted earthenware" available from his 323, Pearl Street store in 1797 (*Daily Advertiser* New York, June 3). Another brother, Cornelius Cauldwell, arrived in New York in c.1806 with a son, Ebenezer, and they focused on the crockery trade. Before moving to New York, Cornelius Cauldwell was listed as a dealer in earthenware and glass at 35, Dale end, Birmingham, England (Chapman 1800). The genealogy of the Cauldwell family is well recorded since Jane Cauldwell, a daughter of Cornelius Cauldwell, married George Colgate in 1824 and thus became linked to the famous Colgate family of New York (Abbe and Howson 1941: 365–70; see Pedigree 2).

Indicative of the importance of individuals such as Ebenezer Cauldwell (as opposed to the sons, or brothers of Staffordshire manufacturers) was that he was described as the "eldest representative of the crockery jobbing business in this country" when he died in 1875. (*The New York Herald* June 20, 1875). In turn, and in a familiar pattern, Cauldwell had an influential role in introducing others into the trade. James M. Shaw became a New York crockery importer from 1838. Though born in New York, he originally worked as a clerk for Ebenezer Cauldwell, thus acquiring a knowledge of the trade. Shaw also attended the same Baptist church as Cauldwell (*New York Tribune* January 12, 1889).

Many of the importers and dealers engaged in the crockery trade became interconnected through marriage. A Birmingham, England, newspaper recorded that in 1806, "At New York, on 23d[sic] of April, Mr. William Hewitt, merchant son of Mr. Hewitt, Lane End, Staffordshire, to Miss Sarah Cauldwell, eldest daughter of Mr. John Cauldwell, merchant, of New York, formerly of this town" (*Aris's Birmingham Gazette* June 16, 1806). A Thomas and William Hewitt ran crockery stores at 263 Broadway and 16 Chambers Street in the early 1800s (*New-York Gazette* May 6, 1805).

It is less clear when William and Thomas Hewitt first arrived in the United States from Staffordshire. An obituary of Gideon Hewitt (a son of Thomas) suggests that the family arrived in New York as early as 1794, when "he was but one year old" (*Daily Milwaukee News* December 30, 1869; see Pedigree 3). However, it was not until the early 1800s that Thomas Hewitt advertised receiving forty-six crates of earthenware from the ship *Diana* (*Republican Watch-Tower*, New York January 8, 1803). On occasion, it was advertised that their stock was suited to the West Indies (*New York Gazette* September 25, 1805), and in 1808, William and Thomas Hewitt advertised the substantial amount of 600 crates and hogsheads of earthenware, including an assortment of "fancy articles," tea and table services, and gold and silver lustre ware (*New York Gazette* September 25, 1805; *Mercantile Advertiser* July 12, 1808).

William Hewitt died in 1810, "at St. Bartholomews [sic], on the way to St. Croix, where he was going for the benefit of this health" (*Mercantile Advertiser,* New York February 13, 1810). Mrs. Sarah Hewitt (the daughter of John Cauldwell and widow of William Hewitt) remarried in 1811, Thomas Cook, who was connected to the firm of Bakewell and Cook (*Public Advertiser*, New York May 15, 1811; see Pedigrees 2 and 3). Yet again, maintaining interconnections with other families involved in selling ceramics was the case. Thomas Cook and Thomas Bakewell had a china and glassware store at 198 Broadway, listed in New York directories (Longworth 1811). Thomas Bakewell also married a member of the Hewitt family, which is discussed in Chapter 7. The Bakewell & Cook partnership ended by c.1815, but Thomas Cook continued to deal in ceramics and glass, independently (Doggett 1848–49).

After the death of William Hewitt, Thomas Hewitt ran the glass and earthenware wholesale and retail store at 263 Broadway (*Mercantile Advertiser* March 8, 1810). With different members of the family involved in the trade, businesses were able to continue. Thomas Hewitt became Thomas Hewitt & Son in 1819, when Gideon was formally admitted into the crockery business (*Mercantile Advertiser* February 5, 1819). Thomas Hewitt died in 1822 aged sixty, at his residence No. 289 Broadway

(*National Advocate* December 17, 1822). By order of the executors, 150 crates and hogsheads of assorted glass and earthenware belonging to Thomas Hewitt, deceased, were sold at auction, and all persons indebted to him were requested to make immediate payments to Gideon P Hewitt. The executors were Mary Hewitt (apparently Thomas's widow, who continued to be involved in running the china store on 289 Broadway), and Thomas Purser, mentioned below (*National Advocate*, New York April 7, 1823). During the 1820s, Thomas Hewitt & Son was run by Mary Hewitt and Gideon Hewitt. Not until 1832 was it announced that a William Butler would continue to run Thomas Hewitt & Son's China, Glass and Earthenware business at 289 Broadway. Overall, the Hewitt family were involved in importing crockery for at least thirty years (see Pedigree 3).

Crockery importers in the United States inevitably marketed ceramics from a variety of manufacturers, but it is interesting to note what was promoted. On one occasion, Thomas Hewitt junior, of Maiden-lane, New York, advertised a range of ceramics referred to as the "celebrated manufactories of Ridgway, Woods, Clews, and Careys, &c." References to Ridgway, Wood, and Clews were common in advertisements, but not in the case of Carey. Perhaps the explanation is that the Hewitts and John Carey & Sons were all ceramic manufacturers from Lane End (Figure 3.6).

The significance of interconnections rather reinforces the point that the ceramic trade was not "anybody's business" (Collard [1967] 1984: 63). There is even a sense that the connections recorded in New York paralleled those that were formed in Staffordshire. For instance, a manufacturing partnership described as William and Thomas Coomer and John Hewitt of Longton existed between c.1799 and 1801. A William Coomer married Ann, daughter of Samuel

CHINA, GLASS & EARTHENWARE

REPACKED for the country trade, from 25 to 30 per cent. less than the regular packing prices of last week : the ware of the first quality, from the celebrated manufactories of Ridgways, Woods, Clews, Careys. &c. The greatest care taken in selecting out and packing.

Shipping supplied at the shortest notice.

THOS. HEWITT, Jun.
51 Maiden Lane.

Figure 3.6 *Evening Post*, New York May 28, 1823.

Bridgwood of Lane End (Hampson 1990: 91). In New York, a Coomer (no Christian name provided) and S. Bridgwood were recorded as running a china store on 208 Broadway, New York, between 1810 and 1813 (*Columbian*, New York April 3, 1810; Longworth 1813).

At the beginning of the Anglo-American War of 1812, British subjects had to declare their occupations, how long they had been in the United States, and if they had applied for naturalization. Samuel S. Bridgewood [sic] of New York indicated that he was an earthenware merchant and had arrived in 1809. Likewise, Thomas Bridgewood, who lived at the same address, declared arrival in New York as 1812, and was listed as a clerk (Scott 1979: 73). Jane Hewitt, daughter of T. Hewitt "merchant of N. York," married Samuel Bridgewood, merchant, in 1810. More interconnections were formed as individuals arrived from England. As Thomas and Samuel Bridgwood became established, they occupied two addresses. Samuel Bridgwood was listed at 246 Greenwich, and Thomas Bridgwood, "china &c st.[store]" at 222 and 246 Greenwich (Longworth 1819–20).

It is vital to begin to appreciate these complex, inter-woven family connections in order to understand how the trade developed. In September 1822, Thomas Bridgewood [sic] advertised china, glass and earthenware from "Messrs. H. Conklin & Co's Store," Poughkeepsie, New York (*The Dutchess Observer*, Poughkeepsie September 11, 1822). The explanation is that Samuel Bridgwood married Jane Hewitt, and her sister, Mary Ann Hewitt, married Henry Conklin of Poughkeepsie (*Weekly Visitor and Ladies' Museum*, New York May 30, 1818; see Pedigree 3). In this instance, the marketing of ceramics and glass at Poughkeepsie would make no real sense without understanding some of these convoluted links. The ability of individuals living around Poughkeepsie to have access to what Thomas Bridgewood described as "the best quality and newest patterns" was not entirely driven by demand but enhanced by family ties. Most definitively, distribution was a reflection of kinship, and there were other influential factors, which are considered in Chapter 6.

Individuals moved around, but they invariably maintained links to the ceramic trade. Whereas Samuel Bridgwood continued as a crockery merchant until at least 1824, Thomas Bridgwood and Charles F. V. Reeve, "late of the City of New York," began advertising china, glass, and earthenware from a warehouse and rooms located on King Street, Charleston, South Carolina, from 1823 (*Augusta Chronicle and Georgia Advertiser* December 27, 1823). Thomas Bridgwood remained involved in the ceramic trade until his death in 1830 (*City Gazette,* Charleston, S.C., June 22, 1830). On his gravestone at St. Michaels Church, Charleston, it states that he was native of Staffordshire, England (findagrave.com #38039162).

For some time, authors have been aware of how kinship provided a level of security and opportunity when conducting an international trade. For instance, T. H. Breen's analysis of "An Empire of Goods: The Anglicization of Colonial America, 1690-1776" raised the question of whether bloodlines were useful in opening up assess to credit (1986: 495). Alternatively, Sheryllynne Haggerty has argued that the "kinship nexus" persisted as a feature of trade and networks because it is reduced "moral hazard" (2012: 165). Haggerty's *"Merely for Money"?:*

Business Culture in the British Atlantic, 1750-1815 also points out how merchants had to be skillful, requiring knowledge of the commodities in which they dealt and the customs of the countries with which they traded (2012: 26). Based on the examples outlined above, bloodlines did provide access to credit, and family members were loyal even if this placed a strain on relationships. A knowledge of ceramics was something of a given if the importer and dealer had connections to the Staffordshire Potteries.

Intermarriage

Peter Mathias in *The Early Modern Atlantic Economy* observes how "marriage often cemented alliances between families with close business interests" (2000: 19). There is ample evidence of marriages serving as a means by which individuals were inculcated into the crockery trade. Robert Charles Wetmore was born in 1799, at Pequannock, Connecticut. In 1819, he was employed in the ceramic trade by his brother-in-law, George Tredwell, who was already a crockery dealer in New York. George, of the house of "John and George Tredwell," married Cornelia Roxanna Wetmore (*New York Daily Advertiser* April 21, 1817). Having obtained knowledge of this trade, Robert Charles Wetmore then formed a partnership with his brother, Prosper M. Wetmore, becoming wholesale crockery dealers in New York from 1826. He retired in 1849, "having amassed a great fortune." (*New York Herald* May 10, 1890). A sister of George Tredwell married into another New York mercantile family called Kissam. George Tredwell's nephew, Timothy Tredwell Kissam, then became a crockery dealer (see Pedigrees 4 and 5).

There are many examples of marriage resulting in links to the crockery trade. Thomas Purser and Thomas Bridgwood (who were both English) ran a china store at 16 Bowery, New York, from at least 1816 (Census, Brooklyn 1855; Longworth 1816). Their partnership lasted until 1818, when they continued independently the crockery trade (*Mercantile Advertiser*, New York February 24, 1818). Thomas Purser married a widow, Mrs. Mary Drummond, and his stepson, James P. Drummond, then became involved in the crockery trade. Thomas Purser and James Drummond became partners, and when Thomas Purser retired from business, Drummond took possession of No. 51 Maiden Lane, previously occupied by Thomas Hewitt junior (*Commercial Advertiser*, New York March 14, 1826). Previously, Purser had acted as executor for Thomas Hewitt, the crockery dealer, who died in 1822. Purser already had links to the Hewitt family (*Commercial Advertiser*, New York December 11, 1823).

Thomas F. Field, a crockery dealer of Utica (and later, New York), married Mary Ann Roberts in 1823, and Mary's sister, Jane Roberts, married Zebinah M. Mason in 1840. Prior to the marriage, Zebinah Mason lived in Utica and was described as a joiner, builder, and lumber merchant (Harrington 1829). However, after Mason's marriage to Jane Roberts, he moved into the crockery business, forming a partnership with his brother-in-law, Thomas F. Field. This partnership operated between 1843–44 in New York. When Zebinah M. Mason moved to Auburn, New York, he continued to be involved in the crockery trade, even stressing how his goods were from Staffordshire (Figure 3.7).

Inevitably, not all crockery importers and dealers in America were from Staffordshire. Nevertheless, there is still evidence of individuals from Staffordshire marrying into the more established New England families involved in the ceramic trade. John Hall junior (of the firm John & Ralph Hall of Burslem) married into the Blanchard family in 1820. A John Blanchard was in partnership with John S. Hastings, and they were crockery dealers. John Hastings had married into the Blanchard family (see Pedigree 6). Joseph S. Hastings and John Hall jr. advertised jointly in Boston, marketing 400 packages of CC, edged, printed, and enameled ware, manufactured by John and Ralph Hall of Burslem and Tunstall (*Boston Intelligencer* July 5, 1823).

CROCKERY!

At No.84 Genesee street Auburn,

THE Subscriber having been engaged in the importing and jobbing crockery trade in the city of New York is now opening at the above stand one of the largest nad best assortments of CHINA, GLASS AND EARTHEN WARE, ever offered in Western New York , which we will put up to the order of Merchants in Auburn, and all others who favor us with a call, at the lowest New York prices. No mistake.

We have bought our stocks of goods of the Staffordshire Manufacturers, England, and at the New York Auction package sales, for Cash, and at prices which will incline us to sell them very cheap. Hotel keepers and Families will here find a most durable assortment to select from, and at prices which canno t fail to please. A variety of DINING SERVICE and fine CHINA TEA SETTS will be open this week. Purchasers are invited to call and examine for themselves. Z. M. MASON.

May 7th, 1814.

N. B. A fine assortment of Table Cutlery, Spoons, Britania, and Stone Ware always on hand.

Figure 3.7 *Auburn Journal and Advertiser*, New York, June 12, 1844.

Business Strategy

Records for the "Association of Earthen Ware Dealers" of Boston exist from 1817 until 1835. It has even been proposed that this association existed before the Anglo-American War of 1812 (Miller 1998: 129). Prominent members included the crockery dealers Henry Wainwright and Thomas Jackson, who often acted as the chair at meetings. In the period covered by the association's records, the membership evolved and increased, but its intention was to regulate the sale prices and discounts on imported earthenware and Chinese porcelain (known as India China) and combat the perennial problem of large of amounts of ceramics being offered for sale at auction. Generally known as "combination," crockery businesses would agree to limit their purchases at auction and fix their selling prices. With a membership fee of two dollars, being part of the Boston association opened up certain privileges (Association of Earthenware Dealers [hereafter Association], February 18, 1822). At one meeting, it was recorded how a dealer called F. Wilby had "offered the dealers 50 crates of earthenware," and these were then purchased by all those in attendance (Association March 21, 1822).

On another occasion, a meeting of the Association was initiated because F. Wilby & Co. had advertised 100 packages of ceramics to be auctioned. It was agreed to "inform them [Wilby & Co.] that the regulation still exists of not attending public sales, and provided Messrs. F. Wilby & Co. will offer the same lot to the Dealers at private sale they will attend at such time and place as may be appointed …" Henry Wainwright and Otis Norcross were appointed to meet with Wilby, and it was determined that he was willing to offer the goods "at very low terms." Some of Wilby's goods apparently included ceramics from Ridgway (Association May 26 and 28, 1823). In other words, while members of the association may not have attended auctions in person, there is evidence of members obtaining goods privately. In one instance, those who attended an association meeting were offered 10 percent under the selling price of 100 crates of earthenware belonging to Martin Brimmer (Association February 23, 1824). Those in attendance included Joseph S. Hastings, Michael Mellen, John Mellen, Henry Wainwright, Otis Norcross, and Robert Briggs.

At one meeting in May 1819, it was agreed to adhere to certain prices of imported CC [cream colored] edged, and printed wares. But extraordinarily, an additional agreement allowed for nineteen crockery dealers outside Boston to be supplied, "without regard to the list of prices" (Association May 13, 1819). The list included George Hill of Providence, Rhode Island, and Charles Blanchard of Portland, Maine. Deacon Charles Blanchard (a devoted member to the church, and crockery dealer of Portland), actually died in Boston (*Portland Daily Press,* Maine November 21, 1876). Interestingly, members of the Boston association, who voted on this clause, were Daniel and Joseph S. Hastings, who had business and family ties to the Blanchard family (see Pedigree 6).

Certainly, family ties existed between the Boston crockery dealers and those located in other regions. This is proved by a meeting held in 1823. On this occasion, it was initially voted to sell "Eagle Chambers" at 24s or 30s and

"American Blk teapots" for 13s 6d. But it was additionally agreed "that the dealers may sell to the following named persons without any restrictions" (Association April 16, 1823). In this instance, a list of twenty-three dealers, including Charles Blanchard of Portland, Maine; Nathan Hastings of Providence, Rhode Island; and women dealers named as Betsey Ward, Sarah Cushing, and Hannah Harris of Salem, Massachusetts, were all exempt from the fixed prices. This agreement was voted on by fifteen members of the Boston Association who attended the meeting on that day, including the crockery dealer Joseph S. Sampson. Conveniently, and somewhat cynically, Joseph S. Sampson was married to Nathan Hastings' daughter (see Pedigree 6). Nathan Hastings was originally a Boston crockery dealer but moved to Providence. Members of the Hastings and Sampson families were located in Boston, but their business interests gradually expanded further afield to Providence, Rhode Island, and Cincinnati, Ohio. While it has been noted before that crockery dealers outside Boston could be supplied at more liberal rates (Miller 1998: 138), the motivation for this behavior was not discussed. The explanation perhaps stems from aiding members of the extended family, connected to the same trade.

Previously, it has been noted that a value of kinship within business structures was opening up access to credit (Mathias 2000: 15–35). There is evidence of this, in the form of Peter Wainwright regularly borrowing money from his brother, Henry. An examination of the British and American cotton industries suggests another way that collective action could be interpreted as helping to stimulate economic activity (Rose 2000: 64). However, attempts at regulating the crockery trade may be considered in a new perspective when it is appreciated that forms of collective action were, in reality, undertaken by individuals who shared close family ties. Once the scope of these interconnections is revealed, it suggests how interrelated families gained, financially. They were collectively able to offer lower prices to dealers outside Boston, who could still be related by intermarriages. As a member of the Boston Earthenware Association, interconnected families were also able to benefit from buying ceramics at discounted prices from auctioneers.

A number of members of the Boston earthenware association were all interrelated. These included the families Norcross, Homer, and Mellen. New business partnerships were continuously formed by members of these families (Figure 3.9 and Pedigrees 7, 8, and 9).

There were also instances of widows continuing to run businesses when their own families were already connected to the ceramic trade. Mary Norcross, nee Homer, ran the firm of Otis Norcross after her husband died in 1827. Mary's brother, William F. Homer, was already involved in the crockery trade, in separate partnership (see Pedigrees 7 and 8).

In a similar manner, New York dealers in "China, Glass and Earthenware" pledged not to purchase ceramics at auction in 1821. A notice was published and signed by thirty-five different firms (Figure 3.9).

As established, Thomas Hewett [sic] & Son (consisting of Thomas Hewitt snr., and his son, Gideon), Thomas Bridgwood, Thomas Cook, Thomas Hewitt junior, Thomas Purser, and E. [Ebenezer] Cauldwell were all linked by intermarriages (See

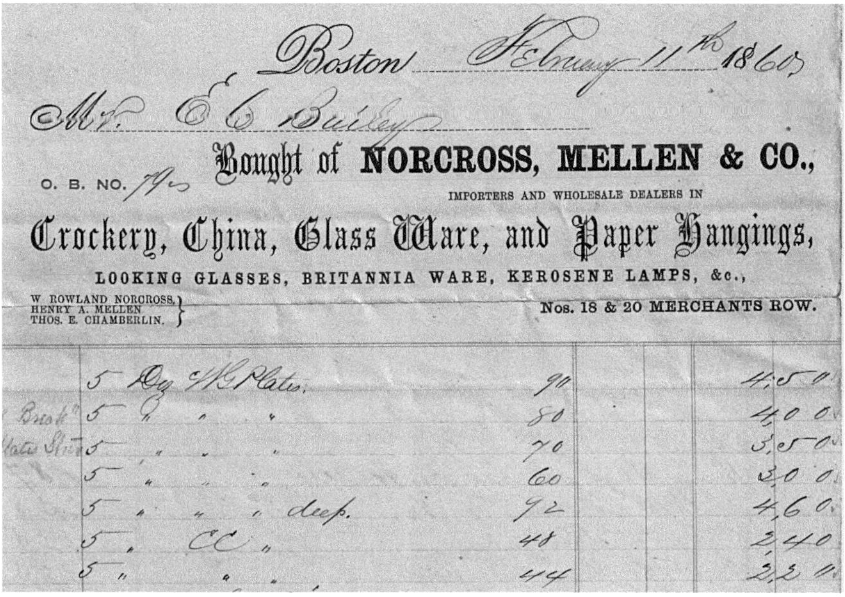

Boston February 11th 1860

Mr. E. C. Bailey

O. B. NO. 79

Bought of NORCROSS, MELLEN & CO.,

IMPORTERS AND WHOLESALE DEALERS IN

Crockery, China, Glass Ware, and Paper Hangings,

LOOKING GLASSES, BRITANNIA WARE, KEROSENE LAMPS, &c.,

W. ROWLAND NORCROSS,
HENRY A. MELLEN
THOS. E. CHAMBERLIN.

Nos. 18 & 20 MERCHANTS ROW.

5 Doz. W.G. Plates	90		4.50
5 " " "	80		4.00
5 " " "	70		3.50
5 " " "	60		3.00
5 " " " deep.	92		4.60
5 " CC "	48		2.40
5 " " "	44		2.2[illegible]

Figure 3.8 Invoice (extract) Norcross, Mellen & Co., importers of crockery, Boston. Dated February 11, 1860. The invoice indicates that the partnership consisted of W. Rowland Norcross, Henry A. Mellen and Thomas E. Chamberlin. See Pedigrees 7 and 9.

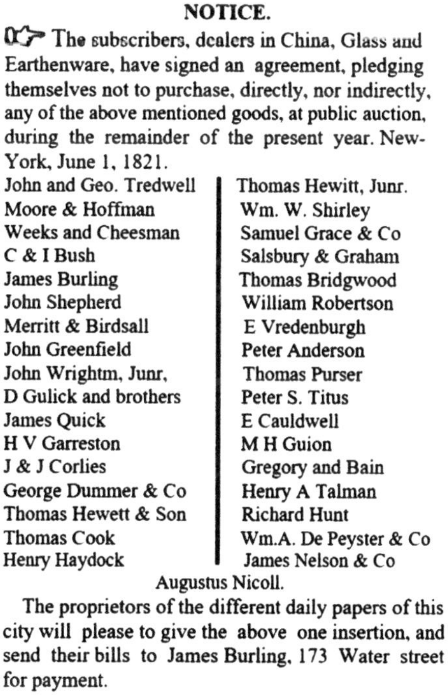

NOTICE.

☞ The subscribers, dealers in China, Glass and Earthenware, have signed an agreement, pledging themselves not to purchase, directly, nor indirectly, any of the above mentioned goods, at public auction, during the remainder of the present year. New-York, June 1, 1821.

John and Geo. Tredwell
Moore & Hoffman
Weeks and Cheesman
C & I Bush
James Burling
John Shepherd
Merritt & Birdsall
John Greenfield
John Wrightm, Junr,
D Gulick and brothers
James Quick
H V Garreston
J & J Corlies
George Dummer & Co
Thomas Hewett & Son
Thomas Cook
Henry Haydock
Thomas Hewitt, Junr.
Wm. W. Shirley
Samuel Grace & Co
Salsbury & Graham
Thomas Bridgwood
William Robertson
E Vredenburgh
Peter Anderson
Thomas Purser
Peter S. Titus
E Cauldwell
M H Guion
Gregory and Bain
Henry A Talman
Richard Hunt
Wm.A. De Peyster & Co
James Nelson & Co
Augustus Nicoll.

The proprietors of the different daily papers of this city will please to give the above one insertion, and send their bills to James Burling, 173 Water street for payment.

Figure 3.9 *Evening Post*, New York June 19, 1821.

Pedigrees 2 and 3). They were also all English, and in the case of the Hewitts and Thomas Bridgwood, from Staffordshire. Another subscriber, William W. Shirley, was also from Staffordshire, and this family is discussed in Chapter 5. Surprisingly little has been written about these individuals in ceramic history literature, even though their families played an important part in developing the New York crockery trade. The only exception to this is John Greenfield of New York, who was known to early writers because he had a recorded backstamp found on wares manufactured by R.& J. Clews of Staffordshire (Slosson 1878: 158; McCauley 1944: 296). (Figures 2.25 and 2.26).

An awareness of kinship then raises the point of whether it caused alternative forms of behavior. On that point, when Thomas Purser of No.16 Bowery, New York, retired from business in 1826, Thomas J. Barrow acquired his crockery store. By contrast, Thomas J. Barrow's advertisements offered "China, Glass & Earthenware, wholesale, as [sic] less than combination prices" (*Commercial Advertiser*, New York February 15, 1827; *Spectator*, New York September 28, 1827). From the late 1820s, Barrow & Co.'s advertisements were directly aimed at "merchants who are interested in the breaking up the *combination in price of Crockery*, [original italics] which has hitherto prevailed in this business" (*Charleston Courier* February 15, 1830). Thomas Barrow's family background was in New York; his grandfather sold artistic prints, composition, and color materials, from at least the 1770s. He does not appear to have married into the other families involved in the New York crockery trade (*New York Gazette, and Weekly Mercury* April 12, 1779; October 22, 1781).

Barrow openly opposed forms of combination in the press, and due to his course of action, he even claimed to have become a target of persecution by others involved in the trade. He published a letter claiming that he had been forced to obtain stock by employing agents in Liverpool, anonymously purchasing ceramics for cash, and how one manufacturer called "R. Griffith" had declined to supply him with an order of teapots because of this opposition to combination (Figure 3.10).

A John and Robert Griffith (claiming to be originally from the Staffordshire Potteries, and more recently, of New Jersey), advertised themselves as earthenware manufacturers, near Pittsburgh, from 1815–17. This firm manufactured black and brown glazed coffee and teapots (Figure 3.11).

At the start of the Anglo-American War in 1812, Robert Griffith stated that he was aged twenty-five, had arrived in the United States in 1810, and was an earthenware manufacturer at Elizabeth Town, New Jersey. Also described as earthenware manufacturers were John Griffith, living in the United States since 1808, and Edward Griffith, arriving as early as 1804 (Scott 1979: 245). Apparently, Edward and John Griffith were in a partnership until 1814 (*New-Jersey Journal* July 12, 1814). In 1815, the teapot and earthenware manufactory of one Jonathan Griffith & Co. (in partnership with Elias Wade) was established at Elizabeth Town (*New-Jersey Journal* November 14, 1815). Evidently, various members of the Griffith family were involved in ceramic production or the ceramic trade. In 1819, a co-partnership between Sampson Tams (originally from

Figure 3.10 *Spectator*, New York September 17, 1830.

NO COMBINATION AND FREE TRADE
EARTHENWARE AND LOOKING GLASSES
THOMAS J. BARROW, & Co. IMPORTERS 88 Water STREET. New York, offer for sale 1,000 packages EARTHENWARE, GLASS, CHINA, and LOOKING GLASSES, com prising the most complete assortment ever offered in this mar ket, and will be repacked to the Country Merchant at the lowest prices. In consequence of having refused to join the *Combination* for regulating the prices of Crockery, in this city, we have been made the subjects of a most intolerent persecution, the object of which is nothing less than our entire ruin and explusion from the trade, our characters have been assailed as men of integrity and fair dealing, our credit as a house of responsibility impeached, and every endeavor made to ruin it, and to crown the whole our importations through the regular channels have been stopped (in consequence of these threats thrown out to the Manufacturers in England) so that we have been obliged to employ Agents in Liverpool to make our purchases in such a manner that our names would not appear in the t ransaction – all the facilities attendant upon obtaining credit for our importations are denied to us, and anything but cash in Liverpool will obtain for us our needed supplies of ware. We are suffering these hardships in the case of the Merchant and Consumer of this description of goods no less than our own ; and to them, as our last resort, we come for aid and assistance ; so long as are enabled to sustain ourselves against more than forty men, who have combined to bring about our ruin in this unheard of manner, we will continue to sell our goods free and independent, at our own rates *for Cash or approved city acceptances only.*

SEPTEMBER 10 THOS J. BARROW & CO.,
No.88 Water street, above Old-slip.

The following letter, received a short time since, is a literal account of the notices which have been served by the trade on all persons who supply us with goods :-

MESSRS T. J. BARROW & Co.

GENTLEMEN – Your favor was received and should have been attended to before this time, *but I was notified by the Crockery Dealers in the city of New York, that, if I supplied you with Tea-pots, I must not expect any orders from them* – You know my opinion on that subject, but it will not do for me to contend with th e trade, as we wish to get along as easy as possible. *I am very sorry* to say I must, (tho' willing to supply you,) decline your orders. I do hope you will make some arrangements with the trade that will be to your mutual advantage. Yours with respect,

[Signed] R.GRIFFITH.

Staffordshire) and John Griffith of 81, Maiden Lane, New York, was dissolved, with Griffith remaining in trade, offering an assortment of imported printed, painted, and edged ware (*New-York Gazette* September 19, 1819).

Whether "R. Griffith" (as mentioned by Thomas J. Barrow) was definitely the same individual as Robert Griffith, originally from Staffordshire, is unclear. But there was a real sense of the trade being tightly controlled, reinforced by the assertion in R. Griffith's letter; if an order for teapots had been supplied, this could potentially result in his being boycotted by other New York crockery dealers. Apparently, this was something that Griffith's business could ill-afford. Thomas Barrow attempted to act in an independent manner.

In 1832, despite Barrow's fears of "expulsion from the trade," an advertisement claimed that a connection had been formed with one of the largest Potteries in England, and he thanked his southern and western friends for their "liberal support" during his "struggle" against the combination of prices (*Georgian*, Savannah January 23, 1832). Barrow's fears of expulsion from the trade were not

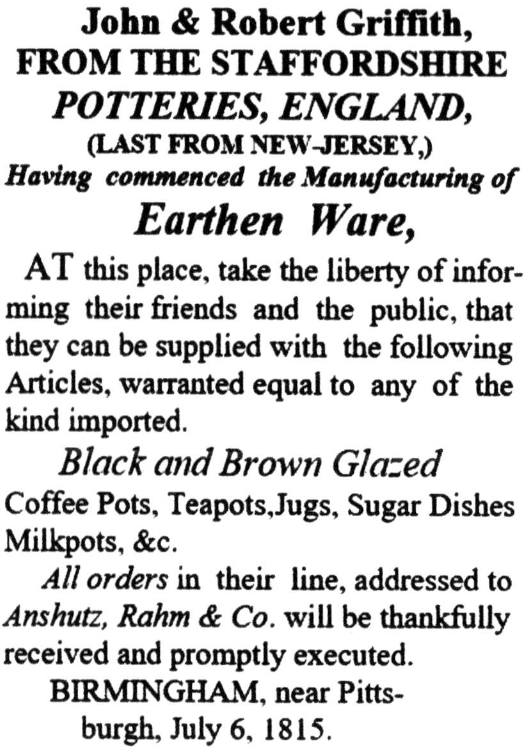
John & Robert Griffith,
FROM THE STAFFORDSHIRE
POTTERIES, ENGLAND,
(LAST FROM NEW-JERSEY,)
Having commenced the Manufacturing of
Earthen Ware,
AT this place, take the liberty of informing their friends and the public, that they can be supplied with the following Articles, warranted equal to any of the kind imported.
Black and Brown Glazed
Coffee Pots, Teapots,Jugs, Sugar Dishes Milkpots, &c.
***All orders* in their line, addressed to *Anshutz, Rahm & Co.* will be thankfully received and promptly executed.**
BIRMINGHAM, near Pittsburgh, July 6, 1815.

Figure 3.11 *Western Monitor*, Lexington, Kentucky July 18, 1815.

without foundation. The *Journal of Commerce* claimed that the New York crockery dealers had been acting together for a long period, and this report was re-published in a number of American newspapers (*Boston Traveler* July 19, 1833). A lengthy article concerned with “Crockery Combination” appeared in the *Morning Courier and New-York Enquirer* in 1833 in response to what had appeared in the *Journal of Commerce*. The article began by quoting from the *Journal of Commerce*:

> … if an auction sale is advertised, the combination will not attend. They require that such sales shall be published no further than their own circle. It is in consequence of this combination, that such advertisements are seldom or never found in newspapers, though auction sales of crockery are of frequent occurrence. The combinants pledge themselves to maintain fixed prices in sale, and any who will not conform to this and all other rules, is followed by whatever mercantile penalties the laws of the fraternity prescribe.
>
> (*Morning Courier and New-York Enquirer* July 13, 1833)

The second half of the article proceeded to vehemently deny that there was such behavior, with the counter-argument concluding that “there is no trade conducted in this city, more justly entitled to the appellation of ‘free,’ than the Crockery; and the prices of the Crockeryware here, are not only loose and irregular, but lower in proportion in cost, than any other city in the Union" (*Morning Courier and New-York Enquirer* July 13, 1833). Based on Barrow's experience, this did not seem to be the case.

A few years later, Thomas Barrow drowned, along with the captain, two mates, seven of her crew and three other passages, when the packet ship, *Pennsylvania*, was shipwrecked shortly after leaving the port of Liverpool, in January 1839 (*Public Ledger*, Philadelphia February 13, 1839). Dying while still in business, rather than retiring, an inventory of Barrow's stock needed to be conducted, providing insight into his range of customers and even how he had ceramic stock held at different parts of America (Inventory, 54.106.4). His ceramic goods in Philadelphia were valued as £105.5.0, and those at Petersburgh, Virginia, amounted to £98.17.10. Based on the "Notes on hand" section of the inventory, there were customers listed, such as H. R. Henry of Aurora, Ohio; F. F. Fagan of Plymouth, North Carolina; and J. G. Dunlap, Augusta, Georgia. Barrow did have a range of southern and western customers. The inventory provides some insight into who were Barrow's more recent Staffordshire suppliers, listing "1 Lot Ironstone Dinner Ware Ridgways" valued at £3.0.0, ironstone plates and twiflers, described as Masons, and ironstone plates, twiflers, and muffins, from Alcocks. The inventory also includes over two dozen "Wedge Wood [sic] Inks" valued at over five dollars. The total of Barrow's ceramic and glass stock was valued at over ninety thousand dollars.

After Barrow's death, the business was continued by James A. Taylor, who advertised "Being entirely disconnected with any combination for the support of high prices, the subscriber will resume the manner of conducting his business, in which he was successful some past years, in the old house of T.J. Barrow & Co." (*Cabinet*, Schenectady, New York March 17, 1840). For some crockery dealers, their marketing strategy celebrated an independence, making it even harder to be certain about the precise prices of ceramics in America.

Connections to the crockery trade

As established in Chapter 1, consideration of the actual importers involved in the ceramic trade developed more slowly, and when this occurred, it was initiated by curiosity over existing backstamps. Dr. Everett J. McKnight's paper on "Peter Morton—An Early American Merchant and Importer" was published in the *Connecticut Magazine* in 1906. The article drew attention to certain printed patterns, and wares manufactured by Enoch Wood of Burslem were alternatively marked as "Peter Morton, Importer of Earthenware, Connecticut" or "Peter Morton, Hartford" (Figure 1.7). Peter Morton was in Hartford, Connecticut, from 1823 until 1832. Dr. Everett McKnight's research concluded that of Morton's "early life and education we know nothing" (1906: 354). However, exploring the backgrounds of individuals assists in explaining their involvement in the crockery trade and establishing why connections existed with specific manufacturers.

Peter Morton's father was Thomas C. Morton, a New York merchant who advertised thread, laces, and muslins from the early 1800s. Evidently, selling ceramics was not a family trade. Nevertheless, Peter Morton advertised that he had purchased the entire china, glass, and earthenware stock of William H. Imlay of Hartford, Connecticut, in 1823 (*Connecticut Mirror*, February 17, 1823). In March 1823, Peter Morton married Ann Tomlinson (a member of a Connecticut family), which might account for why he acquired a business in Hartford (*Connecticut Herald*, April 1, 1823). But the connection to the crockery trade is perhaps more convoluted, highlighting the significance of earlier links and family ties. Connections support the theory that individuals did not become involved in this specialist business by chance.

It was established earlier in this chapter how a price fixing meeting was held in New York in 1834 (Figure 3.4). John Gray was in the chair, described as a representative of Enoch Wood of Burslem. Gray's New York mercantile business typically advertised a range of commodities, such as textiles, clothes, and ceramics (*New York Gazette and General Advertiser*, October 23, 1818: *Mercantile Advertiser*, New York December 6, 1819). By the late 1810s, he had gravitated toward advertising cream colored, painted, and printed wares, even donating, "1 basket of Crockery" to the Fifth Ward Committee, "Relief of the Poor," in 1832 (*Commercial Advertiser*, New York August 7, 1832). Here is further evidence of how ceramics could actually be acquired in more unconventional ways, apart from shopping.

John Gray died at the advanced age of eighty-five in 1851 (*Evening Post*, New York November 11, 1851). An awareness of his age draws attention to how there probably operated a hierarchy within the crockery trade. John Gray, acting as chair, was reflective of his seniority and how he had accumulated long experience of dealing in ceramics and was the representative for Enoch Wood & Sons. His final will and testament shows how money was left to family members in Glasgow, as well as $3,000 to the American Bible Society and $5,000 to John Alexander (another agent for Enoch Wood). Gray appointed Stephen Conover (merchant), Ebenezer Cauldwell (the crockery dealer), Ezekiel C. McIntosh (a crockery dealer of Albany, New York), and John Alexander, as executors. Later, a newspaper notice of 1856 shows that a legal case was raised between the surviving executors of John Gray (Ebenezer Cauldwell and Stephen Conover) against the surviving executors of Thomas C. Morton (John Mortimer jr. and James Paton). Thomas C. Morton had died in 1833, aged sixty-one, and had appointed his sons-in-law, John Mortimer jr. and James Paton, as executors.

Thus, a connection existed between Thomas C. Morton and John Gray, who, incidentally, were both Scottish. It has been suggested that in the early period of American trade, mercantile activity was often dominated by individuals from Scotland, since they had pioneered a successful commercial system whereby merchandise could be acquired on credit, in exchange for American tobacco (Blaszczyk 1984: 9–10). What is clear is that as early as 1805, eighty crates of earthenware were offered for sale by John Gray, described as available from "Mr. Thos. Morton's, Greenwich" (*New-York Gazette* October 19, 1805). The straightforward explanation for why Peter Morton became linked to the crockery trade was that Thomas C. Morton and John Gray were already acquainted.

In fact, New York city directories show that Peter Morton, book-keeper, and John Gray, merchant, shared the same address on 88 Water Street (Longworth 1821 and 1822). Before acquiring the crockery store of William H. Imlay of Hartford in 1823, Peter Morton had gained knowledge and experience of the trade. While it is unclear when John Gray formed a connection with Enoch Wood of Burslem, Peter Morton's own business ties mirrored the networks of his former employer. When Peter Morton moved from Hartford back to New York in 1832, his range of ceramic merchandise was advertised as "in part from Messrs. Enoch Wood & Sons." He was even described as an agent for Enoch Wood & Sons in 1841 (*The New York Journal of Commerce* November 16, 1832; Ripley 1841).

The role of individuals who acted as manufacturers' agents could vary. On occasion, both John Gray and John Alexander sold "English Refined Borax." Indeed, John Alexander advertised that he was an agent for Wood, Kurtz & Co., manufacturers of English borax (*Shipping and Commercial List and New York Price Current,* April 2, 1842). This firm of manufacturing chemists consisted of Enoch Wood senior and his sons, Enoch, Joseph, and Edward of Burslem and Andrew Kurtz of Liverpool (*The Evening Chronicle,* London January 25, 1837). To act as an agent for a Staffordshire manufacturer was not entirely confined to promoting the sale of ceramics.

When the wider links of importers and dealers are traced, it can reveal why different individuals became involved in the ceramic trade, or how businesses expanded.

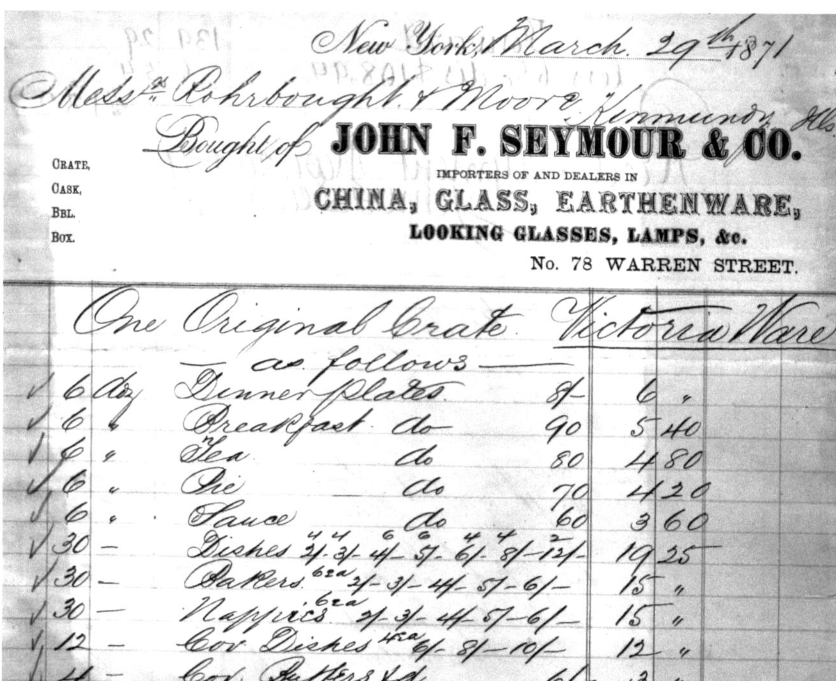
New York, March 29th 1871

Messrs. Rohrbought & Moore, Kinmundy, Ills.

Bought of JOHN F. SEYMOUR & CO.

CRATE, CASK, BBL. BOX.

IMPORTERS OF AND DEALERS IN

CHINA, GLASS, EARTHENWARE,

LOOKING GLASSES, LAMPS, &c.

No. 78 WARREN STREET.

One Original Crate Victoria Ware

as follows

6 doz	Dinner plates	8/-	6	.
6 "	Breakfast do	90	5	40
6 "	Tea do	80	4	80
6 "	Pie do	70	4	20
6 "	Sauce do	60	3	60
30 —	Dishes 3/- 3/- 4/- 5/- 6/- 8/- 12/-		19	25
30 —	Bakers 2/- 3/- 4/- 5/- 6/-		15	"
30 —	Nappies 2/- 3/- 4/- 5/- 6/-		15	"
12 —	Cov. Dishes 6/- 8/- 10/-		12	"
4 —	Cov. Butters &d.	6/-	3	"

Figure 3.12 Invoice (extract) John F. Seymour & Co., New York, to Messrs. Rohrbought [sic] & Moore, Kinmudy, Illinois. Dated March 29, 1871.

As was so often the case, a family member would also become involved in a crockery firm. Joel Seymour, originally from Stillwater, Saratoga County, was a New York crockery dealer from 1834, and was joined by his brother, John F. Seymour, by 1840 (Longworth 1834, 1840). They became a sizeable New York business. In 1840, following a fire along Pearl and Stone Street, the Seymours' loss of stock was estimated at $10,000, though they were insured (*New York Commercial Advertiser* January 29, 1840). Surviving invoices give an indication as to what they sold and provide some sense of their customer distribution. For instance, John F. Seymour, sold a crate of white stoneware amounting to $151.71 to H. F. Robbins, Great Barrington, Massachusetts, in 1867. Later, in 1871, Seymour sold a crate of table, tea, and toilet ware described as "Victoria Ware" for $108.94 to Rohrbough & Moore of Kinmundy, Illinois (Figure 3.12).

What invoices do not convey is how the realities of life could still be harsh, even in the second half the nineteenth century. Joel Seymour died in 1861 aged fifty-six, and although the business continued to be run by John F. Seymour, it had failed by1874 (*New York Herald* November 25, 1861; July 5, 1879). John moved to the residence of his bother-in-law and cousin, the Reverend George F. Seymour of the Protestant Episcopal Church, New York, who lived at the Theological Seminary, only to be shot dead in the grounds in 1879. His wife and brother-in-law discovered his body, and it was her screams that alerted the neighborhood to the

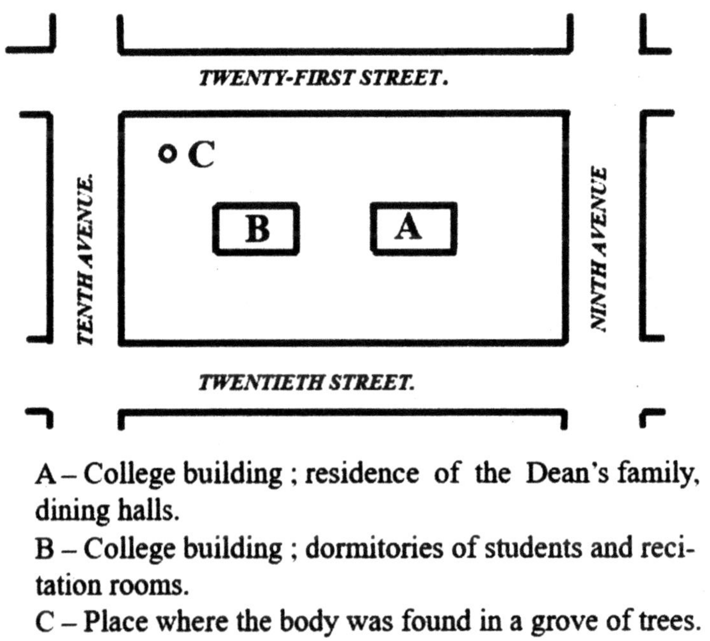

Figure 3.13 *The Sun*, New York July 5, 1879.

crime. At first, robbery was the suspected motive, but nothing was stolen. Suicide was suggested, but no pistol was found. It was even speculated that Seymour had been accidentally shot on the night of July 3, as there was the firing of many guns and pistols around midnight in celebration of Independence Day (*The New York Herald* July 6, 1879). Newspapers even produced diagrams showing the scene of the crime (Figure 3.13).

After a lengthy police investigation, the coroner's inquest concluded that, "Mr. Seymour came to his death from a pistol shot wound accidentally received at the hands of some unknown person, in the grounds of the Theological Seminary, on the night of July 3rd." (*Wheeling Register*, West Virginia July 14, 1879). Consequently, nobody was ever charged. While it has been suggested how the antebellum American city "nurtured violence" (Curry 1981: 96), destructive acts (accidental, or otherwise) remained a feature of society in the late nineteenth century. The past was far from idyllic.

Specialization and movement

Movement from Staffordshire to America was not always one directional. George A. Brown of Baltimore married Mary, daughter of Ralph Stevenson, a manufacturer of Cobridge, at Burslem in 1831 (*Baltimore Patriot & Mercantile Advertiser* April 22, 1831). Ralph Stevenson was involved in the American trade, and accordingly produced wares for the American market (Larsen 1950: 124–40). George A. Brown remained in England after his marriage and became a representative of the firm, Brown, Shipley & Co., of Liverpool, until he died in 1870 (*Liverpool Courier and*

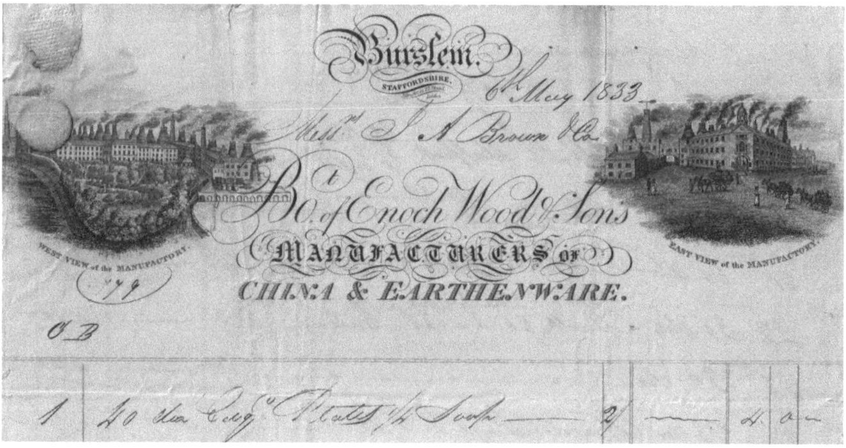

Figure 3.14 Invoice (extract), Enoch Wood & Sons, Burslem, to J. A. Brown & Co., Philadelphia. Dated May 6, 1833.

Commercial Advertiser May 16, 1870). George Alexander Brown was a nephew of Alexander Brown of Baltimore, who originally imported Irish linens and other merchandise from the early 1800s. Alexander Brown & Co. expanded into owning ships, becoming a vast family business with branches in Baltimore, Philadelphia, New York, and Liverpool (Brown 1909: 15–20, 95). A surviving invoice shows that John A. Brown of Philadelphia (a member of the family) imported ceramics manufactured by Enoch Wood & Sons in 1833 (Figure 3.14). It is presumed that the marriage between George A. Brown and Ralph Stevenson's daughter stemmed from connections to the American trade.

There is also evidence of roles being in a state of flux—either manufacturing or selling ceramics in America. In Norman Buck's analysis of the Anglo-American trade, there was no scope to explore how individual roles evolved or changed over time. But as an example, members of the Asbury family, originally from Staffordshire, became crockery importers in Philadelphia. In Stoke, Samuel Asbury, originally a book-printer of Shelton, married Jane, daughter of Ralph Hammersley, a ceramic manufacturer and agent (*Staffordshire Advertiser* December 20, 1828). A ship-passenger document of May 19, 1837, indicates that Mrs. Samuel Asbury, two children, George Hammersley (most likely her brother), and a servant sailed from Liverpool to Philadelphia *(Pennsylvania, U.S., Arriving Passenger and Crew Lists, 1798-1962*). When settled in Philadelphia, Samuel Asbury and George Hammersley shared the same mercantile premises as earthenware importers (M'Elroy 1839; M'Elroy 1861). George Hammersley remained in Philadelphia and died in 1878 aged fifty-nine (*North American* February 26, 1878).

Samuel Asbury returned to Staffordshire in an earlier period. At the end of 1848, a notice appeared in the press offering farms to those anxious to emigrate to the United States as farmers, within six miles of the Sandusky railway in the state of Ohio. Samuel Asbury offered to show plans of these properties and views of neighboring towns from his Hanley residence (*Staffordshire Advertiser* January 6, 1849). He appeared in the Shelton Census of 1851 as an earthenware manufacturer employing over 400 men, women and children. His son, Edward, aged eleven, was described as born in "Philadelphia, America." Ties to his brother-in-law still in Philadelphia, co-existed with links to manufacturing. A partnership between Samuel Asbury and Francis Morley, earthenware manufacturers and merchants of Shelton and Philadelphia, was dissolved in 1853 (*Perry's Bankrupt Gazette* London, June 4, 1853). According to the 1861 census, Samuel Asbury was an earthenware merchant rather than manufacturer. Edward, now aged twenty-two, was described as an "Earthenware Agent."

A surviving invoice dated 1869, for two hogsheads and twenty-nine packages of white granite earthenware with pattern names, Sèvres Chintz, Victory, and Columbia, was sent from "Edward Asbury of Longton agent" to the firm "Asbury & Young" of Philadelphia, showing how Anglo-American business links were maintained by the next generation. Attached to this invoice is a signed and sworn declaration for the value of the goods made at the United States Consular Agency, Tunstall (Figure 3.15). The Philadelphian business was described as being run by

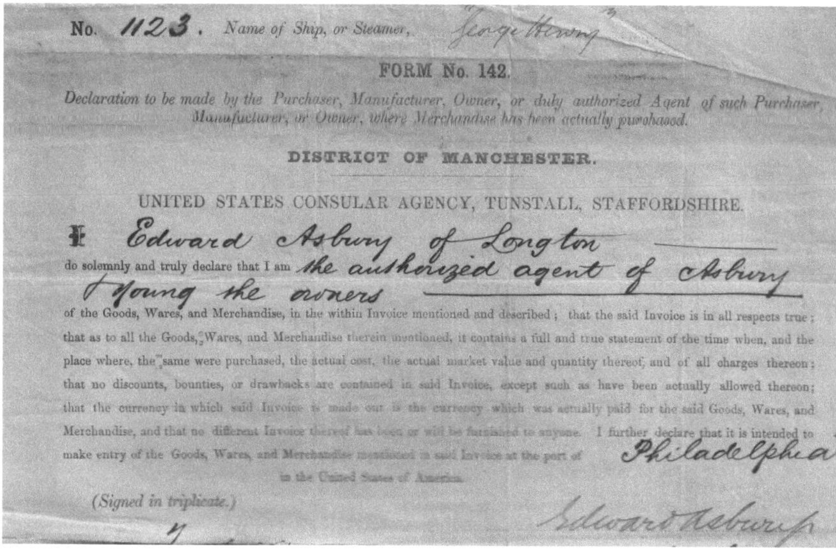

No. 1123. Name of Ship, or Steamer, George Herring

FORM No. 142.

Declaration to be made by the Purchaser, Manufacturer, Owner, or duly authorized Agent of such Purchaser, Manufacturer, or Owner, where Merchandise has been actually purchased.

DISTRICT OF MANCHESTER.

UNITED STATES CONSULAR AGENCY, TUNSTALL, STAFFORDSHIRE.

I Edward Asbury of Longton

do solemnly and truly declare that I am the authorized agent of Asbury & Young the owners

of the Goods, Wares, and Merchandise, in the within Invoice mentioned and described; that the said Invoice is in all respects true; that as to all the Goods, Wares, and Merchandise therein mentioned, it contains a full and true statement of the time when, and the place where, the same were purchased, the actual cost, the actual market value and quantity thereof, and of all charges thereon; that no discounts, bounties, or drawbacks are contained in said Invoice, except such as have been actually allowed thereon; that the currency in which said Invoice is made out is the currency which was actually paid for the said Goods, Wares, and Merchandise, and that no different Invoice thereof has been or will be furnished to anyone. I further declare that it is intended to make entry of the Goods, Wares, and Merchandise mentioned in said Invoice at the port of Philadelphia in the United States of America.

(Signed in triplicate.)

Edward Asbury

Figure 3.15 Declaration (extract), made at the United States Consular Agency, Tunstall, by Edward Asbury of Longton, agent of Asbury & Young, Philadelphia. Dated April 21, 1869. The consignment of earthenware was shipped on the "George Herring," and the total declared vale was £270.9.10.

a John Asbury and Thomas Young (McElroy 1867). Potentially, John was another son of Samuel Asbury.

Yet another shift in role had occurred by the 1870s. The 1871 Census describes Edward Asbury, as born in America, and now as a china manufacturer, living in Stoke. In the following year, *The Public Ledger*, Philadelphia, records that "Samuel Asbury, of Sandon, Staffordshire, late of Philadelphia" had died aged seventy-two (August 20, 1872). Edward Asbury (who became the owner of the Prince of Wales Pottery, Longton) died in 1905. The announcement of his death in the Staffordshire press provides more details of his manufacturing and American connections:

> Mr. Asbury was the son of Samuel Asbury of Hanley, and was born in the United States during a temporary sojourn in that country by his father and mother. About thirty-five years ago he began business as a china manufacturer at Longton in partnership with his uncle, Mr. Titus Hammersley.
>
> (*Uttoxeter Advertiser and Ashbourne Times*, Staffordshire April 26, 1905)

Based on the example of Asbury and Hammersley, their roles were in a constant state of flux. The commonality was that ties to the Staffordshire Potteries enabled individuals to work in different aspects of the trade.

Summary

Elizabeth Collard's opinion that those involved in Anglo-Canadian ceramic trade were "as varied as their stock" does not readily apply to the American market. From at least the late eighteenth century, there existed importers and dealers in America who had ties to Staffordshire. Having these links to Staffordshire appears to have enabled roles to have been more fluid, allowing migration to be not entirely one directional. A link to the Potteries enabled movement between manufacturing or the merchandising aspects of the trade. In an industrial sense, the production of ceramics relied on the efforts of a team rather than the endeavor of an individual. It was even observed how there were as many as twenty separate processes involved in the production of a single ceramic vessel (Arnoux 1853: 382). This interdependency was perhaps carried forward into the sales and merchandising aspects of the trade. In the similar manner to the families involved in manufacturing, individuals connected to importing and dealing, typically intermarried, strengthening their ties to the trade, and in turn, links to Staffordshire.

As the collecting of American-themed ceramics increased, there was an inclination for the early literature to consider the role of importers, but only if the names of importers and dealers had appeared on vessels, as impressed or printed backstamps. Examining the press highlights how a much wider range of individuals were involved in the ceramic trade. This chapter has identified many individuals, who have previously been under-researched or neglected. When their backgrounds are considered, it provides more in-depth sense of who was involved in the trade, laying the foundation for exploring how far marketing ever reflected backgrounds, culture, and identity. The theory examined in later chapters is how intermediaries were not simply importers and dealers who responded to American ceramic fashion and demand but that they marketed or even commissioned ceramics influenced by their own political and religious views. In short, this becomes the explanation for why ceramic designs are more common than others, as observed by the earliest collectors and the earliest publications.

Chapter 4

POLITICS AND MARKETING

Adding to the complexity of understanding the relationship between production and consumption is how ceramics embraced the functional and the mundane, as well as the decorative and the ornamental. Ceramics were often hybrid objects, insofar as they might be based on a functional form, but evidently designed to have a more symbolic purpose. For instance, jugs manufactured in Liverpool or Staffordshire were immediately transformed into something more commemorative, political, or patriotic by the application of images of American politicians, the Revolutionary War, or the naval battles and heroes of the Anglo-American War of 1812–14. Jugs such as these might be large in size and, presumably, their original purchase reflected both the sentiments of the buyer, and in turn, provided ways for the owner to communicate their political or patriotic views to others (Figure 4.1).

Even the most ordinary edged ware plates could have had a painted, printed, or moulded decoration based on American iconography, changing and elevating their significance. These transformations also account for why some ceramics have been more readily preserved compared to others. As ceramics can have such varied functions, describing consumption as determined by either price, or fashion, becomes such a difficult task. It has been suggested that as edged wares were the lowest priced decorated wares, this contributed to their ubiquity, although they were not necessarily the cheapest form of tableware (Miller 2013: 345). An invoice of Mellor, Venables & Co. of Burslem, addressed to S. & J. Tams of Philadelphia, reveals that the cheapest form of tableware was CC [cream colored] wares, priced at 1s 6d per dozen. Blue and green edged plates cost 2s per dozen, whereas printed wares in the "New Canova" pattern were priced at 4s in 1836 (Figure 5.16). But edged wares could be transformed by the addition of an American seal, or the portrait of General Lafayette—the French hero of the American revolutionary wars who made a triumphal return to the United States in 1824. It is unclear whether the addition of these painted, molded, or printed American motifs impacted on the buying and selling price (Figure 4.2).

In Chapter 1, it was determined how the collecting of American-themed ceramics resulted in extensive publications. Some of these earliest American authors found it curious as to why Liverpool and Staffordshire manufacturers willingly incorporated imagery celebrating English defeats, particularly in relationship to the Anglo-American war of 1812–14. However, the degree to

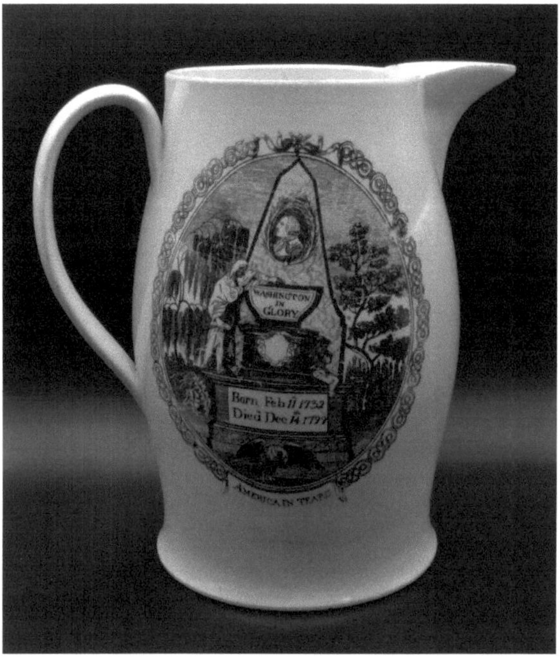

Figure 4.1 Jug, creamware, black printed, commemorating President George Washington, “Washington in Glory, Born Feb.11th 1752, Died December 14, 1799, America in Tears,” with an unnamed ship on the reverse. Staffordshire, or Liverpool, c.1800–10.

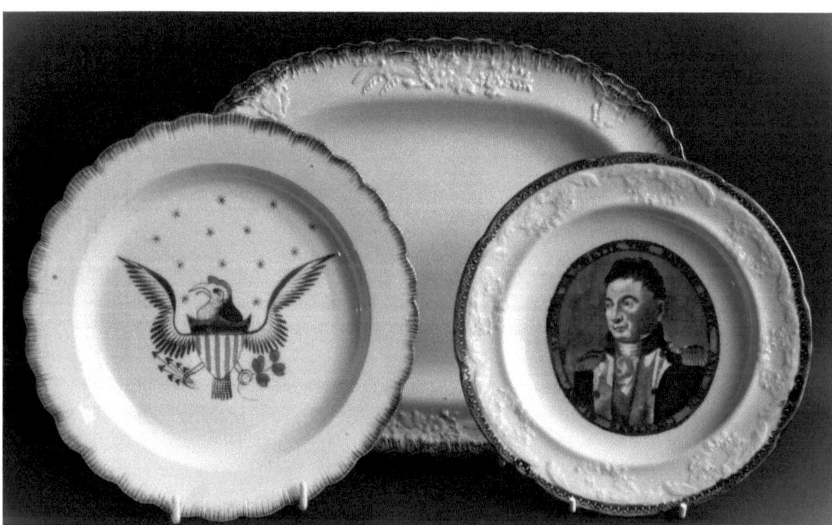

Figure 4.2 Blue edged wares, adapted to the American market. From left to right. Plate, pearlware, painted American Seal, English, c.1810–20. Platter, earthenware, molded decoration incorporating the American Seal, English, c.1820–30. Plate, earthenware, blue transfer printed portrait, inscribed “Welcome La Fayette The Nations Guest and Our Country’s Glory.” Impressed mark, “Clews Staffordshire Warranted,” Cobridge, Staffordshire c.1825.

which "American" dealers may have influenced what was produced was not fully explored (Earle 1892: 142), and the tendency was to assume that importers and dealers were "American," when their backgrounds were clearly more diverse. By the same token, early authors rarely considered who actually marketed American-themed ceramics advertised in newspapers, although it was considerably harder for the earliest researchers and writers to survey advertising, which has been the intention of this book.

It transpires that some "American" crockery importers and dealers were more recent migrants. As discussed in Chapter 3, members of the Hewitt family became crockery dealers in New York and were originally from Staffordshire. Gideon P. Hewitt was born in Staffordshire and became involved in selling crockery. His obituary explains how "During the war of 1812 he took up arms on the side of his adopted country" (*Daily Milwaukee News* December 30, 1869). Ebenezer Cauldwell, a crockery dealer of New York, originally from Birmingham, England, joined the American navy in 1812 (Scott 1979: 80). His cousin, John Cauldwell Jr., whose birth was recorded at the Baptist Meeting House, Cannon Street, Birmingham in 1791, even became an Officer in the United States' Army, and died at Fort George, Niagara, in 1813 (*Commercial Advertiser*, New York September 1, 1813; see Pedigree 2). Families involved in the crockery business might be migrants, but willingly fought on the American side. Both Samuel and Thomas Bridgwood joined the American navy in 1812 (Scott 1979: 73). Peter Morton became a crockery dealer in his own right at Hartford, Connecticut, and later in New York. Although the Morton family were from Scotland, Peter's father, Thomas C. Morton, bequeathed "the family portrait of General Washington" to one of his daughters in his final will and testament (Will, Thomas C. Morton, 1833). The portrait was considered significant enough to be recorded and conveys a level of devotion to their adopted land. It then becomes the question whether the same kind of patriotism filtered down to the business and marketing behavior of crockery merchants.

As explained in Chapter 3, William Shufflebottom arrived in the United States in 1798 and became a crockery dealer in Philadelphia. On one occasion, he marketed ceramics that depicted Washington's home at Mount Vernon in 1823 (Figure 4.3). The wares advertised match extant pieces shown in Figure 4.4.

A straightforward explanation as to why importers (regardless of their own backgrounds or political views) marketed goods that celebrated American society was that this was based on selling goods that appealed to the demands of the market. In this respect, William Shufflebottom's background is irrelevant, as is how he defined himself in his adopted land. Those involved in mercantile pursuits simply marketed goods they hoped would sell in volume. It has not been readily explored whether the political agendas of importers and dealers ever impacted on what was sold. Shufflebottom advertised ceramics printed with images of Mount Vernon as being the "newest patterns," but as shown below, different types of vocabulary were also used when marketing ceramics aimed at the American market.

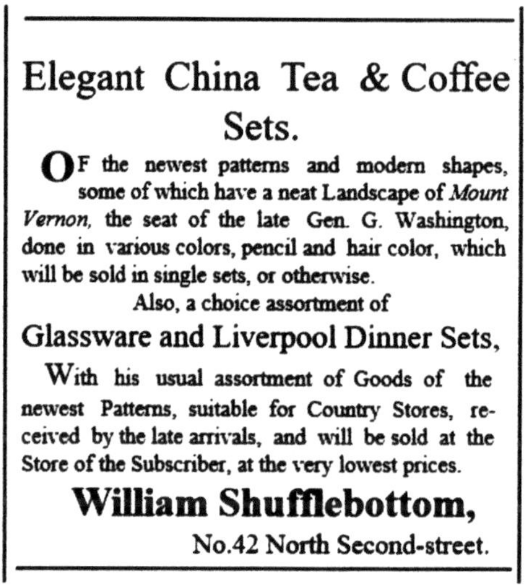

Elegant China Tea & Coffee Sets.

OF the newest patterns and modern shapes, some of which have a neat Landscape of *Mount Vernon,* the seat of the late Gen. G. Washington, done in various colors, pencil and hair color, which will be sold in single sets, or otherwise.

Also, a choice assortment of

Glassware and Liverpool Dinner Sets,

With his usual assortment of Goods of the newest Patterns, suitable for Country Stores, received by the late arrivals, and will be sold at the Store of the Subscriber, at the very lowest prices.

William Shufflebottom,

No.42 North Second-street.

Figure 4.3 *Poulson's American Daily Advertiser,* Philadelphia December 4, 1823.

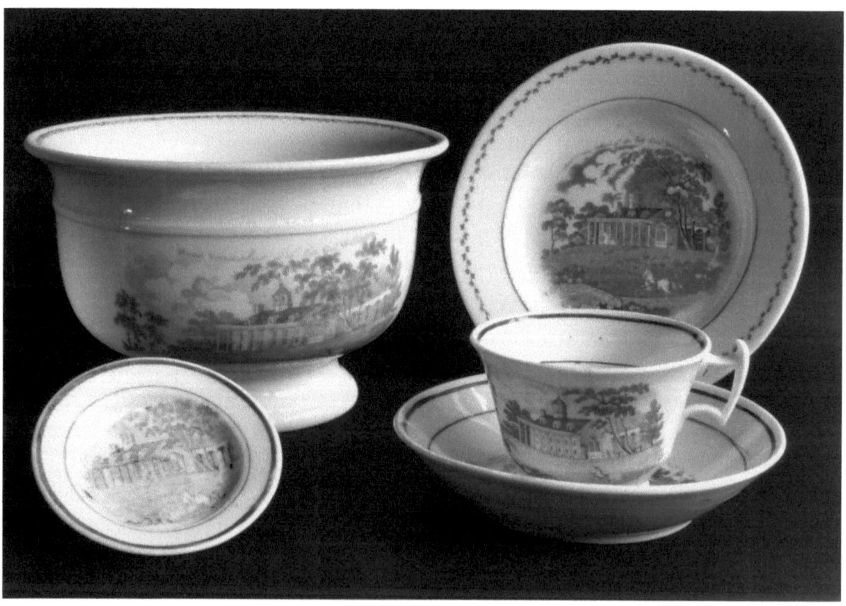

Figure 4.4 Tea-wares, bone china, transfer printed in variety of colors, with enamel and luster decoration. From left to right, top: Slop bowl, light-brown printed, and side plate, dark- brown printed, both titled, "Mount Vernon seat of the late Genl Washington." Probably Staffordshire, c.1820s. From left to right, bottom: Cup plate, purple printed, entitled "Mount Vernon," and tea-cup and saucer, grey-printed, entitled, "Mount Vernon seat of the late Genl Washington." Probably Staffordshire, c.1820s.

Cultural identity

The cultural identity of importers and dealers was far from straightforward. Indeed, the individuals involved in ceramics were sometimes more transient in where they lived. A background in ceramics seems to have facilitated their movement between the Staffordshire Potteries and America. However, in terms of wider debates concerning how new nations were formed, Benedict Anderson's *Imagined Communities* points out:

> There is also no doubt that improving trans-Atlantic communications, and the fact that the various Americas shared languages and cultures with their respective metropoles, meant a relatively rapid and easy transmission of the new economic and political doctrines being produced in Western Europe. The success of the Thirteen Colonies' revolt at the end of the 1770s, and the onset of the French Revolution at the end of the 1780s, did not fail to exert a powerful influence. Nothing confirms this "cultural revolution" more than the pervasive *republicanism* of the newly independent communities.
>
> (1991: 51)

Anderson adds how newspapers (which have also proved so useful as a method of exploring the complex lives of importers and dealers) acted in ways that brought these disparate people together. Anderson usefully describes the characteristics of the earliest American newspapers as:

> They began essentially as appendages of the market. Early gazettes contained—aside from news about the metropole—commercial news (when ships would arrive and depart, what prices were current for what commodities in what port), as well as colonial political appointments, marriages of the wealthy, and so forth. In other words, what brought together, on the same page, *this* marriage with *that* ship, *this* price with *that* bishop, was the very structure of the colonial administration and market-system itself.
>
> (1991: 62)

Based on these observations, Anderson develops the theory that, "from the start the nation was conceived in language, not in blood, and that one could be 'invited into' the imagined community" (1991: 145).

Yet when historians have examined the development of the Anglo-American trade, attention has often been drawn to the reliance of trading communities on kinship. Peter Mathias's chapter on "Risk, credit and kinship in early modern enterprise" explains how strong family ties were an integral part of business due to issues of credit and the high risks involved in trade. In the context of transatlantic trade and the kinship nexus, Mathias even emphasizes the point, stating how "As the common phrase puts it, 'blood is thicker than water'" (2000: 17). Here, rather paradoxically, kinship was important for developing mercantile trade, but not according to Anderson's view of creating a sense of nationhood.

A relationship with the "imagined community" was obviously a complex one. Those already in, and those who joined, came with a range of political views. But provisionally, it may be observed that they were not entirely neutral. The Wainwrights were English, but both married into Bostonian families. Peter Wainwright (the crockery importer, whom Theophilus Smith, earthenware manufacturer of Tunstall, had attempted to murder in 1800) continued to move between Liverpool and Boston. His brother, Henry Wainwright, also became involved in selling ceramics and, in typical mercantile fashion, traveled between Boston and England. In fact, his Boston obituary indicates that he had just returned from Liverpool, "bringing with him a daughter who had been settled in England with her three children" when he died while sea-bathing. As was customary for the time, Wainwright had gone to the bathing house on Western Avenue to hang up his clothes. His naked body found on the flats of the Charles River, in the vicinity of Cambridge, near Boston (*Universalist Magazine,* Boston September 8, 1827). One newspaper notice indicates that the intention of Henry Wainwright's European visit had "… been to make arrangements for further supplies of goods" (*Albany Argus and City Gazette,* Albany, NY September 4, 1827).

In 1790, the firm of Saxton & Wainwright advertised a selection of European and earthen and glass ware from their Boston store (*The Massachusetts Centinel,* Boston April 3, 1790). Prior to this, *The Boston Directory* of 1789, lists separately, Peter Wainwright, as a merchant, and William Saxton as a "grocer and Crockery-ware" dealer (Norman: 39, 44). The *Boston Directory* of 1796 lists "Saxton & Wainwright, crockery ware and dry goods" (West: 90). In 1804, the co-partnership between William Saxton and Henry Wainwright of Boston, and Peter Wainwright of Liverpool was dissolved, and a new partnership of William Saxton, Henry Wainwright, and Thomas Jackson was formed in 1805 (*Independent Chronicle,* Boston January 26, 1804; *Columbian Centinel,* Boston September 18, 1805). At this point, the business of Saxton, Wainwright and Jackson, and Peter Wainwright traded simultaneously in Boston, with both firms continuing to deal in ceramics and glass (*The New-England Palladium,* Boston October 1, 1806). They were substantial businesses. In 1819, Wainwright & Jackson advertised that they had, "imported from the first Manufacturers in Staffordshire, an extensive Assortment, consisting of 300 crates blue, olive and brown printed, lustre, fancy, enamelled [,] edged, and cream colored CROCKERY WARE" (*Columbian Centinel,* Boston January 16, 1819).

What is particularly intriguing is that when William Saxton died toward the end of 1806, his obituary explains how he had been a Boston merchant for upwards of twenty years and was "a native of England" dying at what was then considered the "advanced aged of 62" (born c.1744). Saxton's political dimension begins to emerge. His obituary described him as Dr William Saxton, stating how he:

> … arrived in the early period of our Revolutionary War. Being a decided friend to the rights and liberties of mankind, he of course viewed the conduct of the mother country in a correct light. Her encroachments he considered not only as affecting the colonies, but as indirectly, in their consequences, involving

the liberties of his native land. These sentiments he frequently expressed, and therefore as zealously did he approbate the proceedings of America in making that stand which ultimately secured her freedom and independence.

(*Independent Chronicle*, Boston January 1, 1807)

At this stage, it is unclear whether the political beliefs of individuals ever influenced business and marketing behavior, but this theme will be explored later in this chapter. The obituary also describes how, in terms of his religious beliefs, he was "candid and liberal," and the significance of religion is examined in Chapter 6. A notice that appeared in the press in early 1807 makes it clear that "Dr. William Saxton" was the same individual who was involved in the crockery trade, since his title was used in the notice explaining how Saxton, Wainwright & Jackson had lately been dissolved (Figure 4.5).

Quite why William Saxton—this well-educated and apparently vocal doctor—became involved in the crockery trade is unclear. But, interestingly, Elizabeth Wainwright's half-brother, John C. Howard, was also a doctor, and he became linked to the Wainwright business. During the 1790s and early 1800s, the Liverpool side of

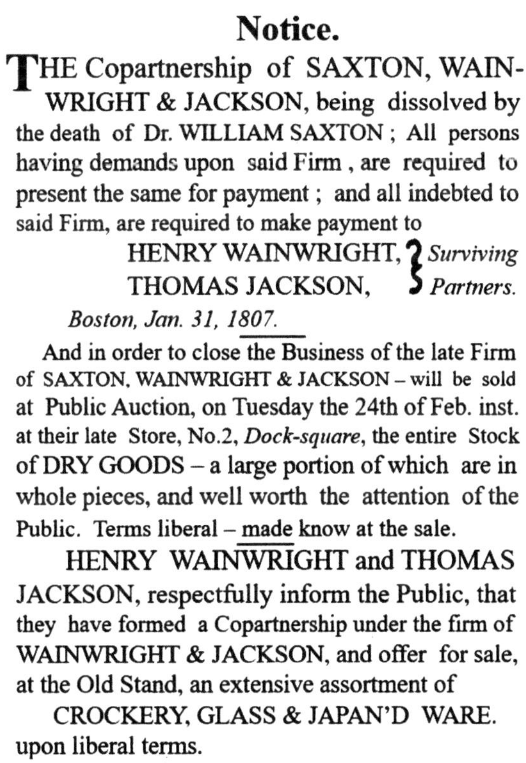

Notice.

THE Copartnership of SAXTON, WAINWRIGHT & JACKSON, being dissolved by the death of Dr. WILLIAM SAXTON ; All persons having demands upon said Firm , are required to present the same for payment ; and all indebted to said Firm, are required to make payment to

HENRY WAINWRIGHT, } *Surviving*
THOMAS JACKSON, } *Partners.*

Boston, Jan. 31, 1807.

And in order to close the Business of the late Firm of SAXTON, WAINWRIGHT & JACKSON – will be sold at Public Auction, on Tuesday the 24th of Feb. inst. at their late Store, No.2, *Dock-square*, the entire Stock of DRY GOODS – a large portion of which are in whole pieces, and well worth the attention of the Public. Terms liberal – made know at the sale.

HENRY WAINWRIGHT and THOMAS JACKSON, respectfully inform the Public, that they have formed a Copartnership under the firm of WAINWRIGHT & JACKSON, and offer for sale, at the Old Stand, an extensive assortment of

CROCKERY, GLASS & JAPAN'D WARE.

upon liberal terms.

Figure 4.5 *The Independent Chronicle*, Boston February 5, 1807.

the business was referred to as Wainwright, Cross and Howard in the British press. However, Howard advertised how he had "resumed the possession of Physic and Surgery" in Boston in 1803 (*Boston Commercial Gazette*, March 10, 1803). Dr John C. Howard became a member of the Boston Board of Health (*Columbian Centinel* Boston April 7, 1804). In Howard's case, the explanation for his temporary change in occupation is provided by a letter written to the *Columbian Centinel*. Here, it was claimed that due to ill-health, he had relinquished his medical profession and become involved in a "respectable mercantile establishment" in Liverpool, which presumably was referring to the firm owned by his brother-in-law, Peter Wainwright (December 16, 1807). Howard claimed that "being in *England* when the celebrated JENNER first promulgated his system of vaccination" inspired him to take an active role in continuing to use this procedure when he returned to Dorchester, just outside Boston. He continued that being "Aware of its slow progress in the country of its birth, and fearing its success would be still more limited here, I proposed gratuitously to inoculate for cow pock" (*Columbian Centinel* December 16, 1807). Howard's letter to the *Columbian Centinel* was motivated by a growing dispute with one Dr. Benjamin Waterhouse, who also claimed to have introduced this process of vaccination to the American public.

In a letter to his sister (Peter Wainwright's wife), John C. Howard mentions:

> "... When I reflect upon what I was and compare it with what I am [,] I can hardly conceive of how I could have overcome that reluctance to application of any kind which has been the Scylla and Charybdis of my early life. But you will perhaps regret that having now acquired some stability of character I should continue to pursue the occupation of merchant and that the prospect of riches and emoluments should bound my views".
>
> (Wainwright, Box 4, Folder 4.2, April 30, 1801)

As Howard explained (drawing on Homer's "Odessey" to emphasize the point), his current occupation was the lesser of two evils. It appears that becoming involved in mercantile activities was not what Dr John C. Howard wanted to do, but it provided some economic stability. Sheryllynne Haggerty's *"Merely for Money"?: Business Culture in the British Atlantic, 1750-1815* makes the valid assumption that merchants had to be skillful and knowledgeable of their trade, but this was not necessarily the case (2012: 26). Howard confessed to his sister how he was "mortified frequently to observe how many of my fellows are superior to me in point of information" (Wainwright, Box 4, Folder 4.2, April 30, 1801). Rather than actual ability, family and kinship remained paramount. In Howard's case, his interest still lay in medicine, but fortuitously, his temporary shift into mercantile activities in Liverpool enabled him to broadened his knowledge of vaccination techniques. Professions could change, and those who became involved in mercantile activity came from a variety of backgrounds.

Due to mercantile activity, life could become split between England and the United States. Peter Wainwright's children were born in Liverpool but largely educated in America (see Pedigree 1). In turn, they were affected by another wave of political unrest created by the Anglo-American War of 1812–14. In fact, Jonathan Wainwright (who later became Bishop of New York) wrote to his brother, Peter Wainwright junior, in Boston:

> You ask what shall I do if drafted. I advise by no means to say you are Englishman for you are not in reality you are naturalised. If you were to say that you were an Englishman they might take it into their heads to make you a prisoner of war. If you are so unfortunate to be drafted I think you had better pay the fine or hire a substitute.You can find out which is cheapest I think the fine is about 50 dollars but any lawyer will tell you. By all means I would recommend to you to call yourself an American and to act as one and it is your duty as you are naturalized and have the protection of the country. Don't meddle in politics I beg of you for it can do you no probable good & may do you harm.
>
> (Wainwright papers, Box 1, Folder 1.4, August 12, 1814)

There is a sense of the difficult decisions that had to be made, and an inescapable impact of the political situation, even for those who came from mercantile backgrounds.

Politics and migration

The possibility that the political situation resulted in the actual movement of people, such as Dr William Saxton, is significant, especially when returning to the issue of what was marketed by crockery importers and dealers. People were not entirely a blank canvas when recalling Benedict Anderson's notion of a new community. As an example, R. junior. & J. Eddowes were listed as "China Glass &c" dealers in the Philadelphia census of 1810, but an astonishing notice that appeared in a variety of English newspapers, such as the *Derby Mercury* and the *Bath Chronicle and Weekly Gazette,* claimed that the Ralph Eddowes, with his wife and five children, accompanied by four other families from Chester, had left England in 1794. They sailed on a ship called *Hope* from Liverpool, and in the case of Ralph Eddowes, had taken with him property valued at twenty-six thousand pounds (*Derby Mercury* September 4, 1794).

After Ralph Eddowes arrived in Philadelphia, he wrote a letter to William Roscoe of Liverpool in 1794, expressing fears that as a newcomer he could not afford to have a poor credit reputation (Haggerty 2012: 112). Initially, Eddowes senior imported a variety of dry goods to Philadelphia, including twenty-five crates of earthenware, in the late 1790s (*Philadelphia Gazette* July 25, 1796). However, as with other merchants, there was a tendency to become more specialized in the range of merchandise sold. By 1805, his two sons, Ralph junior. and John Eddowes, were advertising only ceramics and glass, and Ralph Eddowes senior acquired the stock in trade of George Marr, a Philadelphian "China Merchant" in 1807 (*Poulson's American Daily Advertiser*, Philadelphia May 4, 1807). The following advertisement of 1805 includes the reference to "Jugs, with an elegant print of

R. jun. & I. Eddowes'

Earthen-Ware and Glass-Store,

No. 27, north Third-street,

HAVE received by the Charlotte, and other late arrivals from Liverpool, a handsome assortment of articles in this line; among which are, Brown Line Dinner Setts; Jugs, with an elegant print of the President of the U. States, done by an eminent London artist.

They also offer to the notice of the public, and of the ladies in particular, a few setts of English burnished China (the first imported here) of superior taste; and they are also provided with a great variety of patterns of the same article, by which setts containing any required number of pieces may be ordered from the manufactory.

Japanned Ware of the newest and most elegant patterns.

Common articles in great variety.

Figure 4.6 *Poulson's American Daily Advertiser*, Philadelphia November 6, 1805.

the President of the U. States, done by an eminent London artist," imported from Liverpool (Figure 4.6).

As established in Chapter 1, a tremendous amount has been written about the American-themed Staffordshire wares, reflecting their collectable status and value. However, the location of R. & J. Eddowes' advertisement for jugs printed with the American president has, apparently, not been identified before, and thus remains the only identified advertisement that refers to American wares from this period. Presumably, given the date of the advertisement, the jugs would have depicted a portrait of Thomas Jefferson. It is ironic that it was actually Englishmen, rather than Americans, who advertised these jugs. Creamware jugs incorporating portraits of Jefferson are recorded, and some of these have been attributed to the Herculaneum Pottery, Liverpool (Hyland 2005: 56–65; McCauley 1942: 75–8; Teitelman et al. 2010: 90; see Figure 4.7). But, as Robin Emmerson succinctly argues when considering a Herculaneum invoice of wares dispatched to New York in 1802, "It is important for museums and collectors to realize that the relative proportions of the different types of wares that have survived intact are virtually in inverse proportion to their original share of the market" (2010: 250). Of the two hundred crates, only 3 percent of the total was described as printed wares.

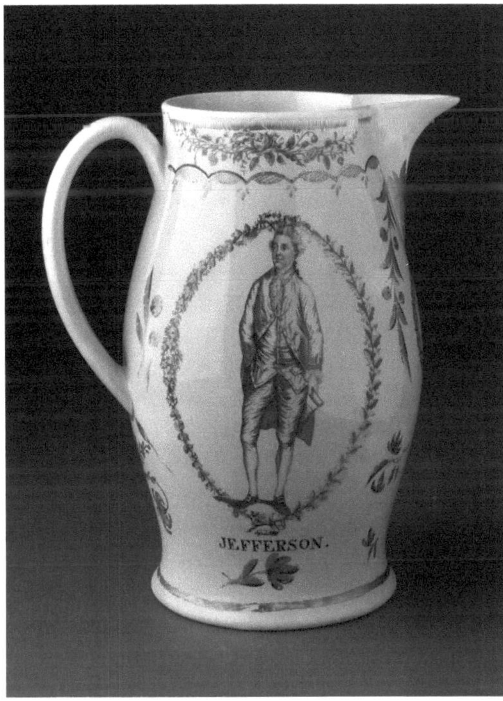

Figure 4.7 Jug, creamware, printed and gilt decoration, entitled "Jefferson." Possibly Herculaneum Pottery, Liverpool, c.1801-09, Gift of S. Robert Teitelman. Courtesy Winterthur Museum, Garden & Library.

The bulk of the invoice was for plain, or edged creamware, and even the printed wares were identified only as "Jugs copperplate" (Emmerson 2010: 250). Eddowes' reference to jugs with a print of the United States President is rare evidence of the marketing of this type of ware when, in the main, advertisements tended to use only generic ware-type terminology.

On another level, it is the political background of the Eddowes family that makes the advertisement more intriguing. Ralph Eddowes senior died in Philadelphia in 1833 aged eighty-two. His lengthy obituary provides evidence of why he migrated to the United States in the first place:

> Mr. Eddowes was born in the city of Chester, England, in the year 1751, where he very early distinguished himself as a Champion of Freedom in the celebrated suit which he instituted (and which was carried to the House of Lords) against the municipal authorities of that ancient city for the corruption of elections, and which resulted partly in his favor: this gained him admiration and respect of the citizens of his native place, and the memory of this act is cherished to this day.
> (*National Gazette,* Philadelphia April 4, 1833)

The legal suit was concerned with the rights of the citizens and freemen of Chester to annually elect the mayor, the alderman, and their council (*Chester Chronicle,* April 23; April 30, 1790). The obituary then explains how he became a merchant in Liverpool and associated with William Roscoe (the Liverpool attorney, historian, and abolitionist) and Dr James Currie (member of the Liverpool Literary Society). However, it then continues:

> … but his enthusiastic love of liberty could not be indulged in his native country, where an intolerant spirit succeeded the French Revolution, and threatened the avowed friends of Freedom, and he embarked with his family for the United States, where they arrived in 1794.
>
> (*National Gazette,* Philadelphia April 4, 1833)

The obituary finishes by explaining how Ralph Eddowes formed a Christian Society following Unitarian views (*National Gazette*, Philadelphia April 4, 1833). In one obituary published in England, it is indicated that Ralph Eddowes was taught by Dr Joseph Priestley when he attended Nantwich school, Cheshire, in the late 1750s (*The Unitarian Chronicle for 1833*: 215–9). Ralph Eddowes junior (who advertised the jugs with the image of the American President) was about twelve when the family emigrated to the United States.

The Eddowes family is evidence of an articulate, well-educated mercantile class whose migration to the United States was a reflection of the political situation. In this instance, understanding their background demonstrates how they were a disaffected English family who, interestingly, marketed politically orientated ceramics when in America. The partnership that existed between Ralph Eddowes junior and John Eddowes was dissolved in 1813 (*Poulson's American Daily Advertiser* April 8, 1813), but both continued to import ceramics independently (*Press*, Philadelphia, May 29, 1816; *Grotjan's Philadelphia Public Sale Report* November 20, 1820).

Inevitably, individuals were of different political persuasions, and this applied equally to those involved in trade. When Thomas Jefferson had just been elected as the American president, Dr John C. Howard wrote to his sister, Elizabeth Wainwright, in Liverpool:

> I cannot rejoice with you that the President's changed and were you upon the spot I think a becoming diference[sic] for the opinions of the approved sages of our country would create even in your mind a degree of scepticism of the propriety of the measure. We are not virtuous to be free as some would explain freedom …
>
> (Wainwright, Box 4, Folder 4.2, April 27, 1801)

Whereas Dr John C. Howard (the partner of Peter Wainwright) was skeptical about Thomas Jefferson, the Eddowes family were strong supporters. Ralph Eddowes senior actually wrote to Thomas Jefferson in 1807, explaining that:

> I was in the earlier part of my life a pupil of the venerable Priestley, and came with alarge family to this country in the same year he did & from motives somewhat similar tho rather of a civil than a religious nature. My attachment to the principles on which the Constitution of the U.S. is founded has gathered

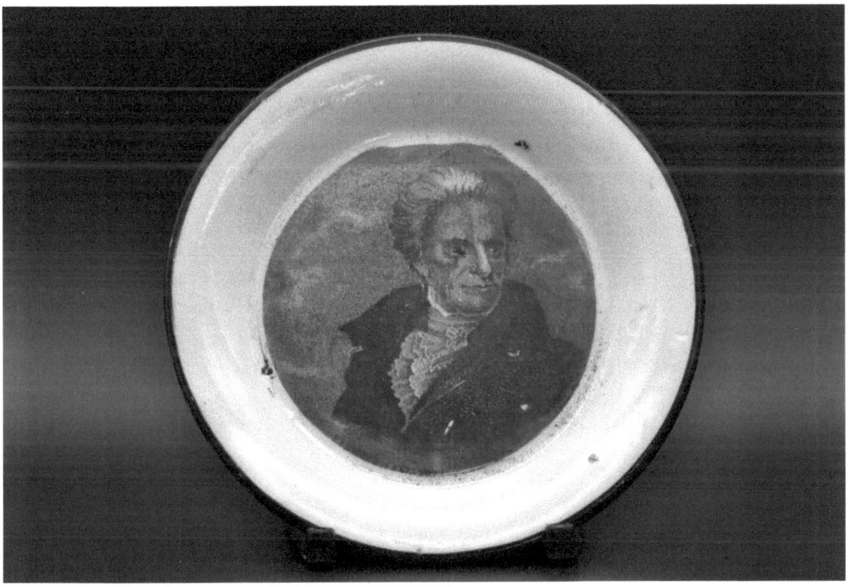

Figure 4.11 Cup plate, earthenware, black printed and black enamel rim, depicting Andrew Jackson. Beneath the portrait is only a fragment of the title, which reads (based on other extant versions) "Hero of New Orleans." This is a reference to General Andrew Jackson winning the battle of New Orleans, against the British in 1815. Impressed "WOOD". Manufactured by Enoch Wood & Sons, Burslem, c.1824–28.

Thus, Robert H. Miller took an active part in the civic debates of that era and was even a member of the Democratic Tippecanoe Club, which supported Harrison and Tyler. He was also involved in the Young Whigs of Alexandria as a member of the organization. Miller proposed that a delegation should attend a Harrison Convention, to be held in Baltimore on May 4 (*Alexandria Gazette and Virginia Advertiser* April 18, 1840). Furthermore, Miller pointed out that since the town of Alexandria was "honored almost daily by an intimate and familiar intercourse with that illustrious man [George Washington] ..." it was resolved that:

> ... as Virginians in heart, and as the sons of Virginians, the Whigs of Alexandria in meeting assembled, repudiate and utterly denounce all and any attempts to hush the voice of their disapprobation of the present Executive, and the party by which he has sustained by any threats whatsoever.
>
> (*Alexandria Gazette* April 18, 1840)

What is significant here is how, just as Miller attended meetings declaring support for General Harrison, he began to market ceramics that depicted "Harrison and Log Cabin engravings ..." Retiring to a log cabin was initially made as a derogatory remark against the elderly General Harrison. However, supporters took this comment and an image of a log cabin to, then, reinforce Harrrison's down-to-earth values and affinity with the common man (Figure 4.12). Miller took the surprising course of even stipulating that "Whig Merchants" would be given credit. Advertisements placed during 1840 and into the early part of 1841 indicated that:

By an early arrival, R. H. M. expects supplies of ware with Harrison and Log Cabin engravings, from designs sent out to the Potteries by himself. Whig merchants will be supplied upon the "*Credit System*" at reasonable prices, in time to celebrate the approaching triumph of correct principles (*Alexandria Gazette* September 19, 1840).

More than simply promote ceramics that might appeal to consumers of the same political persuasion, Robert H. Miller's business behavior even conveys a bias toward the Whig party.

The political dimension of importers should be considered as another way of understanding why certain ceramic designs were produced for the American market. Whereas Ellouise Baker Larsen's *American Historical Views on Staffordshire China* refers to an example of a printed plate bearing the portrait of General Harrison and backstamped "James Tams & Co., Importers, Philadelphia,"

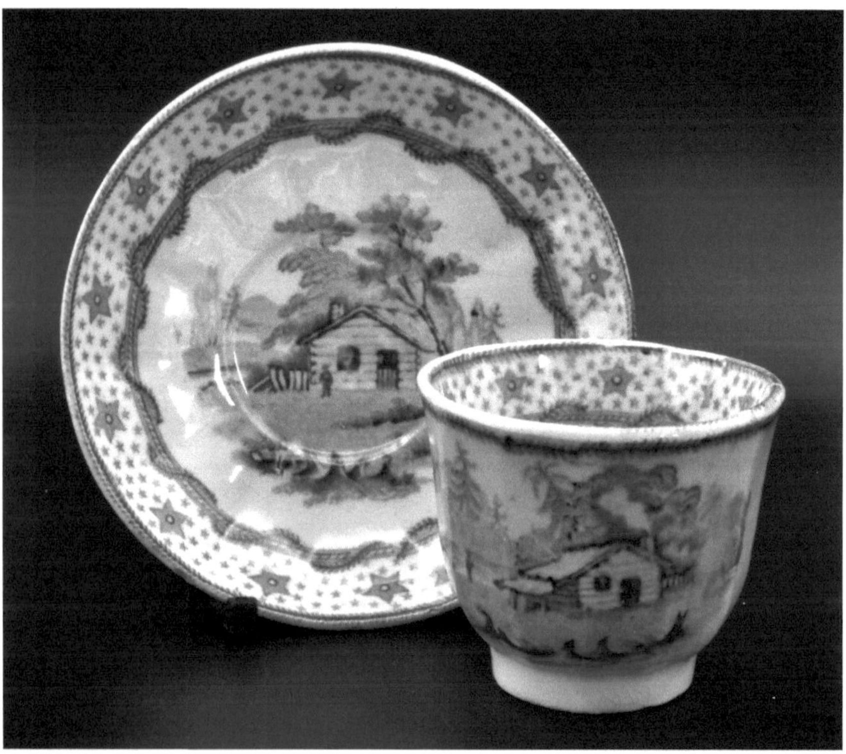

Figure 4.12 Miniature cup and saucer, earthenware, blue printed image of a log cabin. Backstamped as "Columbian Star, 444, Oct [October] 28th 1840, Jno [John] Ridgway." John Ridgway, Shelton, Staffordshire, c.1840.

the belief was that it was ordered by Mr. John Weatherill of Philadelphia, "the purchaser," to be presented to his guests (1939: 177). While this does importantly begin to establish how consumers could influence production, the case of Robert H. Miller introduces the idea that importers and dealers, themselves, occupied a political point of view, which in turn influenced what was commissioned.

Summary

When comparing the backgrounds of crockery importers and dealers with their actual advertising, there is evidence of political sympathies informing marketing strategy. Additionally, political views impacted on what ceramic designs were commissioned from manufacturers. Once the influence of the intermediary is more readily appreciated, it begins to broaden the understanding of why some ceramics were manufactured for the American market. Clearly, the motivation to produce politically related commodities did not entirely stem from manufacturers, though this has often been considered to be the case. Ann Withington's chapter on "Manufacturing and Selling the American Revolution" points out how foreign ceramic producers readily made "use of the American Revolution and republican sentiment to sell their products," arguing that these products helped to "stimulate American appetites and turn Americans into consumers of souvenirs" (1994: 292–3). Perceived in this way, the production of American-themed commodities impacted on consumption, although Withington's interpretation stems from a "focus on the object, its producers, or its owner, who may or may not also have been the buyer" (1994: 288). What actually motivated the production of American-themed wares is even more complex, when the marketing of the intermediary is also considered. Robert Miller apparently commissioned ceramics that referred to Andrew Jackson and William Harrison because these reflected his *own* political views. This is supported by his offering more favorable credit terms to other Whig merchants. It would appear that Miller's motivation was to deploy printed ceramics to further promote a political cause. Apparently, the demand for these goods was rather dependent on the political allegiance of the consumer. It was not necessarily as straightforward as Ann Withington's interpretation of American-themed wares stimulating consumption or reflecting a national culture.

Although Benedict Anderson argued in *Imagined Communities* that language was central to building an identity, he still refers to how "The Protestant, English-speaking creoles to the north were much more favorably situated for realizing the idea of 'America' and indeed eventually succeeded in appropriating the everyday title of 'Americans'" (1991: 63). Here, Anderson briefly draws attention to how religion was an influential factor in shaping American society and contributing to a sense of identity. In theory, while a common language was important, in reality, blood ties and kinship may also be related to religion. It is noticeable how the interrelated families connected to the ceramic trade also belonged to the same religious sects. This leads to a consideration of how far religion impacted on what was commissioned and marketed, to be developed in later chapters.

Chapter 5

DYNASTIES AND INTERCONNECTIONS

It might be reasonably anticipated that in the early periods of conducting the Anglo-American trade, kinship provided a reliable and secure way to carry out business transactions. Indeed, many writers, when discussing the development of the transatlantic trade, have recognized the significance of family ties in creating business networks and facilitating access to credit (Mathias 2000: 25; Rose 2000: 60; Haggerty 2012: 165). Once families were involved in the crockery trade, it was characteristic for them to remain in this business for many years, although this is contrary to how other historians have viewed the broader development of commerce in the United States. For instance, Thomas C. Cochran's *Frontiers of Change: Early Industrialism in America* suggests that American businesses were less inclined to become long-term family dynasties because:

> Few sons felt the obligation, common in continental Europe, to perpetuate the farm or firm as a family enterprise. Money, or "economic rationality," rather than land and family ties, was the common measuring rod of society. New opportunities drew away the ablest young men, and partnerships continually changed.
>
> (1981: 12–3)

While the United States was undeniably entrepreneurial and expanding (1981: 15), Cochran's observations do not apply particularly well with the crockery trade, leading to a consideration as to why this was the case. While interrelated families were capable of moving to different locations, they still remained linked to the crockery trade. For example, the Hastings family of Boston had ties to the Sampson family, who then developed links to Cincinnati (see Pedigree 6). This chapter examines examples of crockery importers and dealers who, as it turned out, had long-term and then interconnected links to the trade, leading to an examination of whether their backgrounds ever impacted on marketing.

Dynastic tendencies

Just as dynastic tendencies occurred within the manufacturing community of the Staffordshire Potteries, the same characteristic continued with those who became the importers and dealers in ceramics. Families involved in the ceramic trade remained so for decades; their businesses were shared between various members of the family, and then passed from one generation to the next. For a short period, Joseph S. Hastings had a business connection with Gilman Collamore in Boston (see Pedigree 6 and 11). Gilman then formed a partnership with his brother, Horace Collamore, which lasted until 1817 (*Repertory*, Boston September 7, 1810; *Columbian Centinel*, Boston April 19, 1817). As an aside to his mercantile activities, Horace Collamore was a Freemason. In this capacity, he arranged for "two accompanying Pitchers to be manufactured" and presented to the Columbian Lodge of Boston in 1819. The Lodge gratefully recorded how the "elegant pitchers had appropriate Masonic emblems" and were a "superb" additional adornment to their interiors (Stelling 2017: 304). The pitchers are still preserved by the Columbian Lodge, proudly bearing the gilt inscription "Presented / to the / Columbian Lodge / by / RW [Right Worshipful] Horace Collamore." Here is more evidence of how importers acted in accordance with their own interests, beyond the needs of the market.

Colonel John Collamore (a brother of Gilman and Horace) had a number of sons who also became involved in the crockery trade. These were Ebenezer, Davis, and Gilman Collamore, dealers in New York (*Evening Post*, New York January 2, 1833), and John junior, George E., and Andrew F. Collamore, based in Boston (see Pedigree 11). Andrew F. Collamore's connection to the trade was tragically cut short, as, along with another thirty pitiful souls, he was lost on board the shipwrecked steamer, *Atlantic*, on its way to New York, in 1846. Andrew was due to spend Thanksgiving with his fiancée (*Christian Watchman*, Boston December 4, 1846). Even taking a short journey was perilous, and all too easily the more comfortable lives of these merchants could be devastated.

When the Boston partnership between Horace Collamore and William Churchill (another crockery dealer) was dissolved in 1824, Horace was immediately replaced by one of his nephews, John Collamore junior, illustrating the importance of the family connection (*Columbian Centinel*, Boston March 3, 1824). When Ebenezer Collamore died in 1884, it is stated that "Most of his life was passed in New York, where he was engaged in the china and glassware trade" (*Boston Morning Journal*, March 6, 1884). Alternatively, the obituary of Gilman Collamore explained how he had imported ceramics for over thirty years in New York from 1854, and he was described as a prominent member of the New England Society (*New York Herald*, March 16, 1888) (see Pedigree 11).

Chapter 3 discussed how marriages cemented links between many of the families involved in the ceramic trade. In addition, women could exercise another crucial role. For instance, Robinson Tyndale was a china merchant in Philadelphia from the early 1810s, but he died in 1842 (Paxton 1813; *The American Sentinel* Philadelphia, May 27, 1842). His wife, Sarah Tyndale, was then listed as china merchant in city directories (M'Elroy 1844). Not unreasonably, it has been argued that Sarah Tyndale (nee Thorn) already had a knowledge of the ceramic trade, since her step-father, Sharon Carter, was a crockery dealer in Philadelphia (Klepp 2021: 245). Carter even established a partnership with Robinson Tyndale in 1815 (*Poulson's American Daily Advertiser*, Philadelphia March 20, 1815).

RICH CHINA DINNER, DESSERT AND TEA SETS, &c., &c., &c.

THE subscriber, (intending to resign business in a few months to the younger branches of her family,) is anxious to dispose of her present stock of rich goods previous to retiring, and will sell her very splendid stock of rich dinner, dessert, tea and toilet sets, rich vases, &c., &c., *at less prices than they can be imported for.*

Persons wishing to supply themselves with china and glass, will find a very large and well-selected assortment, *at prices much below the usual rates.*

SARAH TYNDALE,
219 Chestnut street,
Philadelphia.

Figure 5.1 *The Daily Union*, Washington DC January 2, 1846.

Correspondence also suggests that Sarah was involved in running the store when Robinson was away receiving treatments for cancer before he died (Klepp 2021: 246). More than being a straightforward case of remaining in the crockery trade for her own self-preservation, continuing to run the business enabled Sarah's children to inherit the firm in a later period. Indeed, one advertisement declared how she was "intending to resign business in a few months to the younger branches of her family" (*The Daily Union*, Washington DC January 2, 1846) (Figure 5.1).

American advertising was often so much more than merely listing merchandise. On occasion, advertisements could be revealing of the intentions of a merchant, and in this case, evidence of how women played a significant, and not necessarily inconspicuous role, in carrying out the crockery trade. It was acknowledged in the 1850s how Sarah Tyndale had progressively employed female sales clerks in her store (Klepp 2021: 251–2). After Sarah Tyndale withdrew from the crockery business, the entire stock was acquired by her son, Hector Tyndale, and Edward P. Mitchell (a son-in-law), and the firm became known as Tyndale & Mitchell (*Public Ledger* Philadelphia, July 27, 1846). As Hector Tyndale was born in 1821, he probably lacked the experience to run the crockery business immediately after his father died in 1842.

After Sarah Tyndale retired, aged around fifty-three years, she devoted more attention to issues of social agitation. In a speech delivered at a "Women's Rights Convention" held at Worcester, Massachusetts, it was explained how her husband had died in debt, yet she had risen to be the "proprietor of one of the largest and most beautiful China establishments in this country or the world." Exaggerated as this observation may be, it still highlights how important women could be in the American crockery trade. As an advocate of women's abilities, Sarah Tyndale set about visiting all the houses of bad repute in Philadelphia, encouraging over "three hundred young women to return to the path of virtue" by finding them homes or employment (*National Anti-Slavery Standard*, New York October 31, 1850). She associated with intellectuals, such as the foremost American poet, Walter Whitman, and through her accumulated wealth, financially assisted him in publishing an edition of *Leaves of Grass*. On July 1, 1857, she wrote to Whitman, who resided in Brooklyn, "A friend in the City will send you a check today for fifty dollars Hector would be very glad to do it, but he left the City last Monday" (Kohn, *The Walt Whitman Archive*). (Hector Tyndale also came to know Whitman.) Sarah Tyndale was, in the words of her obituary, "much interested in plans for the reorganization of society, with a view to the better protection of the interests of the laborer against the exorbitant demands of capital" (*National Anti-Slavery Standard*, New York, September 3, 1859).

Meaningful benefits could be derived from a profitable crockery business. However, this was rather dependent on the successful firms being maintained by a single family over a long period of time. How far the crockery trade remained a tightly controlled business is illustrated by the example of the Shirley family. William W. Shirley was baptized in Hanley in 1797 and came from a family background of manufacturing. William arrived in New York in 1818, aged 21 (Scott 1981: 280), and then became a crockery importer (see Pedigree 12). Until 1819, William Shirley was in partnership with Sampson Tams, who is discussed below (*New York Gazette and General Advertiser* August 16, 1819). In 1821, William W. Shirley advertised a wholesale and retail ceramic and glass warehouse at "No.43 Maiden-lane, sign of the large Blue Pitcher" (Figure 5.2).

The use of a shop sign outside the establishment was a practice already adopted by English crockery dealers in London by the eighteenth century (Young 1999: 171). During 1823, William W. Shirley advertised that he stocked "American scenery" table, tea and toilet ware (*Evening Post*, New York June 3, 1823; *New York Daily Advertiser* September 12, 1823). By 1824, Shirley's business had expanded enough to warrant running what was called a "Wholesale Earthen Ware and Glass Store" at No.6 Fletcher and the "Retail Store" at 43 Maiden Lane (*Evening Post* March 15, 1824). The two stores were advertised separately, or the businesses were referred to jointly (Figure 5.3).

William Shirley was able to deal in crockery and glass from more than one New York store because he was in a co-partnership with a brother, Cephas Shirley, who arrived in New York in 1825, aged thirty-one (Scott 1981: 281). Occasionally, Shirley's advertisements mention actual Staffordshire firms, such as Ridgway's table tea and toilet ware and Mayer's table and tea ware in 1830 (*New York Commercial Advertiser* March 31, 1830).

WHOLESALE & RETAIL
CHINA, EARTHEN & GLASS WAREHOUSE,
No. 43 Maiden-lane, sign of the large Blue Pitcher.

WM. W. SHIRLEY has received by the late arrivals, and now opened, a general assortment of the above articles, consisting of rich blue Dinner, Tea and Coffee Services; Pitchers of various sizes and colors ; cut and plain glass Tumblers, Wines, Decanters, &c. of numerous patterns.

N.B. All kinds of Common Ware for Country Stores, sold at the lowest prices.

Figure 5.2 *New York Gazette* June 20, 1821.

WM. W. SHIRLEY'S Wholesale Earthen Ware and Glass Store. No.6 Fletcher, 3d door from Pearl street.

Southern and Country Orders executed at the lowest prices.

Original Packages of Glass and Earthenware on consignment, direct from the manufactories.

RETAIL STORE, No.43 Maiden lane, where families will find a rich and extensive assortment of Cut Glass, China, fine and common Ware, at the lowest city prices.

N.B. The greatest care observed in packing.

Figure 5.3 *Evening Post*, New York April 9, 1824.

Prior to his arrival in the United States, a co-partnership existed between Cephas Shirley and Moses Ellis of Shelton, described as "Printers and Enamellers of Earthenware," until this was dissolved in October 1817 (*The London Gazette* November 1, 1817). Cephas Shirley was then described as an earthenware manufacturer in Pigot's *Commercial Directory* for 1818–20 and was later recorded as a partner in a business called Dean & Co., earthenware manufacturers of Hanley (*Staffordshire Advertiser* June 24, 1820). A notice in *The London Gazette* concerning "Petitions of Insolvent Debtors" described Cephas and Benjamin Shirley as selling ceramics in London, on September 23, 1823.

The Shirley family established a number of ceramic and glass-related businesses, supporting Sheryllynne Haggerty's notion of the "family nexus." A nephew (also called William Shirley) became a ceramic importer in Baltimore from the 1840s (see Pedigree 12). As a result of these family ties, they were in a position to promote one another's different businesses. Interestingly, on one occasion, William W. Shirley of New York mentions the availability of "Shirley & Co's New Brunswick Stone Ware." There is a New Brunswick in the state of New Jersey (Figure 5.4).

From the 1840s, William W. Shirley of New York began to stress that auctioneering was central to his business, and confirming this shift in focus,

Glass Ware, China, Earthen Ware, Furnaces, Stone Ware, &c.

WM. W. SHIRLEY, Commission Warehouse, No. 90 Maiden lane, opposite Gold Street, offers at the lowest market prices –

34 boxes, each an India China Dinner Set
30 crates, do do assortment of Furnaces
30 casks English Flint Tumblers and Wines
4 do do Decanters
5 boxes Plated Castor Frames, low priced
50 do green and red do, a superior article
10 hhds Candle Shades, for exportation.
Furniture Knobs, various patterns, 2 ¼ to 1inch
70 crates assorted Earthen ware

Jno. & Richd. Fisher's Druggist, Chemist, and other Glass Ware, for sale at their prices, and others received for their factory.

Shirley & Co's New Brunswick Stone Ware

Consignments of China, Earthen Ware, and Glass, respectfully solicited.

Cheap storage for one to 200 packages.

Figure 5.4 *Evening Post*, New York June 14, 1830.

NEW YORK,

WM. W. SHIRLEY, AUCTIONEER

GLASSWARE - AUCTION NOTICE to Druggist and Crockery dealers - TUESDAY, September 24th, 10 o'clock, at No. 130 Maiden Lane, corner of Water st. up stairs. Catalogue sale from the shelves of a large and general assortment of Druggist and other glassware, in lots to suit purchasers. Also, 100 packages specie Jars, all sizes, Tinctures, Mortars and Pestles, &c. Also, rich cut Mirror Dishes; Decanters; Tumblers; Bowls; hall Lamps, &c. Sale peremptory, for cash. Goods well packed for shipping at moderate charge.

N. B. - Orders for purchase sent to Mr. W. Shirley, No. 18 Platt street, New York will receive honorable attention. W. W. S. solicits consignments to the auction room, No.18 Platt street for public and private sale; also attends to the purchase of merchandize generally. Catalogues may be had of

Mr. WM. SHIRLEY,
South Calvert st

Figure 5.5 *American and Commercial Advertiser,* Baltimore September 21, 1844.

William Shirley of Baltimore advertised his uncle's New York auction house, even taking responsibility for distributing catalogues (Figure 5.5).

In 1844, William Shirley offered "100 crates printed and common ware" from his South Calvert Street store, supporting a view that he had become a prominent crockery dealer in Baltimore (*American and Commercial Daily Advertiser*, Baltimore September 7, 1844). According to his obituary, William Shirley was actually born in London in 1816 (which relates to the Shirleys having connections to selling ceramics in London), and intriguingly, it was reported how he was "sent to Brussels, Belgium, to learn the queensware business, following the example of nearly all of his family." When he arrived in Baltimore aged eighteen (c.1834), he entered the firm of Earnest & Cowles, wholesale crockery dealers. Nine years later, he purchased the wholesale crockery business of Samuel Clements, on South Calvert Street (c.1843). William's son, Henry C. Shirley, joined this crockery business in 1865 (*The Sun*, Baltimore, February 18, 1865), and his name appears on billheads, even incorporating the phrase "Manufacturers of Stoneware" (Figure 5.6). William Shirley's obituary draws attention to ties to Staffordshire and to other members of the family network who also had links to selling ceramics:

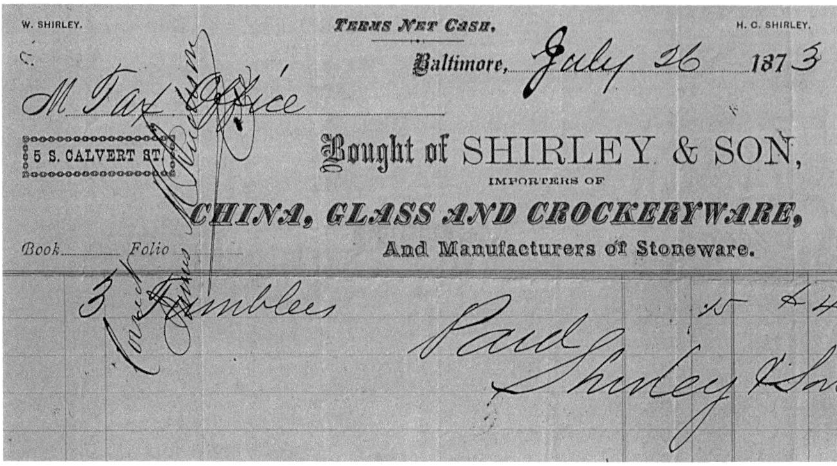
W. SHIRLEY. TERMS NET CASH. H. C. SHIRLEY.

Baltimore, July 26 1873

M Tax Office

5 S. CALVERT ST.

Bought of SHIRLEY & SON,

IMPORTERS OF

CHINA, GLASS AND CROCKERYWARE,

And Manufacturers of Stoneware.

Book Folio

3 Tumblers

Paid Shirley & Son

Figure 5.6 Invoice, Shirley & Son, Baltimore, for glass tumblers sold to the tax office. Dated July 26, 1873.

> He [William Shirley] was descended from the old Staffordshire family of Shirleys, one of the most ancient and respect families of England. He is survived by two sons – Messrs. Henry C. and W. W. Shirley – one daughter – Miss Hannah Shirley – and two grandsons – Capt. Joseph W. Shirley of Troop A. Maryland National Guard, and Mr. Harry Shirley. A brother, Mr. John Shirley, of San Francisco, also survives him.
>
> (*The Sun*, Baltimore December 20, 1900)

The obituary of John Shirley of San Francisco indicates that he was involved with his brother's Baltimore business in 1843, but was based in California from 1849, and allegedly established the first crockery house on the west coast (*San Francisco Chronicle* February 12, 1911). Shirley & Bayley, crockery merchants, advertised in San Francisco in the 1850s (*San Francisco Evening Journal* December 4, 1852; *Daily Placer Times and Transcript*, San Francisco June 14, 1854). The Shirley family, alone, created an elaborate network of ceramic importing businesses, branching from the east coast to developing western markets, and their involvement in the ceramics trade continued into the early twentieth century (*Baltimore American* November 30, 1917). Here is evidence of how inland businesses remained controlled by established specialists rather than moving into the hands of pioneering migrants, carving out new opportunities.

Previous research into the family structure of those involved in the ceramic industry points out how the sons of manufacturers "came to the business early; and they inherited the advantages their fathers had made for them" (Dupree 1995: 187), and this pattern seems to have extended to the importing and selling of ceramics.

Profit

The propensity to remain in the crockery trade rather than Cochran's proposed model of movement into other opportunities offered by American society requires an explanation. In 1860, when aged forty-two, William Shirley, the crockery dealer of Baltimore (and the nephew of William W. Shirley of New York) had real estate worth $5,000 and a personal estate worth $3,000. After approximately fifty years of dealing in china and glass, he had amassed an estate worth $300,000 (Census, Baltimore, 1860; *The Sun*, Baltimore, December 27, 1900). His son also became a crockery dealer (see Pedigree 12). The importers, John Collamore (Pedigree 11), Andrew T. Hall (mentioned in Pedigree 6), and Otis Norcross (Pedigree 7) were all described as millionaires due to their involvement in the Boston crockery trade (*Boston Herald* August 17, 1887). Based on obituaries, the other members of the Collamore family were located in Boston and New York and remained in the crockery business for decades. Henry Winkley of Philadelphia was described as another millionaire crockery dealer, and in this position was able to make a significant contribution to the development of New England education, bequeathing sums such as $50,000 to Williams College and $30,000 to Amherst College, both in Massachusetts, and $20,000 to Dartmouth College in New Hampshire (*Boston Daily Advertiser* August 11, 1888).

Many of the importers and dealers examined above developed successful businesses. Sampson Tams was recorded in Philadelphia in 1846 as "An Englishman by birth; came to this country very poor, and by enterprise and industry in the china and crockery business amassed this large fortune," estimated to be $100,000. Of Kerr & Son it was recorded, "Made their money in the china and crockery business; came to this country poor; are Europeans by birth." Their wealth was estimated to be $50,000 (By a merchant of Philadelphia 1846: 34, 61).

The accumulation of wealth had consequences and opened up various possibilities. Members of the Davenport family first appeared as crockery dealers in New York City directories in 1842 (Longworth 1842). An indication of their growing position in the trade is a backstamp declaring "Manufactured for Davenport Bros. 203 Greenwich St. N. Y.," which appeared on printed ceramics manufactured by Joseph Clementson of Shelton, dating from the 1850s (Figures 5.7 and 5.8). A surviving invoice of 1879 declares that the firm consisted of Thomas, James S. and Samuel W. Davenport (see Figure 5.9). Typically, as this business developed, members of the next generation, or the extended family, became involved. For instance, Thomas's son, William W. Davenport, and his son-in-law, John V. Barkelow, were employed as clerks (Census, Jersey City, 1880).

Despite what was declared on the 1879 invoice, the 1870 census referred to Samuel W. Davenport as a retired merchant, owning real estate worth $30,000. Only Thomas and James Davenport were still active as crockery merchants. Commercial success assisted in diversification. By the 1880 census, Samuel W. Davenport was no longer in retirement but was President of the City Pottery, Trenton (Census,

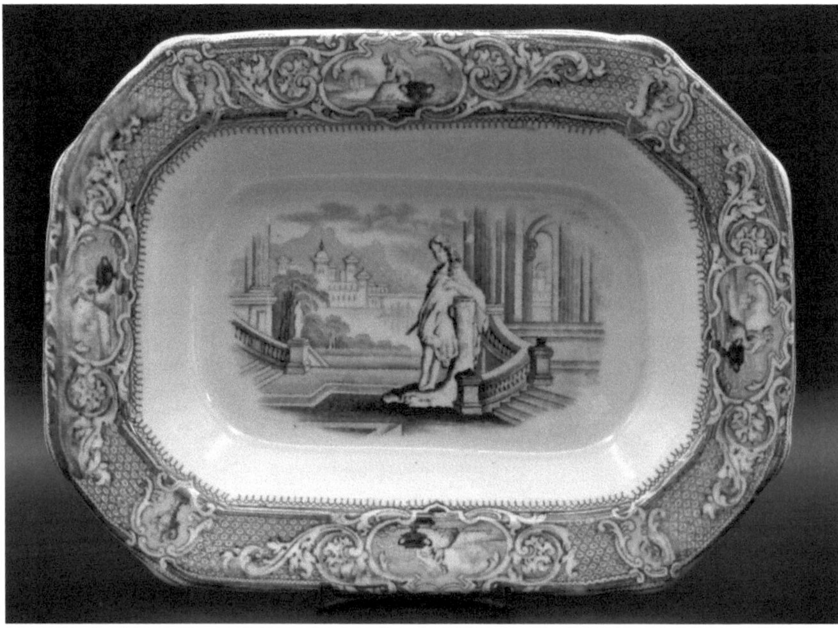

Figure 5.7 Side dish, earthenware, blue printed, "Sydenham" pattern, Joseph Clementson, Hanley, c.1856–70.

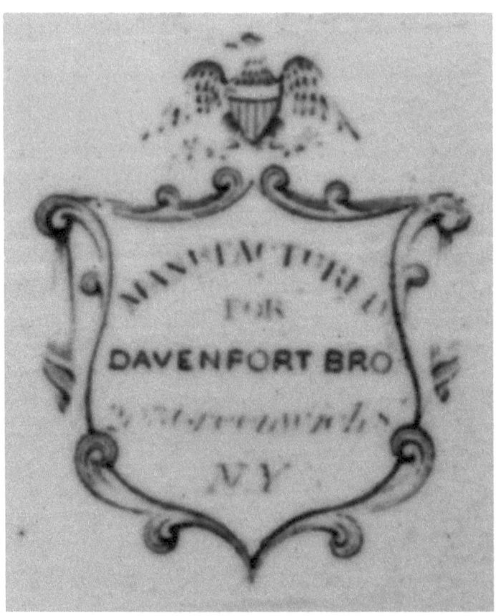

Figure 5.8 Backstamp (of Figure 5.7), "Manufactured For/ Davenport Bro/ 203 Greenwich St / N.Y."

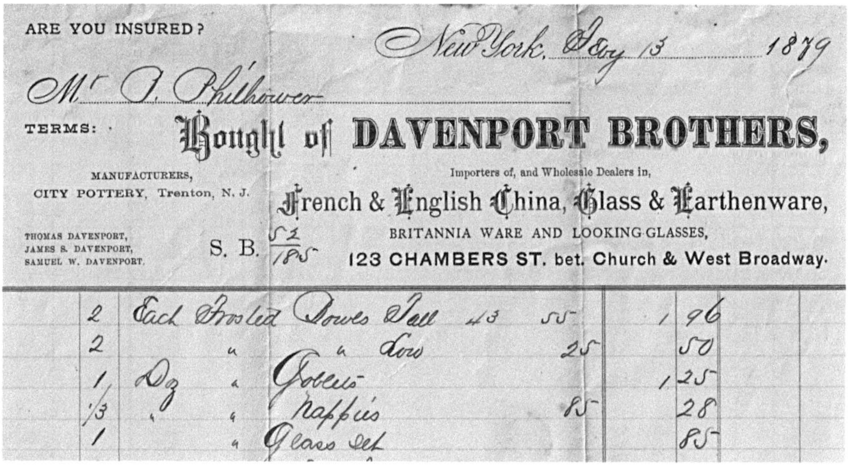
ARE YOU INSURED?

New York, Feby 13 1879

Mr O. Philhower

TERMS:

Bought of DAVENPORT BROTHERS,

MANUFACTURERS,
CITY POTTERY, Trenton, N. J.

Importers of, and Wholesale Dealers in,

French & English China, Glass & Earthenware,

BRITANNIA WARE AND LOOKING GLASSES,

THOMAS DAVENPORT,
JAMES S. DAVENPORT,
SAMUEL W. DAVENPORT.

S. B. 52 / 185

123 CHAMBERS ST. bet. Church & West Broadway.

2	Each Frosted Bowls Tall	43	55	1 96
2	" " Low		25	50
1	Dz " Goblets			1 25
1/3	" " Nappies		85	28
1	" Glass Set			85

Figure 5.9 Invoice (extract), ceramics and glass sold by Davenport Brothers, importers and manufacturers, City Pottery, Trenton, NJ. Dated February[?] 13, 1879.

New Jersey, 1880). This relates to information on the 1879 invoice. Davenport Brothers are described as ceramic importers as well as manufacturers (Figure 5.9).

Whether the Davenport brothers were related to the Davenports of Longport, Staffordshire, is unclear. While the 1880 census declares that Thomas Davenport was born in New Jersey and his father was English, by the time of his death, he had acquired a more notable "American" pedigree. Thomas Davenport's obituary notice states that he was the last surviving member of the firm Davenport Brothers and "a direct descendant of the Rev. John Davenport, a distinguished pilgrim minister" (*The New York Herald* March 7, 1889). With success came certain pretentions, and not everything reported in the press was necessarily accurate or true. But regardless of whether crockery dealers were from England or were born in the United States, at this stage, the most compelling reason for long-term connections, or dynastic tendencies, was profit. The issue of capitalizing on what seemed to be a profitable trade will be returned to in Chapter 6 when discussing the example of an importer who had strong ties to the Baptist faith.

In certain cases, wealth opened up possibilities to exercise a political influence. Chauncey I. Filley's crockery business of St. Louis was featured in *Frank Leslie's Illustrated Newspaper* in 1860 and, evidently, was a successful concern (see Chapter 2, Figures 2.4 and 2.5). In 1870, Chauncey I. Filley was described as a "wh. [wholesale] china ware" dealer who owned real estate worth $70,000 and whose personal estate was valued at $50,000 (Census, St. Louis, 1870). He also became involved in politics. Filley was a Republican and served as the Mayor of St. Louis during the Civil War. Filley was described as being one of the delegates who had signed the ordinance abolishing slavery in the state of Missouri in January 1865, and, allegedly, he was "the first public official to give the Colored man honorable employment" (*The Broad Ax*, Chicago October 6, 1923). Whether this was through his crockery store, or in political capacity, is not clear, although this relates to another aspect of the crockery trade, explored in the last chapter of this book.

Success in the crockery trade encouraged some diversification, but this did not mean abandoning the crockery business. Peter A. Wright established a crockery importing firm in Philadelphia in 1817. His sons, James A. and Edward N. Wright, became involved in the firm, which they continued after Peter Wright retired in 1848. Members of the Wright family became involved in a shipping business, banking, and also dealt in petroleum, but at the same time retained control of the core business, Peter Wright & Sons. Although the family originally came from the slave-owning state of Maryland, James A. Wright (in the manner of Chauncey I. Filley) was "an active anti-slavery man" (*The Philadelphia Inquirer* June 8, 1894).

Interconnections

Until the press is surveyed, it is not immediately obvious how far crockery businesses were interconnected. Partnerships between those families involved in the crockery trade further expanded their influence. In relationship to the American market, the Tams family are well-known because of the existence of ceramics bearing the backstamp, "S. Tams & Co. Warranted Staffordshire" (Figures

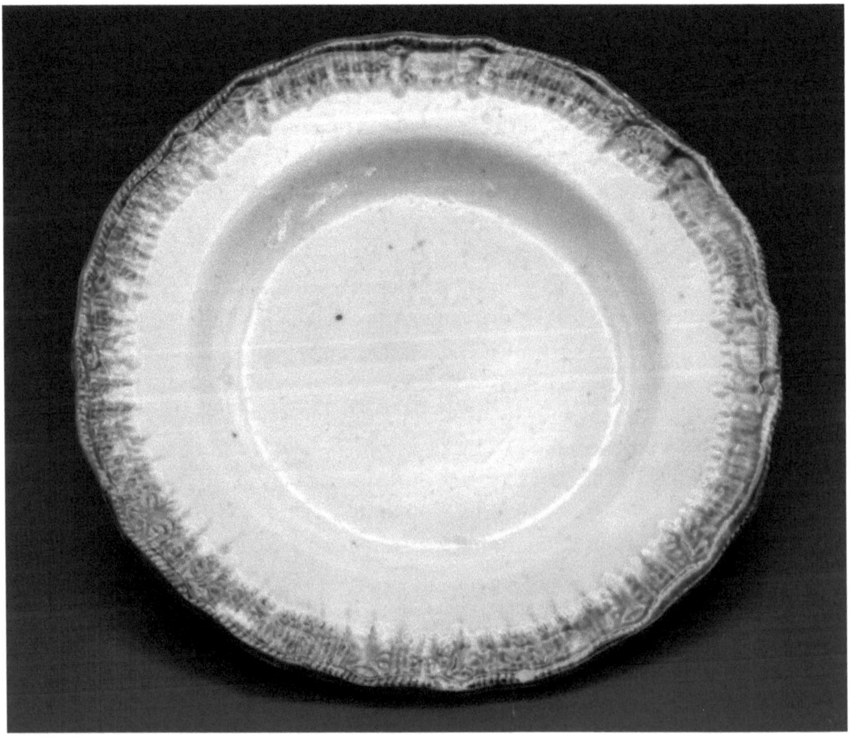

Figure 5.10 Cup plate, earthenware, blue edged, Staffordshire, c.1820–30.

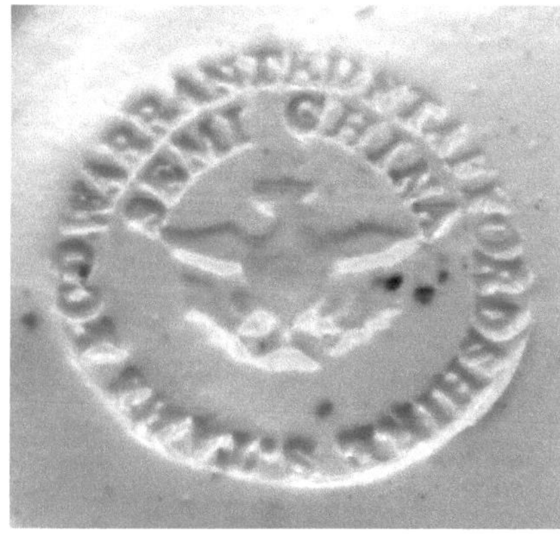

Figure 5.11 Backstamp on Figure 5.10, "S. Tams & Co. Warranted, Staffordshire, Semi China," c.1820–30.

5.10 and 5.11) or "Tams, Anderson & Tams, Warranted Staffordshire" (Figures 5.12 and 5.13). However, it is only the publication of press notices that establishes their other business links. Sampson Tams, originally from Shelton, Staffordshire, arrived in New York in 1816. He began by running a store at 94, William Street (*National Advocate*, New York December 31, 1816; January 18, 1817), followed in 1817 with the establishment of an outlet in Philadelphia, where he advertised lustered, painted, and printed wares from his outlet on 298, Market Street (*Poulson's American Daily Advertiser* December 17, 1817). Simultaneously, Sampson Tams maintained links to New York and Philadelphia, made possible by being in a partnership with William S. Shirley (also originally from Shelton), who apparently ran the New York business.

Sampson Tams' brothers—William, Edwin, and James Tams—also became involved in the crockery and glass trade, but the focus of business was increasingly Philadelphia. They became importers and were occasionally described in American city directories as manufacturers (Ewins 1997: 85–6). In the late eighteenth century and early nineteenth century, Philadelphia was the pre-eminent city, but it had been overtaken by New York in terms of commerce and population by the 1810s (Morison and Commager, 1942: 502). Despite the rapid development of New York (augmented by the opening of the Erie Canal in 1825), Philadelphia still attracted migrant crockery dealers. Observations made by an English traveler perhaps explains why the Tams family were still drawn to Philadelphia. Even though Philadelphia had "... not so much business, not so much gaiety, not so much life," the rents were estimated as being 25 percent less than New York, and this was attributed to "the calculating habits of the society of friends, who reside here in great numbers" (Fearon 1819: 135–6). In other words, it was believed that due to the stronger influence of Quakers, rents remained more affordable.

Flow-blue printed ceramics backstamped "James Tams & Co. Importers Philadelphia" and dating to the 1840s are evidence of a long-term connection to

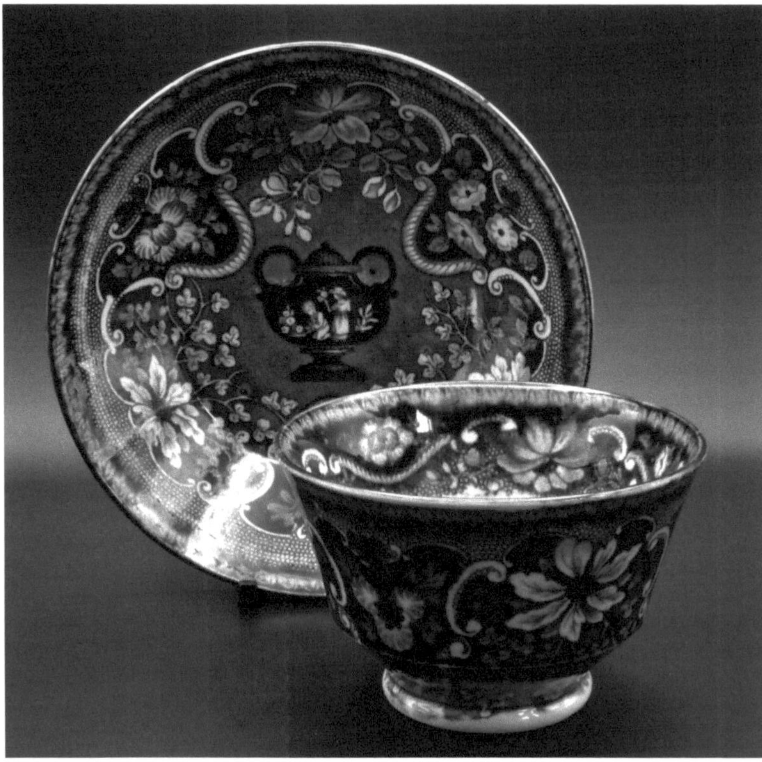

Figure 5.12 Cup and saucer, earthenware, blue printed, floral pattern.

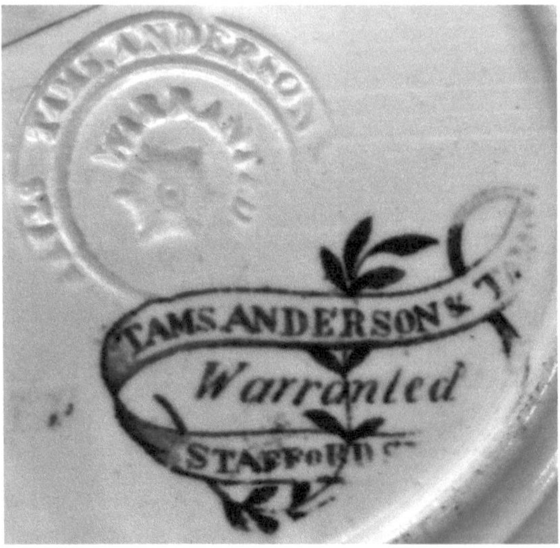

Figure 5.13 Backstamp on Figure 5.12 impressed and printed "Tams, Anderson & Tams Warranted Staffordshire," c.1822–27.

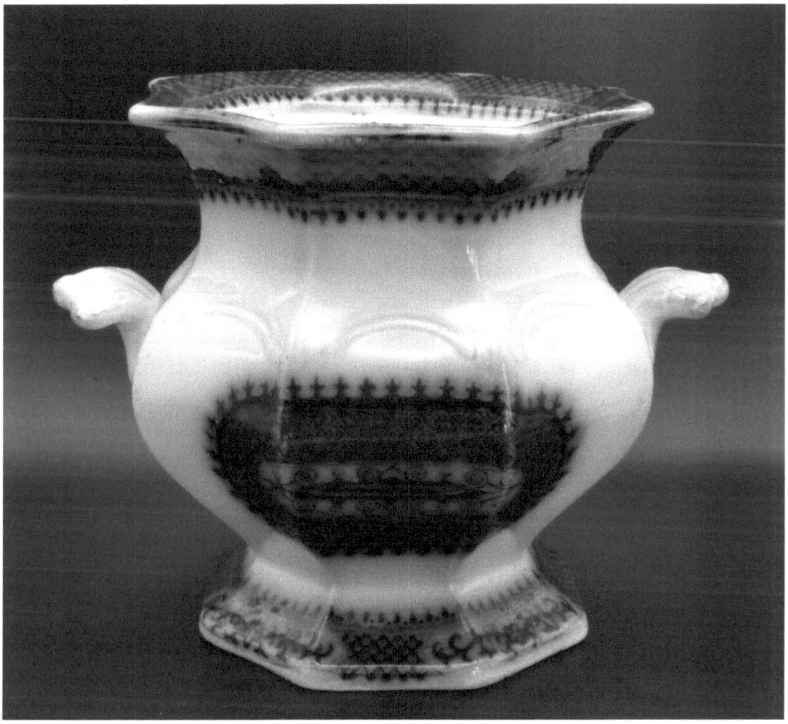

Figure 5.14 Sugar, earthenware, printed flow blue. Staffordshire, 1840s.

Figure 5.15 Backstamp on Figure 5.14, "James Tams & Co./ Importers Philadelphia/ Rock Stone."

Philadelphia (Figures 5.14 and 5.15). Although references to members of the Tams family being actual manufacturers in Staffordshire trade directories are obscure, the marriage certificate of James Tams, merchant of Philadelphia, describes his father, Michael Tams, as a "Manufacturer, Shelton" (Marriage certificate 1843). One Staffordshire trade directory lists "Mr. Michael Tams," High Street, Shelton, under "Miscellany of Gentry, Clergy, Partners in Firms and others not arranged in the List of Trades and Professions" (White 1834). Michael Tams was potentially involved in a partnership with other Shelton manufacturers. This might account for why their name appeared on a variety of ceramic backstamps, even incorporating the phrase "Warranted Staffordshire" (Figures 5.10–5.13). But surviving invoices show that members of the Tams family in Philadelphia regularly purchased ceramics from a variety of other Staffordshire manufacturers, such as Mellor, Venables of Burslem (Figure 5.16).

Once in America, a variety of interconnections were formed with other businesses. A co-partnership between Sampson Tams and John Griffith of 81, Maiden Lane, New York, existed until it was dissolved in 1819 (*New-York Gazette* September 19, 1819). The Griffith family, originally from Staffordshire, became ceramic manufacturers in New Jersey (see Chapter 3). Other connections were

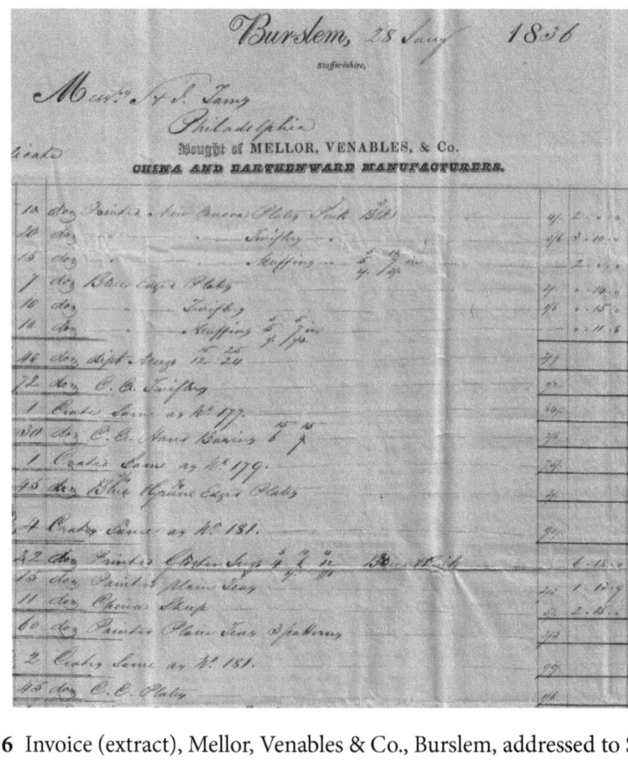
Burslem, 28 Jany 1836
Staffordshire,
Messrs. S & J. Tams
Philadelphia
Bought of MELLOR, VENABLES, & Co.
CHINA AND EARTHENWARE MANUFACTURERS.

10	doz Printed [illegible] Plates Pink Blk	4/-	2 . .
20	doz — Twifflers	3/6	3 . 10 .
15	doz — Muffins		2 . .
7	doz Blue Edged Plates	4/-	. 14 .
10	doz — Twifflers	3/6	. 15 .
10	doz — Muffins		. 11 . 6
46	doz Dipt Mugs 12 24	[illegible]	
72	doz C. C. Twifflers	[illegible]	
1	Crate Same as No 177.	[illegible]	
30	doz C. C. Hand Basins 6 7	[illegible]	
1	Crate Same as No 179.	[illegible]	
45	doz Blue [illegible] Edged Plates	[illegible]	
4	Crates Same as No 181.	[illegible]	
42	doz Printed Coffee Cups [illegible]		6 . 15 .
15	doz Painted Plain Teas	[illegible]	1 . 10 . 9
11	doz China Sheep	[illegible]	2 . 15 .
60	doz Painted Plain Teas 3 patterns	[illegible]	
2	Crates Same as No 181.	[illegible]	
45	doz C. C. Plates	[illegible]	

Figure 5.16 Invoice (extract), Mellor, Venables & Co., Burslem, addressed to S. & J. Tams & Co., Philadelphia. Dated January 28, 1836. This invoice also illustrates the price differentials between printed, edged and C.C [cream colored] earthenware, as mentioned in Chapter 4. It even includes "11 doz China Sheep."

continuously formed. In August 1820, William W. Shirley advertised in New York as "of the late firm of Sampson Tams & Co.," selling an invoice of printed, painted and edged ware from his "New & Cheap China, Earthenware & Glass Store" at 55, Maiden Lane (*New-York Gazette* August 11, 1820).

In another example of evidence of interconnections, a notice of 1843 stated that "Sampson Tams & William J. Kerr of the city of Philadelphia, trading under the firm of E. M. Kerr & Co. China Hall, Baltimore," was now dissolved. In this instance, Sampson Tams had at some point established a partnership with the Kerrs. This notice indicates that E. [Edward] M. Kerr continued at the China Hall, 198, Baltimore Street, Baltimore. As well as family networks, business partnerships provided further ways to expand their crockery markets. Members of the Kerr family originally came from Ireland. It was reported that Joseph Kerr arrived in the United States in 1821 and then established a crockery business in Philadelphia in 1826. During the 1830s, Joseph was in partnership with his brother, John Kerr, and they developed what was called the "China Hall" in Philadelphia (*Sunday Dispatch*, Philadelphia July 10, 1870). Various members of the Kerr family sold crockery in Philadelphia, Baltimore, and Cincinnati.

In 1859, it was indicated that ceramics and glass produced for the Great Eastern steamer and displayed at the China Hall were supplied by the Worcester Porcelain Works, "the English branch of Kerr's establishment" (*The Press*, Philadelphia October 19, 1859). (Figure 5.17).

A marriage between William Henry Kerr (who belonged to a branch of the family who remained as crockery dealers in Dublin) and Caroline Stone (who was related to the Chamberlain family of the Worcester Porcelain Works) resulted

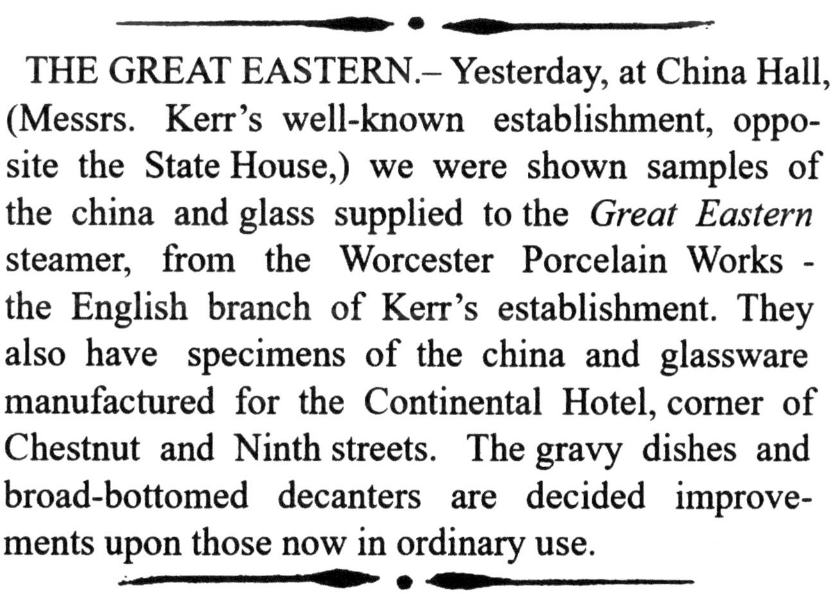
THE GREAT EASTERN.– Yesterday, at China Hall, (Messrs. Kerr's well-known establishment, opposite the State House,) we were shown samples of the china and glass supplied to the *Great Eastern* steamer, from the Worcester Porcelain Works - the English branch of Kerr's establishment. They also have specimens of the china and glassware manufactured for the Continental Hotel, corner of Chestnut and Ninth streets. The gravy dishes and broad-bottomed decanters are decided improvements upon those now in ordinary use.

Figure 5.17 *The Press*, Philadelphia October 19, 1859.

in a business connection that lasted from 1852 until 1862 (Sandon 1975: xx). Understanding interconnections, then, begins to explain why individuals in America came to possess certain ceramic items. In turns out that William J. Kerr of the Philadelphian China Hall was a friend of William E. Burton, an actor, who also lived in Philadelphia. Burton had an extensive library, focusing on publications relating to theatrical themes. Given Burton's background and interests, Kerr presented him with a replica of stoneware jug (believed to have been in the possession of William Shakespeare), which had been manufactured by Kerr & Binns of the Royal Worcester works. This was made more straightforward by the fact that "Mr. William J. Kerr, of the china warehouse, opposite Independence Hall, is the uncle of Mr. Kerr, of Worcester, who alone has the right to, by purchase, to make copies of the Shakspeare[sic] jug ..." (*The Press*, Philadelphia October 2, 1860). An example of the replica Shakespeare jug is in possession of the Museum of Royal Worcester.

In turn, it is interesting how existing invoices for the Kerr's China Hall of Philadelphia perhaps hint at family connections to manufacturing. Instead of the more typical image of the front of the American business establishment, the Kerr invoice of 1862 has three pottery kilns behind a classical-style urn (Figure 5.18).

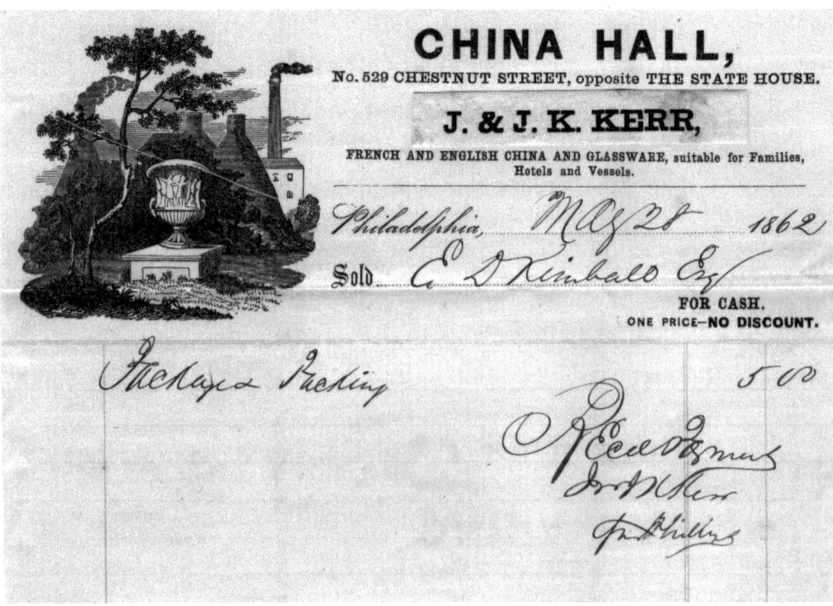
CHINA HALL,
No. 529 CHESTNUT STREET, opposite THE STATE HOUSE.
J. & J. K. KERR,
FRENCH AND ENGLISH CHINA AND GLASSWARE, suitable for Families, Hotels and Vessels.
Philadelphia, May 28 1862
Sold E. D. Kimball Esq
FOR CASH.
ONE PRICE—NO DISCOUNT.

Figure 5.18 Invoice, China Hall, J. & J. K. Kerr. Dated May 28, 1862. The invoice has been altered to reflect a change in the business title. In 1862, the firm William J. Kerr and Joseph Kerr became J. [Joseph] and J. K. [James K.] Kerr (*The Press*, Philadelphia February 18, 1862).

Specialist knowledge

In his analysis of the contributions made by English migrant potters to the development of the American ceramics industry, Frank Thistlethwaite points out how these individuals remained in control of manufacturing in the United States. This phenomenon is attributed to the "unusually high degree of craft skill" involved in this trade (1958: 277). In fact, this relationship was so strong that Trenton, New Jersey, was described as the most English town in the country. It was even noted how:

> At first the English came here a good deal as the Chinamen do, simply to get rich and without much idea of settling permanently. They were clannish, and rarely availed themselves of the privilege of becoming citizens or participated in any way in the politics of the town or the State. They began to get over this peculiarity many years ago, however, and especially within the last two years have been naturalised by the hundred.
>
> (*Sun and New York Press* April 1, 1888)

Crockery importers and dealers had an intimate understanding of the manufacturers, its networks, the products, and then the needs of the market. This appears to have impacted on many aspects of the trade. One crockery seller of St. Louis, Missouri, advertised how his stock, direct from the Potteries and suited to the country trade, was "carefully selected and put up by experienced English packers" (*Illinois Weekly State Journal* August 7, 1845). Even the packing of ceramics—so important to prevent huge damages in transportation—was a considerable skill, and is discussed in Chapter 7. In the case of another St. Louis dealer, the route into the crockery trade may have been influenced by earlier attempts to manufacture ceramics. Giles Filley was born in Connecticut and moved to St. Louis, with his brother Oliver, to manufacture tinware. He subsequently sold his share of this business and became involved in the crockery trade from 1841, only to sell this concern to his cousins, Edward A. and Samuel R. Filley, in 1849. Prior to his involvement in the ceramic trade, Giles Filley had attempted to manufacture pottery, but this was reliant on imported English workmen. However, "Owing to the English workmen leaving from time to time, and no American potters being available, the plant was closed down" (*The St. Louis Republic* February 4, 1895).

Advertisements placed by crockery store owners in the United States occasionally specified that they required individuals that were "active and acquainted with the business" (*Evening Post*, New York April 28, 1825). Although Thomas C. Cochran's *Frontiers of Change: Early Industrialism in America* argued that migration "accentuated" a society that was judged by "what he could do rather than who his parents were" (1981: 12), a family connection to a specialist industry and trade created the opposite effect. Once individuals had formed ties to the ceramic trade, they often remained connected for long periods.

Misconceptions

It transpires that those with a knowledge of manufacturing who became importers contributed to the development of the American pottery industry. A considerable amount of attention was given by contemporaries, and then by ceramic historians, to the Jersey City Pottery of New Jersey, since it was a fairly early attempt at producing porcelain in the United States. Jennie J. Young's *The Ceramic Art* refers to how French artisans had founded the Jersey City Porcelain pottery (1878: 455). Edwin Barber's *The Pottery and Porcelain of The United States* states that this pottery was founded in 1825 by George Dummer, Timothy Dewey, Henry Post jr, William W. Shirley, and Robert Abbatt, and it even includes an illustration of the firm (1893: 118–20) (Figure 5.19).

Barber mentions that a small porcelain bowl produced by this factory was in the Trumbull-Prime collection at Princeton University. As referred to in Chapter 1, William Prime built up a large collection of ceramics, which included the historical Liverpool and Staffordshire wares. According to John Spargo's *Early American Pottery and China*, French artisans were involved in making porcelain at Jersey City, but he believed:

> The first owners of whom there is any record were not French-men. They bore good old American names suggestive of New England. On December 10, 1825, under an act of the New Jersey Legislature, the Jersey Porcelain and Earthenware Company was incorporated, the incorporators being George Dummer, Timothy Dewey, Henry Post, Jr, William W. Shirley, and Robert Abbatt. It is fairly safe to assume that had any of them been potters their names would have been

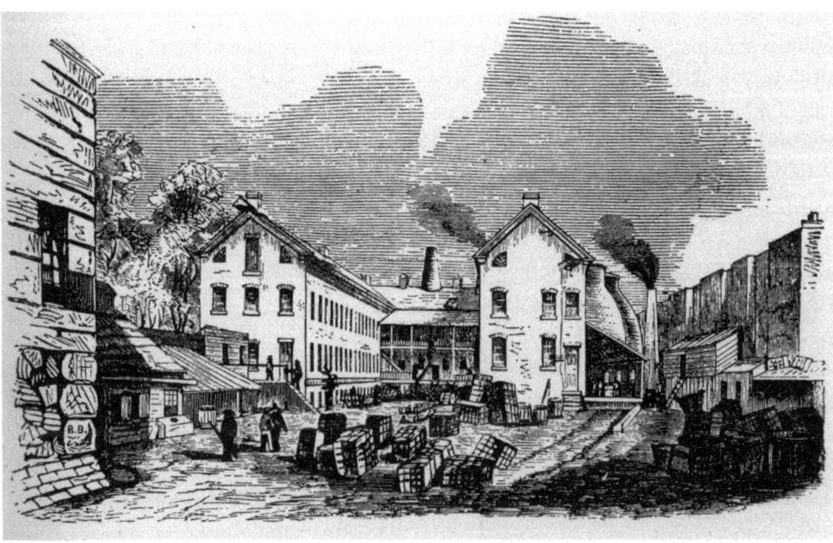

Figure 5.19 Jersey City Pottery, New Jersey. From Edwin Barber's *The Pottery and Porcelain of The United States*, 1893, between pp.118–9.

> encountered in connection with some pottery or other during the ensuing half-century. For this reason the writer believes that they were connected with the enterprise solely on its financial side, as owners, and that the actual potters were the French artisans already referred to (1926: 228–9).

This is an early example of an author actually considering the names of individuals involved from a cultural-identity perspective. Likewise, John Ramsay's *American Potters and Pottery* simply assumed that the Jersey City Porcelain and Earthenware Company was formed by "New Jersey and New York men," using the skills of French potters (1939: 101). But there was evidently a Staffordshire connection, since William W. Shirley was involved in the firm. A closer examination of the press reveals a notice published in November 1824, whereby a company was established to produce porcelain and earthenware with capital given as "*one hundred thousand dollars*," and William W. Shirley referred to as its agent (*The New-York Evening Post* November 29, 1824).

The new establishment was greeted with a degree of enthusiasm in a widely published article titled "American Porcelain," which proclaimed that:

> The manufacture of porcelain, properly so speaking, (for we do not include under this term, the coarse earthen and stone wares of our country,) has been a desideratum among our capitalists even since our national existence …
>
> (*New York Spectator* August 29, 1826)

The article refers to how the exertions had been "crowned with success," involving an agent being sent to Europe to hire artists. It explains how between thirty and forty ladies and gentleman of New York were invited over to Jersey City, and "they were equally astonished and delighted, to find shelves loaded with American china ware, of the most delicate and fashionable models, and of the finest and most beautiful texture" (*New York Spectator* August 29, 1826). The wares ranged from plain cups and saucers to richly painted and gilded wares, including chimney ornaments. At the exhibition of "American Manufactures" sponsored by the Franklin Institute, the "New Jersey Porcelain and Earthenware Company" was awarded a silver medal for "best china from American materials" (*National Gazette and Literary Register,* Philadelphia October 19, 1826). Not only was William W. Shirley involved as a partner, but he was instrumental in the hiring the necessary skilled labour:

> The public are indebted much to Mr. Dummer, Mr. Dewey, and Mr. W.W. Shirley, for the great exertions which they have made in the prosecution of this enterprise. Mr. S. was the gentleman who went as an agent to England.
>
> (*New-York Spectator* August 29, 1826)

George Dummer was a crockery importer and had already founded a glass factory in 1824 (Frelinghuysen 2000: 331). Timothy Dewey acted as the secretary, but as William W. Shirley had only arrived from Staffordshire in 1818, it may be assumed that he still had an invaluable network of contacts.

While early reviews provided positive accounts of the porcelain manufactured at the Jersey Pottery by 1828, there were financial difficulties, and its ownership was transferred to D. & J. Henderson. Of the production of porcelain in the United States, *The Boston Courier* wrote how "there was excellent establishment in full operation near Philadelphia; and another one commenced six or seven years since at Jersey City near New-York, is now used for the manufacture of the printed Staffordshire, and a superior fire proof stone ware" (August 1, 1834).

In the case of the Jersey Pottery, there were even further connections to Staffordshire. When the Franklin Bank of New York failed, allegedly due to malpractices, a libel case was instigated. As the New Jersey Porcelain and Earthenware Company had an account with the Franklin Bank, members of the pottery firm were called as witnesses. Jesse Shirley was a works manager at the New Jersey Porcelain pottery, which in its first inception was in the locality of New York's Tenth Ward (*Spectator*, New York, August 29, 1826). The testimony of a Jesse Shirley declared that:

> On 2d Nov. 1825, witness [Jesse Shirley] received possession of the Porcelain and Earthenware Factory, as Manager in this city [New York]. It remained here about three months, when it was removed to Jersey City. The factory was built in the summer of 1825. After we were at Jersey City, witness [Jesse Shirley] went with letters and checks from Porcelain Co., to Mr. Leggett, at the Franklin Bank, and received the money. Frequently conversed with Mr. Leggett about the funds of the company. Whenever Mr. L. was present, the checks were paid. This was in the spring of 1826. If Mr. L. was absent from the bank, witness went to his house and always got the money …
>
> (*Evening Post*, New York June 26, 1832)

From the evidence reported in the press, the pottery's account was overdrawn by $4,715.63 in August 1825, reaching $25,337.92 by August 1826 (*Evening Post*, New York June 26, 1832). The evidence provided by this libel case shows that more than one member of the Shirley family was involved in this firm. Jesse appears to be a brother of William W. Shirley, and was previously listed as a Staffordshire manufacturer (Holden 1811). Later, a Jesse Shirley was recorded as running a "fancy store" in Philadelphia (Desilver 1835–6). An obituary in *The Sun*, Baltimore, April 8, 1839, indicates that "At Philadelphia, on the 3d instant, Mr. Jesse Shirley, late of Staffordshire, England" had died aged just fifty-two years [born c.1787]. This coincides with reference to Jesse Shirley, son of William and Hannah Shirley, christened on May 21, 1786, Stoke-upon-Trent (see Pedigree 12). The actual development and running of the New Jersey Pottery was more complex than simply involving New England men.

Impact on marketing

Just as historians have become accustomed to recognize how the development of the American ceramic industry often relied on skills transplanted from

Staffordshire to America (Thistlethwaite 1958), the same observation often applied to the selling of ceramics. It is notable that Cephas Shirley (one of William W. Shirley's brothers) advertised his "China Commission Warehouse" on the basis of having a broad knowledge of the "crockery business," initially derived from being a native of the Staffordshire Potteries and also having spent twelve years in the United States (Figure 5.20). Cephas had previously assisted his brother William W. Shirley in New York in the 1820s, and then established his own crockery importing business in Philadelphia in the 1830s. Even his acquaintance with French goods was accounted for because of his time spent in Paris.

Cephas Shirley's advertisement at least provides evidence of how an Englishman could acquire more awareness of French ceramics and suppliers, since French porcelain was widely exported to the American market (Ewins 1997: 46–50).

Perceived in another way, it seems that being a native of the Potteries carried a certain status. This may be illustrated by the case of Edwin and John Tams, who were in a partnership in Philadelphia in the 1840s. Interestingly, a surviving invoice addressed to a buyer located at Tippecanoe, Ohio, of 1849, shows how they maintained in the firm's title a connection to manufacturing (Figure 5.21).

At a certain point, John Tams moved to Leavenworth, Kansas, and acted as an agent for Edwin Tams. When this arrangement ended, John Tams remained in Leavenworth (*Leavenworth Daily Conservative*, Kansas November 30, 1864). In 1867, it was announced that L. G. Terry had opened a new crockery store at

CHINA COMMISSION WAREHOUSE, No.42 and 43 PHILADELPHIA ARCADE – *C. SHIRLEY* offers his services to Merchants and others who have consignments of LIVERPOOL CROCKERY or GLASS WARES, and will attend to the sale or purchase of those articles for a small commission. The knowledge he possesses of the CROCKERY BUSINESS, being a native of the Staffordshire Potteries, England, and having resided in this country for twelve years, will doubtless enable him to be of service to those who may have such articles to dispose of. C. S. has also devoted his attention to the article of FRENCH CHINA. He has resided in Paris, France, and is acquainted with the French Importers who reside in this country.

N. B. The sale of DOMESTIC GLASS, PLATED CASTORS, &c. also attended to.

Figure 5.20 *Public Ledger*, Philadelphia June 27, 1836.

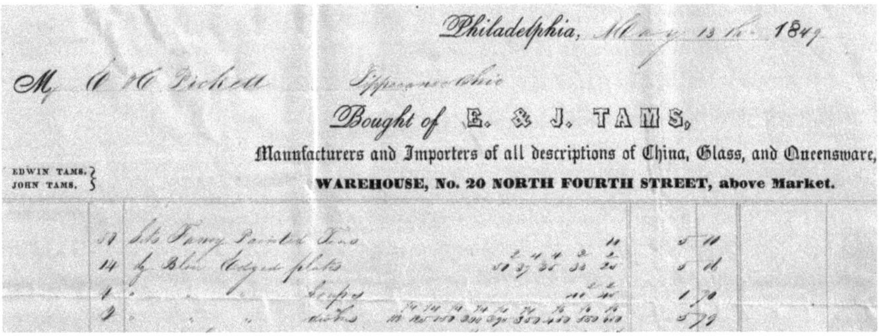
Philadelphia, May 13th 1849

M. E. H. Pickett Tippecanoe Ohio

Bought of E. & J. TAMS,

Manufacturers and Importers of all descriptions of China, Glass, and Queensware,

EDWIN TAMS. JOHN TAMS.

WAREHOUSE, No. 20 NORTH FOURTH STREET, above Market.

Figure 5.21 Invoice (extract) of E. & J. Tams, Philadelphia, addressed to E. H. Pickett, Tippecanoe, Ohio. Dated May 13, 1849. The invoice refers to "Sets Fancy Painted Teas" and "Blue Edged Plates."

Leavenworth, employing Mr. John Tams as a salesman (*Evening Leavenworth Bulletin,* Kansas September 30, 1867). It is significant how one newspaper article described this relationship as:

> LOOK TO YOUR CASH ACCOUNT—The Queensware establishment of L. G. Terry, at 56 Delaware street is being crowded daily by merchants from the interior laying in their fall supplies, while the ladies of the city keep the old Queensware *apostle and prince* John Tams, upon his feet from early morn to we sma' hours of night, attending to their wants. Why is this? Because it is becoming noised abroad that at 56 Delaware street, Queensware can be purchased at 20 per cent lower than any other establishment, not only in Leavenworth, but in the Northwest.
>
> (*Evening Leavenworth Bulletin,* Kansas November 1, 1867)

It seems that John Tams occupied a certain kudos because of his background, when employed by L. G. Terry.

Co-religionists

Frank Thistlethwaite's paper, "The Atlantic Migration of the Pottery Industry," acknowledges how the movement of individuals from Staffordshire to America contributed to the development of the industry in Trenton, New Jersey, and East Liverpool, Ohio. In another contribution, it is suggested that these migrants became active in Republican politics and involved in Methodist and Episcopal churches (1958: 276). Skills, as well as religious connections, were transferred from the old to the new world. An appreciation of religious facilitations might seem superfluous to understanding the Anglo-American trade, but this is not necessarily the case. As Stanley Chapman's structural analysis of the transatlantic economy pointed out:

> So long as communication between trading centres continued to be slow and uncertain, the only way in which merchants could repose confidence in their correspondents' decision making was to employ members of their own families, or, failing that, the "extended family" of co-religionists. Consequently we find that every port was a focus of networks of family connections by means by which goods and credit moved with a degree of assurance.
>
> (1992: 93)

Sharing the same religion was also characteristic of those involved in the crockery trade and an added ingredient of kinship. The Reverend John Williams of the Baptist Church, on Fayette Street (later to be renamed Oliver Street), New York, married a number of individuals described in Chapter 3, who were involved in the crockery trade. They were linked by trade as well as church. In 1805, the Reverend John Williams married Thomas Purser to Mrs. Mary Drummond; William Hewitt to Sarah Cauldwell, in 1806; Thomas Hewitt to Mrs. Burges[sic] also in 1806; Jane Hewitt to Samuel Bridgewood in 1810; Thomas Cook, to the widowed Mrs Sarah Hewitt (nee Cauldwell) in 1811; Mary Ann Hewitt, daughter of Thomas Hewitt, to Henry Concklin of Poughkeepsie in 1818; and Ebenezer Cauldwell to Gloria Anna Garniss in 1819 (*New-York Gazette and General Advertiser* August 16, 1805; *Weekly Museum*, New York April 26, 1806; *New-York Gazette* November 11, 1806; *Mercantile Advertiser* New York, April 3, 1810; *New-York Weekly Museum* May 18, 1811; *The Weekly Visitor, and Ladies' Museum* May 30, 1818; The New-York Evening Post March 16, 1819). The Reverend John Williams even married the Reverend Daniel Sharp, Pastor of the Baptist Church of Newark, New Jersey, to Ann, daughter of John Cauldwell, the crockery dealer of New York (*New-York Weekly Museum* January 6, 1810).

The Reverend John Williams was an influential member of the Baptist community. When he died in 1825, there was a lengthy article published in the *Baptist* about his life and work, where it was commented that the Hewitt and Cauldwell family had been members of his congregation. Ebenezer Cauldwell was christened September 20, 1791, at the Baptist Cannon Street Meeting House in Birmingham, England, and in his case, resulted in a life-long connection to the Baptist faith that continued in New York. When he died aged eighty-four, it was noted how this "well-known crockery merchant" was "probably the oldest representative in the United States," a director of "several banking and insurance corporations in this city," and "for many years an active member of the Baptist denomination" (*New-York Tribune* June 21, 1875). The religious aspect may seem unrelated to interpreting ceramics, but the next chapter explores how it impacted on what was commissioned, and then, on distribution networks.

Summary

Thomas C. Cochran's *Frontiers of Change: Early Industrialism in America* proposed that a reason for alternative business behavior in the United States was due to differences in national culture. He suggests that "the potential for upward mobility no doubt inspired most young men in America in a way not possible in more stratified societies" (1981: 12). While American mobility might have influenced individuals to explore different career paths, the evidence of this chapter shows how crockery-importing firms often remained in the same family for more than one generation. This was not simply to do with the role of men. Women played an important part in linking families together, and on occasion, aided the continuity of crockery firms being actively involved in the business.

Regardless of the role of national culture, dynastic tendencies were rather dependent on the characteristics and history of the trade. The development of the potteries in north Staffordshire region, due to materials, fuel, and the cultivation of generations of skilled laborers, gave the industry a distinctive nature. Dynastic tendencies regularly occurred in the case of the Staffordshire manufacturers. Families involved in the crockery trade in the United States were also dynastic. As shown in this chapter, the Shirley family came from the Potteries. In this respect, it was essentially the same "people" being involved in different aspects of the business. This becomes relevant when backgrounds started to infiltrate approaches to marketing strategy. Boasting of ties to Staffordshire implied to the consumer how the seller could be trusted in this trade because of their background. For other crockery dealers along the Eastern Seaboard who were not from the Potteries (though they might marry into families who were), an incentive to create a new dynasty in this specialist trade stemmed from it remaining a profitable line of business.

What then became another recognizable tendency of the crockery trade was how interlinked families were attached to the same church. This was particularly well illustrated by the community of New York crockery dealers who were married by the same pastor, the Reverend John Williams, of the Baptist church on Fayette Street, which was not far from where their businesses were located, and where they lived. Links to the trade were cemented by intermarriages and further bound by ties to same religion. It is even apparent that these ties stretched beyond New York. One crockery dealer located at Utica was married by Reverend John Williams of the Fayette Street, Baptist Church. The next chapter explores whether religious values impacted on what crockery dealers actually commissioned and marketed.

Chapter 6

RELIGION AND ABOLITIONISM

During the nineteenth century, a variety of printed ceramics were produced incorporating quotes from the maxims of Dr. Benjamin Franklin. A small transfer printed mug, probably manufactured in Staffordshire in the 1840s, combines imagery of children involved in business activities and is accompanied by the phrase, "Keep thy shop, and thy shop will keep thee"—a maxim that was listed under the month of June in Franklin's *Poor Richard … An Almanack for the year of Christ,* 1735. Alternatively, a small plate, also dating from the 1840s, uses imagery and included the phrase, "God helps them, that help themselves," which also appeared in the *Poor Richard's* almanac, in June 1736 (Figure 6.1). Though inspired by the philosophy of Franklin, these designs are not exclusively found in the United States. Franklin's *Poor Richard* almanacs were printed from 1732 to 1758 and then, collectively, as *The Way to Wealth*, in 1758. The maxims were widely circulated, and as these ceramic examples suggest, were used to guide and educate young children in particular ways.

In Max Weber's *The Protestant Ethic and the Spirit of Capitalism* of 1904–5, it was proposed how the advocation of Franklin's maxims of hard work, persistence, and industry were rooted in the ethos of the Protestant faith. Indeed, phrases such as, "God helps them, that help themselves" do imply a religious influence, and Weber supported his theory by drawing attention to Franklin's autobiography. Here it is established that Franklin's father regularly repeated the Biblical phrase, "'Seest thou a man diligent in his business? He shall stand before kings' (Prov. Xxii, 29)" (Weber [1930] 2010: 19). This is cited as evidence of how Franklin's upbringing was shaped by his Calvinist father and how, according to Weber, attitudes to "earning of money" were transformed into an "expression of virtue" ([1930] 2010: 19). In this way, Weber then contends that Protestantism influenced the rise of capitalism and that making money was not entirely divorced from religion. The aim of this chapter is also to explore whether there is evidence of the activities of crockery importers in America being a more complex mixture of businessmen, yet following religious convictions, which in turn impacted on marketing, and even on what was commissioned from manufacturers.

Relevant to developing an understanding of ceramic supply and demand is how Max Weber addressed the impact of Protestantism on consumption. In Weber's opinion, Protestantism "acted powerfully against the spontaneous enjoyment of possessions; it restricted consumption, especially of luxuries" (Weber [1930]

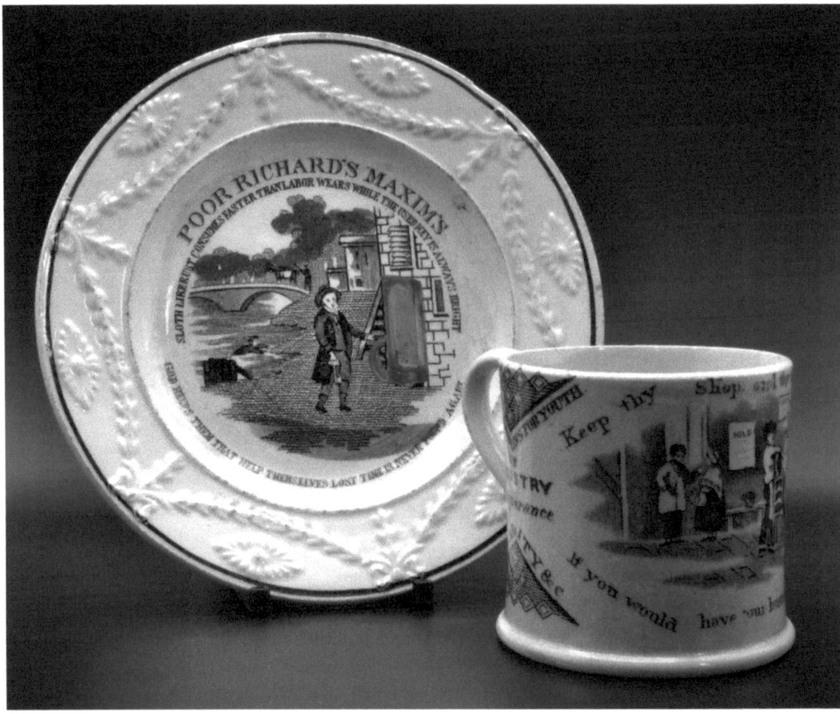

Figure 6.1 Plate and mug, earthenware, transfer printed, with additional enamel decoration on the plate, based on the maxims of Dr. Benjamin Franklin. English, c.1830–40.

2010: 115). Straightaway, there becomes a fundamental problem with Weber's overarching thesis. If the development of a capitalist society was linked in any way to the Protestant values of hard work and self-reliance (as Weber contests), on the other side of this equation was the vital need to consume. In fact, other writers have more readily contributed industrial development and growth to the fundamental role of demand (Gilboy [1932] 1967: 121–38), further stimulated by a rise in fashion-orientated societies (McKendrick et al. 1982). Karl Samuelsson's *Religion and Economic Action*, suggested that "… persons and classes in the most economically advanced countries … were not characterized by thrift in its strict Puritan or ascetic sense" ([1957] 1961: 83). Samuelsson even draws attention to episodes in Franklin's autobiography to highlight inconsistencies in his philosophy. In one instance, it was mentioned how Franklin's wife acquired expensive goods, including Chinese porcelain (Samuelsson [1957] 1961: 58–9). The direct quote from Franklin's 1780s autobiography reads as:

> … our table was plain and simple, our furniture of the cheapest. For instance, my breakfast was a long time bread and milk (no tea), and I ate it out of a twopenny earthen porringer, with a pewter spoon. But mark how luxury will enter families,

> and make a progress, in spite of principle: being call'd one morning to breakfast, I found it in a China bowl, with a spoon of silver! They had been bought for me without my knowledge by my wife, and had cost her the enormous sum of three and twenty shillings, for which she had no other excuse or apology to make, but that she thought *her* husband deserv'd a silver spoon and China bowl as well as any of his neighbors.
>
> ([1868] 1996: 62)

Evidently, the acquisition of desirable, expensive commodities occurred within the Franklin household, and some of the earliest ceramic historians were also aware of inherent contradictions between Franklin's attitudes and what actually occurred. Alice Morse Earle's *China Collecting in America* notes that while Franklin promoted "the wisdom and necessity of great economy," when in England, he purchased a variety of china made by manufacturers, such as Bow and Worcester, for his wife living in Philadelphia (1892: 63–4). Even Max Weber quotes the views of the eighteenth-century Methodist leader, John Wesley, who observed, "I fear whenever riches have increased, the essence of religion has decreased in the same proportion" ([1930] 2010: 118). If anything, there would appear to be a diminishing impact of Puritan values, opening up the possibility to liberally consume, so vital for stimulating production. It is rather ironic that Benjamin Franklin has been credited as being a pioneer of newspaper advertising in the United States, as mentioned in Chapter 2.

According to Joanna Cohen's *Luxurious Citizens: The Politics of Consumption in Nineteenth-Century America*, there was a widespread shift in American values toward consumption (2017: 149–64). However, the existence of ceramics designed for children, as well as the publication of American household-guides, which continued to advocate Franklin's philosophy, raises the possibility of whether everyone was moving in same direction, at the same time. Mrs. Child's *The American Frugal Housewife*, first published in 1829, included quotes from Franklin's maxims (even on the title page), and her advice rather emphasized notions of thrift, purposely aiming her book at poorer housekeepers (1828: 6). In terms of ceramics, she described how to look after new earthenware and how to repair broken china and glass ([1829] 1838: 11, 19). Importantly, books such as these acknowledge that not everyone in America was able to freely consume.

Even if it is disputed that there was not a significant Calvinistic influence on the personal philosophy of Benjamin Franklin, there were still other individuals in America who continued to justify a reticence to overly consume on the basis of following religious doctrine. As shown in Chapter 2, Catherine Beecher published a range of household management books, but it is notable how her views were grounded in religious piety. Beecher maintained that it was "Christianity, which teaches us to 'seek first the kingdom of God,' and to deem food, raiment, and the conveniences of life, as of secondary account" ([1841] 1843: 158). It was even believed by Harriet Beecher Stowe (author of *Uncle Tom's Cabin* and sister of Catharine Beecher) that "There is no country in the world where the religious influence has a greater ascendancy than in America" (1853: 381). It is interesting how Peter Wainwright, ceramic merchant and tobacco dealer, confided to his son, the Reverend Jonathan M. Wainwright of New York, that since "I have been back in England I have not attended the services of any of the churches that have been so acceptable and edifying to me as I have experienced at yours …". Adding that, the English preachers were not fit for office, being, "exceedingly different in practical matter [sic] in seriousness and oratory so that it is not at all surprising to me that the sectarians should have multiplied in the extent they have done" (Wainwright Papers, Box 3, Folder 3.18, June 2, 1831). It then becomes debatable how much religion impacted on those involved in mercantile activities.

Business behavior and religion

It has been appreciated for some time that manufacturers could be influenced by their religious views, which, in turn, affected business behavior (Searle 1998). The ceramic industry was not immune to this, either. In Josiah C. Wedgwood's *Staffordshire Pottery and its History*, a chapter aptly titled "Methodism and the Capitalists" recalls how religion "had a profound effect upon the habits of the pottery people, and permanently changed their affections from cockfighting to psalm singing" (1913: 141–2). In fact, the author (a great-great grandson of the most famous Josiah Wedgwood) refers to the case of one Staffordshire manufacturer, Job Ridgway, who insisted that his employees attended his Methodist chapel, which he had founded (Wedgwood 1913: 143). It is suggested that his son, John Ridgway of the Cauldon Place works, paid special attention to the welfare of employees in terms of housing and education (Stacey (1860): 64).

Historian John Briggs explored how far the Christian convictions of the Ridgway family influenced their employment practices (1988: 47–71), leading to speculation in his chapter, "Nonconformity and the Pottery Industry," of whether religion impacted on business networks and, importantly, on actual production (2003: 58). The Methodist leader, John Wesley, regularly preached in the Potteries in the second half of the eighteenth century (Stacey 1862: 77–81), and Briggs' notes that Staffordshire figurines of Wesley were produced in the nineteenth century (2003: 53, 65–6). The debate then becomes whether "The local may have triggered the potter's mind …", though Briggs concedes how the manufacturer "needed to be certain that there was a large market of would-be buyers with a purchasing desire to be satisfied" (2003: 59). So the question remains: how much of this production was manufacture-led, or market-led?

Joseph Stubenrauch's *The Evangelical Age of Ingenuity in Industrial Britain* of 2016 proposes that there are at least three interpretations as to why ceramics of a religious nature were manufactured: the impact of "local identity" on the manufacturers, how manufacturers wished to influence consumers in a spiritual way, or simply that manufacturers identified a market for these products (2016: 173). In the manner of Briggs, the demands of the market are taken into account. While Stubenrauch's investigation is focused on Britain, this research does importantly question how far the growing consumption of "Trinkets, decorative pottery, glamourous fashions, rich textiles ..." represented "a cultural shift into secularism, away from a religious focus" (2016: 3). Stubenrauch's central argument is that evangelical sentimentalism that embraced ceramics was still a part of nineteenth-century design, referring to examples such as ceramic wall plaques inscribed with the phrase, "Prepare to Meet Thy God," manufactured in Sunderland, in the north-east of England (2016: 172–3). But while other historians have considered the impact of religion on the views of the manufacturers or the desires of the consumer, what appears to be missing from these analyses is whether the motivation to produce ceramics with a spiritual purpose ever stemmed from the religious zeal of the importers and dealers.

As suggested at the end of Chapter 2, some individuals in American society advocated for more restrained consumption based on the influence of religious views. However, historians have proposed how American attitudes, in the main, were moving further away from any sense of constraint. By implication, importers, dealers, and retailers became complicit in developing the sophisticated methods used to tempt consumers with an array of new merchandise (Cohen 2017: 156). In fact, Joanna Cohen proposes that technological advances in production aided this process, so that, "Carpets, stoves, pianos, household textiles, cutlery, mantel clocks, and crockery were all examples of goods that became easier to reproduce in large quantities in the 1840s and 1850s and accordingly became more obtainable by midcentury" (2017: 151). Even before this period, the merchant Peter Wainwright, when in Liverpool, wrote affectionately to his daughter in America:

> I note what your Mama says relative to purchasing you a Piano Fort[sic], on this subject I have not made up my mind, whether to get one here or in Boston, however you may calculate upon my doing it in one place or the other.
>
> (Wainwright Papers,Box 3, Folder 3.12, March 6, 1806)

Here is clear evidence of how those of a mercantile class, when in a financial position to do so, acquired luxury commodities for their families. Merchants were also consumers. But just as the activities of importers and dealers could be shaped by a political dimension, did this ever apply to merchants, importers, and dealers, pertaining to have links to religion?

Verse-a-day crockery

In 1832, there was a lengthy discussion of crockery that would incorporate verses from Scripture. In the *Religious Inquirer*, published in Hartford, Connecticut, an article titled "'Verse-A-Day' Crockery" reported how:

> We have been credibly informed that a Partialist wholesale dealer in Crockery, Queensware, &c., late of this city, has had designs painted illustrative of the verse-a-day system, has forwarded them to Europe with orders to have breakfast, dinner and tea-sets made after them, the use of the *piety*-folks of the land. We know the

> advocates of this uniform system expect, ultimately, to revolutionize the world by it; and that aided by Arthur Tappan, they have begun the establishment of verse-a-day missionaries in every district and department of France, to initiate the people of that *benigted*[sic] reign, (beginning with the conscience-smitten errorist, La Fayette, himself,) into the saving act of committing to memory a particular verse of Scripture every day.
>
> (*Religious Inquirer*, Hartford Connecticut December 8, 1832)

Arthur Tappan, a New York merchant, Calvinist, and leading abolitionist, was even related to Dr. Benjamin Franklin, through his mother. His business gravitated toward importing textiles, although he advertised large amounts of crockery from his Pearl Street store in the 1810s *(New-York Courier,* July 15, 1816). The article was enthusiastic about the scheme, viewing the proposal as an alternative way to spread religious views, and importantly, perceived as something of an antidote to fashion:

> The plan, however, is worthy of its founders and advocates, and deserves a more extensive application at their hands. People of common sense and sobriety are becoming so nauseated with the tracts which are every where so profusely distributed and forced on their notice, that it is with difficulty they can be prevailed on to idle away their time in reading the trash they contain. Can they not be, in some manner, forced to read them; at least while eating and drinking at your daily meals? Attend! they can – He that hath eyes to read it, let him read!
>
> Let the American Tract Society use a part, at least, of its immense funds in bribing the manufacturers of Liverpool, Queens, and other ware to lay aside all their present paterns [sic] and designs, and, instead thereof, to imprint on every pitcher, plate, bowl, mug, cup and saucer some favorite tract addressed to the sinners, impenitent Universalists, &c. Fashion, and a growing scarcity of all others, will soon bring these new wares into general use, and thus the beloved dogmas of unending woe, an endless hell, a partial heaven, an angry God, a personal devil, total depravity and infinite accountability will soon be mixed with our daily food, and mingled with our drink- …
>
> (*Religious Inquirer*, Hartford December 8, 1832)

So called verse-a-day crockery certainly existed in some form. In a later newspaper article concerning religious fairs, "verse-a-day" ceramics were mentioned in the context of appropriate prizes, along with Bibles, Testaments, tracts, and memberships to religious associations (*Gospel Banner and Maine Christian Pilot*, Augusta, Maine, June 10, 1837).

The dilemma of following religious convictions, and at the same time being involved in business and trade, is illustrated by the example of Thomas F. Field. In terms of his background, a notice in the New York's *National Advocate* of 1823, refers to the marriage of Thomas F. Field, "merchant of Utica to Miss Mary Ann, eldest daughter of the late David Roberts of this city," in New York City, as officiated by the Rev. John Williams (April 9, 1823). The Reverend John Williams was connected to the Baptist Church, located at 13 Fayette Street (later to be renamed Oliver Street), New York. Already, it may be observed that he was part of the Baptist community, and how other families associated with the crockery trade, such as the Hewitts and Cauldwells of New York, were also connected to the Fayette Street church (see Chapter 5). Based on Thomas F. Field's obituary, he was "engaged in the crockery business when a mere lad, at Utica, N.Y." and died at his Brooklyn residence, aged eighty-four, in 1877 (*New-York Tribune* September 15, 1877).

When in Utica, Thomas Field was in partnership with Theodore Clark. An article by Robert H. McCauley titled "American Importers of Staffordshire" suggested that Field and Clark opened their crockery store in 1822 (1944: 297). A sugar impressed "Field & Clark, Importers of Earthenware, Utica" illustrates what was imported and how there was demand for blue-printed rural scenes as an alternative to American-themed wares (Figure 6.2).

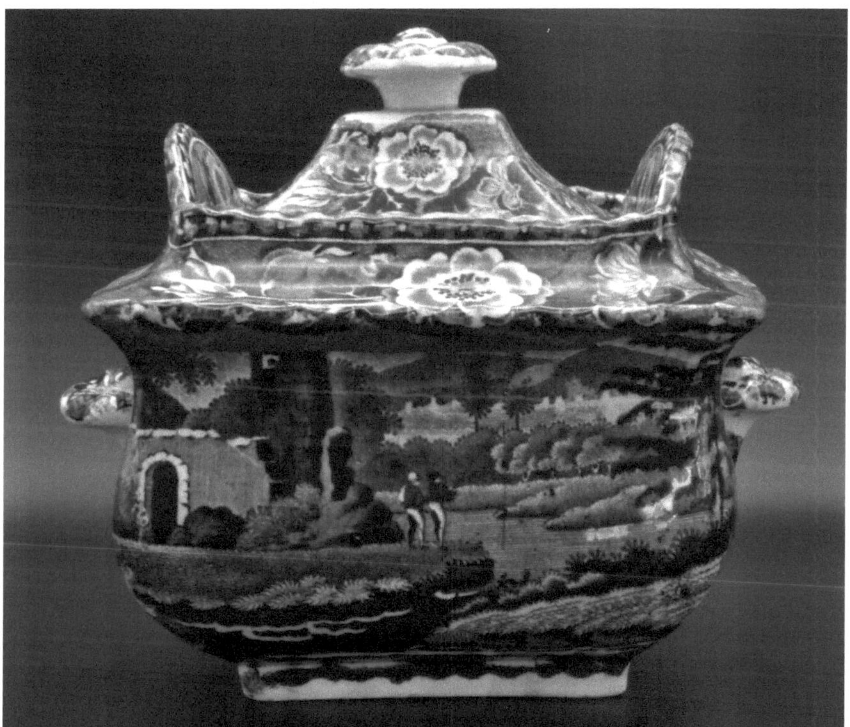

Figure 6.2 Sugar, earthenware, blue printed, depicting two fishermen beside a ruin. This printed pattern occurs on wares manufactured by Enoch Wood & Sons, Burslem, Staffordshire, c.1820s. Impressed with a circular mark, "FIELD & CLARK/ IMPORTERS OF EARTHENWARE/ UTICA." The Field & Clark partnership existed from c.1822–29.

Field & Clark even advertised ceramic designs relating to how advances in transportation were presenting new opportunities for economic progress. In 1824, it was announced that pitchers and plates had been "ordered by" them and were now available. These celebrated the opening of the Erie Canal, enthusiastically described by Field & Clark as creating an "unbroken water conveyance ... between this [Utica] and Liverpool" (*Statesman* June 15, 1824). Printed pitchers and plates mention how De Witt Clinton, the "Late Governor" of New York, had been a significant driving force behind the construction of the Erie Canal, allowing for the expansion of Utica (Figures 6.3 and 6.4).

At first, it would seem that these activities were simply intended to develop the business of Field & Clark. Field's obituary actually referred to how, in 1824, "he made the first transportation of crockery ever carried on the Erie Canal" (*New-York Tribune* September 15, 1877). Thus far, all the evidence would fit into one of expansion and creating opportunities to further consumption. While it has been noted that the Erie Canal ceramic design was orchestrated by Field &

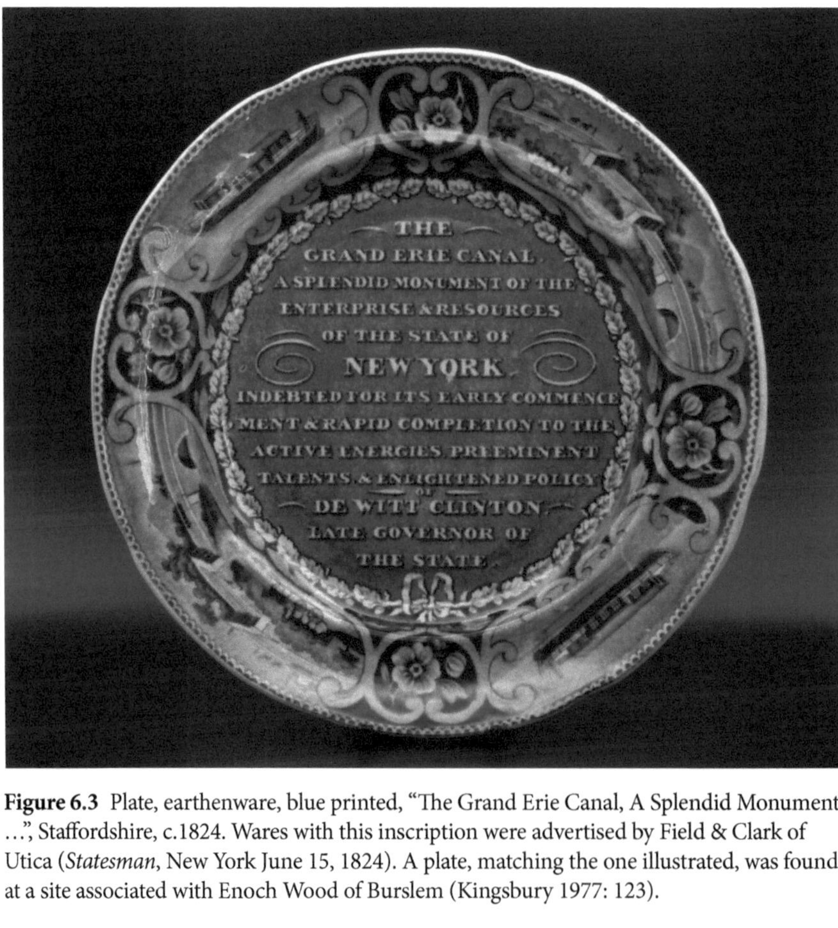

Figure 6.3 Plate, earthenware, blue printed, "The Grand Erie Canal, A Splendid Monument ...", Staffordshire, c.1824. Wares with this inscription were advertised by Field & Clark of Utica (*Statesman*, New York June 15, 1824). A plate, matching the one illustrated, was found at a site associated with Enoch Wood of Burslem (Kingsbury 1977: 123).

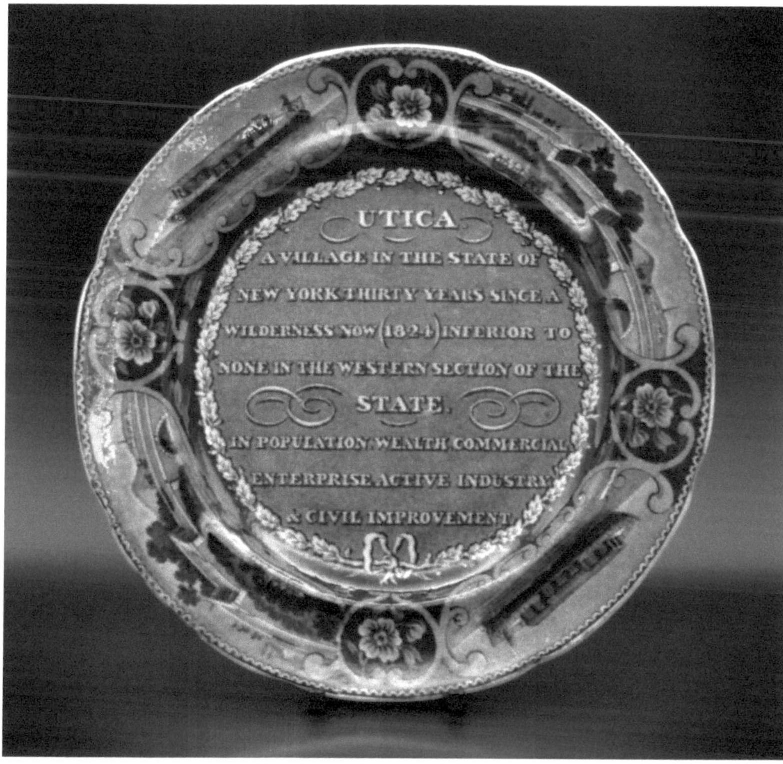

Figure 6.4 Plate, earthenware, blue printed, "Utica, A village in the State of New York ...", Staffordshire, c.1824. Wares with this inscription were advertised by Field & Clark of Utica (*Statesman*, New York, June 15, 1824).

Clark of Utica (*Patriotic America* ...), Thomas Field's wider religious views and sociopolitical interests become relevant at this point.

Orthodox crockery

At a meeting held at the Methodist Chapel, Utica, on February 18, 1828, Thomas F. Field was appointed as one of the commissioners resolved to prevent violation of the Sabbath (*Connecticut Observer*, Hartford March 3, 1828). Field became President of the Baptist Central Tract Society of Utica, founded in April 1828, and secretary of the Oneida Bible Society of New York (*New-York Baptist Register*, Utica November 28, 1828; *Philadelphian*, May 23, 1829). The Baptist Central Tract Society claimed to have distributed 150,000 tracts in 1830, and Field was still active as the President in 1831 (*Christian Watchman* February 12, 1830).

Thomas F. Field's evolving marketing strategy coincides with his religious convictions. In 1829 (McCauley 1944: 297), the partnership of Field & Clark

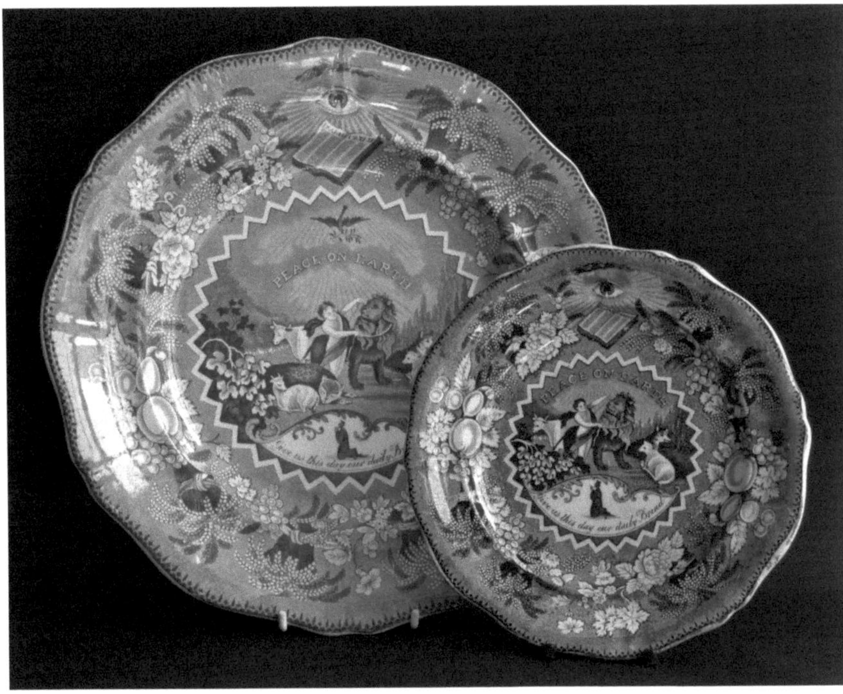

Figure 6.5 Plates, earthenware, pink and brown printed, "Peace on Earth". Printed backstamp, "Millenium" [sic]. Staffordshire, c.1833.

was dissolved, and he moved his crockery business to New York. In May 1833, it was commented on in an article titled "Orthodox Crockery" in the *Trumpet and Universalist Magazine,* of Boston, that Field was launching a ceramic design referring to the Scripture. In this article, Field was reported as stating that, "he has contracted for the manufacture of plates of all sizes" and that the "manufacturers are highly delighted with the pattern" (*Trumpet and Universalist Magazine* May 11, 1833). The orthodox crockery referred to, was actually a pattern titled "Millennium" and was advertised by Thomas F. Field from June 1833 (Figure 6.5).

One advertisement placed by Thomas F. Field for his "Millennium Earthenware" (which included a description), reinforced how plates were of a variety of sizes, "made from designs prepared by himself, principally from Scripture illustrations" and had been received from Staffordshire, by the spring's arrival (*New York Observer* June 8, 1833).

In this instance, reactions to the Millennium design are more significant. A discussion in the *Trumpet and Universalist Magazine,* clearly frowned upon what was perceived as the commercialization of commodities related to a spiritual nature. The article titled "Orthodox Crockery" in the *Trumpet and Universalist Magazine* was far from enthusiastic:

> There will be much money made on this new importation. It is a deep laid scheme for the glory of orthodoxy, and the good of the pocket. But the community is first growing wiser, and such palpable tricks will ere long meet with their deserved reprobation. Merchants may make themselves rich at first in the traffic of modern Babylon, but if the light of truth continues to spread as it has done, they shall "stand afar off for the fear of her torment, saying alas! alas! that great city Babylon, that mighty city! for in one hour is thy judgment come. And the merchants of the earth shall weep and mourn over her; *for no man buyeth their merchandize any more.*" Rev. xviii, 10,11.
>
> (*Trumpet and Universalist Magazine* May 11, 1833)

This above article was reprinted in the *Christian Pilot* (Portland, Maine May 16, 1833), and the controversy was reported in a variety of forms, such as a short article titled "Verse Plates trouble Universalists" in the *Christian Soldier*, Boston, June 22, 1833. One writer in the *Liberator*, Boston, pointed out how Jehovah's command was, "thou shall not make unto thee any graven image, or any likeness, of any thing[sic] that is in heaven above, or that is in the earth beneath …". The article, titled "Moral," continued as:

> I do not know, Mr. Editor, that the same effect would be produced on *every one*, as there was produced on *me* the other day, in receiving a Sabbath-noon refreshment on a millennium plate. I was pleased with those striking emblems of divine promise … but the presentment of the EYE appeared an exception. I could but reflect, this is just like such creatures as we are. We can advance but one step at a time; and that step very often needs mending … - *Western Recorder*.
>
> (*Liberator* September 21,1833)

This writer was not entirely convinced by all the imagery incorporated into the design, though at the same time, there is evidence of how vessels were used. As considered in Chapter 4, some ceramics might be based on a functional form, such as a jug, but given the printed design, may have a more symbolic, display purpose. According to the above article, the Millennium pattern was not simply decorative but was apparently designed to be used, since this writer encountered the design when receiving some food. Moving away from understanding ceramic design as simply responding to fashion, "The Millennium" was introduced by Thomas F. Field as an attempt to promote a religious ethos. It was advertised, but the purpose of this design had nothing whatsoever to do with fashion or being fashionable. When it is broken down, and individual examples are carefully considered, it is increasingly hard to assume that consumers followed one fashion, as a coherent mass.

Only gradually was there a more constructive discussion of the Millennium plates and its appearance. An article titled "The Millennium Ware" appeared in the *Christian Watchman*, Boston, where it was argued how, "at one time it was falsely represented by certain editors." The article included a lengthy description of the imagery but concluded that the design was the result of "a worthy and enterprising importer" and that a quantity of this ware was available for purchase at James S. Barbour's store, 26 Commercial Street, Boston (*Christian Watchman*, Boston August 23, 1833).

Distribution and religion

Judging by the above article, James S. Barbour of 26 (or No. 25 Commercial Street, according to his advertisement below) did not draw attention to the Millennium plate in his own advertising. His advertisements of June and July 1833 simply declared that he was an importer (*Boston Daily Advertiser* July 9, 1833). However, when James S. Barbour married Miss Louisa Harrod in July 1835, it was officiated by the Rev. William Hague, who was the pastor of the First Baptist Church and Society of Boston and had, until 1830, been the pastor of the Baptist Church of Utica (*Boston Recorder* December 22, 1830). Intriguingly, Thomas F. Field's Millennium plate was sold by a Baptist, and one wonders whether Field's connection to Barbour stemmed from the Rev. William Hague's own link to Utica. In this respect, the distribution of the Field's Millennium plate mirrors Stanley Chapman's structural analysis of the transatlantic economy, where he argued:

> … so long as communication between trading centres continued to be slow and uncertain, the only way in which merchants could repose confidence in their correspondents' decision making was to employ members of their own families, or, failing that, the "extended family" of co-religionists.
>
> (1992: 93)

Some advertising referred to the Millennium design. Ezra Chamberlin & Son of Boston advertised China tea sets, and specific advertisements referred to the "Millennium crockery ware", described as a "celebrated" design in 1833 (Figure 6.6). Later, his obituary recalls how "Deacon Ezra Chamberlin" had died aged seventy-six, "a gentleman well known for his correct business habits during a long series of years, and for his connection as one of the oldest and esteemed members of the Second Baptist Church" of Boston (*Manufacturers' and Farmers' Journal* December 28, 1854). Without examining the wider backgrounds of the importers, accounting for why certain patterns of distribution emerged cannot be fully appreciated. It appears that Ezra Chamberlin chose to advertise the Millennium design because of connections to the Baptist faith.

One advertisement placed by Edward E. Huggins of New Haven, Connecticut, emphasized how "Millennium Crockery" was available. Huggins does not appear to have any obvious connections to the Baptist faith, but the possible explanation for his advertisements was that his store and the Baptist Church were both on Chapel Street. In August 1833, an advertisement gave the printed design a special mention (Figure 6.7). By mid-August 1833, Huggins listed his available patterns as Pomerania, Gondola, Italian villa, Millenium, Antiquarian, Tuscan Rose, Indian Temple, Virginia, American Scenery, and Persian (*Columbian Register*, New Haven August 17, 1833).

MILLENNIUM CROCKERY WARE - Ezra CHAMBERLIN & SON, No.8, Union Street, have for sale an assortment of the celebrated MILLENNIUM WARE, which is offered at low prices.

Figure 6.6 *Christian Watchman,* Boston, September 6, 1833.

Millennium Crockery.

THE following is a brief description of this article, by the manufacturer :- On the top of the Plate is the All-seeing Eye shedding rays of light down upon the world ; beneath, is the Bible opened to Isaiah, 11th chap. 6th verse ; next in order, is a Dove descending with an Olive Branch, and the words, "*Peace on earth;*" the centre is filled up with a landscape, and a group of figures, spoken of in the verse representing the Millennium, &c. &c. For sale by

EDWARD E. HUGGINS.

135 *north side of Chapel, 4 doors from State-st.*

Figure 6.7 *Columbian Register,* New Haven August 3, 1833.

Overall, the Millennium design was commissioned by a Baptist, sold by other Baptists, and even sold in locations where it would be easily accessible to a Baptist congregation. Apart from logistical developments in transportation (Tamilia 2016: 185), another way to understand distribution is to appreciate how it could be shaped by religious connections. In addition to servicing fashion, the religious interests of importers and dealers impacted on what they sold, and alternatively, importers might promote goods that would appeal to consumers with stronger religious sensibilities.

No Man Buyeth their merchandise any more

As far as the early ceramic historian, Edwin Barber, was concerned, American-themed wares could be defined as "printing of American scenery, views of prominent buildings and places, and illustrations of historical events on crockery intended for sale in the United States" (1899: 21). From the early 1900s, the umbrella term of "Historical China," or "Historical Staffordshire" was widely used by collectors and authors to describe American-themed wares (Daughety 1927; Larsen 1950: 3). In 1974, David Arman titled a whole book *Historical Staffordshire: An illustrated check list*. The phrase "Historical Staffordshire" was used to describe any printed wares relating to American scenery, or any American events and politicians. This raises an important point as to how these wares should be defined and what may, or may not, be included within this category.

When the Reverend H. W. Hartmann wrote an article concerning "The Millennium Plate" for Sam Laidacker's *The American Antiques Collector*, although he conceded that, "It can hardly be classified as historical since its emblems pertain to the future as prophesied in the Scriptures," the purpose of the article was to draw attention to the iconography of the design (1939: 50). An open Bible provides a reference to Isaiah, Chapter XI, versus 6, which reads, "The wolf also shall dwell with the lamb, and the leopard shall lie down with the kid; and the calf and the young lion, and fatling together; and a little child shall lead them," and thus accounts for why the printed design consists of animals and a child. What the Reverend Hartmann did not know (but has now been established by examining the actual marketing), is how Thomas F. Field instigated the Millennium pattern for the American market. In this respect, a broader definition could be developed of what was produced for the American trade, embracing those printed ceramics that reflected wider cultural themes. Ceramics decorated with printed themes specifically for the American market were not simply places, events, or politicians.

Based on advertisements, and press debate and discussion, Thomas F. Field's Millennium pattern was intended to deliver a religious message—so different from the production of frivolous patterns designed to appeal to fashion. It is interesting how when the religious newspapers first heard of an intention to sell "Orthodox crockery," it was met with some scathing attacks. By all accounts, Field was perceived as someone who had lost integrity by producing a religious design to be sold commercially. Yet there is a paradox here, which contributes to the debate as to what has been perceived as a contradiction between attitudes toward consumption and whether a Protestant ethic did have any relevance to the rise of American capitalism. As has been established, Karl Samuelsson's critique of *The Protestant Ethic and the Spirit of Capitalism* believed that a fundamental problem with Max Weber's theory was that while "Puritanism unquestionably encouraged diligence and thrift (in the sense of low standards of consumption among individuals)," economically advanced countries were "not characterised by thrift" ([1957] 1961: 79, 83). Therefore, for these reasons, Samuelsson's *Religion and Economic Action* begins to fundamentally dispute Weber's thesis. Previously, a way around this apparent contradiction has been to assume that American society simply abandoned the values of ascetic fragility, embracing the possibilities of consumption (Cohen 2017: 149–50).

However, it is not necessarily as straightforward as this. The significance of the Millennium pattern was how it might begin to bridge the gap between the role of religious values in American society and how this still allowed for certain types of consumption. An advertisement placed by Field states that, "Although a considerable extra expense has been incurred in getting up the pattern, it will be sold at the same prices as ordinary patterns of blue printed ware" (*New York Observer* June 8, 1833). Importantly, the printed design was considered to be affordable, and the way it was marketed does not suggest offering the commodity at a lower price to stimulate demand.

The Millennium example conveys how religious views remained significant to some, not in a sense of a Protestant ethic, subscribing to frugality (as originally suggested by Weber), but points toward ways in which there could be a justification for consumption, if the commodities had a religious purpose. Thomas F. Field could defend his Millennium plate on the basis of its ability to spread the gospel. Meanwhile, the consumer (if they were of the same ilk), could rationalize their purchase on religious grounds rather than mere frivolity and fashion. Thus, this example hints at ways in which a Protestant ethos, and possibilities to consume, could coexist. In this way, it perhaps becomes more conceivable to reconcile Weber's notion of a Protestant ethic while not ignoring Samuelsson's observation that the propensity to consume was vital to the development of capitalism. Samuelsson concluded that it is probably "over-hasty" ([1957] 1961: 152) to link the values of Protestantism to the rise of modern capitalism, but the case of Thomas F. Field points toward the potential of religious views continuing to impact on ceramic production, consumption, and distribution, well into the nineteenth century.

Usefully, the Millennium design adds to the theories of why ceramics with a religious theme were produced. Both John Briggs and Joseph Stubenrauch considered the motivation from the perspective of the manufacturer or the demands of the market. But the Millennium design provides another explanation, since it was initiated by the importer—the intermediary. Although some became less hostile to the Millennium design (when viewing the actual pattern), Orthodox crockery was not commissioned on the anticipation of extensive demand. Thomas F. Field was not responding to widespread tastes and purchasing habits but developed an approach to marketing defined by his own connection to the Baptist faith.

Abolition

Framing production and consumption entirely around the concept of fashion, or responding to fashion, can be problematic. Alternatively, assuming that importers and dealers commissioned designs on the basis that they had an acute knowledge of American taste (because of their knowledge of the consumer demand) is also a simplification of their role (Blaszczyk 2000: 36–7). Baptists in north America were traditionally strong campaigners against slavery (Lindman 2000: 142) and once again, it may be suggested that Thomas F. Field's own views impacted on his marketing. In 1838, Field advertised "Blue Printed Earthenware, made expressly to his order" available from his New York outlet. The advertisement describes the wares as being a new pattern and incorporating the phrase "Congress shall make no law ...". This appears on blue printed wares commemorating the death of Rev. Elijah Lovejoy, the proprietor of an abolitionist newspaper at Alton, Illinois, who was murdered by a pro-slavery mob in November 1837 (Figure 6.8).

In the same period that Thomas Field advertised the Lovejoy plate, advertisements occurred for the *Narrative of Riots at Alton* written by the Reverend Edward Beecher, a brother of Harriet Beecher Stowe (Figure 6.9). Given the fact that the impressed mark, "Field & Clark, Importers of Earthenware, Utica," was found on wares manufactured by Enoch Wood & Sons of Burslem (Figures 6.2), it is perhaps possible that the Elijah Lovejoy commemorative design was also manufactured by the same manufacturer. However, currently, no marked pieces have been identified that would confirm an attribution.

It was Field's indignation at the abuse of the American Constitution that resulted in his commissioning these wares. *The Emancipator* also provided a

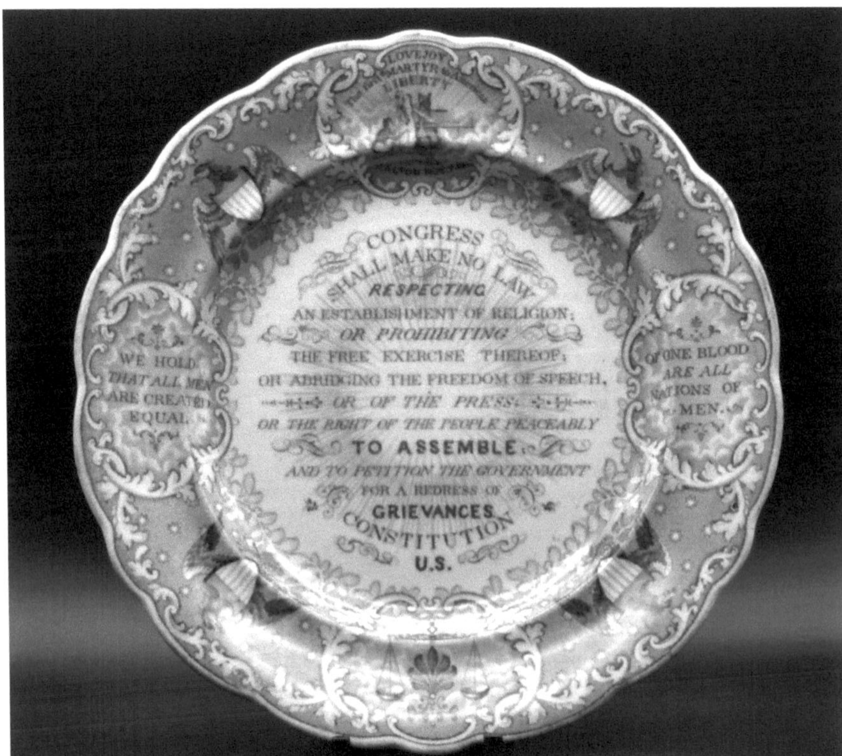

Figure 6.8 Plate, earthenware, blue printed, "Lovejoy ... Congress shall make no law ...", Staffordshire, c.1838. Advertised by Thomas F. Field of New York, in 1838.

NARRATIVE OF RIOTS AT ALTON, in connection with the Death of the Rev. ELIJAH P. LOVEJOY, By the Rev. EDWARD BEECHER, President of Illinois Col-Lege, second edition. Just received and for sale at the Anti-Slavery office, 143 Nassau st. Price - $4,50 per dozen ; 50 cents single.

JOINT STOCK SLAVE BANK LAWS IN THE TERRITORIES OF THE UNITED STATES TO BE REPEALED – The subscriber, at 87 Water street, has just received and for sale, Blue Printed Earthenware, made expressly to his order, of a new pattern, containing suitable devices, with the following article from the Constitution of the United States; "Congress shall make no law respecting an establishment of religion or prohibiting the free exercise thereof, or abridging the freedom of speech, or of the press, or the right of the people peaceably to assemble, and to petition the government for a redress of grievances."

THOMAS F. FIELD

New York, 2d October, 1838.

Figure 6.9 *The Emancipator*, New York October 11, 1838.

further endorsement of the design as advertised by "Mr. Field," including a more detailed description of the "Constitutional Ware," which poignantly mentions how it incorporated a slave kneeling at the figure of liberty pointing to a printing press (New York, October 11, 1838). This may be seen more clearly when examining the plate in detail (Figure 6.10).

A key point is that it seems doubtful that Thomas F Field was responding to American demand when commissioning the Elijah Lovejoy design. The contemporaneous interpretation, pieced together using press commentary, is rather different. In an article in Utica's abolitionist newspaper, *The Friend of Man*, it was reported that specimens of Field's plates had been discovered at the Anti-Slavery Office, New York, in October 1838. The newspaper article (presumably written by the newspaper's publisher, J.F. Bishop), explained how he had proceeded to Field's New York store at 87, Water Street to purchase a dozen plates for his own use. The unwitting testimony is useful here, as some consumers were of the same mindset as Thomas F. Field. But, at the same time, in an article titled, "Anti-Slavery Earthen Ware," the same writer believed that "The pattern was made to his [Thomas Field] own order, and, so far as we know, he is the only man in his

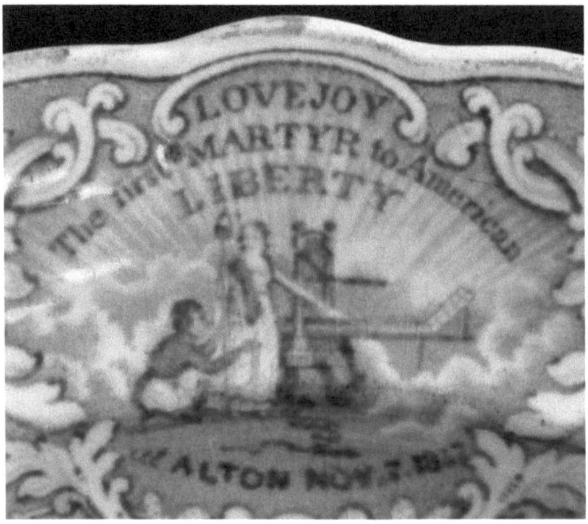

Figure 6.10 Detail of Figure 6.8 showing the inscription "LOVEJOY, The First Martyr to American LIBERTY, at ALTON NOV.7. 1837." Staffordshire, c.1838.

business who has dared to put his finger upon the 'peculiar institution.'" (*The Friend of Man,* Utica October 17, 1838).

One comment, which appeared under the heading of "Scraps," in a Hartford, Connecticut, newspaper mentions how Messrs. Field & Co., were advertising "anti-slavery earthenware" but then asked, "What sort of an animal is that?" (*Times* September 21, 1839). Somewhat paradoxically, it was transfer-printed in a lighter tone (Figure 6.8) following broader shifts in ceramic fashion, but the actual subject matter remained controversial. Thus, it is important to recognize how the design was at that time considered to be touching on an issue of acute sociopolitical tension rather than Field (or a Staffordshire manufacturer) identifying some marketing opportunity.

Awareness of how the sociopolitical views of this crockery importer influenced what Thomas Field commissioned, and what was marketed, complicates John Styles' argument that "specifications were set predominately by the merchants and manufacturers" in response to "changes in fashion ..." (1993: 528). The anti-slavery plate may not have been in enormous demand, but the importance to contemporaries was, according to *The Friend of Man*, that dining tables were furnished with this crockery, and the plates could at least "silently preach abolitionism" to guests and children "on sound principles" (October 17, 1838). Clearly, it was envisaged that the Lovejoy design was for use and not merely for display, and one is reminded of Max Weber's observation that the justification of consumption within a Protestant ethic was often practicality rather than mere pleasure ([1930] 2010: 115–6). To some extent, this also overcomes a criticism of Weber in Karl Samuelsson's *Religion and Economic Action* ([1957] 1961: 83). Instead of straightforward thrift, anti-slavery ceramics are another example of production and consumption being justified based on moralistic grounds. Field's marketing mirrors his sociopolitical views, and he continued to advertise what was termed as his "Anti-Slavery Earthenware" plates and pitchers in the New York *Spectator* from March to June 1839 (Figure 6.11).

ANTI-SLAVERY EARTHENWARE–Plates and pitchers, and a general assortment of China, glass and earthenware, of the latest and best patterns for sale. Country merchants who regard the quality of ware will find it to their interest to call and examine my stock at 87 Water street. THOMAS F FIELD.
New York, 14th March, 1839.

Figure 6.11 *Spectator*, New York, March 18, 1839.

Shocking work among the crockery

While there was agitation for abolition on both sides of the Atlantic, the actual motivation behind their production, and the reactions to ceramics, which expressed these sentiments, varied. Fuchs and Ferguson point out in "'Remember them that are in Bonds': A Plate Made for the Abolition Movement" that a transfer printed ceramic design depicting an enslaved figure was manufactured by Minton of Stoke (2021: 130–9). Fuchs and Ferguson draw attention to *The Fifth Report of the Female Society for Birmingham ... for the relief of British Negro Slaves Established in 1825*, published in 1830, which, apart from listing Herbert Minton as a benefactor, states on the last page:

> Anti-Slavery China may be purchased, at prime cost, of SARAH BEDFORD AND SON, China Rooms, New Street, Birmingham; and Associations and district Treasurers can have any quantity by writing to HERBERT MINTON, China Manufacturers, Potteries, Staffordshire.
>
> (2021: 133)

Sarah Wedgwood, daughter of Josiah Wedgwood I, was a donor and life member of this organization. Some Staffordshire manufacturers were certainly opposed to slavery, and this influenced what they produced. Josiah Wedgwood had previously produced anti-slavery medallions from the 1780s (Klamkin 1973: 102).

However, the Thomas F. Field example reinforces the central argument of this book: that the background, culture, and identity of importers should be considered, rather than perceiving importers and dealers as individuals skillful at anticipating demand and only engaged in pursuing profitable businesses. Field had social convictions, and it was even observed in a Boston newspaper of 1834 that he marketed his New York business as an "Abolition China Store," long before the death of Rev. Elijah Lovejoy in 1837. The reference to a notice in the *Liberator*, Boston, August 30, 1834, as to what the mob might do to Field's crockery store, is a poignant reminder of how the views of merchants were not necessarily in unison with attitudes of the consumers:

> Thomas F. Field, of New York, "offers for sale an amalgamation of colors and qualities of French, English, and India China Tea and Dinning Seats[sic]," and styles his store an "Abolition China Store." If the mob scent out this amalgamation, there may be shocking work among the crockery.
>
> (*Liberator,* Boston August 30, 1834)

Prior to this notice, there were anti-abolitionist riots in New York city during July 1834, when the home of Arthur Tappan—the merchant and abolitionist—was ransacked by a hostile crowd. What makes for uncomfortable reading now, but printed in a New York newspaper, was how some were under no allusion as to the view:

> We have long been of the opinion, and frequently expressed it, that the Abolitionists are *the worst enemies* the blacks of this city have. They are holding out to them the prospect of amalgamation, feeding their pride with impractical hopes, exclaiming and denouncing the prejudice of color, leading them to believe that they are unjustly and cruelly treated by the whites by denial of *equal political* and SOCIAL privileges, fomenting their passions, denouncing all who will not join them in their absurd crusade as kidnappers, villains, manstealers, thieves and pirates, inviting them to sit with the whites indiscriminately, nolens volens, in public assemblies and social parties, and thus attempting to break down the barrier which nature had set up between the races, and which the guardian sentinel is TASTE.
>
> (*New-York Commercial Advertiser* July 10, 1834)

Extreme opinions continued to be expressed, and likewise, ridiculing images still occurred on ceramics. What would appear to be a child's plate titled "the Rule of Three" (though not necessarily only produced for the American market) shows a caricature of three men, dressed in fine clothes, partaking in a toast. This small plate dates from around the 1840s–50s (Figure 6.12).

Despite the views against abolitionism expressed in the New York press, Arthur Tappan was respected by the African American community. In December 1835, his silk-goods store on Pearl Street was destroyed by the catastrophic New York fire. It was later recalled how, such was the support for Tappan, a large party of African Americans specifically saved merchandise from his burning premises (*The Evening Post,* New York, July 24, 1865).

In the manner of Tappan, Thomas F. Field was actively involved in agitation for the abolition cause. Apart from being described as the "oldest crockery merchant or dealer in this State," Field's obituary indicates that he "was at one time prominent in municipal politics, first as a Whig, then as an Abolitionist, and finally, as a Republican" (*New-York Tribune* September 15, 1877). In 1841, Thomas Field was described as President of the Baptist Anti-Slavery Society of New York (*Christian Reflector,* Worcester, Massachusetts January 27, 1841), emphasizing how his sociopolitical and religious views mirrored what he promoted.

Thomas Field even stood as an Abolition candidate for Mayor of New York in 1842, but he received only 136 votes. The Democrat candidate received over 20,000 votes, and the Whig, over 18,000 (*Albany Argus,* Albany, April 22, 1842).

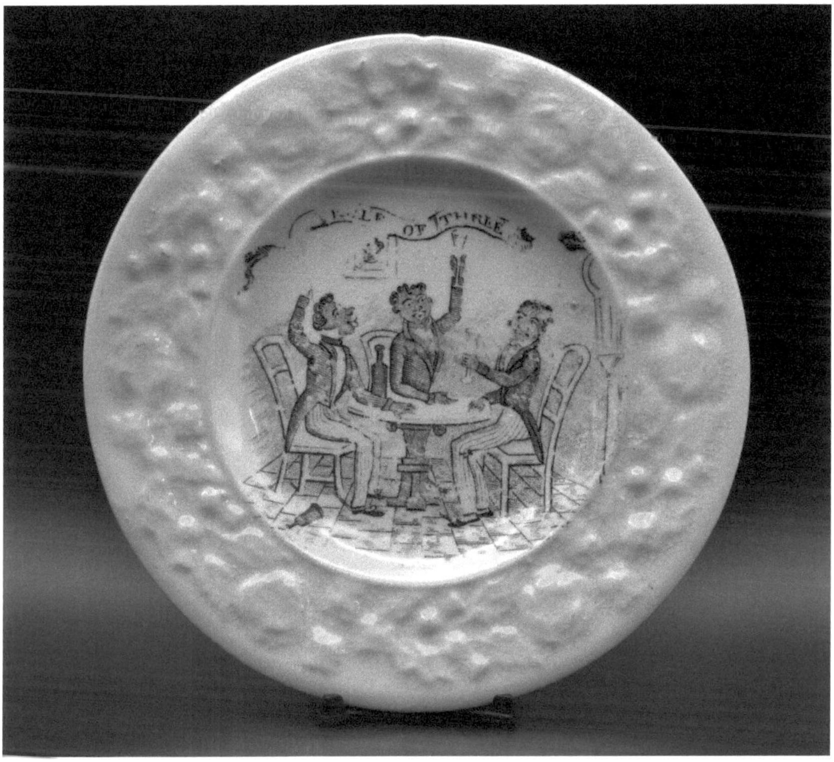

Figure 6.12 Plate, earthenware, black printed, titled "The Rule of Three." English, c.1840–50.

Before the election, an article titled, "New York City, Liberty Nomination, For Mayor, Thomas F. Field" appeared in a Boston newspaper where it is explained how the "pro-slavery spirit was strong," founded on political, commercial, social, and personal need. It was, nevertheless, hoped that when "New York gives way, slavery will soon fall" (*Emancipator and Republican*, Boston March 31, 1842). As Maxine Berg proposed in her *Luxury and Pleasure in Eighteenth-Century Britain*, other "disturbing stories remain to be told" (2005: 330) in terms of consumerism, and the example of Thomas F. Field highlights how the same applies to the United States. Field's response to the murder of the Reverend Elijah Lovejoy was rooted in his beliefs, but not in the changing desires of the market.

Rarity and forgery

The contemporary discussion of the Lovejoy design draws attention to how it touched on an issue of deep sociopolitical tension, rather than Field identifying a marketing opportunity. However, early American ceramic historians developed various unsubstantiated theories as to why the Lovejoy anti-slavery design was produced, which invariably ignored the actual role of the importer and dealer in the process of design-development. Perhaps flavored by post-bellum optimism, Alice Morse Earle wrote how:

> It is asserted that the pieces bearing this design were the gift of the English Anti-Slavery Society to the American Abolitionists, shortly after the death of Lovejoy; that they were sold at auction in New York, and the proceeds devoted to the objects of the Society of Abolitionists. If this account is true, these plates are certainly among the most interesting relics of those interesting days.
>
> (1892: 333)

Later, Ellouise Baker Larsen (the author who produced the most comprehensive survey of printed wares destined for the American market) believed that the design was certainly manufactured in Staffordshire and used to raise money for freeing slaves in the United States (1950: 242). The perpetuation of this view then becomes a convenient re-writing of history. As far as it can be established, nothing in Field's advertisements indicates that any profits were syphoned off in this way. Besides, based on the article in *The Friend of Man,* it is unclear whether there was sufficient demand for the design to benefit those who were enslaved. Nor is there evidence to support the theory that it was a gift from the English Anti-Slavery Society to be sold at auction, although this interpretation still persists in the publications of more modern American ceramic and cultural historians (Klamkin 1973: 102–4; Heneghan 2003: 14). It is noticeable how theories behind the production of the Lovejoy design then became the unquestioned gospel.

In Chapter 1, attention was drawn to Mrs. Alice Maddock owning a version of this plate, and how some American-themed designs were considered by the earliest connoisseurs to be rarer than others. Once appreciating how crockery importers and dealers acted alone, it then becomes possible to appreciate why this could be the case. When discussing the Lovejoy ceramic design, one of the earliest American ceramic historians, N. Hudson Moore, pointed out how:

> … it is unfortunate that this fine old piece was selected for forgery. Any person who is used to handling this old ware gets to detect the differences by mere touch that would escape the casual observer. Not only were the forged plates heavier, but they were thicker, and colder to the hand.
>
> (1903: 79–80)

Different versions of the Lovejoy plates are known, and these seem to support Moore's fear that there were later versions. It is now appreciated by American curators that some surviving plates are of a lighter tone, and of a slightly larger size, such as a 9 ¼ inch plate in the Reeves Museum of Ceramics at Washington and Lee University, Lexington, Virginia (Ewins, 2023: 131). It is thicker and of a more ivory color than what appears to be the originals, clearly made of pearlware, thinner, and printed in a slightly darker blue. Potentially, the larger plates were reproduced later to fulfill a demand for the rare, originals. Hudson Moore believed that:

> This unprincipled act has reduced the price of these plates about one half, and collectors are warned to examine specimens carefully before buying them. The cup- plates of this pattern have escaped the general suspicion and are selling for as highprices as ever.
>
> (1903: 80)

Nevertheless, it appears that interpretations as to why ceramics were produced have often become ingrained, and then, a widely accepted interpretation. Sam Margolin's "'And Freedom to the Slave': Antislavery Ceramics, 1787-1865" of 2002 repeated the idea that the wares were donated by British abolitionists to raise money for the anti-slavery cause and also pointed out how these were faked in the late nineteenth century. Margolin adds:

> Donated by British Abolitionists and shipped to New York to raise money through their sale for the American antislavery movement, the pieces became extremely popular, so much so that forgers manufactured and passed off as original reproductions fabricated in the late nineteenth century.
>
> (Margolin 2002: 97)

For the source of this view, Margolin cites both, Marian Klamkin's *American patriotic and Political China* of 1973, and Ellouise Baker Larsen's *American Historical views on Staffordshire China* of 1975. The narrative has become that the murder of the Rev. Elijah Lovejoy, a Presbyterian minister and editor, created a wave of indignation that led to his becoming a martyr whom the "Staffordshire potters memorialized" in their wares (Margolin 2002: 95–7).

But the reality is that it was not always a case of manufacturers producing goods to appeal to the American market, or cases of manufacturers and merchants responding to demand. It can be something entirely different. Ceramic patterns could be commissioned by a single importer, and the implication of this is that the amount manufactured, sold, and distributed was probably limited. These are transfer-printed industrial products, but not necessarily manufactured, or mass-produced, in the same quantities. So-called industrial products could actually be far more bespoke. The production of copies is not necessarily to do with popularity at the time but more likely an interesting case of how collecting of American-themed wares gradually resulted in a demand for copies, or fakes, as the originals were selling at ever higher prices.

As mentioned in Chapter 1, over the distance of time, American-themed wares have been banded together as "historical Staffordshire," or "historical china." The most typical, early interpretation of the rise of these wares became that they were produced by entrepreneurial manufacturers to appeal to the market. Indeed, when John Ridgway of the Cauldon Place Works visited Boston in 1822, he recorded in his diary, selecting "the best objects for sketching to be applied to a set of American scenery" (Diary, John Ridgway, October 24, 1822). This is unequivocal evidence of how in this case, these patterns were, motivated by the manufacturer. Ridgway noted in Baltimore how, "The People here are proud of their Public Buildings and not without cause" (Diary, John Ridgway, November 11, 1822). Likewise, when Jonathan Wainwright (son of Peter Wainwright, the Liverpool-Boston merchant) visited New York for the first time, he mentions visiting the City Hall, and how, as far as he was concerned:

> This is without exception the most perfect building I have ever seen. It is of solid marble white—& the architecture seems to me without fault.
>
> (Wainwright papers, Box 1, Folder 1.7, July 10, 1817)

J. & W. Ridgway's "American Beauties" series was widely advertised from at least May 1824 in newspaper titles published in Boston, Philadelphia, Portsmouth (New Hampshire), and Charleston (South Carolina). Perhaps not surprisingly, this series included buildings that were admired by contemporaries, including an image of the Baltimore Exchange or the New York City Hall (Figure 6.13).

The problem has been that so-called historical Staffordshire wares have become interpreted as a celebration of an emerging nation, all acting in unison. Carefully scrutinizing the actual marketing of ceramics highlights how the motivation for

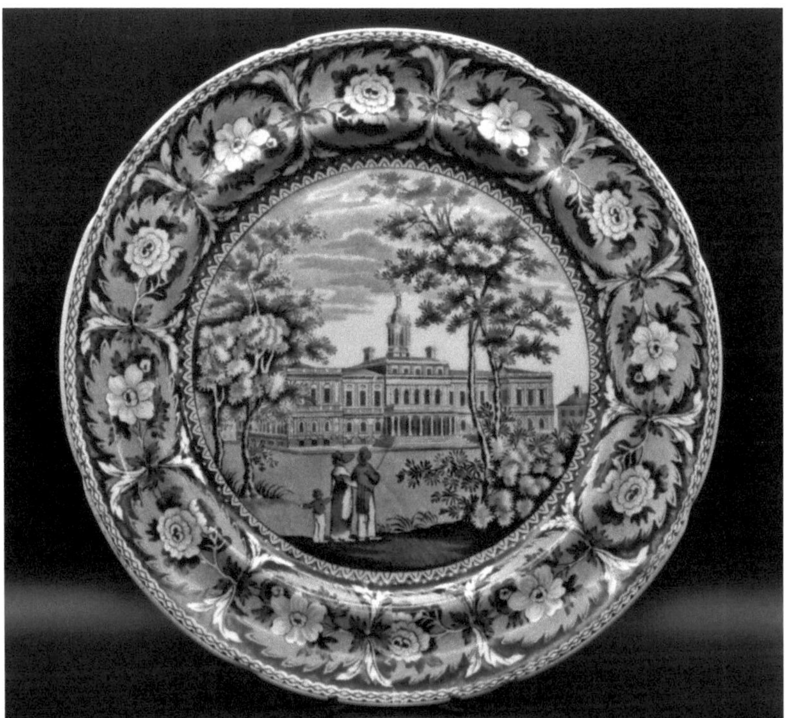

Figure 6.13 Plate, earthenware, blue printed. Backstamped, "Beauties of America/ City Hall/ New York/J.& W. Ridgway." Manufactured by J. & W. Ridgway, Cauldon Place works, Shelton, Staffordshire, c.1823–25.

the production of these types of wares varied. The controversial Lovejoy example was only advertised by Thomas F. Field, who claimed to have originated the design. Thus, there becomes a problem with the overriding theory that wares adapted for the American market were derived from "… the efforts of the Staffordshire potters to compete for the American market after the War of 1812." Adopting such a point of view then creates an inherent contradiction between the role of supply and the impact of demand. It was even observed by the same author how "The potters began to produce large numbers of vessels decorated with American views and national heroes," but that these "… were apparently not very popular, as they almost never turn up in archaeological assemblages dating from this period" (diZerega Wall 1994: 272). The example of the Lovejoy design illustrates how production could be driven by the importer and, at the same time, how there could be variations in their occurrence or popularity.

The outsider

In reality, the comments of contemporaries infer that the Lovejoy subject was a controversial one. This type of behavior was certainly more marginal, but highly significant in the sense that it might begin to explain why the earliest writers and collectors identified certain printed designs, as rare. Apart from being described as the "oldest crockery merchant or dealer in this State," Thomas F. Field's obituary indicates that he was born in England (*New York Tribune*, September 15, 1877). The narrative that ceramics, depicting American themes, were made by entrepreneurial English manufacturers, does not always apply. Neither does the view that intermediaries "harvested meaningful data about tastes and purchasing habits" (Blaszczyk 2000: 33). Field is an example of a crockery importer and dealer who marketed ceramics that reflected his own individual concerns. Rather than adopting the *ways* of his new land, there was an element of alienation expressed through his views and behavior. In the case of the Lovejoy design, when it is understood that Field had English roots, this becomes more akin to an outsider making a personal comment on the ensuing anti-slavery debate. The typical interpretation of early collectors and researchers—that Staffordshire manufacturers produced wares "particularly for the American Market and used incidents and scenes which appealed in a peculiar way to the growing nation" (Daugherty 1927: 277)—assumes that there was already a coherent sense of nationhood. However, the marketing of certain ceramics reveals that this was something of a myth.

Increasingly, by bringing together an examination of the marketing of ceramics, with the backgrounds of those individuals involved in selling certain designs, it becomes less satisfactory to relate a consumer revolution to the all-pervasive model of fashion and emulation. But the extensive work of McKendrick (using the archival material of Wedgwood) has often become the advanced way to interpret the relationship between supply and demand. For instance, using McKendrick's work on Wedgwood, it has then been assumed that "Manufacturers manipulated markets by following fashion trends" (Fullerton 2016: 92–3). While it cannot be disputed that ceramic manufacturers might respond to changing demand and fashion (sometimes, guided by intermediaries), the example of Thomas F. Field shows that not *all* production and consumption operated in this way. Nor is it completely satisfactory to account for consumption on the basis of competitive price (Miller and Earls 2008: 102). Based on Field's advertising, he did not attempt to stimulate demand by offering designs at a lower price compared to other printed wares. Certainly, in the case of the Millennium pattern, Field stressed that it was available at the same price as other blue printed wares (*New York Observer* June 8, 1833). Production could be orchestrated by the importer, and this was clearly expressive of their views and their identity. As a consequence, consumption of more bespoke designs was not a given.

Summary

This chapter highlights how importers and dealers were socially and culturally complex individuals, adding weight to Haggerty's suggestion that merchants "were not pure 'economic men.'" (2012: 236). Exploring the role of importers and dealers and then considering their origins and backgrounds begins to grow in significance, since not all ceramics necessarily emanated from the motivation of the Staffordshire manufacturer, or to requests from intermediaries to meet with the anticipated demands of the consumer. What the ceramic designs linked to Thomas F. Field demonstrate is that not all forms of production and consumption were fashion-based: quite the reverse. Examining the marketing of ceramics, which referred to Biblical or abolitionist themes, has implications on interpreting design. Field's designs cannot be described as manufacture-led, or market-led. It must be recognized, when examining the relationship between production and demand, that intermediaries were also capable of expressing alternative points of view.

The example of ceramics expressing Biblical or abolitionist themes gives weight to what was proposed towards the end of Chapter 2: that there were different possibilities within the marketplace instead of one dominant fashion. Likewise, if marketing is carefully scrutinized, it emerges as something more diverse and segmented. For instance, it was alleged that the New York merchant, Arthur Tappan, approved of "Verse-a-day" crockery of the 1830s. Tappan sold some ceramics. In one advertisement, Tappan's merchandise was described as "from Liverpool, 50 crates assorted Dinner Setts of the most fashionable patterns" (*New-York Courier*, July 15, 1816). As with so many other advertisements, the typical leverage of fashion was used to promote sales. However, as Thomas F. Field's marketing strategy evolved, it aligned much more closely with his religious connections and later moves to become an abolitionist mayor. Apparently, it was down to each individual to decide how they approached their marketing.

Thus, care must be taken not to misread actual ceramic objects from a twenty-first-century perspective. The Elijah Lovejoy anti-slavery design has been cited in David Fischer's *Liberty and Freedom: A Visual History of America's Founding*

Ideas, as one example of the "outpouring" of imagery and print, linking abolition with civil liberties (2005: 280). Semiotically, the image is exactly that, but as shown above, in reality, contemporary commentators believed that this ceramic design had limited commercial appeal. This would then coincide with the earliest ceramic historians who observed how the anti-slavery Lovejoy design was rare. Fischer is assuming that the production, or simply the existence of the object, was a reflection of changing attitudes to slavery, and uses it as evidence of the rise of the abolition movement.

The existence of the object (or the text) becomes evidence of its demand, but this analysis fails to recognize issues of rarity or contemporary reactions to the product. It is the totality of the reading of object that becomes the problem. In the Introduction to this book, it was pointed out how Roland Barthes' essay, "The Death of the Author," opposed the emphasis on understanding the lives of the producer when examining a piece of work, concluding that the text and the reader should assume far greater importance (Barthes [1968] 1977: 148). However, Fischer's interpretation of the Lovejoy design shows the danger of simply focusing on the object without appreciating the wider context and, on this occasion, having knowledge of the role of the intermediary, and their marketing, since they acted as the author. The birth of the reader is not infallible.

Following this point through to the consumer, care must be taken not to assume that everyone acted in fashion conscious and emulative ways. Based on the archaeology of three sites located in Manhattan, New York, dating from the 1790s to 1820s, it was concluded from the evidence of ceramics that, "… the consumers' goal was always to have a flashy tea set." (diZerega Wall 1994: 269). However, this would appear to be a generalized view. Comments in newspapers suggest that the designs orchestrated by Field resonated with some consumers. Rather than simply follow the whims of fashion, some ceramics became reflective of differing views and the debates occurring within society.

Chapter 7

MORALITY AND RACE

By the nineteenth century, the evolution of ceramic advertising in the United States was more complex than simply providing information about the plethora of imported merchandise. An in-depth analysis of marketing has revealed how it could take diverse forms, and in the case of the crockery importers and dealers, phrases were used that indicated how, on occasion, the motivation for production came from the importer and dealer, not the manufacturer.

The possibility has now been raised that crockery importers and dealers were capable of investing (apparently far more than has been previously appreciated) something of themselves into marketing strategies, and even what they commissioned to sell. Marketing could reflect political as well as religious values, even if this was detrimental to maximizing profits. As established in the previous chapter, the crockery dealer, Thomas F. Field, was a member of the Baptist community, and launched his "Orthodox crockery," in the form of the Millennium pattern, in 1833 (see Chapter 6, Figure 6.6). The following article, titled "More Orthodoxy!", appeared in the *Boston Recorder* in 1835, and based on what was stated below, was almost certainly referring to Field:

> An exceedingly pious young man who keeps a crockery ware shop, applied to the managers of the Portland steamer with a proposition to supply her, and receive stock. A bargain was made – a large amount of ware furnished – and lo! the first thing the proprietors knew, the number of shares he had stipulated for were up for sale at auction by his authority. Upon inquiring into the circumstances and asking the reason, they were informed by the orthodox crockery-ware dealer aforesaid, that he couldn't think of *holding shares* in a boat that *travelled Sundays*! There's for you!
>
> (*Boston Recorder* August 28, 1835)

Thomas F. Field was not simply a crockery dealer but was appointed as a commissioner to prevent violations of the Sabbath (*Connecticut Observer*, Hartford March 3, 1828). Although Field provides evidence of how his religious views ethically impacted on his approach to business, the manner in which the story was reported suggests that attempts to reconcile commerce with actions determined by religious values could also evoke a spirit of mockery. As established in the previous chapter, some ceramic importers accumulated significant fortunes because of involvement in this trade. Thomas Field's personal estate was only valued at $500 in 1860 and $1,500 in 1870 (Census, Kings, Brooklyn, 1860, 1870). Peter Mathias points out how there has been a long-argued debate as to whether kinships, additionally connected to the same theology, also acted "as a motivation force for business success" (2000: 32). But in the case of Thomas Field, following his strict Baptist ethos could just as easily curtail mercantile activity. There was a sense of Field attempting to impose his religious values though his Millennium pattern and avoidance of business activities on the Sabbath. Nevertheless, in the typical kinship pattern so prevalent in the ceramic trade, Thomas F. Field junior became connected to the crockery business (Census, New York City, 1880).

While the impact of religious morality on businesses has been examined by both British and American writers, there is more scope to explore how this then impacted on the crockery trade. Searle's *Morality and the Market in Victorian Britain* debates how effective "Christian Churches actually were in influencing the behavior of businessmen" (1998: 259). Searle refers to examples of Quaker corn merchants who attempted to develop their trade and business but were still mindful of their own religious ethos. Even if opposed to, and not directly involved in slavery, Searle also considers some points that dealt with the moral and religious dilemma of dealing in slave-grown produce in Britain. One reaction was the boycotting of West Indian sugar, and this approach was broadened to encompass a wider range of commodities in the mid-nineteenth century. Free-produce stores existed in London and Manchester from the late 1840s (Searle 1998: 61).

Likewise, advertisements for "Free Labor" stores (often owned by Quakers) appeared in Philadelphian abolitionist newspapers as early as the 1830s. Lawrence B. Glickman's paper, "'Buy for the Sake of the Slave': Abolitionism and the Origins of American Consumer Activism," documents advertisements that actually used the phrase "Free Labor," either to describe the merchandise available, or to promote the entire store, making it possible for consumers (if they wished) to be involved in this form of activism (Glickman 2004: 889–93). However, Glickman's research found that these stores were "generally short-lived enterprises" due to problems with sourcing "free-labor" merchandise, and then, with the actual quality of the produce being sold (Glickman 2004: 890–1).

Adopting an ethical approach was not necessarily widespread, or that straightforward, but it did have an impact on advertising. It is probably reasonable to suggest that the way Thomas F. Field acted was more unusual, being a reflection of his own personal and religious conscience. Comments in the press suggest that printed designs relating to the Millennium, or those that commemorated the murder of Reverend Elijah Lovejoy, the abolitionist, should not be interpreted as a huge marketing opportunity.

Expressly for us

As discussed in Chapter 2, the emergence of an American society more willing and able to consume has often been related to a growing desire to follow fashion. The creation of enormous retail emporiums in major American cities, designed to entice buyers to an array of available merchandise, is cited as evidence of some of the techniques that were used (Cohen, 2017: 155–7). The methods by which ceramic stores also became engaged in selling fashionable merchandise is illustrated by the case of Jones, McDuffee & Stratton of Boston. A description of their store in 1874 establishes how their crockery business was gradually transformed into a magnificent emporium. Jones, McDuffee & Stratton was located on Chatham and South Market streets but moved to the corner of Franklin and Federal Street to occupy a five-story building. According to one press description of Jones, McDuffee & Stratton, "no museum that we have ever seen presents so many rare curiosities of art and manufacture," being connected to all the major European potteries (*Boston Cultivator* August 29, 1874). This article, in the *Boston Cultivator*, ended its description by pointing out how on the corner of the store, there was a clock that "can not [sic] fail to attract the attention of all persons passing through that part" of town (*Boston Cultivator* August 29, 1874). Evidently, the store was now on a grand scale, with a magnificent presence, and its gradual expansion was depicted on a plate manufactured by Josiah Wedgwood & Sons, Etruria, Staffordshire, in the 1910s (Figure 7.1).

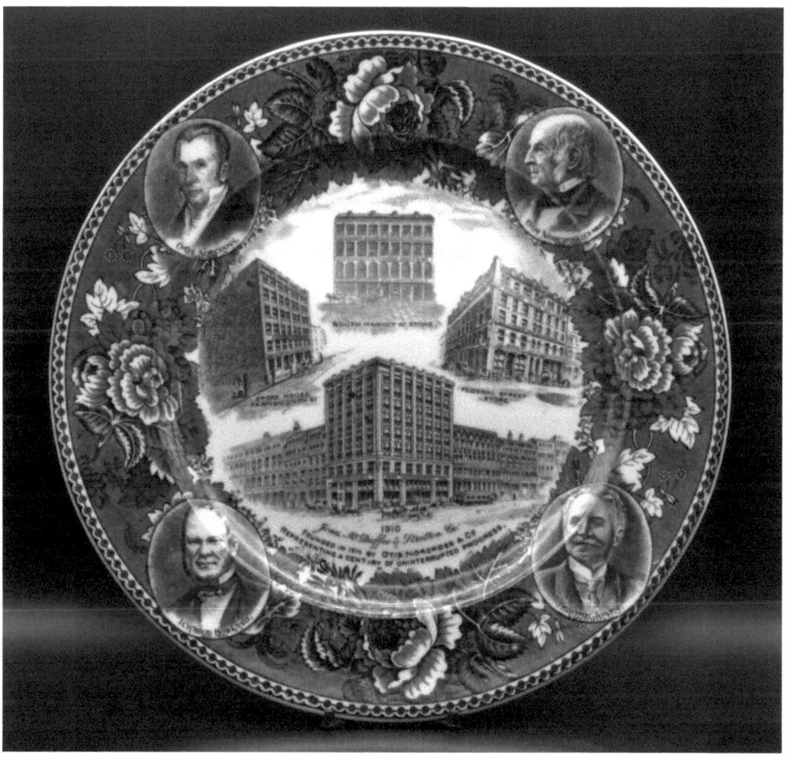

Figure 7.1 Plate, earthenware, blue printed, depicting premises and members of Jones, McDuffee & Stratton, Boston, celebrating one hundred years of business. The lower image depicts the store on Franklin Street. From top left to right: Otis Norcross (1785–1827), and Otis Norcross junior, Mayor (1811–1882). From bottom left to right: Ichabod Howland (1813–1871), and Jerome Jones (b.1837). See Pedigree 7. Impressed "Wedgwood", Etruria, Staffordshire, c.1910.

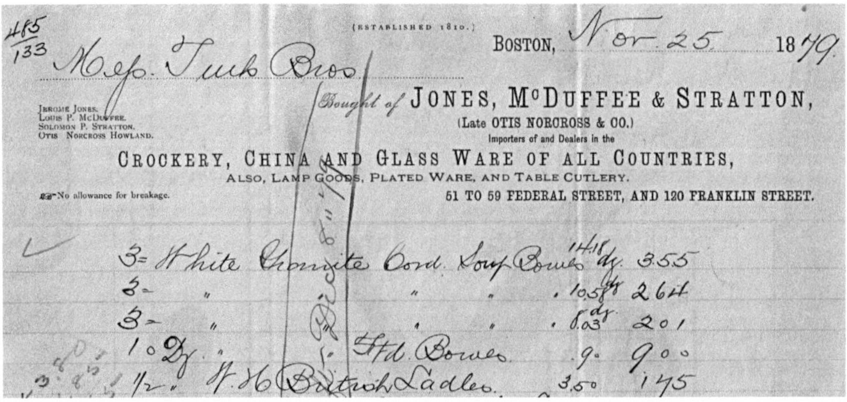

485
133
(ESTABLISHED 1810.)
BOSTON, Nov 25 1879
Mess. Tuck Bros.
JEROME JONES.
LOUIS P. MCDUFFEE.
SOLOMON P. STRATTON.
OTIS NORCROSS HOWLAND.
Bought of JONES, McDUFFEE & STRATTON,
(Late OTIS NORCROSS & CO.)
Importers of and Dealers in the
CROCKERY, CHINA AND GLASS WARE OF ALL COUNTRIES,
ALSO, LAMP GOODS, PLATED WARE, AND TABLE CUTLERY.
No allowance for breakage.
51 TO 59 FEDERAL STREET, AND 120 FRANKLIN STREET.

3 = White Granite Cord. Soup Bowls 1418 dz. 355
3 - " " " " . 1058 264
3 - " " " " . 803 201
10 Dz. " " Fd Bowls 9. 900
1/2 " W. H British Ladles 350 175

Figure 7.2 Invoice (extract) of Jones, McDuffee & Stratton. Dated November 25, 1879. The invoice provides the names of the business partners and how this firm was originally established by Otis Norcross in 1810 (see Pedigree 7).

Originally, the firm of Jones, McDuffee & Stratton was established by Otis Norcross in 1810. As the company evolved, different individuals joined the firm and became partners. Certainly, marriage provided one way to enter into the firm (see Pedigree 7). By the 1870s, the firm consisted of Jerome Jones, Louis P. McDuffee, Solomon P. Stratton, and Otis Norcross Howland. Jerome Jones joined as a clerk and had become a partner by 1861. Otis Norcross jr. was involved in the original firm and formed a partnership with Ichabod Howland. As Norcross jr. retired in 1867 (to become the mayor of Boston), and Ichabod Howland died in 1871, the firm then became known as Jones, McDuffee & Stratton (*The Boston Herald* December 14, 1916). A surviving invoice from the 1870s provides information about when the firm was founded and who was involved in the business by that period (Figure 7.2).

There is no denying that based on descriptions and imagery, Jones, McDuffee & Stratton became a significant Boston emporium. But, on the other hand, an examination of their actual advertising questions whether all ceramics sold was simply fashionable items. In the year that senator Charles Sumner died, Jones, McDuffee & Stratton advertised Parian busts produced for them and manufactured by "Leadbeater, of Staffordshire." Robinson & Leadbeater were Parian manufacturers based in Stoke from around the 1860s. The advertisement placed for "Christmas, Pleasant Surprises …" is worth quoting at some length, since it emphasizes the role that Jones, McDuffee & Stratton apparently had in orchestrating the production of the following wares:

> … Parian Bust, "Wendell Phillips," "Charles Sumner," "John A. Andrew," "Robert Collyer," etc.
>
> The bust of WENDELL PHILLIPS, recently modelled for us in Staffordshire, after the original by Martin Millmore, is of the best English Parian, and as a

likeness and work of art is approved and commended by his friends. On the back of the bust are the characteristic words: "Peace if possible; Justice at any rate," engraved in fac simile with his autograph.

The bust of CHARLES SUMNER, modeled expressly for us is from the same pottery, and is equally commended. On the reverse of it are his famous words. "Equality of Rights is the first of Rights," with his autograph. The price of the size, 10 inches high is, the same as the Phillips bust, $3.50.

We have also the busts of ROBERT COLLYER and JOHN A. ANDREW. On the back of the latter is the characteristic essence: "I know not what record of sins awaits me in the other world, but this I know, that I was never mean enough to despise any man because he was ignorant, because he was poor, or because he was black" ...

(*The Golden Rule*, Boston December 20, 1876)

The phrases "modelled for us" and "expressly ordered for us" are significant, since they provide a sense of their relationship with their European suppliers. The Parian busts available were of lawyers, senators, and preachers—not necessarily connected to Massachusetts or Boston—but all prominent figures in declaring an indefatigable support for abolitionism and racial equality. An anti-slavery speech delivered by Charles Sumner in 1856 so enraged Preston Brooks, a South Carolina senator, that he severely attacked Sumner with a cane. Such was the degree of contention over the issue of slavery. A Parian bust of Sumner, inscribed on the reverse, "Equality of Rights is the first of Rights" matching what was advertised, is shown in Figure 7.3.

Jones, McDuffee & Stratton's advertisements indicate that certain Parian busts were ordered by them. Successful crockery dealers were also becoming powerful figures in their own right. Were the Parian busts (as promoted by Jones, McDuffee & Stratton) entirely responding to demand, or potentially a reflection of their own moral persuasion? John A. Andrew, the Massachusetts lawyer and subject of one of the Parian busts, attended meetings of the Bird Club of Boston. Jerome Jones (of Jones, McDuffee & Stratton) was a life-long member. This political organization was composed of business owners who supported Charles Sumner as a Senator and John A. Andrew as governor of Massachusetts (*Springfield Daily Republican* April 4, 1901; April 28, 1901). Although an 1875 advertisement placed by Jones, McDuffee & Stratton used the phrase "Parian Busts of Gov. Andrew, Sumner, Robert Collyer and 20 other celebrities" (*Christian Register*, Boston November 27, 1875), perhaps inferring a popularity of these individuals, the 11-inch version of Charles Sumner's Parian bust cost $4.00, and the 13 inch, $6.00 (*Spring Republican* December 22, 1875). John A. Andrew, Charles Sumner, and Robert Collyer may have been described as celebrities, but the actual busts were expensive items. In the same era that Jones, McDuffee & Stratton marketed their Parian busts, Guy & Brothers of Boston offered an entire ironstone tea-set of fifty-four pieces for $3.50 (*Christian Register*, Boston October 13, 1877). The price, as well as the scale of the supplier, infer that production and the ability to purchase them were limited. Robinson & Leadbeater of Stoke, who apparently produced the Parian busts for Jones, McDuffee & Stratton, employed only forty-six people (Census, Stoke-on-Trent, 1871).

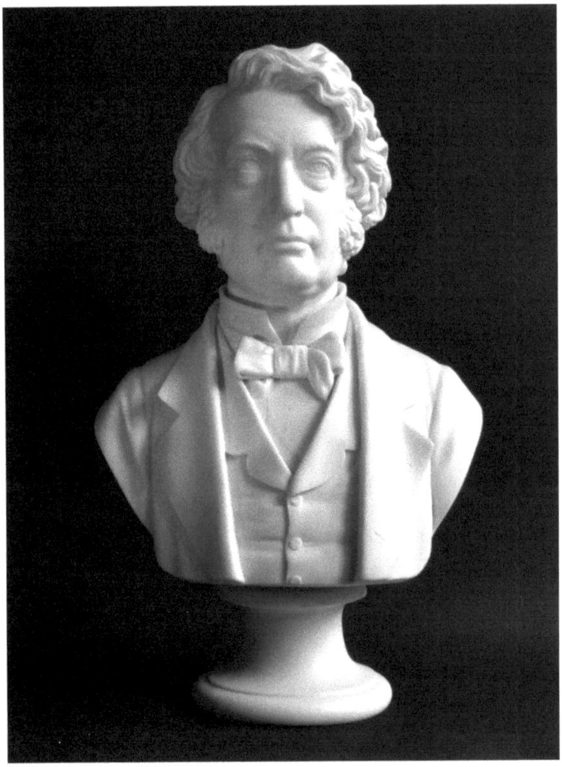

Figure 7.3 Parian, bust of Charles Sumner, impressed, "Published by J McD & S, Equally of Rights is the first of Rights, Charles Sumner, Copyright." Probably manufactured by Robinson & Leadbeater, Stoke-upon-Trent, c.1875.

Examining advertising—not simply the surviving ceramic examples—draws attention to these further instances of importers acting in more individualistic ways. While this has become clearer by examining marketing, it has also been noted above that the crockery importer, Thomas F. Field, did not amass a vast personal wealth. There was perhaps an economic price for pursuing an ethical and moralistic position. However, Jerome Jones (of Jones, McDuffee & Stratton) bequeathed $10,000 to each of his three daughters, and $1000 to both the Young Men's Christian Union, and the Free Hospital for Women at Brookline, Boston (*Boston Journal* December 17, 1916). In other words, Jones was still able to accumulate a significant mercantile fortune and advertise certain ceramics, which may well have reflected the business owners' views and sympathies.

When examining the lives of merchants, it becomes clear just how far they could be multifaceted individuals. Hector Tyndale was a significant figure in the crockery trade in Philadelphia, inheriting a business established by his father, Robinson Tyndale. As Robinson died aged sixty-four, his mother, Sarah, continued to run the business until it was passed to Hector Tyndale. When Hector delivered an address described as "Before the Mercantile Beneficial Association," he was at pains to point out how "Labor in any form, in any condition, still preserves its heavenly origin, for the Father of all of us is the centre of all labor." He continued:

> These are truths, my friend, we cannot impress too strongly on our minds; they are, or ought to be, a part of our religion, and that religion, too, which is not lip service, but which should be graven on our hearts and ever present to our minds; they should accompany us to our temples of labor, to our stores and workshops; there they should most be present, for it is there we are to apply them".
>
> (*North American and United States Gazette* May 15, 1850)

Tyndale was a conscientious individual, originally of a Democrat persuasion. In 1837, as a young man, he visited Texas with his father, and witnessing the slave system, became a member of the Free-Soil party and an opponent of slavery (*The Philadelphia Inquirer* March 20, 1880). Later in life, Hector Tyndale accompanied Mrs. Brown to Harper's Ferry, Virginia, to recover the body of the abolitionist, John Brown, who had been executed for treason in 1859. Tyndale fought in the American Civil War and in 1868 ran for mayor of Philadelphia. It was a campaign hampered by controversy, with Tyndale being accused of blasphemy, when it was reported how:

> ... in the presence of some company, in Mr. Tyndale's own parlor, attention was directed to a likeness of John Brown which graced the walls. In the course of conversation General Tyndale emphatically remarked: "*That Man,*" pointing to John Brown's picture, "*was a better man than Jesus Christ*".
>
> (*Camden Democrat,* New Jersey September 19, 1868)

In Staffordshire, John Brown was immortalized in the form of a ceramic flatback, although there is no indication that this figurine was ever advertised for sale by Tyndale & Mitchell (Pugh 1995: 204–5). Although Hector Tyndale's campaign was ultimately unsuccessful, the above extract provides greater insight into his sentiments and even a sense of what he owned. As Hector Tyndale withdrew from the crockery business to pursue his municipal ambitions (allowing his brother, Harold, and a brother-in-law to continue the Tyndale & Mitchell firm), he still devoted "considerable attention to ceramic art, and acquired the reputation of being an excellent critic in so matters, so much so that he was selected as one of the judges of the Centennial Exposition, and made chairman of the Group in Ceramics" (*The Philadelphia Inquirer* March 20, 1880).

Morality

Awareness of the wider preoccupations of ceramic merchants and dealers leads to moving beyond the consideration of ceramic designs and marketing to begin to explore additional ways in which attitudes potentially influenced behavior. As has been established by previous chapters, Peter Wainwright came from the outskirts of Liverpool and dealt in a variety of commodities, but he often advertised the sale of crockery in Boston during the 1790s and early 1800s. Family letters are revealing of their own attitudes to slavery. Peter Wainwright's sons were also born in Liverpool, and, as teenagers, were pupils of a school in Sandwich, approximately fifty miles south of Boston. The Sandwich Academy advertised as opening in 1805 and described how its curriculum paid attention to "literary, moral and religious improvement" (*Columbian Centinel*, Boston August 21, 1805). On one occasion, the eldest son, Jonathan Wainwright (later to be the Bishop of New York), wrote to his mother:

> Since I wrote my last letter old Titus has died. I believe he has done his duty in this world. He sprung from nothing & died possessed of 1500 dollars, from which (by his will) there is to be a clock put on the meeting house steeple, a monument to be erected over his tomb & the remainder to be given to the parish. Mr. W. Fessenden is the executor. We see that worth is not confined to color. Titus was once a slave. Is it not strange that men will still continue in a trade so discordant with the principles of humanity & justice. And bind them to hard labour with the scourge of cruelty. Men, whose natural abilities if cultivated might make them some of the first of characters.
>
> (Wainwright papers, Box 1, Folder 1.5, March 29, 1808)

Titus was somehow connected to the Academy, or to Sandwich. None of these intended acts of generosity was apparently reported in the local press, although there were references to William Fessenden, who was described as the Treasurer of Sandwich Academy (*New-England Palladium,* Boston February 15, 1805). Jonathan Wainwright's letters are already evidence of how his attitudes were devoid of prejudice, but they are at the same time contradictory, in the sense that his father had previously benefited from slavery. As established in Chapter 3, Peter Wainwright diversified, importing tobacco from the southern states for smoking and chewing, which was refined at his Mill Bridge works, near Boston. Undeniably, the growing of tobacco was extremely reliant on those who were enslaved (Bordewich 2005: 16).

Yet there was still some remarkable consistency in Jonathan's attitudes from his youth to his concerns as an adult. Twenty years later, when Jonathan Wainwright was a reverend in New York, a select group of individuals convened at his house to discuss the unusual case of the "Moorish Prince, ABDUHI RAHHAMAN." The prince, a former slave from Natchez, Mississippi, had been freed so that he could return to Africa. However, the purpose of the meeting was to devise ways in which Rahhaman's five sons and eight grandchildren could also be freed, since they remained in captivity (*New-York American,* October 14, 1828). One of the five who attended the meeting was none other than New York merchant and abolitionist, Athur Tappan.

If individuals moved to the United States from Staffordshire because of involvement in the crockery trade, they inevitably encountered a more multicultural society. Thomas Bakewell's connection to the ceramics probably stemmed from his marriage to Mary Hewitt at Stoke in 1808 (Adams 1926-27). Members of the Hewitt family of Lane End were ceramic manufacturers and had become crockery importers in New York by the early 1800s, as discussed in Chapter 3 (see Pedigree 3). Bakewell was listed as receiving crates of earthenware in New York in 1810

Figure 7.4 *New-York Gazette & General Advertiser* December 8, 1818.

China, Glass & Earthenware, Agency

THOMAS BAKEWELL, having been appointed Agent for a principal Manufactory in England, solicits the attention of those Merchants and Dealers, who have been in the habit of importing the above mentioned articles.

T.B. pledges himself that orders received by him shall be selected with an exactness, and executed with a promptitude, which will entitle his house to a liberal patronage. Terms accommodating.

T.B. tenders his acknowledgments to his former customers, and informs them and the public that his individual stock of China, Glass and Earthenware, he is selling at reduced prices, at public auction. Those who wish to avail themselves of a rare opportunity, for obtaining a cheap assortment will find it to their advantage to attend the sales, which will continue Tuesdays and Thursdays at No. 51 Maiden-lane, until the whole is sold. Terms liberal to whole and other dealers.

(*Ming's New-York Price-Current* October 27, 1810). Based on New York city directories, Thomas Bakewell was in partnership with Thomas Cook from 1811 until 1814, and Cook had married into another crockery importing family, the Cauldwells—who were also connected to the Hewitt family (see Pedigrees 2 and 3).

By 1818, Thomas Bakewell of 51, Maiden Lane was able to advertise that he had secured the agency of a principal manufacturer, presumably a Staffordshire firm (Figure 7.4). Bakewell built up a significant trade, receiving the substantial amount of 134 crates of earthenware from Liverpool in 1820 (*Shipping and Commercial List and New York Price Current* April 7, 1820).

One of Thomas Bakewell's sons, the Reverend William Henry Bakewell (Figure 7.5), wrote an autobiography, providing significant insight into the wider activities and experiences of those involved in the crockery trade (Willett 1892). The Reverend William Henry Bakewell was born in New York in 1817 and stated that:

> My father was well off as regards this world's goods. He was a wholesale dealer in chinaware, in connection with my grandfather Hewitt, (mother's father) who was a manufacturer of the world-renowned "Staffordshire china".
>
> (Willett 1892: 6)

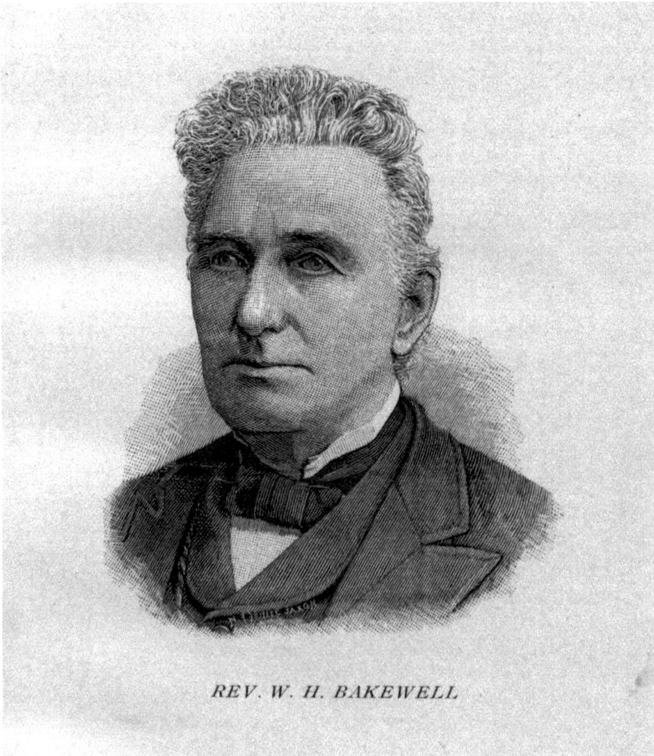

Figure 7.5 Reverend William H. Bakewell, frontispiece, from W.H. Bakewell's *Vision of Faith in the Dream of Time* … 1888.

But, reinforcing the view that those involved in mercantile trade were also multidimensional individuals, Thomas Bakewell was described by his son as:

> … for years a class leader and Sabbath school superintendent in the old John Street Church, New York. That was the first Methodist church built in America (Willett 1892: 5).

The Methodist branch of the New York Sunday School Union Society met at a Chatham Street property near to the John Street Church. Between 1816 and 1818, Thomas Bakewell was regularly listed as a superintendent of the Sunday school, which sometimes had around four hundred pupils, aged between ten and twenty-one, both male and female, and of mixed ethnicity, although the number of pupils listed as "coloured" [sic] was proportionally smaller (Minutes, Methodist Branch of the New York Sunday School Society, 1816–18). The Reverend William Bakewell recalls how, as a child, their home on Chatham Street, New York, was often used as a place to stay by visiting Methodist preachers, such as Joshua Marsden from England, and the Americans, Bishop William McKendree, and Dr. Nathan Bangs.

William Bakewell's account provides revealing evidence of how his father behaved as an Englishman in New York. Whereas Elizabeth (the American wife of Peter Wainwright) employed English "imported domestics" when living in Boston (Wainwright Papers, Box 1, Folder 1.4, September 29, 1807), Thomas Bakewell "purchased" an African-American maid known as Peggy. Slavery in New York was not uncommon. In the eighteenth century, New York City had the second highest slave population after Charleston, South Carolina (Lepore 2005: 60). Only because of laws introduced in 1799 and 1827 was slavery gradually abolished in the state of New York, although due to certain technicalities, it was still possible to be enslaved well into the 1840s (Rael 2005: 132). The Reverend William Bakewell described their maid, Peggy, in the following way:

> Her name was "Peggy." I do not know that she ever had any other name. She was a colored domestic, who had been purchased by my father in New York. The horrible traffic in human beings was not viewed in the same light as it was a few years later. The conscience of the church was not thoroughly awakened to the enormity of the evil. Many Christian people owned slaves and did not deem it inconsistent with a profession of religion, so long as they were treated kindly. My father, however, could not reconcile slave ownership with a profession of Christianity, so he gave Peggy her freedom. In the exercise of her freedom she very gladly accompanied us across the sea ...
>
> (Willett 1892: 8)

Although Thomas Bakewell initially had no qualms about purchasing a slave, connections to Methodist church led him to grant Peggy her freedom. Then, Peggy accompanied the Bakewells back to England, when they visited relatives in Staffordshire in the 1820s. This coincides with an 1822 press announcement, indicating that Thomas Hewitt jr., was returning to "his old establishment" on 51, Maiden Lane, where Thomas Bakewell had previously been located since at least 1816 (*Evening Post*, New York November 2, 1822). Thomas Hewitt junior and Thomas Bakewell were brothers-in-law (see Pedigree 3). Peggy must have exercised a deep and lasting impression on William Henry Bakewell. She was illustrated in his memoirs, and stereotypical (as her portrayal now appears), it is notable how Peggy was the only member of his household specifically chosen for depiction in the publication (Figure 7.6).

As a boy, the Reverand William Bakewell was able to meet his paternal grandfather in England. He ran a lunatic asylum at Spring Vale, near Stone (Figure 7.7), and as "Keeper of the Spring Vale Asylum," even gave lectures on the subject of the "Nature, Causes and Means of preventing, and Cure of Mental Derangement" at the Wheat Sheaf Inn, Cheadle, Staffordshire (*Staffordshire Advertiser* September 28, 1816). As for Peggy, the Reverend William Bakewell indicates that having gained her rightful freedom, she died while still in England, "some years later" (Willett 1892: 8). As a consequence of the Anglo-American ceramic trade, multiculturalism actually existed in England.

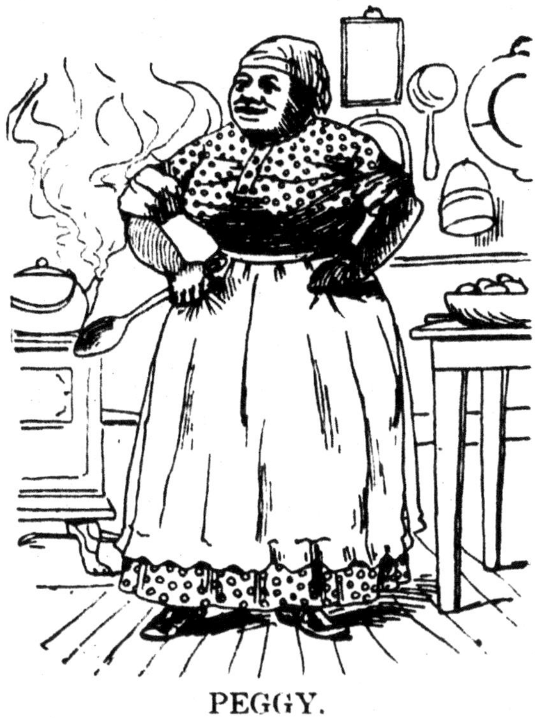

Figure 7.6 Engraving, "Peggy," in Reverend C. Carey Willett, ed., *Memories of Britain By Rev. W. H. Bakewell*, Darius D. Thorp, Lansing, Michigan, 1892, pp. 8–9. Courtesy of John Hay Library, Special Collections, Brown University, Providence, RI.

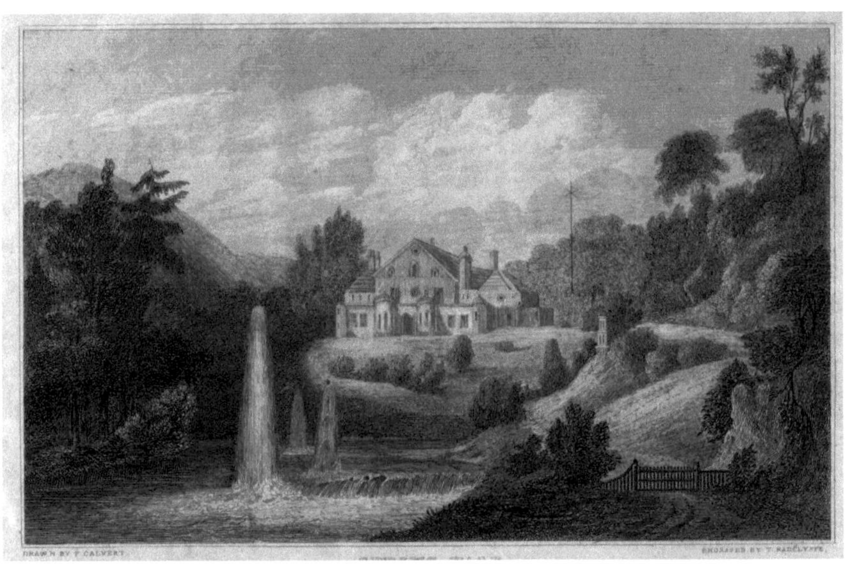

Figure 7.7 Engraving, titled "Spring Vale, near Stone, Staffordshire, seat of T. Bakewell, Esq", c.1830. A similar image of the house is reproduced in Reverend C. Carey Willett's *Memories of Britain By Rev. W. H. Bakewell*, Darius D. Thorp, Lansing, Michigan, 1892.

CROCKERY. – A general assortment of EARTHERN-WARE, CHINA, and GLASS, for sale by the subscribers at their store, 85 Genessee- St. and Canal tow-path, opposite Bleecker's Bason.

THOMAS F. FIELD. & CO.

Utica, 22 Aug. 1828-

Figure 7.8 *New-York Baptist Register*, Utica, December 19, 1828.

However, as pointed out by the Reverend William Bakewell, "many Christian people" continued to own slaves, and it was this troubling contradiction that caused Harriet Beecher Stowe to use her work—most famously, *Uncle Tom's Cabin*—to "bring the subject of slavery, as a moral and religious question, before the minds of all those who profess to be followers of Christ in America" (Stowe 1853: vi). Thomas Bakewell freed his maid, widening the debate over the potential impacts of links to church and religion on the activities of other crockery importers and dealers.

Religious newspapers and advertising

Of the 6,056 American newspaper titles published in 1871, it was estimated that "the religious papers take the lead, and number two hundred and eighty-three" (Greeley et al. 1872: 1221–2). A sizeable proportion of the newspapers maintained that they followed a religious ethos in nineteenth-century America. It is not too surprising, then, to observe how the crockery dealer, Thomas F. Field (with his strong Baptist connections), advertised in a Utica newspaper titled the *New-York Baptist Register* (Figure 7.8).

The tendency to use certain newspapers to advertise merchandise, which coincided with the views of the seller, was even observed by contemporaries. A notice in *The Newark Daily Advertiser* noted how:

> What Next?—A pious trader in N. Y. advertises in the religious papers, "*Millennium Earthen Ware dinner Plates*! of all sizes, made from designs prepared by himself, from scripture".
>
> (June 8, 1833)

This notice is referring to Thomas F. Field, who had moved from Utica to New York by the 1830s and had commissioned the Millennium printed design. But the suggestion is of how the dealers would draw attention to religious goods in religious newspapers. When in New York, Field also advertised in *The New-York Recorder*, specifically described as "A Religious Family Newspaper." The *New-York Recorder* was published weekly from 1845 and was edited by the Reverend Sewall S. Cutting. When it was launched, Cutting described its intentions as:

> I aim to make a *Religious Newspaper*, [Cutting's italics] in the most comprehensive sense of those terms. I shall seek the latest intelligence on all subjects which are suitable to the character of the religious press. As to the denominational character of this paper – it will be Baptist. I shall seek to maintain courtesy towards all branches of the Christian family …
>
> (*The New-York Recorder* July 3, 1845)

As the *Recorder* evolved, it gradually acquired different titles. It was known as the *New-York Recorder & Register* in the 1850s. By 1865, it had become *The Examiner and Chronicle*, but it still boasted that it was "The Largest, Cheapest, and the most Widely-Read Baptist Newspaper in the World" in the 1870s (*The Examiner and Chronicle* February 17, 1870).

Field was not the only ceramic dealer to advertise in this newspaper. In another instance, William A. Francis advertised "China, Glass and Earthenware" available at his New York store (*The New-York Recorder* December 4, 1845). William A. Francis was mentioned in trade directories in the 1850s, as a crockery dealer, who also became treasurer of the New York Montana Mining and Discovery Company. Was a propensity to advertise in certain religious papers a reflection of the ethos of this dealer? As it turns out, a more detailed obituary notice appears for William A. Francis, as he sadly committed suicide due to illness, in 1866. This lengthy article further establishes that he, "for twenty-five years had been an exemplary member of the Twenty Third Street Baptist Church" (*The World*, New York November 3, 1866). There was a clear Baptist connection, and perhaps a tendency to advertise in familiar newspapers. Or, viewed in another way, paying to advertise in a newspaper that was sympathetic to the Baptist cause allowed merchants to give a revenue to newspapers, such as the *Recorder*.

One intriguing advertisement for "crockery, lamps etc." was placed by Ovington Brothers and actually used the phrase, "Respectfully inform the readers of the Recorder," how they had moved to a new store in Brooklyn (*The New-York Recorder* March 27, 1850). The phrase "readers of the Recorder …" was used in the Ovington advertisements placed in this newspaper from between January to April 1850. In one instance, advertisements for Ovington Brothers, as well as Thomas F. Field, appeared in the same column in March 1850 (Figure 7.9).

In another instance, a newspaper titled *The Independent* of New York claimed to have the largest circulation of any religious newspaper in the world. For this reason, newspaper editions suggested that "as a medium for advertising, its columns are unsurpassed." In anticipation of the potential readership, it is interesting that advertisements placed by G. W. Tooker, importer, wholesaler, and retailer of ceramics and glass, Canal Street, New York, offered "A liberal discount to made to Clergymen, Missionaries, and Principals of Schools" (*The Independent* December 18, 1862). The Ovington Brothers of Brooklyn also advertised in *The Independent*.

CROCKERY, LAMPS, &C.

OVINGTON, BROTHERS, RESPECTFULLY INFORM THE readers of the Recorded, that they have removed to their new Store, No 184 Fulton street, between Orange and Pineapple streets, and are now opening Dinner, Tea, and Toilet Ware of the new patterns and superior finish.

Their stock also comprises a full assortment of Solar, Miniature Solar, and others Lamps, Girandoles, Hall Lanterns, Britannia Ware, and a variety of house furnishing articles; and they confidently assure their friends that they can make their purchases at No.184 Ful-Ton street, Brooklyn, as cheap at any store in the city of New-York.

BOWERY LAMP STORE.

THE SUBSCRIBER IS CONSTANTLY RECEIVING FROM CORNELIUS' and other manufactories, all of the latest styles of Solar and Land Lamps, Hall Lamps, Girandoles, &c, which he is prepared to sell at the lowest cash prices. Britannia Metal, Glass and Camphene Lamps, Camphene, Oil Burners, Fluid, Globes, Wicks, Chimneys, &c, always on hand.

CHARLES A. BALDWIN, 59 ½ Bowery.

CHINA, GLASS AND EARTHEN WARE.

A VERY GENERAL ASSORTMENT OF CROCKERY CONSTANTLY for sale, suitable for housekeeps, at the current prices of New-York or this city – At the store, 167 Atlantic street, corner of Clinton, South Brooklyn.

N.B. Goods loaned for the use of parties.

THOMAS F. FIELD.

Figure 7.9 *The New-York Recorder* March 27, 1850.

This leads to questions as to whether the owners of Ovington Brothers had any religious affiliations of their own.

Ovington Brothers was established by Henry A. Ovington (a secretary to the New York City Chamberlain) with his sons, Theodore Tweedy and Edward Judson Ovington, in Brooklyn in 1846. Another son called William H. Ovington ran a Chicago branch of the firm from the 1870s until 1889 (*Daily Inter Ocean* March 4, 1889). Pedigree 13 shows the various members of the Ovington family. Henry A. Ovington was from Springfield, New Jersey, and had been a colonel of the militia regiment, which paraded on the arrival of General Lafayette at New York in 1824 (*Truth* January 7, 1883; *New York Tribune* February 22, 1886; *The New York Herald* February 22, 1886). Evidently, Ovington Brothers became a successful business. Both Theodore T., and Edward J. were, on occasion, described as millionaires (*Waterbury Evening Democrat* April 29, 1908; *Kansas City Times* December 4, 1887). When a huge fire occurred at Ovington Brothers in 1883, their losses were estimated at $250,000, giving some indication of the size of the business by that period (*Truth* January 7, 1883). Charles K. Ovington recorded in his personal diary that:

> January 6th 1883. Store Burned. Secured a lease of a church in Clinton street the same day. Opened the church in about a week and continued in business there until November, when the new store opened.
>
> (Diary, Ovington, 1882–83)

Even the amount of rescued stock sold in the "White Church on Clinton St. around the corner from the ruins of their old buildings" was described as consisting of fifteen-thousand decorated cups and saucers and twenty-thousand decorated plates (*New York Tribune* February 5, 1883). It is curious that ceramics were sold, albeit temporarily, from a church building. Nevertheless, ceramics backstamped as "Ovingtons" were often supplied by the high-end European and English manufacturers, such as Josiah Wedgwood & Sons (Figures 7.10 and 7.11).

Intermittently, Ovington Brothers continued to advertise in the *Recorder* in the 1860s and 1870s. In 1865, they offered "Decorated Dinner Services, of choice and new designs from $90 to $500" (*The New-York Recorder* March 2, 1865). For the holiday Christmas trade in 1874, tea and toilet-sets and Parian statuettes were all available (*The New-York Recorder* December 17, 1874). Advertisements placed in the *Recorder* (alongside Ovington Brothers) were for "Portable Pipe Organs for

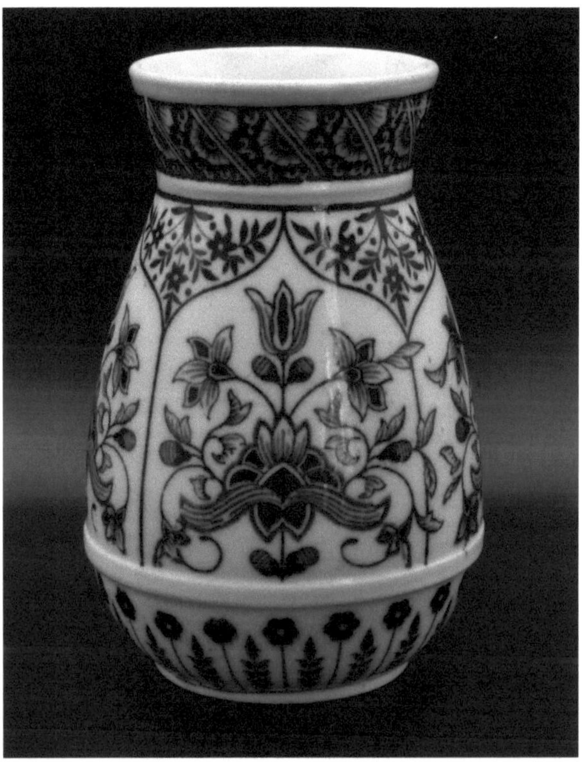

Figure 7.10 Toothbrush holder, earthenware, blue printed. Josiah Wedgwood & Sons, Etruria, Staffordshire, c.1870–80.

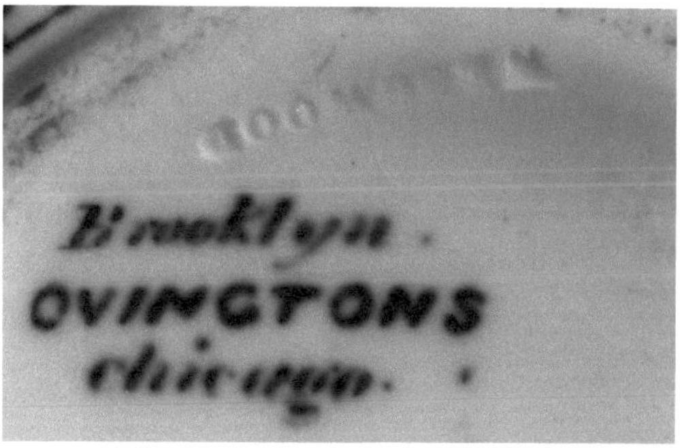

Figure 7.11 Backstamp and printed mark on Figure 7.10. Impressed "Wedgwood" and blue printed mark, "Brooklyn/ Ovingtons/ Chicago."

churches" available from Charles B. Derby of New York, and chimes and church bells sold by Jones & Co. of Troy, New York (*The New-York Recorder* December 19, 1867). While this conveys a tendency to promote merchandise with some religious functions, there is no evidence, at this stage, that Ovington Bothers marketed ceramics that responded to a religious or social cause.

Church connections

Nevertheless, the Ovington family had strong church connections. Henry A. Ovington was a member of Pierrepont Street Baptist Church of Brooklyn (*New York Tribune* February 22, 1886). His son, Edward, became a deacon of the Plymouth Congregationalist Church, Orange Street, near to the Ovington Brothers business on Fulton Street. It is significant that the Reverend Henry Ward Beecher became the minister of Plymouth Church in 1847 (*Harper's Weekly* August 11, 1866) and remained in this position until his death in 1887 (*The New York Herald* March 11, 1887). A cousin of Henry Ward Beecher, the Reverend Luther F. Beecher, even formed a joint ownership of *The New-York Recorder*, with Reverend Sewall S. Cutting from 1853 to 1855 (*The New-York Recorder* August 3, 1853; January 31, 1855).

Henry Ward Beecher's father, Lyman, was a Presbyterian minister at Lichfield, Connecticut (Merideth, R. (1965): vii), and many members of this family were connected to the abolition cause. One of Lyman's sons, Reverend Edward Beecher, wrote a *Narrative of Riots at Alton* of 1838, which outlined the events surrounding the murder of the abolitionist, Reverend Elijah Lovejoy, whom he knew. Both Reverend Edward Beecher and his brother, Reverend Thomas K. Beecher, were described as frequent visitors to Plymouth Church (*Daily Graphic* January 26, 1875). The most well-known child of Lyman was Harriet Beecher Stowe, the author of the influential book, *Uncle Tom's Cabin*, first published in 1852. Although twentieth-century African American writers have considered it a "very bad novel," chiefly because of its "sentimentality" and its failure to address

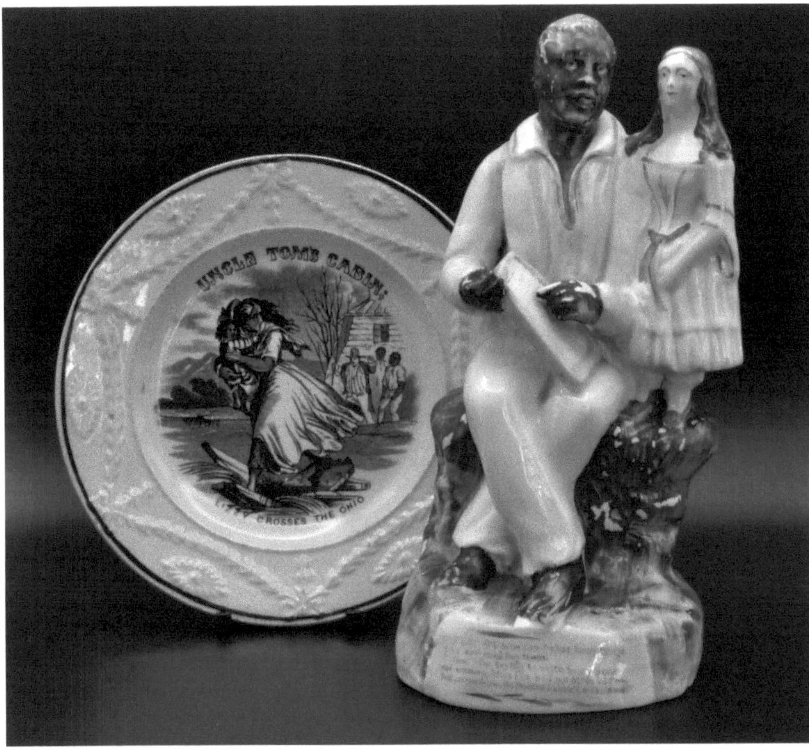

Figure 7.12 Plate and figurine based on Harriet Beecher Stowe's *Uncle Tom's Cabin,* c.1852–60. From left to right. Plate, earthenware, black printed, with relief moulded decoration, titled "Uncle Tom's Cabin; Lizzy crosses the Ohio," taken from, *Uncle Tom's Cabin,* Chapter VII. English, c.1852–60. Figurine, earthenware, enamel and gilt decoration, Eva and Uncle Tom printed quote from *Uncle Tom's Cabin,* Chapter XIX, reading, "Eva: 'O Uncle Tom! what funny things you are making there.' Tom: 'I'm trying to write to my poor old woman, Miss Eva and my little children, but somehow, I'm feared I shan't make it out.'" Probably Staffordshire, c.1852–60.

why white people behaved as they did, it was an extremely provocative publication of that era (Baldwin [1955] 2012: 14). From an early period, editions of *Uncle Tom's Cabin* were illustrated, and these served to inspire imagery used on ceramics and figurines manufactured in England, questionable by today's standards (Figure 7.12). The imagery and characterization are now outmoded, but it sensationally and effectively drew attention to the treatment of those who were enslaved. The extent to which figurines based on *Uncle Tom's Cabin* were sold or were available across the United States is somewhat unclear, since they were not widely advertised. However, in one instance, Samuel T. Crosby advertised Parian statuettes described as "Uncle Tom and Eva" in the *Christian Register* (yet another overtly religious newspaper), published in Boston (January 16, 1858).

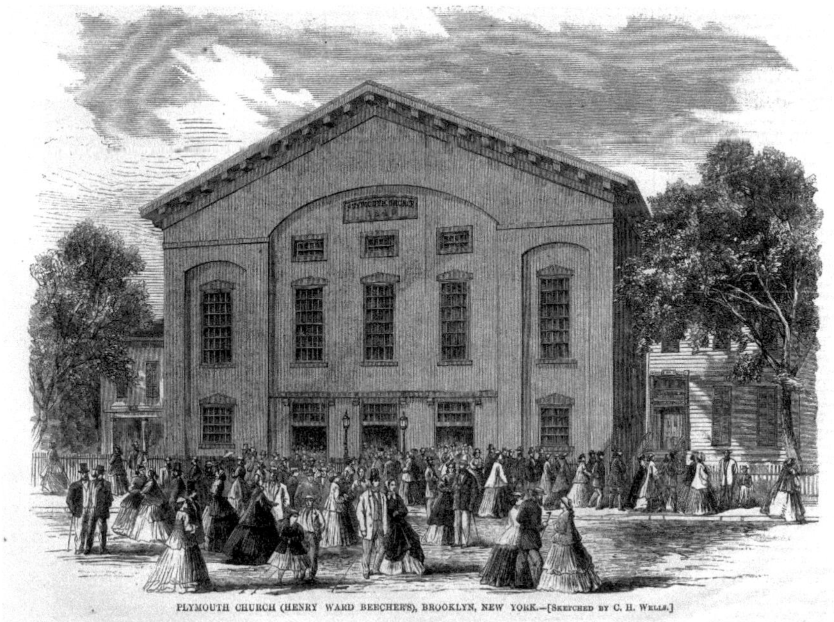

Figure 7.13 Engraving, "Plymouth Church (Henry Ward Beecher's), Brooklyn, New York," *Harper's Weekly*, August 11, 1866, p. 500.

Through the influence of Reverend Henry Ward Beecher, Plymouth Church became a center of abolitionist activity in Brooklyn. Beecher was a charismatic figure, and his theatrical, sometimes humorous style of preaching attracted much attention (Furman 2015: 258–9). An engraving that appeared in *Harper's Weekly* of August 1866 titled "Plymouth Church (Henry Ward Beecher's) Brooklyn, New York" depicts a sizeable crowd of followers outside the building (Figure 7.13). It was already reported that Beecher's congregation was too large for the church. *Harper's Weekly* reported:

> The 300 pews, together with the aisle and wall seats, give sittings for about 2700. After cramming the doorways and stairs the total audience numbers of about 3000. The sum-total of pew rents for the current year is the rather astonishing figure of $42,000.
>
> (August 11, 1866)

In a complete reverse of a scene from *Uncle Tom's Cabin*, where a young individual called Emmeline was sold at public auction (Figure 7.14), Plymouth Church raised substantial amounts of money to free those who were enslaved (Decker 2013: 20–1). On one occasion, a nine-year old girl, nicknamed as "Pink" by her owner, was presented to the congregation in the manner of an auction.

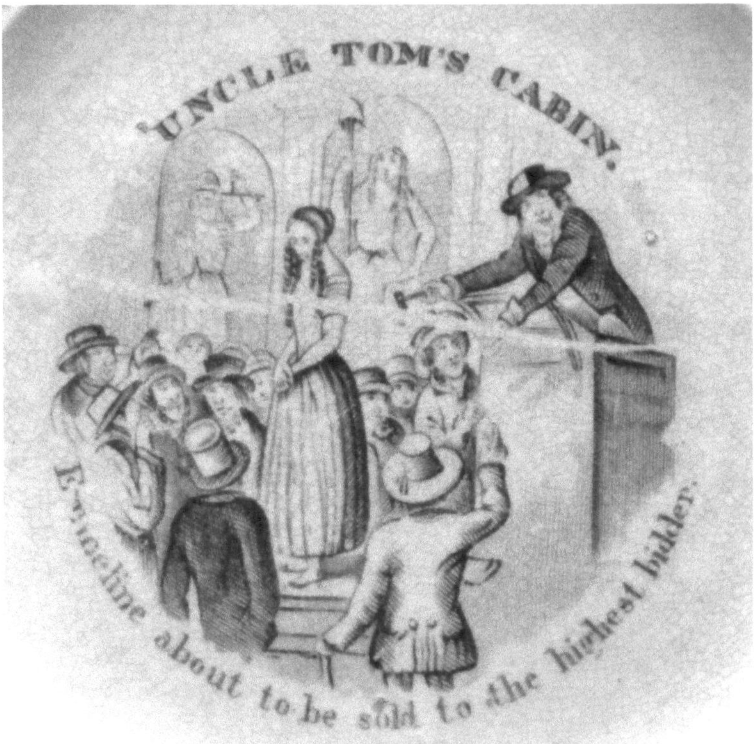

Figure 7.14 Plate (detail), earthenware, blue printed image entitled, "Uncle Tom's Cabin. Emmeline about to be sold to the highest bidder." English, c.1860s.

Her name alluded to an additional sinister risk of enslaved pale-skinned girls being forced into prostitution (Woods 2016: 44–5, 49–53). Theodore Tilton was described as a superintendent of Plymouth Church and introduced the girl to the Sunday School, and a collection was taken (*Albany Evening Journal* February 2, 1860). After Beecher's sermon, Pink was taken up to the pulpit, when a further collection raised money. Even jewelry, in the form of a gold and opal ring, was donated. It was reported how, "This was placed on the child's finger and she was told always to keep it and remember it as her 'freedom ring.'" (*New-York Commercial Advertiser* February 6, 1860). With sufficient funds collected, Pink's ransom was paid, and her freedom was secured.

Prior to being elected as president of the United States, Abraham Lincoln was invited by Plymouth Church to speak, and because of the demand, a larger New York venue had to be found (Decker 2013: 95–7). It was even alleged that people escaping from the slave states of Delaware, Maryland, and Virginia were hidden in the Plymouth church's cellar (Decker 2013: 42). Different members of the Ovington family remained connected to Plymouth Church. When Mrs. E. J. Ovington died in 1881, a memorial service was held there (*The New York Herald* June 6, 1881), and Irene H. Ovington (a sister of Theodore, Edward and William) wrote "Personal Memories of Henry Ward Beecher," in which a firsthand account is provided of how Beecher had been actively involved in aiding escaped slaves. As she states:

> And what a friend he was to the slave. How fearless he was in his defence! Many times, fugitives from the horrors of bondage, were secreted by him, until they could safely continue their way by what we then called "The underground railway" from the south to the freedom of Canada. Many times the Plymouth congregation, stirred by his eloquent appeals, raised large sums to buy freedom for an enslaved one.
>
> ("Personal Memories ...", Ovington, 1895)

As a member of Plymouth church, Irene Ovington published arrangements of Beecher's sermons ([1884] 1892) and acted as a secretary for the Plymouth Foreign Missionary Society (Annual Reports 1895).

Employment and race

As indicated, Ovington Brothers originally consisted of Theodore T. and Edward J. Ovington of Brooklyn and William H. Ovington of Chicago. One of Theodore's sons, Charles Ketcham Ovington, became involved in Ovington Brothers and eventually became president of the firm (see Pedigree 13). Rather typical of other importers and dealers involved in the crockery trade, he made visits to Europe to acquire stock. Charles' diary notes, "I went to Europe in the Spring on the steamer *Arizona*, a number of crockery men were on board, but no one of interest to me." (Diary, Ovington 1882–83). He stayed at the Railway hotel at Stoke, seeing unspecified manufacturers, before crossing the channel to visit Meissen and Limoges.

However, Charles clearly had wider interests; Mr. and Mrs. Charles Ovington paid $1,000 to become lifetime members of the National Association for the Advancement of Colored People (NAACP) (*Truth* January 7, 1883; *The Topeka Plaindealer* May 3, 1929; *The New York Times* January 30, 1930). Charles' sister, Mary White Ovington, wrote (among other books) *Half a Man; The status of the Negro in New York* published in 1911 and was also a co-founder of the NAACP formed around 1910. Mary Ovington's *Half a Man* was dedicated to her father, Theodore Ovington, and provides a vivid account of the condition of African Americans in New York and Brooklyn from the nineteenth century to the 1910s. When Theodore died, one obituary stated that "in early life he became identified with the anti-slavery movement, and gave practical support to the cause," and for a while he attended Plymouth Church (*The Brooklyn Daily Eagle* May 20, 1909). Thus, various members of the Ovington family had long-term commitments to issues of emancipation and equality. However, since it is not obvious through their marketing whether Ovington Brothers marketed any ceramics relating to the abolitionist cause, is it possible that religious and moralistic concerns were expressed through their business practice?

Ovington Brothers employed at least one African-American china packer, who also, importantly, was an active church minister. His name was Voss Neal, and he appears in press articles because of a case that occurred when he was asked to officiate at the marriage of a saleswoman to a clerk, while at work, in 1882. The controversy (as reported in the press) was whether the actions of Voss Neal were legally binding. The lengthy article, titled "Married only in Jest: Complications over a knot that a colored preacher tied," stated:

> The Rev. Voss Neal, an aged colored man is very old, of 63 Troy avenue, Brooklyn, is on six days of the week a packer in Ovington Bros.' china store at 248 Fulton street, Brooklyn. On the seventh day he preachers in Bethel Methodist Episcopal Church, at Schenectady and Dean avenues. He is very old, very moderate in his movements, and his scanty locks are sprinkled with grey. He is of accommodating disposition, and when pretty Gussie Cropsy, the little black eyed saleswoman, presented herself before him in the basement last Friday, accompanied by Will Everingham a clerk, who is the nephew of Ovingtons and the reputed heir to a large estate, and with great merriment, requested him to "marry them," the old man put the usual questions with great solemnity, and sent them away with the injunction to go and get a marriage certificate and he would fill it out. When a few hours later Miss Cropsey[sic] was accosted by her fellow clerks as "Mrs. Everingham," she professed to be amused, but the day after was very indignant, and said she was no longer carrying the fun any further.
>
> (*The Sun,* New York November 17, 1882)

Since Voss Neal was also actually interviewed by a reporter, this article provides additional evidence of how he had often conducted marriage services:

> The Rev. Voss Neal was sitting last evening in the rear of the chamber of his dwelling. His coat was off, and his stocking clad feet rested in a chair. He laid aside his newspaper as the reported entered, and looked up over his glasses. "Did I marry Will and Gussie? Come now, this thing has gone far enough … it was all in fun. There's no marriage to it. They haven't got a certificate, and I haven't returned one of these blanks to the Health Department. Why, I do lots of marryin'. I'm too old to make such a mistake as that."
>
> (*The Sun,* New York November 17, 1882)

Voss then explains how he was sitting by the stove in the basement eating his dinner when Cropsy and Everingham came in to request a marriage. When asked how Miss Cropsy felt, it was stated:

> She cried once or twice about it, but lately she has been more resigned. Mr. Hall, the floor walker, fined them both 50 cents for leaving the floor without permission. Fact is, it has been a pretty rough joke all 'round, and when they all ask me who I'm goin' to marry next I feel like giving 'em a piece of my mind.
>
> (*The Sun,* New York November 17, 1882)

It transpired that Everingham was not related to the Ovington family, based on more details published in *The Sun* by the following day. Here, it was also reported how:

> Miss Gussie Cropsy, the young saleswoman in Ovington Brothers' China store at 248 Fulton street, Brooklyn was married in jest to Will Everingham, stood behind the counter yesterday. Two Sevres china vases and a porcelain card receiver showed in contrast with her flushed cheeks. Mr. Hall, the floor walker said at noon on Nov. 10 Everingham went into the basement to wash for lunch. Miss Cropsy and a fellow clerk went there for the same purpose. Voss Neal, the colored minister, employed as a packer, and an Irishman were talking religion by the furnace. Two or three cash boys were standing about. Everingham suddenly proposed in jest that Neal should marry them …
>
> (*The Sun,* New York November 18, 1882)

These reports have been recounted in detail since they reveal the scope of interracial relationships that existed within an up-market china store. In the account provided by *The Sun,* Miss Cropsy was reported as saying, "I knew Mr. Neal was a minister," and it was because he was "talking religion" that Everingham said, "Let's go over and have him marry us" (*The Sun,* New York November 18, 1882). Later in the same article, it was reported how Neal had reassured Mr. Ovington that no actual marriage had taken place. The legality of the marriage is unimportant; it is how a basement of a Brooklyn crockery store became the stage for a mock-wedding, inspired by Voss Neal's conversation.

Further details concerning Voss Neal may be established from trade directories and census records. In the 1850 census, Voss Neil [sic] was living in the culturally mixed district of south of Brooklyn called Flatbush, Kings, with his wife and children. The family was designated as "B" and described as originating from New York. In 1850, Voss was only described as a laborer, aged thirty-nine, with six children, including a child, also called Voss Neil [sic] aged three. Remarkably, Voss Neal's neighbor was Job Jackson, the ceramic importer. The census record records Job Jackson as a merchant, aged forty, born in England. A New York city directory provides Job Jackson's business address as 113 Water Street and his home address as Flatbush (Doggett 1850–1).

Job and his brother John Clews Jackson were previously earthenware manufacturers at Cobridge, near Burslem in the Staffordshire Potteries. After the manufacturing business of J. & J. Jackson was declared bankrupt in 1835 (*The Staffordshire Advertiser* September 26, 1835), both brothers migrated to United States and imported ceramics for various other Staffordshire firms (Ewins 1997: 95–6). Even Job and John C. Jackson's parents moved to the United States and died in Brooklyn in the 1840s. Their mother, Mary Clews [Jackson], was a sister of Ralph and James Clews. The Clews were well known for producing goods tailored toward the American market, including a design depicting the parade to commemorate the arrival of the French General Lafayette at New York City in

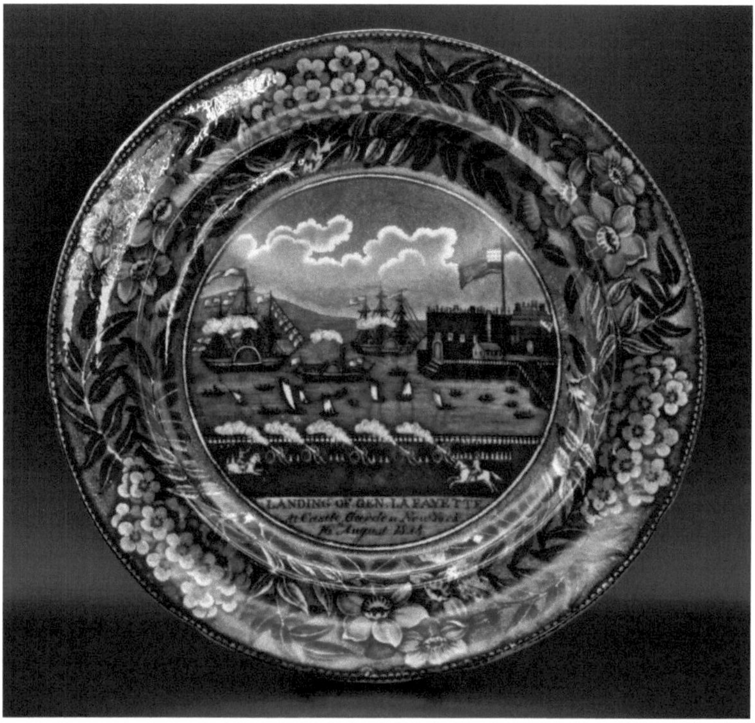

Figure 7.15 Plate, earthenware, blue printed, depicting the arrival of General La Fayette at New York on "August 16, 1824." Impressed, "R. & J. Clews", Cobridge, Staffordshire, c.1825.

1824, which Henry A. Ovington had also attended as a colonel (Figure 7.15). It was said that Henry Clews, the New York banker and son of James Clews, became a collector of ceramics (see Chapter 1).

The Jackson-Clews family were also a well-respected Christian family. It was particularly noted in the *Protestant Churchman*, of New York, that:

> On Wednesday last, at Prospect Hill, Brooklyn, at the residence of her son, Job Jackson, Esq. Mrs. MARY JACKSON, in the 67th year of her age.
>
> In the death of this excellent Christian lady a large and most respectable family circle, and numerous attached friends, are called to mourn. She was an ardent friend and pious member of the Church, who privileges and ministrations, we trust, have been exchanged for the glories of the Church triumphant in heaven. "Blessed are the dead who die in the Lord, even so saith the spirit for they rest their labors".
>
> (October 23, 1847)

A version of this notice with the above quote appeared in *The Staffordshire Advertiser* (November 20, 1847).

The example of Job Jackson residing next door to Voss Neal, supports research that suggests how racial segregation in early American cities was less pronounced. The clustering of African Americans in Brooklyn and New York began to intensify in the second quarter of the nineteenth century (Curry 1981: 72–8). It is, at least, feasible that Neal's connection to the crockery trade may have stemmed from being a neighbor of Job Jackson.

The 1855 census shows how Voss Neal was living in Kings, Brooklyn, with no trade recorded. However, a Brooklyn Directory lists Voss Neil [sic] as a "(col.), packer," living on Warren Street (Smith 1855: 238). Voss Neal's link to ceramic packing may be traced back to at least the mid-1850s, and connections to the church, probably from the mid-1840s. In 1891, Neal was described as "for nearly forty years" the minister for the African Methodist Episcopal Church at Weeksville, east Brooklyn, and was certainly documented as a probationer of this church in 1847 (*The New York Age* May 9, 1891; Payne 1891: 199). This church became known as the Bethel African Methodist Episcopal Church (Wellman 2014: 53). An article concerning the "Colored Camp-Meeting at Flushing" (east of Brooklyn), on Sunday, August 18, 1867, describes how various "discourse" were delivered, among others, by "Rev. Voss Neal of Baltimore":

> At 4 o'clock pm probably not less than 2,000 persons were on the ground. Although the meeting was ostensibly one of colored people, and was gotten up and managed by them, at least, four-fifths of the audience was whites, of both sexes and ages, and classes.
>
> (*New York Tribune* August 19, 1867)

Although Voss Neal had been Brooklyn for some time, the reference to Baltimore may relate to what was recorded by later census records. In 1870, Voss Neil[sic] of Brooklyn, Kings was described as aged sixty-one, mulatto china packer, born in Maryland—not New York, as previously indicated by the 1850 census. Neal's wife, Martha, was also listed as born in Maryland, although all of their children were still listed as born in New York. It is possible that Voss and Martha Neal escaped from a slave state. Alternatively, one of Voss Neal's children indicated that both his parents were born in South Carolina (Census, Providence, RI, 1900). Recalling some of the disturbing details mentioned by Stowe's *The Key To Uncle Tom's Cabin*, perhaps Neal and his wife were sold as children and unclear of their place of birth (1853: 84–90). Or, as suggested by Judith Wellman's *Brooklyn's Promised Land: The Free Black Community of Weeksville, New York*, African Americans provided different places of birth as a way of purposely obscuring backgrounds (2014: 57–60). Across the United States, the draconian Fugitive Slave Act of 1850 allowed any individual identified as being enslaved to be returned to their "owners." Those identified were not allowed to testify on their own behalf (Wellman 2014: 99).

In 1875, Neal was just a "chinapacker"[sic], without indicating his ethnicity (Lain, 1875). While many individuals were described as "packers," Neal appears to be the only specifically designated "china" packer listed in Brooklyn. The 1880 census lists Neal as a "china packer" aged seventy, born in Maryland, and his wife, Martha, now described as born in Delaware.

It was not unheard for African Americans to be involved in the crockery trade. William W. Shirley (originally from Shelton) advertised in New York for "A stout active white or coloured [sic] boy 16 to 18 years old" to "act as porter and drive and take care of a horse, at a crockery store" located at 43 Maiden Lane (*The Evening Post,* New York May 9, 1826). Prior to this, and using only the contact address of "43 Maiden Lane," a newspaper notice requested a white or colored boy to act as a porter and a "white or coloured [sic] man, as packer for a crockery store in Virginia, one that can write & capable of acting as a salesman prefered" (*The Evening Post,* New York September 1, 1824). Here it is suggested how a degree of education was required in this aspect of the crockery business.

When James M. Shaw & Co., of New York advertised for ceramic packers, it was stipulated that they required "Two strong men wanted who understand packing crockery; none others need apply" (*The New York Herald* September 6, 1890). Having experience of the trade was advantageous. In a slightly later period, an article titled, "The Retail Delivery Clerks," explained how china packers were normally charged for any breakages, and how they were subject to respiratory illnesses due to working long hours in basements, breathing in dust and dirt from straw. The working hours, somewhat flexible due to customer demand, averaged twelve hours per day, receiving between $9 and $12 per week, with sick pay (*Daily People* September 20, 1903). These wages were not the lowest in New York at this time. Wages for a kitchen or lunchroom worker were advertised as from $8 to $9 per week, and those of a clerk were given as $20 per week (*New York American* April 1, 1904).

Thus, the circumstance of Voss Neal's employment at Ovington Brothers leads one to suspect that this was for more social rather than practical reasons. China packing was a physically demanding job, involving a great deal of dexterity, suiting younger individuals. Neal was aged around seventy-two years at the time of the marriage incident in 1882, although it is the case that he offered his services, independently, as a china, glass, and earthenware packer, in 1881 (Figure 7.16).

KEEP THIS CARD - FAMILIES R E - moving can have their china, glass and earthen ware repacked and warranted to go safe any distance. Address *VOSS NEAL, at Mr. Campbell's, corner of Fulton* and Nevins sts.

Figure 7.16 *The Brooklyn Daily Eagle* April 21, 1881.

A Brooklyn directory described Voss Neail [sic] as a clerk (Lain 1884), but the following press article referred to him as a preacher. In 1885, Neal was in Trenton, New Jersey, attending a meeting at Mount Zion Church, where he was robbed:

> Voss Neal, a local preacher of Brooklyn, has been attending the revival services at Mount Zion M. E. [Methodist Episcopal] Church. Last evening Charles Blackwell, who happened to be boarding in the same house with Neal, entered the preacher's sleeping apartment and stole $5.35. Blackwell has been held for trial.
>
> (*The Trenton Times* February 7, 1885)

The Mount Zion Church of Trenton had a long relationship with African American rights. Other visiting clergy even gave lectures on subjects such as "a plan for the elevation of the colored race" (*Trenton State Gazette* November 22, 1864). A further article indicated that Voss Neal:

> … an old colored clergyman of Brooklyn, has been in the city for a few weeks past, and sojourned with a colored family in Rose Street. He was not rich in worldly goods, and what little he had of filthy lucre he needed sadly.
>
> (*Trenton Sunday Advertiser* February 8, 1885)

When Charles Blackwell (the thief who was held in custody at the City Hall) sent for Voss Neal, he confessed to how the stolen money was hidden among the attic rafters at the Rose Street property (*Trenton Sunday Advertiser* February 8, 1885). Blackwell was subsequently sentenced to thirty days imprisonment (*The Trenton Times* March 5, 1885).

The incident at Trenton, New Jersey, in 1885, suggests that Neal was able to spend time away from Ovington Brothers to pursue his spiritual work. In 1889, Voss Neal was a packer, living at 83 Troy Avenue (Lain 1889), whereas in 1890, he was listed as "Rev. Voss Neal" at the same address (Lain 1890). It was reported that the "Rev. Voss Neal of Brooklyn gave a very practical and stirring sermon" at Allen African Methodist Episcopal Church of Jamaica, Queens (*The New York Age* January 18, 1890), although the Kings, Brooklyn Census of 1892 continued to described Neal as a china packer, now aged eighty-two. It is notable how the census records never appear to acknowledge Voss Neal's actual links to the clergy.

In a section titled "Pottery and Porcelain" in *Great Industries of the United States* of 1872, there is an illustration of an interior of a retail store. Not attributed to any business, it appears to depict a woman serving another woman, and in the background, a young white man is packing wares into a basket. There is a full basket on the left of the image in the foreground (Figure 7.17). Any of the ethnic diversity that existed in stores such as Ovington Bros. was not obvious from imagery such as this, or the interior of Chauncey I. Filley's store of St. Louis, shown in Figure 2.5.

Neal's wider preaching activities and his ability to conduct matrimony services was obviously known to the employees of Ovington Brothers. People described as "colored" were listed in Brooklyn and New York city directories in the nineteenth

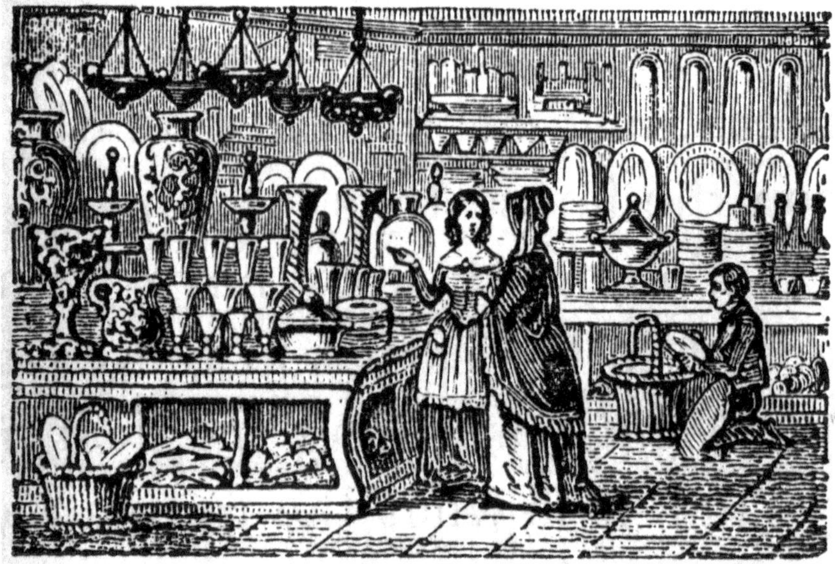

Figure 7.17 Engraving, "Crockery ware and vases," Horace Greeley et al., *The Great Industries of the United States*, 1872, plate 345, p. 833.

century and carried out a variety of trades. But, apart from Voss Neal, only four others, including a woman called Susan Richardson, were described as "colored" packers in a Brooklyn directory of 1855 (Smith: 238, 246, 267, 270, 307). In fact, Mary Ovington's *Half a Man* observed how the employment of African Americans as servants and waiters "have long been identified in America," and this remained the case ([1911] 2019: 55). From the 1870s, only a "little group" had acquired land in Brooklyn, which was cheaper than Manhattan (1911 [2019]: 18). There were still limited possibilities of progress for African Americans according to her research, even by the 1910s.

Judith Wellman's *Brooklyn's Promised Land: The Free Black Community of Weeksville, New York*, suggests that well-educated African Americans (who had trained as teachers or preachers) continued to work in low-paying jobs in order to subsidize their families. It was the inability to progress that led the Reverend James W. C. Pennington (a former Maryland slave) to write in an open letter of 1831, along with other African Americans, to raise the question, why have so many of us not "advanced into different branches of business; or taken into merchant houses, manufacturing establishments etc … ?" (Wellman 2014: 40). Ministers working in laboring jobs was not uncommon (Curry 1981: 191). However, china packing was not simply menial labor. It was classed as a specialist trade—to the extent that some crockery dealers boasted of employing "English packers" (*Illinois Weekly State Journal*, 1845). Or, conversely, in the "Situations Wanted," it was emphasized by someone seeking work, "CROCKERY Packer, with long experience" (*New York*

Journal and Advertiser October 25, 1898). In England, a United Potters' Packers Union was established in 1887 (Burchill and Ross 1977: 153), and a union of pottery packers was formed at the center of American ceramic production—Trenton, New Jersey (*Trenton Times* June 11, 1900).

Conceivably, the employment of Voss Neal coincides with Ovingtons' wider interest in emancipation and advancement. An interpretation of Ovingtons' actions could be that they were putting into practice what Henry Beecher preached, or what Harriet Beecher Stowe had argued as early as the 1850s—that Christian business owners should employ African Americans in order to help provide "a respectable means of livelihood" (1853: 496). An elderly Voss Neal was provided with an income by Ovington Brothers, and they were aware of his religious role. The behavior of the Ovington family was progressive for that era. For instance, it was reported how Theodore Ovington "dined with negroes," while his daughter (Mary White Ovington) lived for part of the week at Phipps' "model tenement of negroes" at 233 West Sixty-third Street in the "heart of the uptown 'black belt.'" Mary Ovington only stayed with her family in Brooklyn at the weekend (*Waterbury Evening Democrat*, Connecticut April 29, 1908). On one occasion, Mary White Ovington was described as the Harriet Beecher Stowe of her age (*Kansas City Advocate* February 4, 1921).

Potentially, religious beliefs, church attendance, and running a crockery business were far more intertwined. Some of Ovington Brothers' profits were ploughed back into Plymouth Church. It has been mentioned already how Plymouth Church was able to raise the huge sum of $42,000 for pew rents in 1866. References show that the Ovington family were involved in this form of fundraising. Edward Ovington paid $300 for pew No.102 at Plymouth Church in 1869 and $275 for-rent in 1870 (*New York Tribune* January 6, 1869; *The New York Herald* January 5, 1870). H. A. Ovington (apparently Henry A. Ovington, father of Theodore, Edward, and William) paid $110 for a pew in 1885 (*The New York Herald* January 7, 1885), even though his obituary indicates that he was a member of Pierrepont Street Baptist Church. In turn, from 1865 to 1874, Plymouth Church donated money to the American Missionary Association, aimed at providing the funding of schools required to educate freed people in the southern states (Decker 2013: 117–18).

An African-American customer

Although the merchandise of Ovington Brothers was apparently aimed at the upper echelons of society, connections to an African American customer can be demonstrated. There were reports of a legal case involving Reverend Henry M. Wilson, an African American preacher, who was connected to Brooklyn's "colored church at East New-York" (*The Sun* March 9, 1869). Wilson was also a founding member of the African Civilization Society and General Manager of the Brooklyn Colored Orphan Asylum (*The Evangelist* November 28, 1861; *New York Commercial Advertiser* April 27, 1868). The African Civilization

Society was founded in 1858 and based at Weeksville, where a community of free African Americans had evolved since the 1830s and 1840s. Importantly, the African Civilization Society's goal was to promote the emigration of African Americans to Africa, with the intention of creating a Christian, free-labor cotton economy. Unlike other colonization movements, the African Civilization Society was entirely led by African Americans (Wellman 2014: 45–8, 106).

When acting as a secretary for the Civilization Society, Wilson was given the ownership of a six-piece communion set provided by Ovington Brothers, which was kept at his house and then carried to church when required. Subsequently, after Wilson left his secretarial role, he was accused by other members of the society of stealing the communion set, along with two pitchers, two dozen dishes, four dozen tumblers, four dozen plated forks, three dozen knives and forks, and two and a half dozen tea cups and saucers. The goods were valued in total at $48.25 (*The World* March 11, 1869). An alternative account in *The New York Journal of Commerce* interpreted the transaction as a gift, stating:

> The little knot of communicants connected with the Society, which Mr. Wilson so ably represented, owned a little plated communion set, which had been presented to them through the charity of Ovington Bros., of Brooklyn. After each communion this was taken to Mr. Wilson's house for safe-keeping. When he was deposed an order came to his house for the service. He replied to the messenger that he would send them over … He did so not many minutes thereafter … Towards the evening of the same day he was arrested on charge of stealing this service!
>
> (March 27, 1869)

Wilson was honorably discharged of larceny by Justice Lynch of Weeksville, Brooklyn. A misunderstanding had simply arisen regarding the whereabouts of the communion set and the other items (*The World* March 11, 1869).

The actual circumstances of how these goods were acquired is more revealing. In one account, it was mentioned how Wilson had himself procured the communion service from a "Fulton Street establishment," which was where Ovington Brothers was located (*The New York Herald*, November 15, 1870). Apparently, Reverend Wilson had shopped in Ovington's store, which might otherwise be reserved for a privileged white, middle and upper class. Whether Wilson's purchases included all of the ceramics and glass is not clear, although the question of the cost is solved by the point expressed in the press that "the party from whom it [the communion set] was obtained was a subscriber to the society, and they agreed to relieve him from his annual subscription if he would allow them to retain the set" (*The New York Herald* November 15, 1870). In other words, the Ovington Brothers were subscribers to the African Civilization Society, and any payment for the goods was waived in lieu of their membership fee.

If consumption is only perceived on the basis of economic transactions, it neglects how commodities, even in that period, could cut across different social and cultural spheres in rather more unexpected ways. Ovington Brothers sold

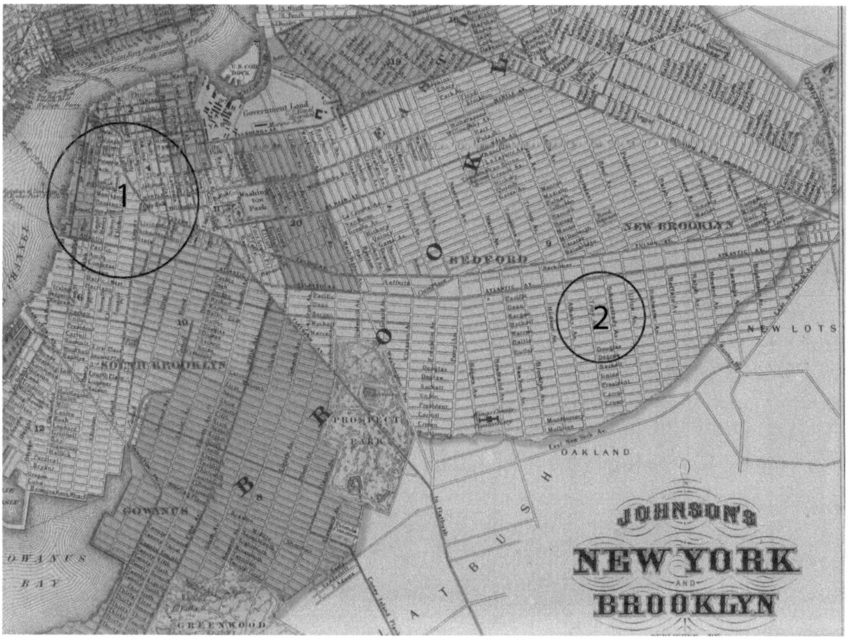

Key
District 1: Addresses in Brooklyn Heights area.
Ovington Brothers, crockery store – 240 Fulton Street.
Edward J. Ovington – 95 Livingston Street.
Henry A. Ovington – 47 Sidney Place.
Theodore T. Ovington – 170 Livingston Street.
Theodore Tilton – 48 Livingston Street.
Rev. Henry W. Beecher – 82 Columbia Street.
Plymouth Church – Congregational, Orange Street, near Hicks Street.

District 2: Addresses in Wyckoff Street and Troy Avenue district.
Rev. Voss Neal (china packer) – Troy Avenue, near Atlantic Ave.
Rev. Henry M. Wilson – Wyckoff Street, near Troy Avenue.

Addresses from Lain, G. T (1867), *The Brooklyn City and Business Directory for the Year Ending May 1st, 1867*, **Brooklyn and New York: Lain & Co.**

Figure 7.18 The Brooklyn district with key addresses. Johnson's *New York and Brooklyn* map, published by Johnson and Ward, 1866. New York's East River, on left.

ceramics and glass, along with metal goods and cutlery (*New York Observer* December 10, 1868). Whether the communion set was acquired as a bartered exchange, or it was simply a gift, it provides further evidence of links between Ovington Brothers and advancement organizations, and importantly, connections to other African-American preachers.

Members of the Ovington family had clear connections to African Americans, although ironically, segregation was becoming more pronounced in major cities in the second half of the nineteenth century (Curry 1981: 76). Members of the Ovington family lived in the vicinity of Livingston Street—near to their business on Fulton Street and to Plymouth Church—in the wealthy, predominantly white district of Brooklyn Heights, while Reverend Henry Wilson lived on Wyckoff Street, near to Troy Avenue. The Reverend Voss Neal also lived on Troy Avenue, eastern Brooklyn, from the mid-1860s (Figure 7.18). Despite this geographical separation, their lives have been shown to be surprisingly interconnected. It was even stated that funds for the African Civilization Society were chiefly contributed by European Americans, and how Reverend Wilson made the collections in person, being "the life and soul of the Society." He was even educated at Princeton, before becoming a minister in the Presbyterian Church (*The New York Journal of Commerce* March 25, 1869). The instances of the Reverend Henry Wilson and the Reverend Voss Neal provide rare insight into ways in which African Americans actually interacted with the owners of a crockery business.

Trial

From a greater contextualization of the families involved in the crockery trade arrives a richer understanding of ceramics. This may then be shown in 1875, when Edward J. Ovington was called as a witness to a scandalous court case between Theodore Tilton and Reverend Henry Beecher. Tilton (a member of Plymouth Church) accused Beecher of having an affair with his wife, Elizabeth Tilton. When Mrs. Tilton left her husband, she lived with the Ovington family (*The World* March 3, 1875). Previously, Beecher and Tilton had been co-editors of *The Independent* of New York in the early 1860s.

During the trial, Edward Ovington stated in his court case evidence how he had known Beecher for at least twenty-five years. Mrs. Maria Ovington (who was also called as a witness) claimed to have known Mr. and Mrs. Tilton more intimately since 1867 (*The New York Herald* March 3, 1875). The trial was nationally reported, and *Frank Leslie's Illustrated Newspaper* even included images of the Ovingtons and the Beechers (Figure 7.19).

An occupying article in *Frank Leslie's Illustrated Newspaper* noted:

> The first witness called was Edward J. Ovington. He is deacon of Plymouth Church, and has been very intimate with the family of Mr. Tilton. He is a tall, erect man, with light red hair, beard and mustache, pale eyes and whitish

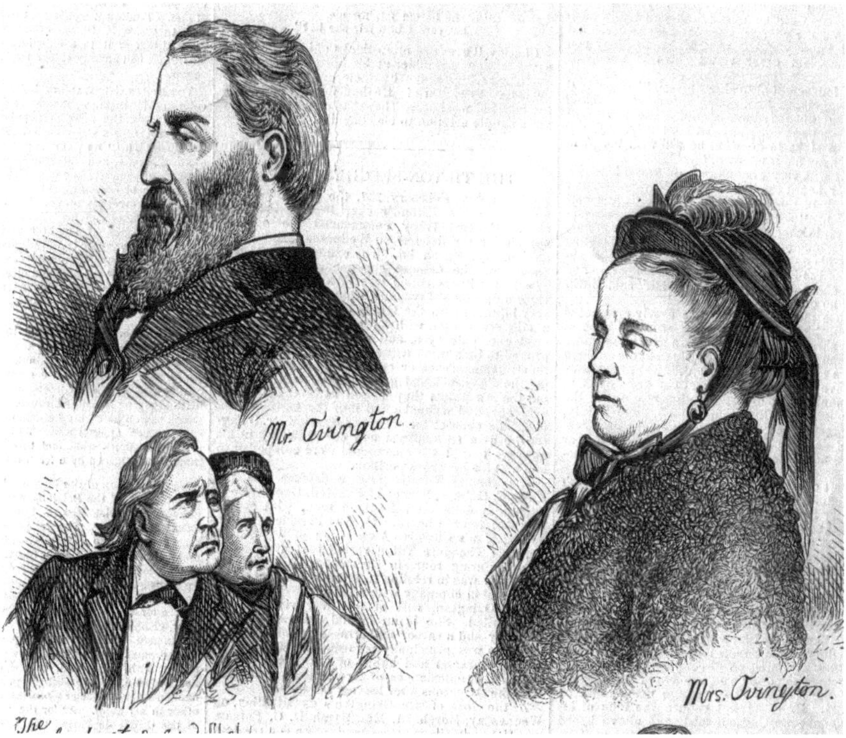

Figure 7.19 Engraving, "The Tilton-Beecher Trial—Portraits and Incidents," *Frank Leslie's Illustrated Newspaper* March 20, 1875, p. 24. Top left, Mr. [Edward J.] Ovington. Bottom left Mr. & Mrs. Beecher, titled "The defendant and his wife." Bottom right, Mrs. [Maria] Ovington.

> eyelashes. He proved to be a weak witness. He could not easily recall names, dates or circumstances … Mr. Ovington became so confused and contradictory in his answers, that all the court-room were compelled to laugh at his ludicrous position.
>
> (*Frank Leslie's Illustrated Newspaper* March 20, 1875)

In due course, the *New-York Recorder* reported how a committee from Plymouth Church exonerated Beecher of adultery, and later, after the six-month trial, he was also acquitted (*The New-York Recorder* September 3, 1874; July 8, 1875). Coinciding with the end of the trial a Parian bust of Rev. Henry Ward Beecher was produced with the impressed mark, "Ovington Bros. Brooklyn, W.T. Copeland and Sons" of Stoke, dated August 1875. The wording of the backstamp implies that the bust was commissioned by Ovingtons, and on this occasion, how it is advantageous to be aware of the family's wider milieu. It seems unlikely that this Parian bust was simply ordered by Ovington Brothers, at this point in time, due to sheer chance (Figure 7.20).

As shown at the beginning of this chapter, Jones, McDuffee & Stratton advertised Parian busts with the phrase "expressly for us," whereas advertisements for a bust of Beecher seem to be conspicuously absent. It is almost as if the Parian bust was commissioned by Ovington Brothers as a mark of respect for their personal friend and religious leader, but given the controversy of the court case, it was downplayed. Apart from a reference to "Brother Ovington is back from Europe with a bust of Beecher" (*Springfield Republican* July 24, 1875), no advertisements placed by Ovington Brothers that specifically mention a Parian bust of Beecher have been located. It was manufactured, available, but not obviously marketed. Although the court case was inconclusive, the Beecher trial was controversial, and his reputation was damaged (Fox 1999: 38). There was the additional problem of the Ovington family being directly involved as witnesses, and Mrs. Tilton moving into the Ovington home.

Whereas there existed ceramics commissioned and promoted by Jones, McDuffee & Stratton, the Parian Beecher bust for Ovington Bros., was apparently not marketed in newspapers, at all. This highlights, once again, a difficulty in the ways in which Regina Blaszczyk's *Imagining Consumers: Design and Innovation*

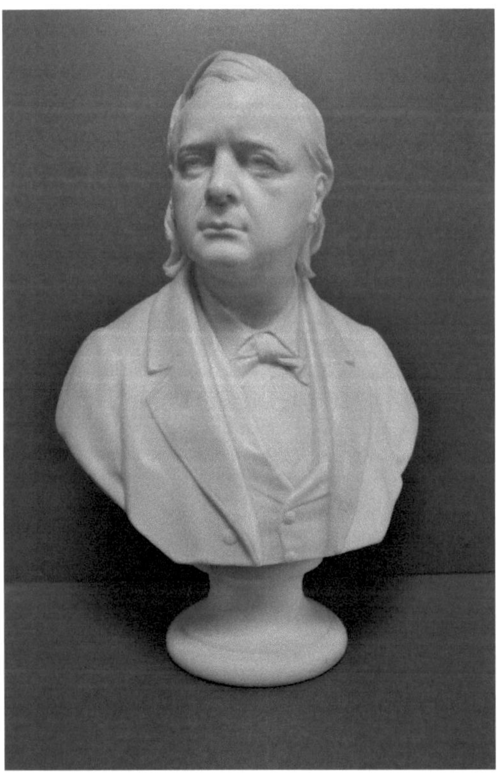

Figure 7.20 Parian, statuette of Henry Ward Beecher. Impressed mark on reverse, "Ovington Bros. Brooklyn/ W.T. Copeland and Sons/ Stoke upon Trent/ 1875/ Registered, August 31, 1875/ No.37", Staffordshire, c.1875. Courtesy of The Green-Wood Historic Fund Collections, Brooklyn, New York.

from Wedgwood to Corning, interprets the role as importers and dealers as "fashion intermediaries" (2000: 12). This would exclude how the Ovington Brothers apparently operated in more personal ways, based on their own loyalty to Henry Ward Beecher, and how their actions were not simply a reflection of widespread demand.

Summary

Once the lives of importers and dealers are understood, it then becomes more apparent to observe how the relationship between supply and demand was not always that straightforward. Not all intermediaries behaved in ways that followed a model of commissioning designs that would appeal to the market and ultimately increase their profits. The activities of the Ovington family mirrored their wider, socio-religious concerns, which in turn was also put into practice through their own employment record, or gifts to an African American customer. Knowledge of this context also helps explain why a Parian figure of Beecher was produced for Ovington Brothers. Evidence of Ovington's interactions has come to light through references in the press, providing an alternative narrative to the expressions of prejudice and negative stereotypes openly discussed in New York newspaper articles, such as "Unpalatable Counsel" of 1855, or "Crime among our Colored Population" of 1860 (*New-York Daily Tribune* September 22, 1855; *The New York Herald* April 1, 1860). Or, indeed, the cases of ceramic and glass thefts linked to African Americans mentioned in Chapter 2. Previous research has shown how African Americans were more likely to be convicted of a crime than the rest of the population, but this must be placed in a context of a justice system dominated by European Americans (Curry 1981: 113–4). Unlike some of the prevailing attitudes and imagery of that time, not all people were racist.

Accounts of a wedding in the basement of Ovington's ceramic store caused a great deal of interest at the time. An interview with Henry J. Hall, the floor walker at Ovington's, stated:

> No one who is in the possession of the facts can imagine the annoyance which that little lark has caused to Miss Cropsey [spelt as Cropsy in some accounts]. Not less than 300 people, many of them from out of town, have visited the store in the last fortnight for the express purpose of getting a look at her. I have received letters from strangers living as far West as Chicago asking if the published accounts were correct. The SUN'S story has been copied into newspapers all over the country. Woodcuts of Neal and the young couple, not of course resembling them in the remotest degree, have appeared in the illustrated newspapers. In such circumstances it seems to have it settled in the most positive manner that the young couple are not legally married.
>
> (*The Sun*, New York December 1, 1882)

Temporarily, at least, the individuals involved (but not the owners) became the celebrities. The story was printed in a variety of newspapers, from Indiana, Missouri, South Dakota etc., though woodcuts of Neal and the "married" couple have not been located. Voss Neal died in Brooklyn in November 1898, with the coroner's death certificate giving his advanced age as ninety-eight and eleven months—even older than that declared in the cited census records. He was described as "colored," a native of the United States, and the son of American parents, named as Voss and A. Neal. No occupation was declared on the certificate, and as far as can be seen, he died in obscurity without any reference made to his death in the press. He was buried at the Evergreen cemetery in Brooklyn (Death Certificate 1898). Members of the Ovington family were buried at the Green-Wood cemetery of Brooklyn, along with Reverend Henry Ward Beecher.

CONCLUSION

In 1877, a Salt Lake City newspaper called the *Deseret Evening News* published an article titled "Home Manufacturers, Earthenware, China and Glass—what shall we do with our Boys?" As the title indicated, the fundamental question addressed was whether ceramic production in the state of Utah could begin to supply domestic demand, which would provide alternatives to imported goods and meaningful employment. The article's author, Osmond B. Shaw, was acutely aware of the role of competition, describing "The products of the Staffordshire potteries rank, and justly too, among the foremost of England's manufactures, being known and prized among all the nations of the world." For Utah to begin to compete with the ceramics produced in Staffordshire was a considerable challenge. Indeed, it was even conceded that Utah's growing prosperity had contributed to the acquisition of "those manufactures" (March 22, 1877).

By the 1870s, views that espoused the cultivation of American manufacturing industries were far from new. However, in this instance, it is the writer who made these remarks which is of significance. Osmond B. Shaw was a son of Simeon Shaw, the author of the *History of the Staffordshire Potteries: and the Rise and Progress of the Manufacture of Pottery and Porcelain*, first published in 1829. Simeon Shaw moved to the Potteries from Salford, Lancashire, initially as a schoolmaster, and then became the most significant early historian of the ceramic industry. He recognized the importance of the Staffordshire Potteries, and as one obituary recorded, possessed a "considerable original genius" (*The Wolverhampton Chronicle* ... April 20, 1859). Although Osmond B. Shaw emigrated to the United States, he was born in the Potteries, and this context explains the expectation of his being able to write informedly on ceramics. First and foremost, the focus of this book has been on recognizing the importance of the backgrounds, culture, and identity of intermediaries. This can equally be applied to writers or collectors as to how they formulated knowledge, interests, and interpretations. Rightly or wrongly, Osmond Shaw's background gave him an authority to write about ceramics.

The original promotion of Simeon Shaw's *History of the Staffordshire Potteries* ... in the *Staffordshire Advertiser* mentions how this new publication included "Biographical Sketches" of the individuals involved in the development of the industry (November 28, 1828). In a sense, Shaw's work did much to shape subsequent approaches to the subject. The role and contribution of manufacturers has often been emphasized, until writers such as Neil McKendrick explored the role of marketing, fashion, and demand (McKendrick, N., J. Brewer and J. H. Plumb (1982): 100–45). Likewise, Blaszczyk's *Imagining Consumers: Design and Innovation from Wedgwood to Corning,* drew attention to the role of "fashion intermediaries," such as shop keepers, salesmen, retailers, showroom managers, etc. She even argued how these intermediaries should be recognized as having a "major responsibility for the way things looked" (2000: 12).

While Simeon Shaw drew attention to how certain Staffordshire manufacturers had developed and refined various bodies, glazes, and forms of decoration, Blaszczyk focused on how fashion and demand shaped these new products of ingenuity. In a way, it is ironic how more recent ceramic historians have arrived at this point of view, when those involved in the ceramic trade in the nineteenth century had already suggested how intermediaries and distributors were crucial. For instance, as pointed out in a trade article in the *Pottery Gazette*:

> Of course, to please the consumer is the great aim of the manufacturer or producer and of all the intermediaries between them and the consumer. The best way to please him is a matter that is more within the knowledge of the distributor than any other parties to the business.
>
> (August 1, 1896)

The distributor was perceived as holding "the key to the trade," being closer to the consumer. This article also suggested that "Sometimes that taste can be led, and occasionally it can even be diverted from a line it was evidently taking, but very frequently, far more frequently than some manufacturers are aware of, the prevailing taste of the public must be judiciously met" (*Pottery Gazette* August 1, 1896).

Although manufacturers produced the goods, they were not necessarily the sole authors of these wares. This book has attempted to consider the importance of the distributors who could act variously as either the merchant, auctioneer, wholesale importer, or retail dealer. More than simply assume, in the manner of Blaszczyk, that intermediaries had a knowledge of demand, the aim has been to explore their backgrounds as a way of providing additional ways to understand and interpret the process of authorship in ceramic design. Intermediaries had closer contacts to the consumer, but their actions were not always connected to servicing the demands of the market. It has been shown how there are instances of importers and dealers commissioning and marketing ceramics that reflected their own sociopolitical views, even if these had limited appeal. What might, at first, seem absurd and extraordinary, apparently occurred. This book has examined various intermediaries, just as nineteenth-century ceramic historians attached an importance to knowing the biographical details of manufacturers (Meteyard 1865–66). Exploring the cultural backgrounds of crockery importers and dealers can explain why certain ceramics were produced and marketed. Thus, exploring the perspective of the intermediary can be fruitful, and the view that production is either steered by the entrepreneurial manufacturer, or was a response to the evolving tastes and fashions of the consumer, has to be modified.

Using a combination of sources has provided more information about the backgrounds and cultural identities of ceramic importers. While scrutinizing these records remains a lengthy process, the results show how marketing strategy can vary and that generalizations concerning English or American advertising should now be avoided. Advertising was anything but "straight-forward" (McKendrick et al. 1982: 118) and can provide a window into the multi-dimensional lives of the crockery dealers. Thoroughly examining advertising in all its diversity, in conjunction with what can be determined about the lives of the sellers, reveals how marketing and behavior could reflect backgrounds, culture, and identity.

This view then begins to resonate when turning back to publications written by the earliest collectors and connoisseurs. The identification by the earliest ceramic writers of how some patterns were rarer than others makes far greater sense when it is appreciated that ceramic patterns could be commissioned by a single importer. This has been shown by a careful analysis of marketing. Printed wares that depicted American themes (such as the murder of Elijah Lovejoy) were seemingly only a small proportion of the overall volume of the ceramic trade and were only advertised by the importer who commissioned the design. This is different from the entrepreneurial manufacturer producing ceramic designs for the envisaged consumer, as distributed through a network of agents. The relationship between the maker and the consumer is more complicated than has been outlined before. Successive collectors, writers, and curators have banded together American-themed ceramics as one category, when they were produced for a range of different reasons. Consequently, to compartmentalize ceramic designs, even if they appear to conform to a certain type, is now revealed as problematic, since the actual motivation for production might vary. This, in turn, has implications on how curators organize and manage collections formed in the past.

Regina Blaszczyk points out how "Generations of connoisseurs have studied high-style craftsmen, self-appointed reformers, and high-profile 'name' designers" (2000: 12). While this is probably true, at the same time, this observation does not fully convey other reasons for collecting. There were individuals in America who had ties to the ceramic trade, collecting American-themed ceramics. Backgrounds and identity impacted on what has been preserved. If these collections were then donated to museums, they were influential on notions of consumption and demand. In the manner of Osmond Shaw, the circumstances of backgrounds have continuously shaped behavior, interests, and ideas, which have been the underlying theme of this book.

Just as backgrounds might influence the collecting of ceramics, culture and identity could shape the attitudes of importers and dealers. Referring to them as "American importers and dealers" immediately implies that they all shared the same identities, which was not the case. It should not be assumed that all crockery dealers were "American" and, therefore, automatically patriotic. Crockery dealers might be Americans, and pro-American, or from England, politically dispossessed and keen to assimilate. Other importers and dealers might have English origins, and occasionally, were not entirely in agreement with the conditions of American society. As outsiders, they wished to comment on issues such as the continuation of slavery, although differing attitudes to abolitionism were also expressed by Americans.

Max Weber's *The Protestant Ethic and the Spirit of Capitalism* of 1904–5 argues that the United States represented the "highest development" of capitalism, "stripped of its religious and ethical meaning" ([1930] 2010: 124). Yet some "American" crockery importers and dealers were still attached to religious denominations in the nineteenth century, which, in turn, impacted on marketing, distribution, the designs commissioned, and their business practices. For instance, the Parian figure of the Reverend Henry Ward Beecher, impressed with the "Ovington Bros" backstamp, coincides with their having strong ties to Plymouth Church and their concerns for racial equality. Ovington Brothers of Brooklyn had ties to an Africa-American preacher, providing new insight into other levels and processes of consumption, when previous research has tended to focus on the array of marketing devices and merchandising establishments developed to serve the white middle class (Cohen 2017: 149–80). Evidently, Ovington Brothers were attempting to make a difference, and this points toward how, moving forward, ceramic history can address issues of race.

It appears that the next generation was not entirely immune from inheriting the attitudes, culture, and identity of their parents. Would Mary White Ovington have written a play entitled *The Spode Cup* if she did not come from the family background of the ceramic trade? She was a daughter of one of the Ovington brothers and became an important civil rights activist, with a stamp released by the American postal service in recognition of her work in 2009. There are no press references to Mary's play ever being performed or published, but the typed manuscript, among the papers of the Ovington family, appears to date from the 1940s. Set in a mansion owned by the Fleming family in Charleston, South Carolina, the play likewise implies a modern period, with its references to motor cars, railways, and the country club. It centers around the discovery that their daughter's school friend, who had just been a house guest, was descended from a slave. Urged by her cousin, Mrs. Mary Fleming demands the removal of the bed from the guest room, and embarks upon destroying anything that the girl had touched or used, including:

> The Spode cup that Lafayette drank from. That was used in this room at the first tea party to make money for the confederacy! The cup that General Beauregard held in his hand when he was called to the front! Oh, you are heroic! And you are right. Fling it into the fire!
>
> (Ovington, unknown date: 19)

The French general Lafayette fought in the American Revolutionary War and upon returning to the United States in 1824 visited every state, while Beauregard was a Confederate general during the Civil War. In the ludicrous situation of the play, Ovington explores how inanimate objects, such as a Spode cup, can absorb residues of race simply by being handled and used. It is as if a southern desire for segregation, associated with the Jim Crow laws, had collided with the world of antiques and ceramic heirlooms. Although Mrs. Fleming's own son was quick to point out some of hypocrisies of this situation, by stipulating, "I reckon plenty of colored folk have drunk out of that on the sly, when they were washing it," according to his mother, this was less of an indiscretion because they were their own servants. In the final part of the play, it transpires that the girl was not descended from a slave after all, and their colored servant is instructed to reinstate the bed that General Beauregard had slept in, but the precious Spode cup had been lost forever.

Ultimately, the backgrounds, culture, and identities of ceramic importers and dealers impacted on what was commissioned, approaches to marketing, and even how intermediaries behaved. This leads to a theorization as to why this became the case. Conceivably, with the inevitable geographical divide between the suppliers and the American market, English manufacturers were obliged to respond to requests from importers and dealers. Guidance from importers and dealers was perhaps welcomed, and presumably manufacturers would have readily accepted commissions from intermediaries as a means to make additional money. Then, as a result of the gap between the producer and the market, American marketing began to evolve in ways that reflected this situation. Potentially, the entrepreneurial nature of the United States encouraged marketing to become more individualized, and this reflected how the market itself consisted of different sociopolitical sensibilities. The varied and unusual qualities of ceramic advertising in the United States reflected the diversity of cultures and ideas sharing or occupying different points of view. Far more than what has been previously recorded, marketing became a reflection of different backgrounds and identities of the intermediaries, and perhaps most significantly of all, the culture of the United States fostered an environment whereby different ideologies could be expressed.

At this stage, determining who actually consumed ceramics with a political, religious, or anti-slavery significance is harder. The assumption might be that these ceramics would have been acquired by consumers who shared the mindset as the importer and dealer who made the commission. However, as pointed out in Chapter 2, an English traveler observed how Seneca Indians owned blue printed Staffordshire pottery in the nineteenth century. The style of the patterns was potentially meaningless to other cultures who did not share the same reference points or sociopolitical concerns. Conceivably, to outsiders, they were simply decorative vessels. A precise archaeological investigation of a household site where the attitudes of the family are well documented might help solve this problem and establish whether, for instance, a family known for supporting the abolitionist cause ever owned ceramics based on an anti-slavery theme. This would help to demonstrate how consumption habits varied, questioning an all-pervasive model of a fashion-orientated world. Certainly, acknowledging that production could be steered by intermediaries in more individualized and expressive ways helps account for why certain ceramic designs were then perceived as rare by early collectors.

Henceforward, based on this research, it is proposed that there are at least three ways to understand the development of ceramic design. It cannot be denied that entrepreneurial manufacturers created designs intended to appeal to the American market. Alternatively, there is evidence of how intermediaries commissioned or steered the production of manufacturers on the basis of possessing a more informed view of changing consumer demand. But, the third way, as outlined in *Alternative Narratives …*, is how importers and dealers commissioned and marketed goods that reflected their own backgrounds, identities, and cultures. The key point is that this was not necessarily responding to demand but could parallel their own views and consciences. This has been revealed by bringing together an examination of marketing with an attempt to gain a greater understanding of the lives of the intermediaries.

The proposed third way, then, helps unify earlier types of ceramic history, which were far more fixated on what was being collected, with contemporary forms of literature that have considered broader patterns of production and consumption on the basis of fashion and price. If production was entirely driven by a consumer's desire to have goods that were fashionable or sold at a reasonable price, it becomes harder to account for why some designs were more unusual and rarer than others. Conventional wisdom might relate this distortion to changing levels of collecting, but this book has argued that the answer to this conundrum lies in the role of the intermediary, who ordered ceramics that reflected their own ideologies.

What began as an alternative narrative of ceramic history actually becomes a way to link past and present literature together. If the contribution of intermediaries is acknowledged, the recognition of why some ceramics were rare by the earliest collectors and writers and then the more recent interpretation of ceramics as reflecting demand becomes less of a contradiction. It was feasible to have ceramics that were promoted as either serviceable or fashionable, as well as those that were more marginal, contentious, and expressive. There were (for want of a better expression) "intermediary commodities" that existed between ceramics marketed as new and fashionable and those that were simply ordinary, functional, and cheap. Theoretically, "intermediary commodities" existed because merchants wanted to contribute to social and political debates or convey support for individuals and causes. Here, there emerges another interesting paradox. Regardless of the subject matter, the actual English manufacturer accepted the commission for financial gain, whereas the behavior of the crockery importer and dealer was not necessarily motivated by sheer profit. The intention of the intermediary was not always to sell the greatest amount of merchandise to the greatest number. By their very nature, "intermediary commodities" were not that common, and they occurred in ceramics where it was possible to assign a subject and literal meaning.

From the examples discussed in this book, the intermediary, in the form of the importer and dealer, has been shown to be capable of acting as an "author," in terms of steering the manufacturer to produce particular designs, in ways that were a concern to them, rather than what was dictated by the market. As established, older forms of ceramic history literature have tended to assume that production was guided by the entrepreneurial producer, but given the tempo of communication between America and Britain, this would have not been without its problems. When Peter Wainwright wrote to his son in Boston, he would often mention, at the end of a letter, how he was enclosing "a few News Papers" from England (Wainwright Papers: Box 3, Folder 3.17, November 30, 1830). From a producer's perspective in Staffordshire, it would have been problematic to keep pace of the various evolving social and political movements in the expanding American market. For instance, the murder of Elijah Lovejoy at Alton, Illinois, was discussed in a variety of English newspapers at the end of 1837. Some accounts were lengthy, but only a short article appeared in the *Staffordshire Advertiser* titled "Slavery in America—Riot and Murder of the Rev. Mr. Lovejoy &c" (December 23, 1837). Lacking any precise dates of when the actual assassination took place (unlike the versions of the transfer printed design (Figure 6.10)), it illustrates some of the difficulties faced by English producers in keeping abreast of worldwide events, if it is always assumed that it was the Staffordshire manufacturer who took the initiative in creating the design.

Although the interventions of intermediaries may not account for all of the instances of ceramics identified as rare (by the earliest collectors and writers), the value in understanding the backgrounds of importers and dealers has been demonstrated. Whenever possible, the "reader" can benefit from having a more comprehensive range of information; otherwise, the interpretation of the object will be incomplete, or sometimes incorrect. Contrary to the theory of Roland Barthes, this can only be achieved by gaining a wider knowledge of the backgrounds and beliefs of the intermediary. For the purposes of this book, an examination of advertising has been brought together with the biographical details of the importers and dealers as an additional way to consider ceramic history. Instances of advertising that mentioned precise designs, or the use of phrases such as, "expressly for us," reveals how the motivation behind production can be varied and complex. Potentially, authorship can be positioned in different places and was not simply in the hands of the producer.

Whether this third approach was a characteristic of other global markets supplied by Staffordshire or was peculiar to the American market and a phenomenon of the nineteenth century remains to be seen. At this stage, the point is that, based on the case study of the Anglo-American trade, manufacturers did not simply produce goods to appeal to the market, and neither did manufacturers or merchants simply respond to demand. Between the manufacturer and the market, there is now evidence for the contribution of intermediaries shaping production based on their own backgrounds, culture, and identity.

REFERENCES

Books

Abbe, T. and H. A. Howson (1941), *Robert Colgate: The Immigrant: A Genealogy of the New York Colgates and Some Associated Lines*, New Haven: Tuttle, Moorehouse and Taylor & Co.

Adams, P. (1925), *Stoke-upon-Trent Parish Register*, Part III, Staffordshire: Staffordshire Parish Registers Society.

Adams, P. W. L. (1926-27), *Stoke-upon-Trent Parish Register*, Part IV, Staffordshire: Staffordshire Parish Register Society.

Anderson, B. (1991), *Imagined Communities: reflections on the origin and spread of nationalism*, London: Verso.

Applegate, E. (2012), *The Rise of Advertising in the United States: A History of Innovation to 1960*, Plymouth, UK: The Scarecrow Press Inc.

Arman, D. and L. Arman (1998), *Anglo-American Ceramics Part 1: Transfer Printed Creamware and Pearlware for the American Market 1760-1860*, Portsmouth, RI: Oakland Press.

Arnoux, L. (1853), *Lectures on the Results of the Great Exhibition of 1851 … On Ceramic Manufactures, Porcelain and Pottery*, London: David Bogue.

Baldwin, J. ([1955] 2012), *Notes of a Native Son*, Boston: Beacon Press.

Barber, E. A. (1893), *The Pottery and Porcelain of the United States: An Historical Review of American Ceramic Art from the Earliest Times to the Present Day*, New York and London: G. P. Putnam's Sons.

Barber, E. A. (1899), *Anglo-American China*, Indianapolis, Ind: Press of The Clay-Worker.

Bakewell, W. H. (1888), *Vision of Faith in the Dream of Time: An Epic-Dramatic Poem in Books and Cantos*, Jackson, Michigan: Daily Citizen Printing and Publishing House,

Barthes, R. ([1968]1977), *Image Music Text*, London: Fontana Press.

Beecher, C. E. ([1841] 1843 revised), *A Treatise on Domestic Economy for the use of Young Ladies at Home and at School*, Boston: Thomas H. Webb & Co.

Beecher, C. E. (1846), *Domestic Receipt Book: Designed as a Supplement to her Treatise on Domestic Economy*, New York: Harper & Brothers.

Berg, M. (2005), *Luxury and Pleasure in Eighteenth-century Britain*, Oxford: Oxford University Press.

Blaszczyk, R. L. (2000), *Imagining Consumers: Design and Innovation from Wedgwood to Corning*, Baltimore and London: The Johns Hopkins University Press.

Boardman, J. (1833), *America and the Americans*, London: Longman, Rees, Orme, Brown, Green and Longman.

Bordewich, F. (2005), *Bound for Canaan: the Epic Story of the Underground Railway: America's First Civil Rights Movement*, New York: Harper Collins.

Brewer, J. and R. Porter, eds. (1993), *Consumption and the World of Goods*, London and New York: Routledge.

Briggs, J. (2003), "Nonconformity and the Pottery Industry", in D. Bebbington and T. Larsen (eds.) *Modern Christianity and Cultural Aspirations*, London: Sheffield Academic Press, Continuum International Publishing, pp.47–77.

Brown, J. C. (1909), *A Hundred Years of Merchant Banking: A History of Brown Brothers and Company; Brown, Shipley & Company and the Allied Trades*, New York: Privately Printed.
Buck, N. S. ([1925] 1969), *The Development of the Organisation of Anglo-American Trade 1800-1850*, Devon: David & Charles.
Burchill, F. and R. Ross (1977), *A History of the Potters' Union*, Hanley, Stoke-on-Trent: Ceramic and Allied Trades Union.
Butler, F. G. (1885), *A History of Farmington, Franklin County, Maine, from the Earliest Explorations to the Present Time, 1776–1885*, Farmington: Press of Knowlton, McLeary and Co.
By a merchant of Philadelphia (1846), *Memoirs and Auto-biography of some of the Wealthy Citizens of Philadelphia*, Philadelphia: Published by the Booksellers.
Carey, M., L. Beecher, and S. Jackson (1820), *Addresses of the Philadelphia Society for the Promotion of National Industry*, Philadelphia: James Maxwell.
Camehl, A. W. ([1916] 1946), *The Blue China Book: Early American Scenes and History Pictured in the Pottery of the Time*, New York: Tudor Publishing Company.
Campbell, C. (1987), *The Romantic Ethic and the Spirit of Modern Consumerism*, Oxford: Blackwell Publishers.
Campbell, C. (1993), "Understanding traditional and modern of consumption in eighteenth-century England: a character-action approach", in J. Brewer and R. Porter (eds.), *Consumption and the World of Good*, London and New York: Routledge.
Chapman, S. (1992), *Merchant enterprise in Britain from the Industrial Revolution to World War I*, Cambridge: Cambridge University Press.
Child, Mrs. [L. M] ([1829] 1838), *The American Frugal Housewife, dedicated to those who are not ashamed of economy*, New York: Samuel S. & William Wood.
Cochran, T. C. (1981), *Frontiers of Change: Early Industrialism in America*, Oxford: Oxford University Press.
Cohen, J. (2017), *Luxurious Citizens: The Politics of Consumption in Nineteenth-Century America*, Philadelphia: University of Pennsylvania Press.
Collard, E. ([1967] enlarged 1984) *Nineteenth-century Pottery and Porcelain in Canada*, McGill-Queen's University Press, Kingston and Montreal.
Collard, E. (1983), *The Potters' View of Canada*, Canada: McGill-Queen's University Press.
Coysh, A. W. (1972), *Blue-Printed Earthenware, 1800-1850*, Plymouth: David & Charles.
Cressey, P.J., J. F. Stephens, S. J. Shephard and B. H. Magid (1982), "The Core-Periphery Relationship and the Archaeological Record in Alexandria, Virginia", in R. S. Dickens (ed.), *Archaeology of Urban America: The Search of Pattern and Process*, New York and London: Academic Press.
Cunningham, jr., N. E. (1994), "Political Dimensions of Everyday Life in the Early Republic", in C. E. Hutchins (ed.) *Everyday Life in the Early Republic*, Winterthur, Delaware: Henry Francis du Pont Winterthur Museum, (1994), pp. 3–33.
Curry, L. P. (1981), *The Free Black in Urban America 1800-1850*, Chicago and London: The University of Chicago Press.
Daugherty, G. E. (1927), "Grandmother's Old Blue Historical China and Its Makers", Lebanon County Historical Society, October 28, Vol. IX, 8, pp.271–86.
Decker, F. (2013), *Brooklyn's Plymouth Church in the Civil War Era: A Ministry of Freedom*, Charleston and London: The History Press.
Dinnerstein, L. and D. M. Reimers (1999), *Ethic Americans: A History of Immigration*, New York: Columbia University Press.
diZerega Wall, D. (1994), "Family Dinners and Social Teas: Ceramics and Domestic Rituals" in C. E. Hutchins (ed.) *Everyday Life in the Early Republic*, Winterthur, Delaware: Henry Francis du Pont Winterthur Museum, 1994, pp.249–84.

Dupree, M. W. (1995), *Family Structure in the Staffordshire Potteries 1840-1880*, Oxford: Clarence Press.

Dyson, S. L. (1982), "Material Culture, Social Structure, Changing Cultural Values: The Ceramics of Eighteenth- and Nineteenth-Century Middletown, Connecticut", in R. S. Dickens, Jr. (ed.), *Archaeology of Urban America: The Search for Pattern and Process*, New York: Academic Press, Inc., pp.361–80.

Earle, A. M. (1892), *China Collecting in America*, New York: Charles Scribner's Sons.

Emmerson, R. (2010), "The Jonathan Aborn Invoice: September 1802", in S.R.Teitelman, P. Halfpenny, and R. W. Fuchs (eds.), *Success to America: Creamware for the American Market featuring the S. Robert Teitelman Collection at Winterthur*, Suffolk: Antique Collectors' Club, pp.250–61.

Fearon, H. B. (1819), *Sketches of America: A Narrative of a Journey of Five Thousand Miles Through the Eastern and Western States of America*, London: Longman, Hurst, Rees, Orme and Brown.

Fischer, D. H. (2005), *Liberty and Freedom: A Visual History of America's Founding Ideas*, Oxford: Oxford University Press.

Foster, C. ([1835] 2011), *An Account of the Conflagration of the Principal part of the First Ward of the City of New York*, British Library: Historical Print Editions.

Fox, R. W. (1999), *Trials of Intimacy: Love and loss in the Beecher-Tilton Scandal*, Chicago and London: The University of Chicago Press.

Franklin, B. ([1868] 1996), *The Autobiography of Benjamin Franklin*, Mineola, New York: Dover Publications, Inc.

Frelinghuysen, A. C. (2000), "Empire City Entrepreneurs: Ceramics and Glass in New York City", in C. H. Voorsanger and J. K. Howat (eds.), *Art and the Empire City: New York, 1825-1861*, New York: The Metropolitan Museum of Art.

Fuchs, R.W. and P. F. Ferguson (2021), " 'Remember them that are in Bonds': A Plate Made for the Abolition Movement", in P. F. Ferguson (ed.), *Pots, Prints and Politics: Ceramics with an Agenda, from the 14th to the 20th Century*, London: The British Museum, pp.130–39.

Fullerton, R. A. (2016), "Segmentation in Practice: An historical overview of the eighteenth and nineteenth centuries" in D. G. B. Jones and M. Tadajewski (eds.), *The Routledge Companion to Marketing History*, London and New York: Routledge, pp.85–95.

Furman, R. (2015), *Brooklyn Heights: The Rise, Fall and Rebirth of America's First Suburb*, Charleston, SC: The History Press.

Gilboy, E. W. ([1932] 1967), "Demand as a Factor in the Industrial Revolution", in R. M. Hartwell (ed.) *The causes of the Industrial Revolution in England*, 1967, London: Methuen & Co. Ltd., pp.121–138.

Glennie, P. (1995), "Consumption within Historical Studies", in D. Miller (ed.), *Acknowledging Consumption: A Review of New Studies*, London and New York: Routledge.

Godden, G. (1979), *Oriental Export Market Porcelain and its influence on European wares*, London, Toronto, Sydney and New York: Granada.

Goldberg, A. F. and J.P. Witkowski (2006), "Beneath His Magic Touch: The Dated Vessels of the African-American slave Potter Dave", in Robert Hunter (ed.), *Ceramics in America*, Milwaukee: Chipstone Foundation, pp.58–92.

Greaser, A. and P.H. Greaser (1973, fourth ed.), *Homespun Ceramics: A Study of Spatterware*, Des Moines, Iowa: Wallace-Homestead Book Co.

Greeley, H. et al. (1872), *The Great Industries of the United States: Being an Historical Summary of the Origin, Growth, and Perfections of the Chief Industrial Arts of this Country*, Hartford, Chicago and Cincinnati: J. B. Burr & Hyde.

Haggar, R. and E. Adams (1977), *Mason Porcelain and Ironstone 1796-1855*, London: Faber & Faber.

Haggerty, S. (2012), *"Merely for Money"? Business Culture in the British Atlantic, 1750-1815*, Liverpool: Liverpool University Press.

Halfpenny, P. A. (2010), "Creamware and the Staffordshire Potteries", in S. R.Teitelman, P. Halfpenny, and R. W. Fuchs (eds.), *Success to America: Creamware for the American Market featuring the S.Robert Teitelman Collection at Winterthur*, Suffolk: Antique Collectors' Club, pp.30–59.

Haines Halsey, R. T. ([1899] 1974), *Pictures of Early New York on Dark Blue Staffordshire Pottery*, Canada: General Publishing Company, Ltd.

Heard, J. H. (1856), A *Historical Account of Columbian Lodge of Free and Accepted Masons of Boston, Mass.* Boston: Alfred Mudge & Son.

Heneghan, B. T. (2003), *Whitewashing America: Material Culture and Race in the Antebellum Imagination*, Mississippi: The University Press of Mississippi.

Henrywood, R. K. (2002), *Staffordshire Potters, 1781-1900: A Comprehensive List Assembled from all known Contemporary Directories with Selected Marks*, Woodbridge, Suffolk: Antique Collectors' Club Ltd.

Hollenback, K. L., and M. B. Schiffer (2010), "Technology and Material Life", in D. Hicks and M. C Beaudry (eds.), *The Oxford Handbook of Material Culture Studies*, Oxford: Oxford University Press, pp. 313–332.

Horn, J. and P.D. Morgan (2005), "Settlers and Slaves: European and African Migrations to Early Modern British America", in E. Mancke and C. Shammas (eds.), *The Creation of the British Atlantic World*, Baltimore, Maryland: Johns Hopkins University Press.

Howard, D. S. (1984), *New York and the China Trade*, New York Historical Society: Columbia Publishing Co.

Hudson Moore, N. (1903), *The Old China Book*, New York: Frederick A. Stokes Company.

Hutt, W.H. (1936), *Economists and the Public: A study of Competition and Opinion*, London: Jonathan Cape.

Hyland, P. (2005), *The Herculaneum Pottery: Liverpool's Forgotten Glory*, Liverpool: Liverpool University Press.

Kissam, E. (1892), *The Kissam Family in America from 1644 to 1825*, New York: Dempsey & Carroll's Art Press.

Klamkin, M. (1973), *American Patriotic and Political China*, New York: Charles Scribner's Sons.

Klepp, S. E. (2021), "Sarah Thorn Tyndale", in C. Dallett Hemphill and R. Hessinger and D. K. Richter (eds.), *Philadelphia Stories: People and Places in Early America*, Philadelphia: University of Pennsylvania Press, pp.243–67.

Kowalsky, A.A. and D. E. Kowalsky (1999), *Encyclopedia of Marks on American, English, and European Earthenware, Ironstone, and Stoneware (1780-1980)*, Atglen, PA: Schiffer Publishing Ltd.

Laidacker, S. (1938), *The Standard Catalogue of Anglo-American China from 1810 to 1850*, Scanton, PA, Sam Laidacker, 711 Linden Street.

Larsen, E. B (1939), *American Historical Views on Staffordshire China*, New York: Doubleday, Doran & Company, Inc.

Larsen, E. B. (1950, revised and enlarged), *American Historical Views on Staffordshire China*, New York: Doubleday & Co., Inc.

Lepore, J. (2005), "The Tightening Vise: Slavery and Freedom in British New York" in I. Berlin and L.M. Harris (eds.), *Slavery in New York*, New York: The New Press, pp.57–89.

Leslie, Miss ([1840] 1844), *The House Book, or a Manual of Domestic Economy*, Philadelphia: Carey & Hart.

Lindman, J. M. (2009), *Bodies of Belief: Baptist Community in Early America*, Pennsylvania: University of Pennsylvania Press.

Lockett, T. A. (1997), "English Porcelain for the U.S.A.", *Northern Ceramic Society Journal*, Kendal, Cumbria: Titus Wilson & Son, pp.87–103.

McCauley, R. H. (1942), *Liverpool Transfer Designs on Anglo-American Pottery*, Portland: The Southworth Anthoensen Press.

McCusker, J.J. and K. Morgan, eds. (2000), *The Early Modern Atlantic Economy*, Cambridge: Cambridge University Press.

McKendrick, N., J. Brewer and J. H. Plumb (1982), *The Birth of a Consumer Society: The Commercialization of Eighteenth-century England*, London: Europa Publications Limited.

Majewski, T. and M. J. O'Brien "The Use and Misuse of Nineteenth-century English and American Ceramics in Archaeological Analysis", *Advances in Archaeology Method and Theory*, Volume 11, pp.97–209.

Mancke E., and C. Shammas, eds. (2005), *The Creation of the British Atlantic World*, Baltimore: Johns Hopkins University Press.

Mandel, E. ([1968]: 2nd impression, 1971), translation by Brian Pearce, *Marxist Economic Theory*, London: Merlin Press.

Marchand, R. (1985), *Advertising the American Dream*, Berkeley: University of California Press.

Marryat, J. (1816), *Thoughts on the Abolition of the Slave Trade and Civilization of Africa; with remarks on the African Institution and the Examination of the Report of the Committee, recommending a general Registry of Slaves in the British West India Islands*, London: J. M. Richardson, Cornhill, and J. Ridgway, Piccadilly.

Marryat, J. (1850), *Collections Towards a History of Pottery and Porcelain in the 15th, 16th, 17th and 18th Centuries: With a Description of the Manufacture, a Glossary, and a List of Monograms*, London: John Murray.

Mathias, P. (2000), "Risk, credit and kinship in early modern enterprise", in McCusker, J.J. and Morgan, K. (eds.), *The Early Modern Atlantic Economy*, Cambridge: Cambridge University Press, pp.15–35.

Mayhew, J. (1763), *Christian Sobriety: Being Eight Sermons on Titus II. 6*, Boston: Richard and Samuel Draper.

Merideth, R. (1965), *Narrative of Riots at Alton by Edward Beecher*, New York: E. P. Dutton & Co., Inc.

Meteyard, E. (1865-66), *The Life of Josiah Wedgwood from his Private Correspondence and Family Papers*, 2 volumes, London: Hurst and Blackett.

Miller, G. L., A. S. Martin and N.S. Dickinson (1994), "Changing Consumption Patterns: English Ceramics and the American Market from 1770 to 1840", in C. E. Hutchins (ed.), *Everyday Life in the Early Republic*, Winterthur, Delaware: Henry Francis du Pont Winterthur Museum, pp. 219–48.

Miller, G. L. (2013), "A Revised Set of CC Index Values for Classification and Economic Scaling of English Ceramics from 1787 to 1880", in R. Allen, J. Huddleson, K. J.

Wooten, and G.J. Farris (eds.), *Ceramic Identification in Historical Archaeology: The View from California, 1822-1940*, Germantown, MD: The Society for Historical Archaeology.
Morgan, K. (2000), "Business networks in the export trade to North America, 1750-1800", in J. J. McCuster and K. Morgan (eds.), *The Early Modern Atlantic Economy*, Cambridge: Cambridge University Press, pp.36–62.
Morison, S. E. and H. S. Commager (1942), *The Growth of the American Republic*, Vol.1, New York and London: Oxford University Press.
Nöel Hume, I. ([1974] 2009), *All the Best Rubbish: The Classic Ode to Collecting* New York: Harper.
Ovington, I.H. ([1884] 1892), *Comforting Thoughts Spoken by Henry Ward Beecher in Sermons, Addresses, and Prayers*, New York: Fords, Howard and Hulbert.
Ovington, M. W. ([1911] reprint 2019), *Half a Man: The Status of the New York Negro*, New York ; London: Longmans, Green, and Co.
Parke-Bernet Galleries (1938), "The William Randolph Hearst Collection: Part II, Early American Furniture and Historical Blue Staffordshire Ware", New York.
Payne, D. (1891), *History of the African Methodist Episcopal Church*, Nashville, Tennessee: Publishing House of the A. M. E. Sunday-School Union.
Presbrey, F. ([1929] 1968), *The History and Development of Advertising*, New York: Greenwood Press.
Price, J. M. (1989), "'What Did Merchants Do?' Reflections on British Overseas Trade, 1660–1790", *The Journal of Economic History*, Volume XLIX, Number 2, June, pp. 267–84.
Prime, W. C. ([1877] 1879), *Pottery and Porcelain of all Times and Nations*, New York: Harper & Brothers.
Pugh, P. D. G. (1995), *Staffordshire Portrait Figures and the Allied Subjects of the Victorian Era*, Woodbridge, Suffolk: Antique Collectors' Club Limited.
Rael, P. (2005), "The Long Death of Slavery", in I. Berlin and L. M. Harris (eds.), *Slavery in New York*, New York: The New Press, pp.111–146.
Ramsay, J. (1939), *American Potters and Pottery*, Clinton, Mass: Colonial Press Inc., Hale, Cushman & Flint.
Richards, S. (1999), *Eighteenth-century ceramics: Products for a civilised society*, Manchester and New York: Manchester University Press.
Robacker, E. F. and A. F. Robacker (1978), *Spatterware and Sponge*, Cranbury, New Jersey: A. S. Barnes and Co., Inc.
Robineau, S. (1901), *Old China*, published, Syracuse, New York: Keramic Studio Publishing Co.
Rose, M. B. (2000), *Firms, Networks and Business Values: The British and American Cotton Industries since 1750*, Cambridge University Press, Cambridge.
Rosenstein, L. (2009), *Antiques: The History of an Idea*, Ithaca and London: Cornell University Press.
Sandon, H. (1975), *Royal Worcester Porcelain: from 1862 to the Present Day*, London: Barrie & Jenkins.
Samuelsson, K. ([1957] 1961), *Religion and Economic Action* [translated by E. Geoffrey French], London, Melbourne, Toronto: William Heinemann Ltd.
Scott, K. (1979), Compiler: *British Aliens in the United States during the War of 1812*, Baltimore: Genealogical Publishing Co. Available at Ancestry.com. [database on-line]. Provo, UT, USA: Ancestry.com Operations Inc, 2006.
Scott, K. (1981), *Early New York Naturalizations: Abstracts of Naturalization Records from Federal, State, and Local Courts 1792–1840* Baltimore: Genealogical Publishing Co. Inc.

Searle, G.R. (1998), *Morality and the Market in Victorian Britain*, Oxford: Clarendon Press.
Shaw, S. (1829), *History of the Staffordshire Potteries; and the Rise and Progress of the Manufacture of Pottery and Porcelain; with References to Genuine Specimens, and notices of Eminent Potters*, Hanley: G. Jackson.
Shi, D. E. (1985), *The Simple Life: Plain Living and High Thinking in American Culture*, Athens, Georgian: The University of Georgia Press.
Slosson, A. T. (1878), [Originally published as by "The Youngest Member"], *The China Hunters*[sic] *Club*, New York: Harper & Brothers.
Smith, A. ([1776] 1871), *An Inquiry into the Nature and Causes of the Wealth of Nations*, London: Alex. Murray & Son.
Smith, M. W. (1924), *Anglo-American Historical China*, Chicago: Robert O. Ballou.
Snyder, J. B. (1995), *Historical Staffordshire American Patriots & Views*, Atglen, PA: Schiffer Publishing Ltd.
Spargo, J. (1926), *Early American Pottery and China*, New York and London: The Century Co.
Stacey, J. (1862), *A Prince in Israel; or Sketches of the Life of John Ridgway, Esq.*, London: Hamilton, Adams and Co. [reprint of original edition by Hansebooks].
Stefano, F. ([1974] 1980), "James Clews, nineteenth-century potter: Part II, The American Experience", in Paul Atterbury ed. *English Pottery and Porcelain: An Historical Survey*, London: Peter Owen, pp.207–9.
Stelling, H. A. (2017), "Ambassadors of Elegance: English Transfer-Printed Presentation Pitchers in Massachusetts Lodges", in John S. Wade (ed.), *Reflections on 300 Years of Freemasonry*, London: Lewis Masonic, pp.291–307.
Stowe, H. B. (1853), *The Key to Uncle Tom's Cabin; Presenting the Original Facts and Documents upon which the Story is Founded…* London: Clarke, Beeton and Co.
Stubenrauch, J. (2016), *The Evangelical Age of Ingenuity in Industrial Britain*, Oxford: Oxford University Press.
Styles, J. (1993), "Manufacturing, consumption and design in eighteenth-century England", in J. Brewer and R. Porter (eds.), *Consumption and the World of Goods*, London and New York: Routledge, pp.527–54.
Tamilia, R. D. (2016), "History of channels of distribution" in D. G. B. Jones and M. Tadajewski (eds.), *The Routledge Companion to Marketing History*, London and New York: Routledge.
Teitelman, S. R., Halfpenny, P. and R. W. Fuchs (2010), *Success to America: Creamware for the American Market featuring the S. Robert Teitelman Collection at Winterthur*, Suffolk: Antique Collectors' Club.
The Wealth and Biography of the Wealthy Citizens of the City of New York (1846), New York: The Sun Office.
Trustees of The Wedgwood Museum (1973), *Letters of Josiah Wedgwood, 1762-1770*, Volume 1, Manchester: E.J. Morten.
Turner, E. S. ([1952] 1968), *The Shocking History of Advertising*, Middlesex: Penguin Books.
Ward, J. (1843), *The Borough of Stoke-upon-Trent … its History, Statistics, Civil Polity, & Traffic*, London: W. Lewis & Son.
Weber, M. ([1930] 2010), *The Protestant Ethic and the Spirit of Capitalism*, London and New York: Routledge.
Wedgwood, H. (1877), *Romance of Staffordshire: A Collection of Historical, Biographic & Descriptive Sketches …* Vol1, Manchester: John Heywood, Deansgate.

Wedgwood, J. C. (1913), *Staffordshire Pottery and its History*, New York: McBride, Nast & Company.
Wellman, J. (2014), *Brooklyn's Promised Land: The Free Black Community of Weeksville, New York*, New York and London: New York University Press.
Wetherbee, J. (1996), *White Ironstone: A Collector's Guide*, Dubuque, Iowa: Antique Trader Books.
Williams, P. (1971), *Flow Blue China: An Aid to Identification*, Jeffersontown, Kentucky: Fountain House East.
Withington, A. (1994), "Manufacturing and Selling the American Revolution", in Catherine E. Hutchins (ed) *Everyday Life in the Early Republic*, Winterthur, Delaware: Henry Francis du Pont Winterthur Museum, 1994), pp. 285–315.
Witkowski, T. H. (2016), "A history of consumption in the United States", in D. G. B. Jones and M. Tadajewski (eds.) *The Routledge Companion to Marketing History*, London and New York: Routledge.
Witkowski, T. H. and D.G.B. Jones (2006), "Qualitative Historical Research in Marketing" in Belk, R. W. (ed.), *Handbook of Qualitative Research Methods in Marketing*, Edward Elgar Publishing, Cheltenham, pp. 70–82.
Wulf, K. (2005), "'Of the Old Stock': Quakerism and Transalantic Genealogies in Colonial British America", in Mancke E. and C. Shammas (eds.), *The Creation of the British Atlantic World*, Baltimore, Maryland: Johns Hopkins University Press, pp.304–20.
Young, H. (1999), *English Porcelain 1745–95: Its Makers, Design, Marketing and Consumption*, London: V&A Publications.
Young, J. J. ([1878] 1879), *The Ceramic Art: A Compendium of the History and Manufacture of Pottery and Porcelain*, London: Sampson Low, Marston, Searle & Rivington.

Articles, Annuals and Journals

Anderson, A. (2013), "The Romance of Old Blue: collecting and displaying Old Blue Staffordshire China in the American Home c.1870-1938", *Interpreting Ceramics*, Issue 15, Available at: http://www.interpretingceramics.com/issue015/conf_contents.htmonlinejournal.
Blaszczyk, R. L. (1984), "Ceramics and the Sot-Weed Factor: The China Market in the Tobacco Economy", *Winterthur Portfolio*, Vol. 19. No. 1 (Spring), pp. 7–19.
Breen, T.H. (1986), "An Empire of Goods: The Anglicization of Colonial America, 1690-1776", *Journal of British Studies*, October, Vol. 25, No. 4. pp. 467–499.
Briggs, J. (1988), "'The Radical Saints of Shelton': The Ridgway family, Methodist Pottery Manufacturers", in D. J. Jeremy (ed.) *Business and Religion in Britain*, Vol. 5, Aldershot: Gower, pp. 47–71.
Ewins, N. (1997), "'Supplying the Present Wants of Our Yankee Cousins' Staffordshire Ceramics and the American Market 1775-1880", *Journal of Ceramic History*, Volume 15, City Museum & Art Gallery of Stoke-on-Trent, pp.154.
Ewins, N. (2023), "Hidden Histories: the case of Elijah Lovejoy and the Production of Anti-Slavery Ceramics", in R. Hunter and R., Fuchs II (eds.), *Ceramics in America*, Milwaukee: Chipstone Foundation, pp. 124–33.
Glickman, L. B. (2004), "'Buy for the Sake of the Slave': Abolitionism and the Origins of American Consumer Activism." *American Quarterly* 56, no. 4, December, pp. 889–913.

Hampson, R. (1990), "Longton Potters 1700–1865", *Journal of Ceramic History*, Volume 14, Stoke-on-Trent: City Museum & Art Gallery, pp. 236.
Hartmann, H. W. (1939), "The Millennium Plate", in S. Laidacker (ed.), *The American Antiques Collector*, May, Vol. 1, No.3, pp. 50–51.
Hudnut, A. M. (1907), "Some Notable Collections of Old Blue Staffordshire China, Decorated with American Views, Syntax and Wilkie Designs, and the Arms of the Thirteen Original States", *American Homes and Gardens*, Vol IV, No 1., January, pp. 21–27.
Hudnut A. M. (1917), "Accessions: Staffordshire Historical China Presented", *Bulletin of the Detroit Museum of Art*, Vol. 11, Number 7-8, April-May, pp.69–71.
McKendrick, N. (1960), "Josiah Wedgwood: An Eighteenth Century Entrepreneur in Salesmanship and Marketing Techniques", *The Economic History Review*, New Series, Vol. XII, No. 3, 1960, pp. 409–33.
McKendrick, N. (1964), "Josiah Wedgwood and Thomas Bentley: an Inventor-Entrepreneur Partnership in the Industrial Revolution", *Royal Historical Transactions*, Vol. 14, December, pp. 1–33.
Magid, B. H (2006), "Commemorative Wares in George Washington's Hometown", in R. Hunter (ed.), *Ceramics in America*, Milwaukee, WI: Chipstone Foundation, pp. 3–39.
Magid, B. H. (2008), "Robert H. Miller, Importer: Alexandria and St.Louis", in R. Hunter (ed.) *Ceramics in America*, Milwaukee, WI: Chipstone Foundation, pp. 143–161.
Margolin, S. (2002), "'And Freedom to the Slave': Antislavery Ceramics, 1787–1865", in R. Hunter (ed.), Milwaukee, WI: Chipstone Foundation, *Ceramics in America*, pp. 80–109.
Miller, G. L. (1998), "The Association of Earthen Ware Dealers of Boston", in K. A McLeod and J. R. Boyle (eds.), *The Heritage of Wedgwood*, Proceedings of the Wedgwood International Seminars, Charlotte, #36, Boston #37 and Dallas #38, pp. 126–147.
Miller, G. and A. Earls (2008), "War on Pots: The Impact of Economics and Politics on Ceramic Consumption Patterns" in R. Hunter (ed.) *Ceramics in America*, Milwaukee: The Chipstone Foundation, pp. 67–108.
Pomfret, R. (2010), "Letter Books of Matthew Smith 1806-32", *The Northern Ceramic Journal*, Volume 26, 2010, pp. 33–107.
Schwartz, G. (2011), "Digging up Salem's Golden Age: Ceramic Use Among the Merchant Class" in R. Hunter (ed.), *Ceramics in America*, Hanover and London: Chipstone Foundation, University Press of New England, pp. 71–99.
Schwind, A. (1984), "The Ceramic Imports of Frederick Rhinelander, New York Loyalist Merchant" *Winterthur Portfolio: A Journal of American Material Culture*, Volume 19, Number 1, Spring 1984, pp. 21–37.
Smith, S. (1974), "Norwich China Dealers of the Mid-Eighteenth Century", *English Ceramic Circle Transactions*, Vol.9, No.2, pp. 193–211.
The Unitarian Chronicle for 1833 (1833), London: Charles Fox, 67, Paternoster Row.
Thistlethwaite, F. (1958), "The Atlantic Migration of the Pottery Industry", *Economic History Review*, Second Series, December, Vol. XI (2): pp. 264–278.
Walthall, J.A. (2013), "Queensware Direct from the Potteries: US Importers of Staffordshire Ceramics in Antebellum America 1820–1860", *Studies in Material Culture No.*1, Historical Archaeology, Illinois: Illinois State Archaeological Survey.
Willett, C. Carey, ed. (1892), *Memories of Britain By Rev.* W. H. Bakewell, Lansing, Michigan: Darius D. Thorp.
Woods Jr., N. F, (2016), "Pink and the Fancy Gal: White Slavery, the Abolitionists' Crusade, and the Painter's Canvas," *Nineteenth-Century Art Worldwide* 15, no. 3, Autumn, pp. 37–60. Available at: https://doi.org/10.29411/ncaw.2016.15.3.4.

Magazines

Kingsbury, P. D. (1977), "Enoch Wood earthenware found in St.Paul's Church, Burslem", *The Magazine Antiques*, July, pp.122–7.
Laidacker, S. (1939a), "How Can I Learn About Historical Staffordshire", *The American Antique Collector*, Volume 1, October-November, No 6., p.125.
Laidacker, S. (1939b), "Importer's Marks", *The American Antique Collector*, Volume 1, December, No 7., p.150.
McCauley, R. H. (1944), "American importers of Staffordshire", *The Magazine Antiques*, June, Vol. XLV, No.6, pp.295–7.
McKnight, E. J. (1906), "Peter Morton – An Early American Merchant and Importer" *Connecticut Magazine*, Vol. 10, pp.350–8.
Norman-Wilcox, G. (1931), "Staffordshire Views of the Boston State House", *The Magazine Antiques*, December, Vol. XX, No.6, New York: The Magazine Antiques, Incorporated.
Norman-Wilcox, G. (1934), "American-Historical Staffordshire Rarities", *The Magazine Antiques*, May, pp.178–182.

Census Sources

All available from Ancestry.com Operations, Inc.

Census, Baltimore, 1860.
Census, Jersey City, New Jersey, 1880.
Census, Kings, Brooklyn, 1850.
Census, Kings, Brooklyn, 1855.
Census, Kings, Brooklyn, 1860.
Census, Kings, Brooklyn, 1870.
Census, Kings, Brooklyn, 1875.
Census, Kings, Brooklyn, 1880.
Census, Kings, Brooklyn, 1892.
Census, New York City, 1860.
Census, New York City, 1870.
Census, New York City, 1880.
Census, Philadelphia, 1790.
Census, Philadelphia, 1810.
Census, Providence, Rhode Island, 1900.
Census, St.Louis, 1870.
Census, Stoke-on-Trent, 1851.
Census, Stoke-on-Trent, 1861.
Census, Stoke-on-Trent, 1871.

Trade Directories

Allbut, J. (1802), *The Staffordshire Pottery Directory*, Hanley: J. Allbut and Son.
Barfoot, P., and Wilkes, J. (1791), *The Universal British directory of trade, commerce, and manufacture*, Volume 2, London: Printed for the Patentees, the British Directory Office.

Chapman, T. (1800), *Chapman's Birmingham Directory; or Alphabetical list of merchants …* Birmingham: T. Chapman.
Desilver, R. (1831), *Desilver's Philadelphia Directory and Stranger's Guide*, Philadelphia: Robert Desilver.
Desilver, R. (1835–6), *Desilver's Philadelphia Directory and Stranger's Guide* for 1835 & 1836, Philadelphia: Robert Desilver.
Doggett, J. (1843–44), *The New-York City Directory for 1843 & 1844*, New York: John Doggett, Jr., 79 Nassau Street.
Doggett, J. (1844–45), *The New-York City Directory for 1844 & 1845*, New York: John Doggett, Jr., 79 Nassau Street.
Doggett, J. (1848–49), *New York City Directory 1848-49*, New York: J. Doggett.
Doggett, J. (1850–1), *Doggett's New York City Directory, for 1850-1851*, New York: John Doggett, Jr.
Frost, J. H. A and C. Stimpson (1825), *The Boston Directory*, Boston: John H.A. Front Printer.
Gore (1796), *Gore's Directory of Liverpool or Alphabetical List, of The Merchants, Tradesman …* Liverpool: Gore.
Harrington, E. (1829), *The Utica Directory*, Utica, New York: Dauby & Maynard.
Hodge, R., T. Allen and S. Campbell (1789), *The New-York Directory and Register for the Year 1789*, New York: Hodge, Allen and Campbell.
Holden, W. (1805), *Holden's Triennial Directory …* London: W. Holden, No.8, Corner of Northampton Buildings, Rosoman Street, Clerkenwell.
Holden, W. (1809), *Holden's Triennial Directory …* London: William Holden, 122 Newgate Street.
Holden, W. (1811), *Holden's Annual London and Country Directory of the United Kingdom and Wales …* London: William Holden, 122 Newgate Street.
Lain, G. T (1867), *The Brooklyn City and Business Directory for the Year Ending May 1st, 1867*, Brooklyn and New York: Lain & Co.
Lain, G. T. (1875), *The Brooklyn City and Business Directory for the Year Ending May 1st, 1875*, Brooklyn and New York: Lain & Co.
Lain, G. T. (1884), *The Brooklyn City and Business Directory for the Year Ending May 1st, 1884*, Brooklyn: Lain & Co.
Lain, G.T. (1886), *Lain's Brooklyn Directory: for the Year Ending May 1st, 1886*, Brooklyn: Lain & Co.
Lain, G. T. and C. J. Healy (1889), *The Brooklyn City and Business Directory for the Year Ending May 1st, 1889*, Brooklyn: Lain & Co.
Lain, G.T. (1890), *The Brooklyn City and Business Directory for the Year Ending May 1st, 1890*, Brooklyn: Lain & Co.
Longworth, D. (1798), *Longworth's American Almanac, New-York Register and City Directory*, New York: David Longworth.
Longworth, D. (1811), *Longworth's American Almanac, New-York Register and City Directory …* New York: David Longworth.
Longworth, D. (1813), *Longworth's American Almanac, New-York Register and City Directory …* New York: David Longworth.
Longworth, D. (1816), *Longworth's American Almanac, New York Register and City Directory …* New York: David Longworth.
Longworth (1819–20), *Longworth's American Almanac, New-York Register and City Directory …* New York: Published for Jona Olmstead.
Longworth, T. (1821), *Longworth's American Almanac, New York Register and City Directory …* New York: Thomas Longworth.

Longworth, T. (1822), *Longworth's American Almanac, New York Register and City Directory* … New York: Thomas Longworth.
Longworth, T. (1824), *Longworth's American Almanac, New York Register and City Directory* … New York: Thomas Longworth.
Longworth, T. (1825), *Longworth's American Almanac, New York Register and City Directory* … New York: Thomas Longworth.
Longworth, T. (1826), *Longworth's American Almanac, New York Register and City Directory* … New York: Thomas Longworth.
Longworth, T. (1834), *Longworth's American Almanac, New York Register and City Directory* … New York: Thomas Longworth.
Longworth, T. (1840), *Longworth's American Almanac, New York Register and City Directory* … New York: Thomas Longworth.
Longworth, T. (1842), *Longworth's American Almanac, New York Register and City Directory* … New York: Thomas Longworth.
McCarty and Davis, (1821), *The Philadelphia Directory and Register for 1821* … , Philadelphia: McCarty and Davis.
M'Elroy, A. (1839), *Philadelphia Directory for 1839*, Philadelphia: Isaac Ashmead & Co.
M'Elroy, A. (1844), *Philadelphia Directory for 1844*, Philadelphia: Edward C. Biddle.
M'Elroy, A. (1861), *Philadelphia City Directory*, Philadelphia: E. C. & J. Biddle & Co.
McElroy, A. (1867), *Philadelphia City Directory for 1867*, Philadelphia: E. C. & J. Biddle & Co.
Norman, J. (1789), *The Boston Directory, Containing A List of Merchants, Mechanics, Traders, and others of the Town of Boston* …. Boston: John Norman.
Paxton, J. A. (1813), *The Philadelphia Directory and Register for 1813* … Philadelphia: B. & T. Kite.
Pigot, J. (1818–20), *The Commercial Directory*, Manchester: James Pigot and R. & W. Dean.
Ripley, F. F. (1840), *The New York Business Directory, for 1840 & 1841, wherein the Names and Occupations of the Principal Business Men* … New York: New York Publication Office.
Smith, W.H. (1855), *Smith's Brooklyn Directory for the Year ending May 1st, 1856*, Brooklyn: W. H. Smith.
Trow, J. F. (1876), *Trow's New York City Directory*, New York: The Trow City Directory Company.
Underhill, T. (1816), *Biennial Directory, Class Trade* … London: Thomas Underhill, 11 Coleman Street.
West, J. (1796), *Boston Directory, containing the Names of the Inhabitants, their Occupations, Places of Business, and Dwelling-Houses*, Boston: Manning & Loring.
White, W. (1834), *History, Gazetteer and Directory of Staffordshire* … Sheffield: Robert Leader, Independent Office.
Wilson, H. (1855), *Wilson's Business Directory of New York City*, New York: John F. Trow, Printer & Publisher.
Woods, T. W. (1860), *Woods' Baltimore City Directory*, Baltimore: Printed by John W. Woods.

Archival and Primary Sources

Annual Report for the Year 1917, Detroit Museum of Art, report for the year 1916-17. Available at: Detroit Museum of Art, Annual Report for the year 1917.pdf

Annual Reports, Plymouth Church, New York, 1895. Author's collection.
Association of Earthenware Dealers records, 1817-1835. Association of Earthenware Dealers. Ms. N-2018 (Tall), 1 Volume, Massachusetts Historical Society, Boston, MA.
Death Certificate, Voss Neal, Borough of Brooklyn, November 4, 1898. Available from Death Certificates - NYC Health.
Diary, John Ridgway, 1822, The Potteries Museum and Art Gallery, Hanley, Stoke-on-Trent.
Diary, John Fanny Watson, 1835, Winterthur Museum and Archive, Delaware.
Diary, Charles K Ovington, 1882–3, Mary White Ovington Archive, Walter P. Reuther Library, Wayne State University, Detroit, Michigan.
Findagrave.com database and images https://www.findagrave.com/memorial/38039162/thomas-bridgwood:accessed 05 January 2024, memorial page for Thomas Bridgwood (1794–17 Jun 1830),Find a Grave Memorial ID 38039162, citing Saint Michaels Church Cemetery, Charleston, Charleston County, South Carolina, USA; Maintained by Saratoga (contributor 46965279). Available at: Ancestry.com.
https://www.findagrave.com/memorial/58036818/henry-stevenson:accessed 02 November 2024, Green-Wood Cemetery, Brooklyn, Kings County, New York. Available at: Ancestry.com.
Green-Wood Collections, Brooklyn, New York.
Inventory, 54.106.4 "The Goods, Chattels & Credits which were of Thomas. J. Barrow, Dec'd [deceased] filed 24 May 1839". Appraised by John C. Jackson and John Wright. Winterthur Museum and Archive, Delaware.
Kohn, Denise, "Tyndale, Sarah Thorn [1792–1859]", *The Walt Whitman Archive*. Gen. ed. Matt Cohen, Ed Folsom, & Kenneth M. Price. Accessed 08 March.2025 http://www.whitmanarchive.org.
Letter book, Benjamin Eaton, 1805-7, Vol. 1 c.1. TN: 257064, David M. Rubenstein RareBook & Manuscript Library, Duke University, Durham, North Carolina, USA.
Marriage certificate, James Tams and Sarah Antoinette Wade, November 16, 1843, Toxteth, Lancaster. From General Register Office.
Minutes of the Methodist Branch of the New York Sunday School Society, Vol. 89, 1816–18.
New York and Vicinity, United Methodist Church Records, 1775-1949. Available at Ancestry.com.
Ovington, M. W. (Unknown date), Play transcript, *The Spode Cup*. From, Mary White Ovington Archive, Walter P. Reuther Library, Wayne State University, Detroit, Michigan.
Pennsylvania, U.S., *Arriving Passenger and Crew Lists, 1798-1962* [database on-line]. Lehi, UT, USA: Ancestry.com Operations, Inc., 2006. Original data: *Selected Passenger and Crew Lists and Manifests*. The National Archives at Washington, D.C. Available at: Ancestry.com.
Pennsylvania, U.S., Federal Naturalization Records, 1795-1945 [database on-line]. Lehi, UT, USA: Ancestry.com Operations, Inc., 2011. Original data: Naturalization Records. National Archives at Philadelphia, Philadelphia, Pennsylvania. Available at: Ancestry.com.
"Personal Memories of Henry Ward Beecher", Ovington, I. H. (1895), Plymouth Church of the Pilgrims and Henry Ward Beecher collection; ARC.212; Series 1, Section 10, Folder 2; Brooklyn Public Library, Center for Brooklyn History.
Presbyterian Historical Society, Philadelphia, Pennsylvania, *U.S., Presbyterian Church Records, 1701-1907;* Book Title: *Arch Street Burying Ground 1777-1830;* Accession

Number: *V M146 P533ar*. Available at: Ancestry.com *U.S., Presbyterian Church Records, 1701-1907* [database on-line].
Printed Circular, March 19, 1834, English pottery industry: miscellaneous broadsides 1833-1846, Kress Collection, Baker Library, Courtesy of, Harvard Business School.
Thomas Jefferson Papers, Library of Congress: Series 1, General Correspondence, R. Eddowes to Thomas Jefferson, November 14, 1807, Microfilm Reel: 039.
Available at: http://hdl.loc.gov/loc.mss/mtj.mtjbib017883.
Wainwright Family Papers, Boxes 1-5, Manuscripts and Archive Division, New York Public Library.
Will, Thomas C Morton, New York, U.S., Wills and Probate Records, 1659-1999, Wills, Vol. 070, April 26, 1833. Available at: Ancestry.com.

Web Sources

Patriotic America: Blue Printed Pottery Celebrating a New Nation. Available at https://www.americanhistoricalstaffordshire.com/

PEDIGREES

Pedigree 1 Wainwright family

Peter Wainwright = Elizabeth Spence
m. 1755, Warrington,
England.

Elizabeth Clark = 1. Rev. Jonathan Mayhew, m. 1756, Boston.
d. 1766.
2. Rev. Simeon Howard, m. 1771, Boston.
d. 1804.

Peter Wainwright = Elizabeth Mayhew
b. 1759, Farnworth,
near Liverpool.
d. 1841, Farnworth.
The Liverpool business
was described as
**Wainwright, Cross
and Howard,** in the
1790s.

Elizabeth Mayhew
b. c.1759, Boston.
m. 1790, Boston.
d. 1829, Liverpool.

Dr. John Clark Howard
(half-brother)
Had mercantile links
with the Wainwrights,
as well as being a
physician.[1] A co-
partnership was
dissolved between
**Thomas Jackson and
John C. Howard** in 1804.[2]

Henry Wainwright = Lucretia Green
b. 1767, Farnworth.
d. 1827, Boston.
**Saxton, Wainwright
and Jackson** of Boston,
existed from 1805. This
became **Henry Wain-
wright & Thomas
Jackson** in 1807.

Lucretia Green
m. 1795, Boston.

Rev. Jonathan Mayhew Wainwright
Bishop of New York.
b. 1792, Liverpool.
d. 1854, New York.

Peter Wainwright jr.
b. 1794, Liverpool.
d. 1878, Boston.

Eliza Wainwright
b. 1794, Liverpool.
d. 1834, Boston.

Lucretia Wainwright = Frederic H. Bradlee
m. 1831.[3]

Key: Names in bold, dealt in ceramics.

---

[1] *Columbian Centinel*, Boston, December 16, 1807.
[2] *Columbian Centinel & Massachusetts Federalist*, Boston August 25, 1804.
[3] *Boston Commercial Gazette*, April 14, 1831.

Pedigree 2 Cauldwell family

Cornelius Cauldwell, Linen-draper.[1] = Jane Edwardley of Wednesbury, Staffordshire. m. 1760, Birmingham, England.

John Cauldwell b. c.1763, Birmingham. d. 1822, New York. = Deborah Low[2] m. April 1787, Birmingham.

Joseph Cauldwell b. 1766, Birmingham. = Maria Lea m. October 1787, Birmingham.

Cornelius Cauldwell jr. b. 1770, Birmingham. d. 1818, New York. = Elizabeth [Thompson[3]] m. 1789, Birmingham.

Others

Children of John Cauldwell and Deborah Low:

Sarah Cauldwell b. 1788, Birmingham. = 1. **William Hewitt**, m.1806, New York, son of Mr. Hewitt, Lane End, Staffordshire (see **Pedigree 3**). 2. **Thomas Cook**, m. 1811, of **Bakewell & Cook.**

Jane Cauldwell = Charles L. Roberts m. 1825, New York.[5]

John Cauldwell d. 1813, Fort George, Niagara.

Cornelius J. Cauldwell

Henry W. Cauldwell.[4] d. 1843, New York.

Children of Cornelius Cauldwell jr. and Elizabeth [Thompson]:

Jane Cauldwell = George Colgate m. 1824, New York.

Ebenezer Cauldwell b. 1791, Birmingham. d. 1875, New York. = 1. Glorianna Garniss 2. Maria Alburtis 3. Ann Milbank[6]

Children of Ebenezer Cauldwell:

Thomas G. Cauldwell (b. c.1822–1858)

William Alburtus Cauldwell (1827–1893, New York)

Key: Names in italics, dealt in ceramics in England. Names in bold-italics, dealt in ceramics in England, and then in USA. Names in bold, dealt in ceramics in the USA

[1] *Derby Mercury*, February 2, 1781.

[2] Abbe T. and H. A. Howson (1941), p.366. Deborah Lea, sister of Maria Lea. However, according to Birmingham Parish Records, her name appears as 'Deborah Low'.

[3] Abbe T. and H. A. Howson (1941), p.367.

[4] Abbe T. and H. A. Howson (1941), p.336. Cornelius and Henry W., described as sons of John Cauldwell.

[5] *Statesman*, New York December 20, 1825 "Mr. Charles L. Roberts of the house Freeman, Cobb & Co. Boston, to Miss Jane, daughter of the late John Cauldwell Esq of this city" Gorham L. Freeman, Nathaniel R. Cobb and Charles L. Roberts were dealers in "English goods" (Frost & Stimpson 1825).

[6] Abbe T. and H. A. Howson (1941), p.368. The spelling of Maria Alburtis differs from the obituary of "William Alburtus Cauldwell".

Pedigree 3 Hewitt family

Brothers?

Thomas Hewitt = Mary …… died 1849, aged 75.[1]
b. c.1762.
d. 1822, aged 60, New York.
Will provides the names of children.

'**Hewitt,** widow of Thomas, 289 Broadway.
Hewitt & Son, Thomas china store, 289 Broadway'.[3]

John Hewitt[2] = Grace (parents provided by William Hewitt's will of 1810).
(A John Hewitt and Grace Bridgewood, both of Stoke, married August 18, 1782, Whitmore, Staffordshire).

Children of John Hewitt and Grace:

Thomas Hewitt

Mary Hewitt m.1808, Stoke. = **Thomas Bakewell**

Rev Henry W. Bakewell.
b. 1817, New York.
d. 1899, Michigan.

William Hewitt = Sarah Cauldwell
d. 1810, St. Bartholomew, Caribbean.
"of the firm Thomas and William Hewitt, merchants".[4]
His will of 1810 mentions a brother and uncle, both called Thomas Hewitt.

Sarah Cauldwell m. 1806, New York. (see **Pedigree 2).**

John Cauldwell Hewitt

Children of Thomas Hewitt and Mary:

Thomas Hewitt jr. = Clara Pierce
b. c.1789.
d. 1826.

Jane Hewitt = **Samuel Bridgewood (Bridgwood)**
b. c.1791

Gideon P. Hewitt = Mary C. Hunter
b. c.1793.
d. Milwaukee, Wisconsin, 1869.[5]
In partnership with Nehemiah Hewitt.

Nehemiah Hewitt

Mary Ann Hewitt = Henry Conklin, Poughkeepsie.

John Hewitt

Eliza Hewitt

Margaret Hewitt

William Hewitt

Edward Hewitt

Key: Names in bold, dealt in ceramics.

[1] *Commercial Advertiser,* New York January 8, 1849, "At Williamsburgh on the 6th inst. Mrs. Mary Hewitt, relict of the late Thomas Hewitt, in the 75th year of age."
[2] Allbut J. (1802), earthenware manufacturers, Hewit [sic] and Comer, and John Hewit [sic], Lane-end; Holden, W. (1805), Coomer, Sheridan and Hewit [sic], earthenware manufacturers, Green Dock, Lane end; Hampson, R. (1990) , indicates that John Hewitt & Son existed from 1811 to 1823 , p.91.
[3] Longworth, T. (1824).
[4] *Mercantile Advertiser,* New York February 13, 1810.
[5] *Daily Milwaukee News* December 30, 1869, states that G.P. Hewitt was born Staffordshire, August 1793, and came to New York when, "he was but one year old." It is added that, "During the War of 1812, he took up arms on the side of his adopted country". He was commissioned as an officer, and deacon of the First Baptist church in Milwaukee.

Pedigree 4 Wetmore and Tredwell family

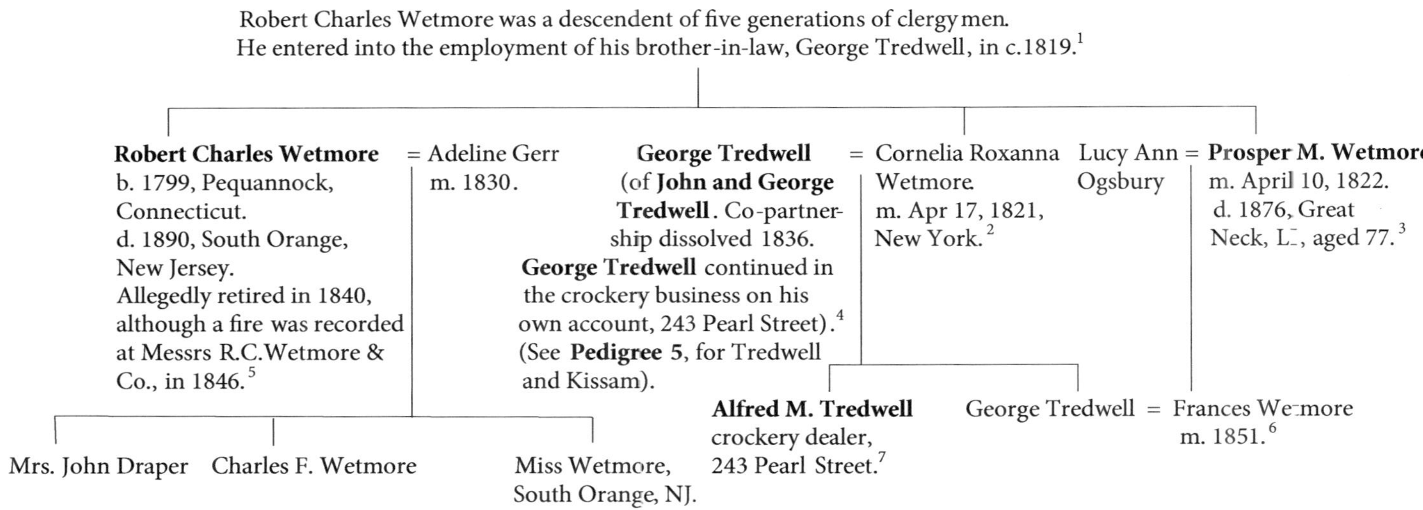

Key: Names in bold, dealt in ceramics.

[1] *New York Tribune*, May 10, 1890.
[2] *New York Daily Advertiser*, April 21, 1817.
[3], *Evening Post*, New York March 16, 1876, name given as Prosper Montgomery Wetmore.
[4] *Evening Post*, New York, February 17, 1836.
[5] *Spectator*, New York, September 30, 1846.
[6] *New York Observer*, March 6, 1851.
[7] *The New York Journal of Commerce*, March 4, 1841. Alfred M. Tredwell purchased the ceramic and glass stock belonging to his father.

Pedigree 5 Tredwell and Kissam family

Dr. Benjamin Tredwell, = Elizabeth Seabury
North Hempstead,
Long Island.
Died 1830, aged 95.[1]

Daniel Whitehead Kissam = 1. Elizabeth Tredwell
m. 1787. d. 1803.
2. Phebe Wilmot.[3]

John Tredwell

George Tredwell = Cornelia Roxanna Wetmore
d. 1848, aged 61.[2]

see **Pedigree 4.**

Samuel Kissam
Hardware merchant,
of the firm, Tredwell,
Kissam & Co, New York.

Timothy Tredwell Kissam[4]
(1800–1878)
Advertisement placed by
Timothy T. Kissam & Son,
145, Maiden Lane, New York,
Agents for Mason's Patent
Ironstone China.[6]

= 1. Sarah Betts,
m. New York, 1822.[5] Died 1848.
2. Mary Sayles.

Others

Peter Betts Kissam

Lambert Holland Kissam

Key: Names in bold, dealt in ceramics.

---

[1] *Evening Post*, New York June 25, 1830.

[2] *Long Island Farmer, and Queens County Advertiser*, New York, May 9, 1848, "In New York, on Wednesday, George Tredwell, son of the Late Dr. Tredwell, of North Hempstead, aged 61 years." Other notices declare that he was aged 65.

[3] Kissam, E. (1892), p.36-37.

[4] Kissam, E. (1892), p.36 and p.67.

[5] *New York Daily Advertiser* September 24, 1822 .

[6] *Times-Picayune*, New Orleans, Louisiana, March 24, 1846. The advertisement refers to the strength and durability of Mason's ironstone , and how this ware had already been supplied to hotels in New York, Philadelphia, Boston, Baltimore, New Orleans etc.

Pedigree 6 Hastings, Blanchard, and Sampson family

Daniel Hastings, d.1803, aged 54, Newton, MA.[1]

Daniel Hastings jr. = 1. Dorcas Blanchard. 2. Deborah Hammond
Partnership, **Blanchard & Hastings,** Boston.[3]

Nathan Hastings (Providence, RI, from c.1821–31. Cincinnati, from 1835).

George Hastings d. 1825.

Rebekah Hastings = Isaac Coolidge
m. 1804.

Charles Hastings

Joseph S. Hastings = Harriot Blanchard
Connected to **Gilman Collamore.** (See **Pedigree 11**).
Co-partnership existed between **Joseph S. Hastings & John Blanchard .**
d. 1872, aged 85, Hoboken, NJ[4]

Sisters ? (Harriot Blanchard, Caroline Blanchard)

Caroline Blanchard = **John Hall jr.** of Burslem.
m. 1820, Boston.[2]

(There was also a **John Hall,** crockery dealer, Boston, b. 1823, Burslem, d. 1891, Boston).

Presumably brothers.

Joseph S. Sampson = Mary Ann Hastings
m. 1824, Providence, RI.[5]
Co-partnership with **W.S. Sampson**
Later, in Cincinnati, a crockery-dealing partnership existed between **Jos. S. Sampson, Wm. S. Sampson and B.P. Hunt.**

Ann Maria Coolidge = **William S. Sampson**
b. 1808, Newton, MA
m. 1831, Cincinnati.[6]
Boston, then Cincinnati.
d. 1878, aged 79, Cincinnati.[7]

Nathan Sampson
Cincinnati.

Key: Names in bold, dealt in ceramics.

---

1 *Boston Commercial Gazette* May 30, 1803.
2 *Repertory*, Boston April 27, 1820, "John Hall jr. Esq. of Burslem to Miss Caroline Blanchard of this town."
3 *Columbian Centinel*, Boston February 3, 1802, partnership of John Blanchard and Daniel Hastings, jun., dissolved.
4 *New York Herald* December 20, 1872, "Joseph S. Hastings of Newton, Mass., … formerly and for many years one of the largest importers of earthenware. "
5 *Boston Telegraph* April 15, 1824, "In Providence, Mr. Joseph S. Sampson, of this city, to Miss Mary Ann Hastings eldest daughter of Mr. Nathan Hastings, of the former place."
6 *Boston Traveler*, September 16, 1831, "In Cincinnati, Mr. William S. Sampson to Miss Ann Maria Coolidge, late of is city. "
7 *Cincinnati Commercial Tribune*, October 28, 1878.

Pedigree 7 Norcross family

Daniel Norcross = Abigail Chapin.

Joel Norcross (1767–1837)

Otis Norcross = **Mary Cunningham Homer,** daug. of Eleazer Homer
b. 1785, MA.
d. 1827, aged 42.
A partnership existed between Otis Norcross, John Mellen, and Eliphalet Jones. After the death of Otis, the firm was run by **Mary C. Norcross** and **Eliphalet Jones.** **J. Addison Norcross** was admitted into the business.[3] (see **Pedigree 8**).

Chapin Norcross = Susan Danforth
d. 1822, Phil.,
formerly of Boston

Josiah Norcross [1] = Ann Homer Mellen.[2] (see **Pedigree 9**).
d. 1862

William Rowland Norcross
(1820–1889).
Involved in **Michael Mellen & Co.,** with **Thomas G. Caldwell, H.A.Mellen,** and **T.E. Chamberlin.**

George Lane

Otis Norcross jr. = Lucy Lane [4]
d. 1882, aged 71.
Otis Norcross & Co., consisted of Otis Norcross, Daniel Webster Norcross and Ichabod Howland. This became **Howland & Jones,** and then **Jones, McDuffee & Stratton** of Boston.[6]

Maria Lane = **Ichabod Howland**

Otis Norcross Howland.
Involved in **Jones, McDuffee & Stratton.**

J. Addison Norcross
d. 1849.

Daniel Webster Norcross [5] = Delia A. Bruce.
b. 1826.

Joseph E. Norcross.
Involved in **Jones, McDuffee & Stratton.**

Key: Names in bold, dealt in ceramics in the USA.

[1] *Boston Daily Advertiser* November 10, 1818, partnership between Josiah Norcross and Eliphalet Jones formed, wholesale and retail, earthenware, china and glass.
[2] *Christian Register*, Boston December 26, 1823, Josiah Norcross, merchant, Boston, to Ann Homer Mellen, daughter of Abner Mellen, of Framingham.
[3] *Worcester Daily Spy*, Massachusetts May 15, 1903.
[4] *Nantucket Inquirer*, Massachusetts, December 19, 1835, Otis Norcross to Lucy Ann Lane, daughter of George Lane.
[5] *Worcester Daily Spy*, Massachusetts May 15, 1903. Described as descended from a colonial family; the first being Jeremiah Norcross of Watertown, MA.
[6] *Worcester Daily Spy*, Massachusetts May 15, 1903.

Pedigree 8 Homer family

Eleazer Homer, merchant, Battery Wharf, Boston. d.1847. = Mary Barlett. m.1786, Boston.

see **Pedigree 7.**

Otis Norcross = **Mary Cunningham Homer**[1]
Co-partnership formed with **Eliphalet Jones.**[2] d. 1827.
b. c.1790. d. 1869 aged 79, Boston.

William Flagg Homer = Adeline M. Wellington. m. 1831, Boston.
b. c.1803. d. 1883, Belmont. Co-partnership, **Isaiah Atkins and Wm. F. Homer**, formed in 1825. The firm became **Homer, Lane & Co.**

Eliza B. Homer = Charles Lane, merchant
m.1821, Boston.

Harriet Homer d. 1846, Madison, Indiana. = **John Mellen** d. 1851, Madison, Indiana.[3]

see **Pedigree 9.**

Horace Holly Homer (1842–1903) = Georgian E. Gray (m. 1867, Arlington, MA).
Homer, Caldwell & Co., consisting of **Wm. F. Homer, Horace H. Homer**, and **Thomas G. Caldwell**, formed in 1862.

Key: Names in bold, dealt in ceramics.

---

1 *The Evening Gazette*, Boston March 1, 1828. After the death of Otis Norcross in 1827, Norcross & Co., was run by Eliphalet Jones and Mary C. Norcross; *Boston Daily Advertiser*, March 1, 1833, partnership between Eliphalet Jones and M. C. Norcross, dissolved.

2 *Boston Daily Advertiser* April 11, 1820.

3 *Madison Daily Banner*, Indiana January 1, 1851; *Christian Register*, Boston, September 20, 1851, John Mellen died aged 61, Madison, Ind, formerly of Boston. The business was continued by Charles E. Mellen and John H. Mellen at Madison.

Pedigree 9 Mellen family

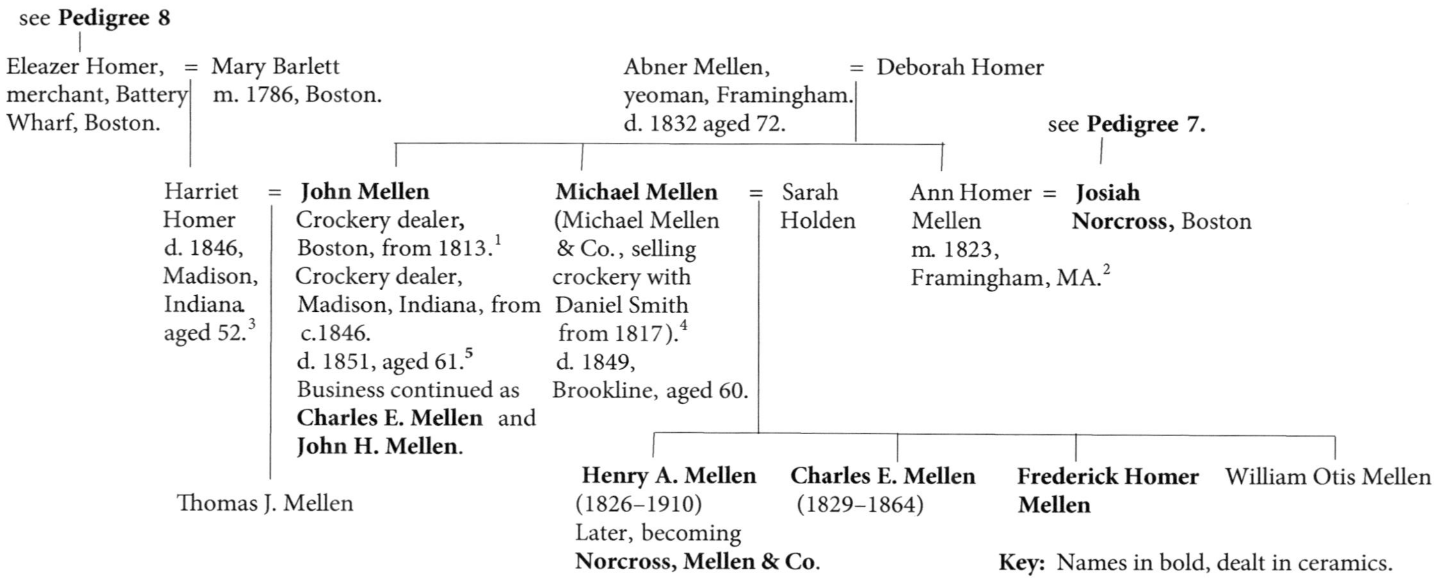

---

1 *Boston Daily Advertiser* April 22, 1813.
2 *Concord Gazette and Middlesex Yeoman* , Massachusetts December 27, 1823.
3 *Weekly Messenger*, Boston November 11, 1846.
4 *Columbian Centinel* May 7, 181 ; *Boston Intelligencer*, December 12, 1818, co-partnership dissolved.
5 *Madison Daily Banner* , Indiana, January 1, 1851.

Pedigree 10 Eddowes family

John Kendrick esq. of Wynnhall, Denbighshire, Wales

John Eddowes, grocer or tobacconist.

Ralph Eddowes = Sarah Kenrick
b. Chester, 1751.
Educated at Nantwich by Dr. Priestley.[1]
Moved to America in 1794. d. 1833, Phil.
Described as "Rev. Ralph Eddowes" in John Eddowes' 1871 obituary.

Sarah Kenrick
m. 1777.

Rev. Timothy Kenrick

thirteen children, in total.

Ralph Eddowes jr. = Louisa Thornton
b. Chester, 1784.
d. 1841, Phil.

Louisa Thornton
m. 1820, Phil.

John Eddowes = Lydia Naudain
b. Chester, 1785, bpt. 1786.
1850 Census, described as a "notary public".
d. 1871, Geneva, Illinois.

Lydia Naudain
m. 1816, Delaware.

Roger Eddowes
b. 1792, Chester
Farmer, Moorland Township, Pennsylvania
d. 1856.

Ralph Eddowes III
(1821–1898)
Wheelwright, Phil.,

Thomas Jefferson Eddowes
(1826–1893)
Bookbinder, Phil., in 1850.

Timothy Eddowes, preacher, Geneva, Illinois.[2]

Key: Names in bold, dealt in ceramics.

[1] *The Unitarian Chronicle for 1833: And companion to the Monthly Repository*, London, pp.215-19.

[2] *Christian Register*, Boston, November 16, 1866, "Timothy Eddowes, grandson of that Eddowes who with, John Vaughan, once founded the church in Philadelphia for which Dr. Furness now preaches".

Pedigree 11 Collamore family

Capt. Enoch Collamore = Hannah …
b. 1745, Scituate, MA.
d. 1824.

Col. John Collamore = 1. Michal … 2. Polly …
b. 1775, Scituate.
d. 1859, aged 83, Scituate.

Gilman Collamore
b. 1789, Scituate.
Formed co-partnership with with **Joseph S. Hastings** , 1810.[2] (see **Pedigree 6**). Dissolved, 1813.[4]

Horace Collamore = Laura Briggs, Pembroke, m. 1821.[1]
b. 1791, Scituate.
In business as **Collamore & Churchill**.[3]

Other sons

Children of Col. John Collamore:

John Collamore jr.
b. 1802, Scituate.
Involved in **Churchill & Collamore**, from 1824,[6] later **John Collamore & Co.**
d. April, 1884.

Ebenezer Collamore
b. 1809, Scituate.
In New York.
d. March, 1884.

Andrew Collamore
b. 1817, Scituate.
In Boston.
d. 1846.

Davis Collamore
b. 1820, Scituate.
In New York.
d. 1887.

George Collamore[5]
b. 1828, Scituate.
In Boston.
d. 1881.

William Collamore
b. 1830, Scituate.

Gilman Collamore
b. 1834, Scituate.
In New York.
d. 1888.

Key: Names in bold, dealt in ceramics.

---

[1] Heard, J. H. (1856), p.445.

[2] *Independent Chronicle* , Boston October 25, 1810, "Joseph S. Hastings and Gilman Collamore have formed a connection in business under the firm of Hastings & Collamore."

[3] *Columbian Centinel*, Boston, March 3, 1824 , connection between Horace Collamore and William Churchill dissolved, but continued as William Churchill and John Collamore, junior.

[4] *Boston Patriot* June 19, 1813.

[5] *Boston Post* July 15, 1861, co-partnership between George E. Collamore, John Curtis, and William Hope, formed.

[6] *Boston Intelligencer* September 22, 1827, co-partnership formed between Churchill, Collamore & Co. of Boston, and Churchill, [Ferdinand] Sands & Co., of New York.

Pedigree 12 Shirley family

William Shirley = Hannah …
of Shelton.[1]

- ***Jesse Shirley***
  bapt. 1786,
  Stoke-upon-Trent.
  d. 1839, Philadelphia.
- John Shirley = Eliza …
  bapt. 1790, Hanley.
  Dealer in earthenware, London.
  - **William Shirley** = Ellen G. Davis
    b. 1816, London.
    d. 1900, Baltimore.
    Shirley & Robert Cook,
    Calvert St., Baltimore.[5]
    m. 1840, Baltimore.
    - **William W. Shirley**
      d. 1917, Baltimore.
    - **Henry C. Shirley**
      Baltimore.
  - **John Shirley**
    d. 1911, San Francisco.
- ***Cephas Shirley*** *
  bapt. 1793, Hanley.
  d. 1863, Baltimore.[2]
- Benjamin Shirley
  bapt. 1795, Hanley.
  Dealer in earthenware, London.
- **William Wright Shirley** = Eliza Garrick Coddington,
  bapt. 1797, Hanley.
  d. 1865, New York.
  m. 1818, New York.[3]
  - William Faircio Shirley
    d. 1903, New York.[4]

* Cephas Shirley was initially in New York, followed by Philadelphia in c.1836, and then resided, Calvert St., Baltimore.

Key: Name in italics, had connections to ceramic manufacturing. Names in bold italics, had connections to manufacturing, and then dealing in ceramics in the USA. Names in bold, dealt in ceramics in the USA.

---

[1] Holden, W. (1809), William Shirley, earthenware manufacturer, Shelton, pp.367-71; Underhill, T. (1816), W. & J. Shirley, potters, Hanley and Shelton, p.215; *Staffordshire Advertiser* September 7, 1816, William and Jesse Shirley, potters and co-partners, bankrupt.
[2] *Sun*, Baltimore, October 3, 1863, "Cephas Shirley, aged 70", born c.1793; Woods, J. W. (1860), p.349. Cephas Shirley was located at 16 s. Calvert, on the same street as Shirley & Cook, wholesale queensware house, 5 S. Calvert.
[3] *New York Gazette*, August 19, 1818.
[4] *The New York Times*, November 16, 1903.
[5] *Sun*, Baltimore, August 11, 1860, co-partnership between Robert Cook and William Shirley dissolved. William Shirley to continue at 5 South Calvert Street.

Pedigree 13 Ovington family

Henry A. Ovington = Mary Hubbard White
b. Springfield, NJ, 1796.
Secretary to the New York Chamberlain. Member of the First Baptist Church, Pierrepont St., Brooklyn.
d. Brooklyn, 1886.

Children of Henry A. Ovington and Mary Hubbard White:

- **Theodore Tweedy Ovington** (1828-1909). Ovington Bros. was established in Brooklyn, 1846. = Louisa Ketcham
- **Edward Judson Ovington** b. c.1831, NY. Deacon of Plymouth Church. d. 1909, Paris. = 1. Maria Lewis. 2. Georgia Maize, m. 1887.
- **William H. Ovington** b. 1822, NY. Established a Chicago branch of Ovington Bros., in 1872, as **H. Clay Scott & Ovington Bros**. Operated as **Ovington Brothers and Ovington** in 1874. d. 1880, Chicago. The Chicago branch was closed in 1889.[1]
- Mrs. S. Randle, Brooklyn.
- Mrs. I. Evans, New Haven. = Rev. P.S. Evans
- Irene H. Ovington (1836-1905)

Children of Edward Judson Ovington:

- Carter L. Ovington
- **Edward J. Ovington jr.** Involved in the Chicago house.

Children of Theodore Tweedy Ovington and Louisa Ketcham:

- **Charles Ketcham Ovington** (1856–1930) President of Ovington Bros. Member of National Association for the Advancement of Colored People.
- **Theodore T. Ovington jr.**[2]
- Mary White Ovington (1865–1951)[3] Author of *Half a Man*, 1911.
- Mrs. James H. Merritt
- Helen Ovington = Edward W. Kingsbury m. 1894.

Key: Names in bold, dealt in ceramics.

[1] *Daily Inter Ocean* , Chicago, November 18, 1888.
[2] Lain, G. T. (1886), Ovington, Theodore T. jr, china, 246 Fulton, h. 69 Willow, p.809.
[3] *Evening Star*, Washington DC, July 16, 1951. Described as Co -founder of the National Association for Advancement of Colored People (NAACP).

GLOSSARY

Original terms used on documents and advertisements can be confusing, especially for readers less familiar with ceramics. The following are a selection of words used throughout the text with a definition.

Chambers An abbreviated term for chamber pots. The phrase, “cov’d [covered] chambers” also appears on invoices (Frontispiece and Figure 2.28).
China Normally used in connection with any ceramic-body that was translucent. The term covers imported Chinese hard-paste porcelain, European soft-paste porcelains, and English bone china. European porcelains and English bone china were more expensive than earthenwares.
China dealer A phrase used to describe anyone selling ceramics, not necessarily confined to dealing in translucent porcelains.
Crockery A collective word for ceramics. The word crockery was often used in conjunction with terms such as importer or dealer.
Cream-colored [CC] Cream-colored or creamware was a form of earthenware first developed in the eighteenth century. It was often abbreviated to “CC” on invoices.
Earthenware A non-translucent ceramic body fired at a low temperature. It requires a glaze to be non-porous. Earthenware covers creamware, pearlware, edged ware ironstone china, etc.
Edged One of the cheapest forms of tableware available in the eighteenth and nineteenth centuries. Vessels have a molded edge, typically colored blue or green (Figure 4.2).
Enamel Ceramics (earthenware, stoneware, and china) can be decorated with additional enamel colors. These would be applied by hand on to the surface of the vessel. Some colors, such as blue, withstand high-temperatures of firing and would be applied under the glaze. Alternatively, enamel colors, such as yellow, pink, and green, would be applied over the glaze and fired at a lower temperature (Figure 2.21).
Flow-blue, or flowing blue [FB] A form of blue printed earthenware where the design under the glaze is purposely blurred (Figure 5.14).
Liverpool ware Apart from Liverpool being the main shipping port for Staffordshire goods to the United States (certainly by the nineteenth century), ceramics were manufactured in the Liverpool region. The most well-known firm was the Herculaneum factory.
Luster, (UK spelling, **lustre**) Ceramics decorated with metal oxides. The typical colors created were copper, pink and silver (Figures 1.8-1.10, 2.10, and 4.8).
Muffins Small plates used to serve bread and butter or muffins.
Mulberry A mulberry-colored version of flow-blue printed ware.
Nappies Shallow, bowl-shaped vessels.
Potteries A region in North Staffordshire renowned for its concentration of ceramic manufacturers. The district consists of six towns namely, Longton (Lane End), Fenton, Stoke-upon-Trent, Hanley, Burslem, and Tunstall. Other districts between the six towns (where there were additional ceramic manufacturers) included Shelton,

Cobridge, and Longport. In the twentieth century, the towns were amalgamated to form the City of Stoke-on-Trent.

Printed The application of an image taken from an engraved surface onto ceramics. Different types of printing techniques were employed by manufacturers. Bat printing involved applying the image to the surface of the vessel (Figure 4.2), whereas transfer printing was applied under the glaze (Figure 1.2).

Queen's ware A marketing term first employed by Josiah Wedgwood to describe his refined cream-colored earthenware. The term Queen's ware or queensware was widely used by crockery dealers, simply indicating the availability of cream-colored ware, and latterly ceramics, in general.

Stoneware A high-fired ceramic body, which is non-porous. American stoneware vessel were made by country potters and decorated with high-firing cobalt blue and iron oxide.

Trenton A region in New Jersey, USA, associated with extensive ceramic production.

Twiflers (twifflers) Plates used for serving deserts.

White granite [WG] A form of white ironstone, which was molded, and largely undecorated. White granite became particularly popular in the American market from the 1840s onwards (Figure 2.6). Often abbreviated to "WG" on invoices (Figure 3.8).

INDEX

Abbatt, Robert 162
Abolitionism 134, 153, 154, 174, 183–9, 194, 201, 203–4, 213, 215, 217, 235, 237
Abolitionism, attitudes toward 188–9, 194–5, 235–6
Adams 22
Adams, Mary 92
Adams, William 55, 92, 103, Figure 1.2, Figure 2.3
Advertising 3, 8, 50, 51, 171, 235, 237, 239
Adultery trial 228–31, Figure 7.19
African Americans 14, 188, 204, 207, 213, 217–18, 221, 223–8, 231, 236, Figure 6.12
African Civilization Society 225–6, 228
African Methodist Episcopal Church 221
Agents, Liverpool 112
Ahrenfeldt, Charles 40
Alcock, manufacturers 115
Alcock, Richard Edward 100, 101, Figure 3.4
Alcock, Samuel 100, Figure 3.4
Alexander, John 116, 117
Allen, Charles J. F. 31
Allen African Methodist Episcopal Church 223
American consumption behavior 85
American Bible Society 116
American naval and war heroes, 1812–14 War 61, 193, Figure 2.10
American Missionary Association 225
American printed themes 17, 18, 19, 62, 63, 65, 66, 74, 86, 87, 132, 133, 135, 141, 146, 180, 182, 185, 191–2, 193, 219–20, 235, Figures 1.2, 2.1, 2.14, 2.15, 4.1–4.4, 4.6–4.8–4.12, 6.5–6.11, 6.13, 7.15
American porcelain 163
American Seal Figures 1.10, 4.2, 5.8, 5.11
American Stamp Act 49
Ames, Fisher 34, Figure 1.9
Anderson, Benedict 127, 141
Andrew, John A. 200–1
Anglo-American trade, organization 5–7
Anglo-American War (1812–14) 123, 131, 193
Anti-consumption 82, 174
Anti-slavery imagery 86, 183–7, 194, 237 Figures 6.8–6.11
Applegate, Edd 50
Archaeology 11, 12, 237
Arman, David 182
Asbury family 120
Asbury, Edward 120, 121, Figure 3.15
Asbury, Samuel 120
Asbury & Young 120, 121, Figure 3.15
Association of Earthen ware Dealers 109, 110
Astbury 22
Atkins, Isaiah 63
Atwell, Amos 52
Auctions 51, 71, 72, 73, 74, 109, 110, 114, Figure 2.22, 3.9
Auction catalogues 73, Figure 2.23
Author, the 1–2, 11, 195, 234, 238–9

Bakeware, Thomas 104, 204–5, 207–8, Figure 7.4, Pedigree 3
Bakewell, Rev. William Henry 205–8, Figures 7.5, 7.7
Bakewell & Cook 104
Bangs, Dr. Nathan 206
Baptist Anti-Slavery Society 188
Baptist Central Tract Society 177
Baptists 86, 104, 125, 153, 167, 175, 177, 180–1, 183–4, 197, 208, 210
Barber, Edwin 23, 24, 28, 162, 182
Barbour, James S. 180
Barclay, Henry & George 63
Barnard, Alfred D. 26
Barrell, Charles 64, Figure 2.12

Barrow, Thomas J. 112, 113, 115, Figure 3.10
Barrow, Thomas & Co. 113
Bartered, exchanges 228
Barthes, Roland 1–2, 11–12, 195, 239
Baylis, William 91
Beaureguard, General 236–7
Bedford, Sarah & Son 187
Beecher, Catharine 9, 80, 82, 83, 87, 171, Figure 2.29
Beecher, Rev. Edward 184–5, 213
Beecher, Rev. Henry Ward 213, 215, 216–17, 225, 227–32, 236, Figures 7. 13, 7.19–7.20
Beecher, Irene H. 216–17
Beecher, Rev. Luther F. 213
Beecher, Lyman 1, 9, 83, 213
Beecher, Thomas K. 213
Belleek 22
Bennington pottery 24
Bennoch, John 90
Bentley, Thomas 3, 4, 48, 50
Berg, Maxine 51, 53, 86–7, 189
Bespoke, industrial products 191, 194
Bethel African Methodist Episcopal Church 221
Bethel Methodist Episcopal 218
Billheads 58, Figures Frontispiece, 2.9, 2.20, 2.28, 3.8, 3.12, 5.6, 5.9, 5.16, 5.21, 7.2
Bird Club 201
Birmingham, England 103, 167
Bishop, J. F. 185
Bissell, Josiah 31
Blackwell, Charles 223
Blanchard, Charles 109
Blanchard family 110, Pedigree 6
Blaszczyk, Regina 3, 4, 12, 53, 230, 234–5
Bolton, Curtis 99
Borax 117
Bow porcelain 40, 171
Bowen & Richards 103
Brand value 67, Figure 2.17
Breen, Timothy H. 8, 47, 79, 82, 88, 106
Brewer, John 2, 3, 8, 9, 49
Bridgwood, Samuel 106, 125, 167
Bridgwood, Thomas 125
Bridgewood, Samuel S. 106, 167
Bridgewood, Thomas 106, 110, 112
Bridgham, Ebenezer 90
Briggs, John 172, 182
Briggs, Richard 4, 5
Briggs, Robert 109
Broadway 106
Brooklyn 228
Brooklyn Colored Orphan Asylum 225
Brooklyn Heights 228
Brooks, Preston 200
Brown, Alexander 120
Brown, Alexander & Co. 120
Brown, Edward 52
Brown George Alexander 119, 120
Brown, John 203
Brown, John A. & Co 120, Figure 3.14
Brown, Mrs. 203
Brown, Shipley & Co. 119
Brussels 149
Buck, Norman 6, 7, 10, 89–90, 101, 120
Burges[sic], Mrs. 167
Burton, William E. 160
Butler, William 105

Calvinist 86, 169, 171, 174
Camehl, Ada Walker 26, 29, 39
Campbell, Colin 81
Canadian market 89
Capitalist 12, 236
Carey, John & Sons 105, Figure 3.6
Caritat, H. 48
Carter, Sharon 144
Cartlidge, Charles 99, Figure 3.4
Catholics 86
Cauldwell, Ann 167
Cauldwell, Cornelius 103
Cauldwell, Ebenezer 103, 104, 110, 116, 125, 167
Cauldwell, H. W. 74
Cauldwell, Jane 103
Cauldwell, John 103, 104, 125
Cauldwell, Joseph 103
Cauldwell, Sarah 104, 167
Cauldwell family 103, 175, 205, Pedigree 2
Centennial Exposition 203
Ceramic collecting 17
Ceramic, craft skills 161
Ceramic history literature 17–20, 23–31, 238–9
Ceramic packing Figure 5.3
Ceramic specialization 90–1

Ceramics, English labor 161
Chamberlain family (Worcester Porcelain Works) 159
Chamberlin, Ezra 180, 181, Figure 6.6
Chapman, Stanley 166, 180
Chatham Street 206
Chauncey, Florence I. 26
Chelsea porcelain 17
Chestnut Street 78, Figure 2.28
Child, Mrs. 171
China packers 14, 161, 218–19, 221–4
Chinese porcelain (Indian China) 5, 20, 40, 47, 52, 170–1, 187
Christian Society 134
Christie, James 90
Christie's 19
Churchill, C. W. 65, 66, Figure 2.15
Churchill, William 144
City directories 12
Civil War, American 153, 203, 236
Clark, Theodore 175
Clay, Henry 138
Clements, Samuel 149
Clementson, Joseph 151, 152, Figures 5.7–5.8
Clews, Henry 23, 219
Clews, James 23, 24, 30, 65, 75, 76, 105, 112, 124, Figures 1.2, 1.5, 2.25, 2.26, 3.6, 4.2, 7.15
Clews, Mary 219
Clews, Ralph 23, 30, 65, 75, 76, 105, 112, 124, Figures 1.2, 1.5, 2.25, 2.26, 3.6, 4.2, 7.15
Clinton, De Witt 176
Cochran, Thomas C. 143, 151, 161, 167
Cohen, Joanna 56, 77, 82, 83, 171, 173
Colgate, George 103
Collamore, Andrew F. 144
Collamore, Davis 144
Collamore, Ebenezer 144
Collamore, George E. 144
Collamore, Gilman 144
Collamore, Horace 26, 62, 144
Collamore, John 144, 151
Collamore, John Jr. 144
Collamore family 61, 151, Pedigree 11
Collard, E. 89, 121
Collectors, impact 87, 191, 235, 237
Collyer, Robert 200–1
Colonial Williamsburg 39
Combination 109, 110, 112, 113, 114, 115, Figure 3.10
Concklin [sic], Henry 167
Confederate 236
Conklin, H. & Co. 106
Conover, Stephen 116
Constitutional ware 184–186
Consumer revolution 2–3, 6, 9, 11, 68, 82, 193
Consumption, influences on 48, 237
Cook, Thomas 77, 104, 110, 167, 205, Pedigree 2
Coomer, William & Thomas 105
Coomer & Bridgwood 106
Copeland 63, 229–30
Cornwallis, Lord Charles 41, 136–7, Figure 4.8, 4.9
Cotton, Elijah 103
Coutan & Pillivuyt 40
Coysh, A. W. 80
Credit 106, 110, 116, 140, 167, Figure 2.27
Cresson, Ben 91
Cresson, James and John H. 26, 91
Cresson, Joseph 91
Cresson family 102
Crocker, Joseph Allen 35, Figure 1.11
Crockery stores 56–58, 61, 77, 145, 198–200, 218–24, 231, 269, Figure 7.17
Cropper, Benson & Co. 89
Cropsy (Cropsey), Gussie 218, 231
Crosby, Samuel T. 214
Croswell & Sampson 1
Cunningham, Ann 77
Cup plates 80, 81, 88, 191, Figures Frontispiece, 1.12–1.15, 1.17, 2.6, 4.11, 5.10
Currie, Dr. James 134
Cushing, Sarah 110
Cutting, Sewall S. 210, 213

Dark-blue printed 25–7, Figures 1.2, 1.5, 1.6, 5.12
Dave, African-American potter 14
Davenport 22, 68, Figure 1.11
Davenport, H. & W. Figure 3.4
Davenport, James S. 151, 153
Davenport, John & James 67, Figure 2.16
Davenport, Rev. John 153

Davenport, Samuel T. 151, 153
Davenport, Thomas 151, 153
Davenport Brothers 151–2, 153, Figures 5.7–5.9
Dayton, Giles 52
Dealers, definition of 9–11, 235
Deblois, Gilbert and Lewis 52
Decatur, Captain Stephen Figure 2.10
Demand, market-led 2–5, 48–9, 172, 182, 193–4, 231, 234, 238
Democratic Tippecanoe Club 139
Democrats 188, 203
Derby, Charles B. 213
Detroit Institute of Arts 42–43
Dewey, Timothy 162, 163
Dickens, Charles 85
Digital search tools 12–13, 30
Dillen, George 77
Dillinger, James A. 77
Distribution, ceramics 180, 236
Donations to poor, ceramics 116
Drake family 14
Dresden 17, 40
Drummond, James P. 107
Drummond, Mrs. Mary 107, 167
Dummer, George 162, 163
Dunham, David & Co. 71, 72, 73, Figures 2.22–2.23
Dunham, Edgar & Co. 72
Dunlap, J.G. 115
Dynasties 143, 150, 153, 168

Earle, Alice Morse 24, 29, 32, 41, 171, 190
Earls, Amy 6
Earnest & Cowles 149
Eaton, Benjamin 95
Eddowes, John 131, 134
Eddowes, R. jr. & J. 91, 131, 132, 133, 134, Figure 4.6
Eddowes. Ralph 131, 133, 134–5
Eddowes, Ralph jr. 131, 135
Eddowes, Thomas Jefferson 135
Eddowes family 131, Pedigree 10
Edgar & Leffingwell 73
Edged ware 123, 269, Figures 4.2, 5.10–5.11, 5.21
Edinburgh 101, 103
Ellis, Moses 148
Emmeline 215
Emmerson, Robin 132
Emulative behavior 48, 84–5, 193
Enamelers 148, 269
English Anti-Slavery Society 22, 190
English china 188
English consumption behavior 84
Episcopal churches 166
Erie Canal 155, 176
Ethnic backgrounds 83, 84
Ethical production and consumption 198, 202, 236
European ceramics 5, 17, 19, 20
Everingham, Will 218–19
Ewins, Neil 6–7

Fagan, F. F. 115
Family nexus 148
Far Eastern ceramics 17, 19
Fashion 49, 65, 69, 70, 82–4, 86–8, 174, 182, 183, 186, 193–5, 198, 200, 231, 234, 237
Fennesden, William 204
Ferguson, Patricia F. 187
Field, Thomas F. 35, 107, 174, 177–9, 182–4, 187–8, 193–4, 197–8, 202, 209, 210–11, Figures 6.8–6.11, 7.9
Field, Thomas F. & Co. 209, Figure 7.8
Field & Clark 44, 175–7, 184, Figures 6.2–6.4
Filley, Chauncey I. 56–60, 87, 153, 154, Figures 2.4–2.8
Filley, Edward Augustus 57–9, 81, 161
Filley, Giles F. 57, 161
Filley, Oliver 161
Filley, Samuel Roberts 57–9, 81, 161
Fires 74, 75, 77, 188, 211, Figure 2.24
Fischer, David 194–195
Fleming, Mrs. Mary 236–7
Flow blue 65, 155, 157, 269, Figures 5.14–5.15
Flow mulberry 69, 269
Fogg, J. & W.P. 70, Figure 2.20
Forgeries 189–91
Francis, William A. 210
Franklin, Dr. Benjamin 27, 51, 82, 170, 171, 174, Figure 1.4
Franklin Dr. Benjamin's maxims 87–8, 169, 17, Figure 6.1
Franklin Bank 164

Franklin Institute 163
Free Hospital for Women 202
Free-produce stores (free-labor) 198
Free-Soil Party 203
Freeman, Watson 55, 56, Figure 2.3
Freemasons 144
French, Abram 58, 60, Figure 2.9
French artisans 162
French china 66, 83, 84, 165, 188, 217
French porcelain 48, 165, 219
French Revolution 134
Frothingham, Ebenezer 90
Fuchs, Ronald W. 187
Fugitive Slave Act 221
Fuller, Mrs. 52

Garniss, Gloria Anna 167
Garretson, Henry V. 53
German immigration 86, 88
German porcelain 17, 40, 217
Gilliland, James 90
Ginder, Samuel 102–3
Glasgow 101
Glennie, Paul 50
Glickman, Lawrence B. 198
Godden, Geoffrey 4
Gracie, Robert Figure 3.4
Gray, John 99–100, 116, 117, Figure 3.4
Greenfield, John 32, 35, 75, 76, 77, 112, Figures 2.25–2.26
Greenfield John V. 77
Griffith, Edward 112
Griffith, John 113, 158
Griffith, John & Robert 112, 113, 114, Figure 3.11
Griffith, Jonathan & Co. 112
Griffith, R. 113
Grosvenor, Rev. Ebenezer 1
Grosvenor, Mary 1
Grundy, George 66, 67, Figure 2.16
Guy & Brothers 201

Haggerty, Sheryllynne 7, 97, 106–7, 130, 194
Hague, Rev. William 180
Hall, Andrew T. 151, Pedigree 6
Hall, Henry J. 218–19, 231
Hammersley, Jane 120
Hammersley, George 120
Hammersley, Ralph 120
Hammersley, Titus 121
Hammond, Debby 95
Harley & Sackerson 71, 72, 74, Figure 2.22
Harris, Hannah 110
Harrison, General Wiliam Henry 136, 138, 139, 141
Harrison & Hall 90
Harrod, Louise 180
Hartmann, Rev. H. W. 182
Harvey, R. Wistar 42
Haslam, John Buckley 101, Figure 3.5
Hasley, Haines R. T. 24, 29, 44
Hastings, Joseph S. 109, 144
Hastings, Nathan 63, 110
Hastings family 95–6, 143, Pedigree 6
Hearst, William Randolph 41, 42, Figure 1.16
Henderson, D. & J. 164
Henderson & Gaines 35
Heneghan, Bridget T. 84, 85
Henry, H. R. 115
Henshall & Williamson Figure 3.4
Henshaw & Jarves 32, 34, 53, Figures 1.8–1.10
Herculaneum pottery 19, 40, 89, 132, 133, 269, Figures 1.1, 4.7
Hewitt, Gideon 104, 105, 110, 125
Hewitt, Jane 106, 167
Hewitt, Mary 105
Hewitt, Mary Ann 106, 167
Hewitt, Sarah 104, 167
Hewitt, Thomas 105, 106, 110, 167
Hewitt, Thomas jr. 107, 110, 207, Figure 3.6
Hewitt, Thomas & Sons 104, 110
Hewitt, William 104, 167
Hewitt family 104, 110, 175, 204, Pedigree 3
Hewlett, Lewis 77
Hill, George 109
Historical Staffordshire (*see* American printed themes) 191–192
Hochst porcelain 40
Homer family 110, Pedigree 8
Homer, *Odessey* 130
Homer, William F. 56, 110
Horn, James 7
Howard, Dr. John C. 93, 94, 128, 129, 130, 134, Pedigree 1
Howland, Ichabod 199–200

Howland, Otis Norcross 200
Hudnut, Alexander M. 20, 42
Huggins, Edward E. 180–1, Figure 6.7
Huggins & Bradley 53, 54, Figure 2.1
Hume, Ivor Nöel 39
Humphrey clock patterns 85
Hutt, William H. 4

Identity, cultural backgrounds 7–9, 127–31, 135, 141, 163, 165, 193–4
Imlay, William H. 116, 117
Importers, definition of 9–10, 235
Independence Day 119
Indian China (*see also* Chinese porcelain) Figure 5.4
Industrial products 191
Intermarriage 107–8, 110
Intermediaries, types of 9–11, 234
Intermediary commodities, theory of 238
Interracial connections 219
Invoices, imagery on 58, Figures 2.9, 2.20, 3.14, 5.18
Ironstone 201, 270

Jackfield pottery, Shropshire 40
Jackson, General Andrew 138, 139, 141, Figure 4.10
Jackson, Job 100, 101, 219–21, Figure 3.4
Jackson John Clews 100, 101, 219, Figure 3.4
Jackson, Mrs. Mary 220
Jackson, Thomas 94, 109, 128, 129, Figure 4.5
Japanese pottery 40
Jefferson, Thomas 61, 132, 133, 134–5, Figures 4.6, 4.7
Jenner, Edward 130
Jersey City Pottery, New Jersey 162, Figure 5.19
Jim Crow laws 236
John Street Church 206
Jones, Captain Jacob Figure 2.10
Jones, Jerome 199–202, Pedigree 7
Jones, McDuffee & Stratton 199–202, 230, Figures 7.1–7.2
Jones, & Co. 213

Keeling & Morris 51
Kellogg, George 41
Keppel, Admiral 49
Kerr, Edward M. & Co. 159
Kerr, J. 66
Kerr, J. & J. K. Kerr 160
Kerr, John 159
Kerr, Joseph 159, 160
Kerr, William Henry 159
Kerr, William J. 159, 160
Kerr, W. R. & Co. 56
Kerr & Binns 160
Kerr & Son 151
Kerr's China Hall 36, 79, 160, Figures 5.17–5.18
Keyes, Homer Eaton 29
Kinship 94, 95, 103–107, 112, 130, 141, 143, 198
Kissam, Timothy Tredwell 35, 38, 107, Pedigree 5, Figure 1.14–1.15
Klamkin, Marian 26, 191
Kurtz, Andrew 117

Lafayette, Marquis de 17, 23, 28, 41, 123, 124, 136, 137, 174, 211, 219–20, 236, Figures 1.2, 1.17, 4.2, 4.8, 4.9, 7.15
Laidacker, Sam 32, 182
Larsen, Ellouise Baker 26, 29, 30, 32, 65, 140, 190–1
Lea, Jacob 103
Lea, Maria 103
Lea & Cauldwell 103
Leslie, Miss 80
Limoges 217
Lincoln, President Abraham 216
Lind, Jenny 70, 71, Figures 2.20–2.21
Lindsay, William 91
Liverpool creamware 28, 269
Liverpool Literary Society 134
Liverpool pottery 40, 269
Lovejoy, Rev. Elijah 184–5, 189–91, 193–4, 198, 213, 235, 239, Figures 6.8–6.10
Lowestoft porcelain 40
Lutherans 86
Lynch, Justice 226
Lyon, Caleb 17

McCartney, James 51
McCauley, Robert H. 29, 32, 39, 175
McDuffee, Louis P. 200
McKendree, Bishop William 206

McKendrick, Neil 2, 3, 9, 49, 50, 51, 53, 65, 82, 87, 233–4
McKnight, Dr. Everett J. 32, 115
McIntosh, Ezekiel C. 116
Maddock, Alice 21, 41, 190
Maddock, Betsy 21
Maddock, Henry 21
Maddock, John 21
Maddock, John & Sons, Burslem 21
Maddock, Sidney 21
Maddock, Thomas 20, 21, 22
Maddock, Mrs. Thomas 20
Maddock, William B. 21
Maddock & Co. 21, Figure 1.3
Maiden Lane 90, 99, 105, 107, 113, 146, 158, 159, 205, 222, Figure 5.4
Mandel, Ernest 5
Marchand, Roland 8
Margolin, Sam 191
Marketing, as linked to identity 165, 235, Figure 5.20
Marketing approaches 3, 55, 74, 165, 192–4, 199, 202, 230, 234-5, 236, Figures 1.3, 2.18
Marketing history 12
Marr, George 131
Marryat, Joseph 17, 23
Marsden, Josuha 206
Martin, Millmore 200
Mason, E. B. 53, 54, Figure 2.2
Mason, C. J. 36, 103, 115, Figures 1.14–1.15
Mason, Miles 103
Mason, Zebinah M. 107, 108, Figure 3.7
Masonic emblems 144
Mathias, Peter 198
Mayer, John 100, 101, Figure 3.4
Mayer, T. J. & J., Longport 58, 146
Mayer, Thomas 100, Figure 3.4
Mayhew, Elizabeth 96
Mayhew, Dr Jonathan 8, 9, 96
Meigh, Charles 70, 71, Figure 2.21
Meissen 217
Mellen, John 109
Mellen family 110, Pedigree 9
Mellen, Michael 109
Mellor, Venables, & Co. 123, 158, Figure 5.16
Men's Christian Union 202
Merchants, definition of 9–11
Merchants, as consumers 173
Meredith, Sir William 49
Meteyard, Eliza 2, 11, 28, 49
Methodism 86, 166, 171, 172, 206–7
Methodology 11–13
Middle class 48, 77, 81, 82
Millennium pattern 178–83, 194, 197–8, 209, Figures 6.5–6.7
Miller, George 6
Miller, Mordecai 138
Miller, Robert H. 33, 135–41, Figures 4.9, 4.10
Miller, William H. 138
Millington 22
Minton, Herbert 23, 187
Minton, Thomas 2
Mitchell, Edward P. 145, 203
Mitchell, Nathan 55, 56, Figure 2.3
Mitchell & Freeman 55, Figure 2.3
Moore, N. Hudson 29, 39, 41, 80, 190
Morgan, Phillip D. 7
Morley, Francis 120
Morrell, John 90, 91
Morrell, John jr. 91
Mortimer, John jr. 116
Morton, Peter 10, 32, 35, 40, 115, 116, 117, 125, Figure 1.7
Morton, Thomas C. 115, 116
Mount Vernon 125, 126, 136, 137, Figures 4.3, 4.4
Mount Zion Church 223
Muffin plates 81, 269

Napoleonic themes, printed ceramics 61
National Association for the Advancement of Colored People (NAACP) 217
Nationhood, myth 193
Neal, A. 231
Neal, Matha 221–2
Neal, Rev. Voss (china packer) 218–19, 221–5, 227, 232, Figure 7.16, 7.18
New Hall porcelain 40
New York Montana Mining and Discovery Company 210
Newspapers 12–13, 50, 51, 209–13
Norcross family 110, Pedigree 10
Norcross, Mary 110
Norcross, Mellen & Co. 111, Figure 3.8

Norcross, Otis 61, 109, 151, 199–200
Norcross, Otis jr. 199–200
Norman-Wilcox, Gregor 41

Ogden, Jonathan 44
Oneida Bible Society 177
Orthodox crockery 177–83, 197
Ovington, Charles Ketcham 211–12, 217, 219
Ovington, Mrs. Charles 217
Ovington, Mrs. E. J. 216, Figure 7.19
Ovington, Edward Judson 211, 213, 216–17, 224, 227–9, Figure 7.19
Ovington, Henry A. 211, 213, 225, 227
Ovington, Irene H. 216
Ovington, Mrs. Maria 228–9
Ovington, Mary White 217, 224–5, 236
Ovington, Theodore T. 211, 216–17, 225, 227
Ovington, William H. 211, 216–17, 225
Ovington Brothers 210–13, 218, 223, 225–7, 229–30, 231, 236, Figures 7.9–710
Ovington family 13, 225, 232, Figure 7.18, Pedigree 13

Parker, Dr. Henry 1
Parker, Isaac H. 1, 9, Frontispiece
Parian ware, American themes 200, 229–31, 236, Figures 7.3, 7.20
Paton, James 116
Patriotic 123, 235
Patten, Alice 20
Pearl Street 71, 72, 73, 74, 75, 78, 118, 174, 188, Figures 1.13, 2.26, 2.27, 5.3
Peggy 207–8, Figure 7.6
Pennington, Rev. James W. C. 224
Philadelphia Museum of Art 43, Figure 2.10
Phillips, George Figure 3.4
Phillips, Wendell 200
Pierce, Samuel B. 69, Figure 2.18
Pierrepont Street Baptist Church 225
Pink 215
Pitt, William 48, 49, 50
Plumb, J. H. 3, 9, 49
Plymouth Congregational Church 213, 215–17, 225, 227, 228, 236, Figures 7.13, 7.19
Politics 123, 131, 134, 135, 153, 197, 235
Pope, Mrs. Gustavus D. 42
Porter, Roy 3, 8
Portland steamer 197
Post, Henry jr. 162
Postal stamp 236
Poulson, Thomas 98
Presbyterian 213, 228
Price factors 48, 66, 69, 70, 86, 194
Price fixing (*see also*, Combination) 114
Priestley, Dr. Joseph 134
Prime, William C. 19, 24, 25, 28, 39, 40
Printed circulars 69, Figures 2.18, 3.14
Printers 148
Princeton University 25, 162, 228
Profits 151
Production, *see* Supply
Protestants 82, 118, 141
Protestantism, impact on consumption 169–70
Puritan 170–1
Purser, Thomas 105, 107, 110, 112, 167

Quakers 155, 198
Queen's ware (Queensware) 52, 66, 91, 99, 103, 166, 270, Figures 3.3, 3.5

Racial equality 200, 236
Rahhaman, Abduhi 204
Railway Hotel, Stoke 217
Ramsay, John 163
Ramsay, Gatchell & Barcroft 98
Rarity 22, 87, 189–90, 193, 195, 237–9
Reader, the 195, 239
Reeve, Charles F. V. 106
Religion 141, 166–7, 169, 171, 172, 188, 194, 209, 219, 236
Religion, ceramic imagery 173–5, 177–80
Religion, impact on business behavior 172–3, 180, 194, 197, 217–18
Religious newspapers 209–13
Republican 153, 166, 188
Retail 10, 146
Revolutionary War 128
Richardson, Susan 224
Ridgway 22, 63
Ridgway, Job 172
Ridgway, John 5, 6, 24, 55, 99, 101, 102, 105, 109, 115, 146, 172, 191, 192, Figures 1.2, 4.12, 6.13

Ridgway, William 99, 101, 105, 109, 115, 146, 192, Figures 1.2, 3.4, 6.13
Rhinelander, Frederick 4, 50
Robbins, H. F. 117
Roberts, David 174
Roberts, Jane 107
Roberts, Mary Ann 107, 174
Robinson & Leadbeater 200–2, Figure 7.3
Rogers, John 62, Figure 2.11
Rohrbough & Moore 117, 118
Roscoe, William 130, 133
Rosenstein, Leon 20
Rothschild family 17
Rouen pottery 40
Rural printed themes 175
Rushton, John Y. 77

Sadler & Green 50
Sampson, Joseph S. 110, Pedigree 6
Samuelsson, Karl 170, 182, 186
Sandwich Academy 203–4
Saxton, Dr. William 90, 128–9, 131, Figure 4.5
Saxton & Wainwright 90, 94, 128
Saxton, Wainwright & Jackson 128, 129, Figure 4.5
Schwind, Arnold 4
Scotland 101, 116, Figure 1.7
Scott, John 53
Searle, G.R. 198
Seneca Indians 84, 237
Sevres 17, 40, 219
Seymour, Rev. George F. 118
Seymour, Joel 118
Seymour, John F. 117, Figures 3.12–3.13
Shakespeare, William 160
Sharp, Rev. Daniel 167
Shaw, James M. 77, 104, 222
Shaw, Osmond B. 233, 235
Shaw, Simeon 2, 92, 233–4
Shelton, R. 52
Shi, David E. 9
Shirley, Benjamin 148
Shirley, Cephas 146, 148, 165, Figure 5.20
Shirley, Hannah 150
Shirley, Harry 150
Shirley, Henry C. 149, 150
Shirley, Jesse 164
Shirley, John 150
Shirley, Joseph W. 150
Shirley, W. W. 150
Shirley William 148–9, 151, Figure 5.5
Shirley, William W. 112, 146–8, 151, 155, 158, 162, 163, 222, Figures 5.2–5.5
Shirley & Bayley 150
Shirley & Son 150, Figure 5.6
Shirley family 146, Pedigree 12
Shufflebottom, Ralph 98, 99
Shufflebottom, Ralph Hammersley 98
Shufflebottom, William 97–8, 99, 101, 102, 125, Figures 3.3, 4.3
Simpson & Caldwell 68, 69, Figures 2.18–2.19
Slavery 204
Slosson, Annie Trumbull 20, 28, 30
Smith, Adam 4
Smith, Mabel 61, 135
Smith, Matthew 25, 102
Smith, Sheenah 51
Smith, Theophilus 91, 93, 97, 128
Soper, Mrs. Arthur W. 42, 43, Figure 1.17
Soper, Mary 42
Spargo, John 39, 162
Spode, Josiah 2
Spode 63, 236–7
Spring Vale Asylum 207–8, Figure 7.7
Sproston, John Figure 3.4
Staffordshire origins 10, 97–9, 101, 146–50, 165, 168, 204, 233, Figures 3.11, 5.20
Staffordshire pottery 19, 40, 84, 205, 233, 269–70, Figure 3.7
Stansbury, Joseph 90
Stratton, Solomon P. 200
Steel, William 21
Stevenson, Andrew 101
Stevenson, Henry 78, 100, 101, Figures 2.27, 3.4
Stevenson, James 101, 103
Stevenson, Mary 119, 120
Stevenson, Ralph 100, 101, 103, 119
Stillman, Benjamin Morgan 90
Stone, Caroline 159
Stowe, Harriet Beecher 171, 184, 208, 213, 221, 225, Figure 7.12
Stubbs, Joseph 22, 62, Figure 3.4
Stubbs & Kent 103
Stubenrauch, Joseph 172–3, 183

Styles, John 3, 52, 53, 186
Sumner, Benjamin 90
Sumner, Charles 200–1, Figure 7.3
Sumner, Samuel 66
Sumner, William 90
Supply, Producer-led 2–5, 172, 182, 191, 193–4, 231, 234, 238–9
Sunderland lusters, wall-plaques 173

Talcott, N. & D. 72
Tams, E. & J. 77, Figure 5.21
Tams, S. & J. 123, 158, Figure 5.16
Tams, Edwin 155, 165
Tams, James 77, 140, 155, 157
Tams, James & Co. 155, Figures 5.14–5.15
Tams, John 165, 166
Tams, Michael 157
Tams, Sampson 77, 112, 146, 151, 154, 155, 158
Tams, William 155
Tams & Anderson 101
Tams, Anderson & Tams 155, Figures 5.12–5.13
Tams family 101
Tappan, Arthur 174, 188, 194, 204
Taylor, James A. 115, Figure 3.4
Terry, L. G. 165–6
Thistlethwaite, Frank 39, 161, 166
Theft 77, 226, 231
Tilton, Elizabeth 228, 230
Tilton, Theodore 216, 227, Figure 7.18
Titus 204
Tobacco dealing 95, 116, 204
Tomlinson, Ann 116
Tooker, G. W. 210
Trade card 21, Figure 1.3
Treason 203
Tredwell, John and George 35, 36, 37, 107, Pedigree 4 and 5
Trenton potteries 25, 161, 225, 270
Trenton City Museum 23
Trenton School of Industrial Arts 21
Trumbull-Prime Collection 25, 162
Truxton, Thomas 52
Turner, Lane End 103
Turner, Ernest S. 10, 11
Tyler, John 139
Tyndale, Harold 203
Tyndale, Hector 145, 146, 202–3
Tyndale, Robinson 144, 202
Tyndale, Sarah (nee Thorn) 144–6, 202, Figure 5.1
Tyndale & Mitchell 78, 145, 203, Figure 2.28

Uncle Tom's Cabin 27, 171, 208, 213–14, 215–16
Uncle Tom's Cabin, themed ceramics 214, 216, Figures 7.12, 7.14
Unitarian 134
United States Consular Agency 120, Figure 3.15
Universalists 179
University, printed views 63, Figures 2.12–2.13

Wainwright, Eliza 97
Wainwright, Elizabeth Mayhew 93, 129, 134, 207
Wainwright, Henry 94, 95, 96, 109, 110, 128, 129, Figure 4.5
Wainwright, Rev Jonathan Mayhew 95, 96, 172, 192, 204
Wainwright, Peter 8, 9, 13, 90, 92, 94, 95, 96, 110, 128, 130, 172, 173, 203, 238–9, Figures 3.1, 3.2
Wainwright, Peter jr. 96, 97
Wainwright, Cross & Howard 90, 92, 130
Wainwright, Howard & Co. 90
Wainwright & Jackson 94, 128, Figure 4.5
Wainwright family 13, 130, 131 Pedigree 1
Walsh, Alexander 65, Figure 2.14
Walthall, John A. 10
Ward, Betsey 110
Wardwell, Hettie Mann 42
Warehouses 55, 74, Figure 2.3
Washington, Bushrod 136–7
Washington, President General George 17, 52, 125, 126, 136, 137, 139, Figures 1.1, 1.4, 1.17, 4.1
Washington, Martha 17
Water Street 101, 185, 219, Figures 1.14, 6.9, 6.11
Waterford, Ireland 98
Waterhouse, Dr. Benjamin 130
Watson, John F. 75, 77
Weatherill, John 141
Webb, Charles W. 77

Weber, Max 81, 83, 86, 169, 171, 182, 236
Wedgwood 19, 66, 103, 115
Wedgwood, Henry 92, 97
Wedgwood, Josiah 2, 3, 4, 11, 28, 49, 50, 66, 89, 187
Wedgwood, Josiah, Montreal 89
Wedgwood, Josiah C. 172
Wedgwood, Josiah & Sons 199, 212–13, Figure 7.1, 7.10–7.11
Wedgwood, Sarah 187
Weeksville 221, 226
Wellman, Judith 221, 224
Wesley, John 171, 172
West Indian sugar 198
West Indies 68, 104
Wetmore, Cornelia Roxanna 107
Wetmore, Robert Charles 74, 107, Pedigree 4
Wharton, Thomas I. 79, Figure 2.28
Wheat Sheaf Inn 207
Whig party 138, 140, 188
White granite 65, 69, 78, 84, 85, 120, 270, Figures 2.6, 2.28, 3.8
White-ware 85, 86, 88, 270
Whitman, Walter 146
Wholesale 10, 146, 153
Wilby, F. & Co. 109
Williams, Rev. John 167–8, 175, Figure 7.18
Williams, Joseph 78
Wilson, Rev. Henry M. 225–8
Winkley, Henry 151
Winne & Evertsen 52
Winslow, Hubbard 1
Winterthur Museum, Garden & Library 33, 35, 89, Figures 1.11–1.13, 4.7
Withington, Ann 141
Witkowski, Terrence H. 82
Wolfe, Thomas 68
Women's Rights Convention 146
Wood, Amos 89
Wood, Edward 117
Wood, Enoch 19, 22, 24, 40, 62, 65, 116, 117, Figure 1.17
Wood, Enoch & Sons 99, 105, 116, 117, 120, 139, 175, 176, 184, Figures 1.2, 1.17, 2.11, 3.4, 3.6, 3.14, 4.11, 6.2–6.4
Wood, Joseph 117
Wood, Kurtz & Co. 117
Wood & Caldwell 32, 34, 35, Figures 1.8–1.10
Worcester Porcelain 40, 159, 171, Figure 5.17
Wright, Edward N. 154
Wright, James A. 154
Wright, Peter A. 154
Wright, Peter & Sons 154
Wulf, Karin 7

Young, Hilary 3, 11
Young, Jennie J. 19, 162
Young Whigs 139